THE NEW KNIGHTS

The Development of Cavalry in Western Europe, 1562–1700

Frédéric Chauviré

'This is the Century of the Soldier', Fulvio Testi, Poet, 1641

Helion & Company

Helion & Company Limited
Unit 8 Amherst Business Centre
Budbrooke Road
Warwick
CV34 5WE
England
Tel. 01926 499 619
Email: info@helion.co.uk
Website: www.helion.co.uk
Twitter: @helionbooks
Visit our blog http://blog.helion.co.uk/

Published by Helion & Company 2021
Designed and typeset by Serena Jones
Cover designed by Paul Hewitt, Battlefield Design (www.battlefield-design.co.uk)

Text © Frédéric Chauviré 2021
Black and white images © as individually credited.
Colour artwork by Giorgio Albertini © Helion & Company 2021
Maps by Alan Turton © Helion & Company 2021

Every reasonable effort has been made to trace copyright holders and to obtain their permission for the use of copyright material. The author and publisher apologise for any errors or omissions in this work, and would be grateful if notified of any corrections that should be incorporated in future reprints or editions of this book.

ISBN 978-1-913336-48-6

British Library Cataloguing-in-Publication Data.
A catalogue record for this book is available from the British Library.

All rights reserved. No part of this publication may be reproduced, stored in a retrieval system, or transmitted, in any form, or by any means, electronic, mechanical, photocopying, recording or otherwise, without the express written consent of Helion & Company Limited.

For details of other military history titles published by Helion & Company
Limited, contact the above address, or visit our website: http://www.helion.co.uk

We always welcome receiving book proposals from prospective authors.

Contents

Introduction   v

Part I: The Heavy Cavalryman Within the Context of the Era
1. The Men, Their Arms and Tactics   13
2. Man and Horse   30
3. Organisation and Training   54

Part II: How Did the Charge Change?
4. The Triumph of Firepower   79
5. Enter Gustavus Adolphus   95
6. The Relative Stability of Cavalry Tactics   117
7. A Question of Shock   139

Part III: An Essential Place on the Battlefield
8. The French Wars of Religion   157
9. The Thirty Years' War and New Ideas   179
10. Cavalry During the Wars of Louis XIV   207
Conclusion   229

Bibliography   232

Introduction

An image stuck in the mind: the impetuous Francis I of France and his gendarmes, cocooned in their heavy armour, being used as if for target practice by the arquebusiers of the Marquess of Pescara, who shoot them at point-blank range. The King is unhorsed, thrown to the ground, and forced to surrender. The battle had to this point been favourable to the French, but suddenly fortunes turned, and it turned into a rout. Francis doubtless saved his honour, but he lost the flower of his gendarmes. The trauma of the defeat at Pavia in 1525 confirms, after the failures of Bicocca in 1522 or Cerignola in 1503), the evolution of tactics from Courtrai (1302) or the Hundred Years' War. Cavalry no longer dominated the battlefield, and the infantry had become 'the queen of the battles'. The cavalry was condemned to a supporting role. Even Machiavelli seems to have anticipated the lessons of Pavia. In his *Art of the war*, published five years earlier, he made no case for the men-at-arms. 'We do not more have to consider it than we made it formerly', he asserts.[1] 'And the peoples who give to their cavalry a privileged place in their armies only give it as a token of their weakness.'[2] This view is shared by some modern historians. Geoffrey Parker asserts that following Pavia 'in all the western European countries, the heavy cavalry men-at-arms or gendarmes were subject to a rapid and absolute decline.'[3] The same author connects this phenomenon with the overall revolution being seen within the military, the driving elements of which were the bastioned fortifications and improvements in artillery from the fifteenth century, and the part taken by firepower generally, which led to the eclipse of the heavily armoured cavalryman in favour of the infantry in many armies.[4] It is not up to us here to take a stand defending nor supporting this notion but we can at least explore what has happened.[5]

---

1 Niccolò Machiavelli, *L'Art de la guerre*, in *Œuvres complètes* (Paris: Gallimard, La Pléiade, 1954), p.762.
2 Machiavelli, *L'Art de la guerre*, p.763.
3 Geoffrey Parker, *La révolution militaire; la guerre et l'essor de l'Occident, 1500–1800* (Paris: Gallimard, 1993, French edition),p.51.
4 Parker, *La révolution militaire*, p.99.
5 The main contributions in the debate were gathered in the collective published work supervised by Clifford J. Rogers, *The Military Revolution Debate, Readings on the Military Transformation of Early Modern Europe* (Boulder: Westview Press, 1995). Jean Chagniot also reviews this debate in 'La Révolution militaire des temps modernes', *Revue Historique des Armées*, 2, 1997, and in

THE NEW KNIGHTS

It is important to note that this 'military revolution' maintained a distanced relationship with the cavalry. Analyses generally favour the infantry, firearms, artillery, or fortifications, but the mounted part of this 'military revolution' suffers from a lack of study. This did not escape the attention of Laurent Henninger, who reminded us that the transformations in the structure, the equipment, the recruitment, and the tactical role of western cavalry are to be studied in the same way as the changes cited above, 'that we tend maybe too much to consider as exclusive.'[6] Finally, cavalry is often presented as a secondary, even unimportant arm. The mounted troops, and particularly the heavy battle cavalry, would be affected by an inevitable and obvious decline.

Other historians however, distance themselves from this idea. 'Let us not bury either too fast the cavalry', Jean Chagniot warns. He perceives, after 1640, a revival of mounted troops, which he interprets as a 'denial' imposed on the military revolution.[7] In support of this remark, Chagniot reminds us that between 1644 and 1648 the cavalry of Turenne was his main asset in the face of Imperial troops. By 1691, large formations of heavy cavalry are seen facing each other on the battlefield, 'without being too much disturbed during the battle by artillery or muskets'. Louis A. Di Marco considers it is also necessary to return to the idea that the period 1500–1800 sees the mounted arm fading in front of the increasing power of the infantry and artillery. He writes that 'This vision is not only exaggerated, but also false.'[8] This point prompted some authors to envisage the sixteenth century as the start of a new golden age for cavalry.[9]

The question arises therefore of what exactly the role of the cavalry was in the early modern period of warfare? It is a vast and complex subject, but one that can be understood by the analysis of a single common battlefield practice: the charge. A cavalry charge was generally brief, limited to the short time required to cover the distance separating two bodies of opposing horse. Sometimes the term denotes only the very last pre-contact stage of this attack. We can add to this the melee itself, which followed the initial contact. But it is above all things a significant moment. When the charge was sounded, the point of no return was quickly reached, and it is a question from now on of fighting, of killing, or of falling dead or wounded. Yet the charge constitutes the prime modus operandi of cavalry on the battlefield. It is, reminds the Comte de Guibert, 'the action of fighting of the cavalry, and consequently his important and decisive movement.'[10] It is, confirms an

---

Guerre et société à l'époque moderne (Paris: PUF, Nouvelle Clio, 2001). See also Jean Bérenger (ed.), *La révolution militaire en Europe* (Paris: Economica-ISC, 1998).

6   Laurent Henninger, 'Une conséquence de la guerre de Trente Ans en Europe centrale et Balkanique: le renouveau de la cavalerie dans les armées occidentales', in L. Henninger (ed.), *Nouveaux regards sur la guerre de Trente Ans, Actes du colloque international organisé par le CEHD à l'Ecole militaire le 6 avril 1998* (Paris: ADDIM, 1998), pp.94–95.

7   Jean Chagniot, *Guerre et société à l'époque moderne* (Paris: PUF, Nouvelle Clio, 2001), p.291.

8   Louis A. Di Marco, *War Horse: A History of the Military Horse and Rider* (Yardley, Pa: Westholme Publishing, 2008), p.191.

9   Frédéric Chauviré et Bertrand Fonck (ed.), *L'âge d'or de la cavalerie* (Paris: Gallimard, 2015).

10 Jacques-Antoine-Hippolyte, Comte de Guibert, *Essai général de tactique* (Paris: Economica, 2004 [from 1772 edition]), p.112.

INTRODUCTION

anonymous report of 1769, the main purpose of the cavalry in battle, 'all the others which it is used on the war are accessories of that one, and must by this reason be dependent on it.'[11] The relevance of studying the development of the mounted arm appears immediately to the historian, who can see, as Daniel Roche writes, 'a revelation of all the problems met by the European cavalries.'[12] To study the charge and its evolution during the early modern period, is to get to the heart of the cavalry and, beyond that, at the heart of the art of the war, the essential objective of which is to win in battle.

Rather than to embrace the whole early modern period, from the Italian Wars to the French Revolution, it seemed better to concentrate this study over a period from the middle of the sixteenth century to the beginning of the eighteenth. This is the decisive time for cavalry, that, confronted with the improvements in firepower, had to adapt itself to protect its place on the battlefield. Until the middle of the sixteenth century the fundamental principles of the heavy cavalry charge remained essentially the same as those in the twelfth century: the men-at-arms, heavily protected, charged in line, at the gallop (at least by the end of the charge). The charge relied on the power of the shock, of what Claude Gaier calls the 'missile man-horse' and the search of 'the effect of a ram.'[13] But, in the second half of the century, a portion of heavy cavalry adopted the pistol. This led to radical changes, in the form of both new tactics and an evolution of the social composition of the cavalry. By studying these phenomena within the framework of the Wars of Religion in France (1562–1598) it gives us the opportunity to research a period sometimes neglected by military historians. The hundred years which follow the end of the French Wars of Religion are influenced directly by these transformations. The mounted arm tries hard during the seventeenth century to develop the tactical changes now prevalent in a charge and to adapt these to the general evolution of the art of the war. Can we look for and understand to what extent cavalry were allowed to keep a decisive place on the battlefield.

The scale of this subject requires some fairly tight geographical parameters. We shall give priority to France, its authors, and its army. The military history and the literature of this country offer a rich field of study which could alone fill the pages of this book. It is obvious however that the authors and the armies of other nationalities must be considered. This will enrich the overall story: how, for example, to study the French cavalry of the Thirty Years' War without also investigating the Swedish model as seen in Gustavus Adolphus' cavalry? Setting the chronological and geographical framework must mesh with the methodology used.

This presents a potential stumbling block which the historian must take the measure of. Multiple images immediately come to mind when we consider the moment of the charge: furious waves of riders launched at a full gallop, rearing horses, the stabbing and slashing of glittering swords.

---

11 Service Historique de la Défense/Direction de l'Armée de Terre (SHD/DAT), Mémoires et Reconnaissance 1732, f°90, 'Petit mémoire anonyme sur l'équitation de la cavalerie', 26 Février 1769.
12 Daniel Roche, *La gloire et la puissance, Histoire de la culture équestre, XVIe–XIXe siècle*, Tome 2ème (Paris: Fayard, 2011), p.302.
13 Claude Gaier, *Armes et combats dans l'univers médiéval* (Brussels: De Boeck, 1985), pp.66–68.

These representations are less than useful. On one hand they take us back to the time of the glorious episodes of the French First Empire and are not necessarily relevant when applied to the early modern period under review. On the other hand, and especially on a superficial and fragmentary basis, these records do not assist in a scientific analysis of the cavalry charge.

This subject is clearly more complex than it initially appears. How then to approach the subject without returning to the wanderings of 'the former' battle history, 'overloaded with anecdotes, with witty remarks and with edifying scenes'.[14] It is here that one finds all the interest of the rich historiographical perspectives drawn by the revival of the military history and the study of battles, marked by the works of André Corvisier, Jean-Pierre Bois, Jean Chagniot and more recently with Hervé Drévillon, Olivier Chaline and Laurent Henninger. The common object of all these studies is to consider the study of battles 'as the decisive moment around which are organised all the activities of [military history] studies.'[15] It appears from now on in everybody's view that 'the battle history can be made only in the term of the study of a convergent process of military, social, political and cultural changes marked by the evolution of the mentalities and sensibilities.'[16] The battle history is no longer just a matter of scratching the surface, but the opposite, and it reveals the answers if we know how to ask the right questions.[17] To write about the history of the charge is to pose a series of elementary questions: what elements were essential to a successful charge ? How does it take place? How does the charge inform us about the role of the cavalry in the battle?

Therefore, this requires us to understand all the dimensions brought into play by the charge; to reconcile, according to Jean-Pierre Bois' words, the 'emotional' and 'technical' aspects.[18] It is important to recognise the contribution of contemporary culture.[19] For example to understand the constraints related to the use of weapons, and their effect. This aspect is essential if we claim to wish to penetrate to the very heart of the fight. How to fully understand it if we ignore what a cavalry sword is, the way it is used and the wounds it inflicts? The technical aspect also includes horse riding, the style of riding and the use of horses in the fight, and the speed of the charge. It also covers administrative or tactical structures and, how these drive the armies. Finally, the tactics themselves, the art of developing and manoeuvring units, and how to manage them in battle. How to arrange the

---

14 Hervé Drévillon, *Batailles. Scènes de guerre de la Table Ronde aux Tranchées* (Paris: Seuil, 2007), p.11.
15 Etienne De Durand, 'De quelques difficultés de l'histoire militaire', *Cahiers du Centre d'études d'histoire de la défense*, n°9 (1999), p.192.
16 Jacques le Goff, quoted by Laurent Henninger, 'Pour une nouvelle histoire bataille', *Cahiers du centre d'études d'histoire de la défense*, n°9 (1999), p.12.
17 Gorges Duby, *Ledimanche de Bouvines* (Paris: Gallimard, Folio, 1985), pp.8–9. It is obviously necessary to also quote the pioneering work of John Keegan, *The Face of Battle* (London: Jonathan Cape, 1976).
18 Jean-Pierre Bois, 'L'homme dans la bataille à l'époque moderne', in *Cahiers du Centre d'études d'histoire de la défense*, n°9 (1999), p.132.
19 This material culture defined by Daniel Roche, consists of applying to objects of current life the practices of cultural history.

INTRODUCTION

riders in the squadron, and the squadrons in the battle plan? What is the doctrine being followed for the use of cavalry on the battlefield?

The 'emotional' issues are also vast. It is for example the 'elementary fight': 'the sphere in which the learned calculations can break on uncontrollable primary reactions.'[20] It is the fear, the strength, the courage, the elements without which the actual tactics are pointless. As underlined by Jean-Pierre Bois, modern historiography does not focus enough on the degree of courage, the moral firmness that the horrifying experience of pitched battles of the wars of *Ancien Régime* were expected of the soldiers.[21] We cannot limit ourselves to the emotions or feelings of the cavalrymen. Even if they are more difficult to comprehend than those of the officers, it is nevertheless necessary to wonder about their identity and their social origins. These men are the anonymous actors in the charge, those whom the officers have at all costs to lead into battle. Naturally, the very nature of the subject leads us to ask similar questions about their mounts. Does the heavy cavalry charge require horses with particular characteristics? Did these characteristics evolve in time?

As we see it, this is a very wide subject, which leads us to approach a point of view that is not only historic but also anthropological and sociological. In considering all these dimensions of the charge, this is moment when we can measure the true value of cavalry.

This study inevitably falls within the scope of our chosen chronological parameters. However, an exclusively chronological approach would not be without dangers. We would for example risk not being able to fully understand the complexity of the charge, to fall into the ways of describing the 'old' battle history: the narrative of the battles, the anecdotes. That is why a more thematic approach has been used. This has the advantage of being able to emphasise the particular factors which underpin the charge. This work will thus appear in three parts.

It is important at first to remind ourselves that if the charge is a key part of the battle, the success or failure is due to factors which sometimes have seemingly only a rather indirect connection with the battle itself. We shall examine first of all these essential prerequisites, situated 'upstream' from the charge: the armament (offensive and defensive), the recruitment of the riders and the horses, the organic structures, and the instruction. The second part will attempt to analyse the evolution of the charge. Three basic principles structure and organise this: the choice of weapons, the speed at which the charge is led and 'shock' of impact and the way it is conceived. It is the answer to these questions which, by their own mechanisms and their interaction, determine the development of the charge. To better grasp these changes, these three principles will be combined in three chronological chapters, the first organised around the reforms of Gustavus Adolphus. The second will try to give a particular perspective on the complex question of 'shock'. Finally, the third part will change the scale of the analysis. After considering the charge from only the point of view of the squadron, we will set this within

---

20 Hervé Coutau-Bégarie, *Traité de stratégie* (Paris: Economica, 1999), p.102.
21 Bois, 'Approche historiographique de la tactique à l'époque moderne', *Revue Historique de l'Armée*, n°2 (1997), p.24.

the wider framework of the battlefield. This extension allows us to ask the question about the doctrines applied to the use of cavalry and its role in battle. Here too we shall favour a chronological approach: the role during the French Religious Wars, the appearance of new concepts and models during the Thirty Years' War and the development of cavalry during the wars of Louis XIV of France.

Part I

The Heavy Cavalryman Within the Context of the Era

1

The Men, their Arms and Tactics

How were armaments shaped by the adoption of firearms? The study of weapons and equipment can provide a better understanding of the practical realities of the evolution of the cavalry charge. The analysis of weapons – their use and constraints – provides a unique insight into the perspective of the men who employed these arms, whilst in the midst of battle with their lives at stake. This type of study is also essential to better comprehend the mechanics of the charge and its evolution, plus the relationship between weapons and the charge. It is obvious for example, that the introduction and development of firearms influenced the way a charge was conducted, from the perspective of the principles of speed and shock.

However, this area of investigation is vast. We shall therefore favour elements that allow us to better understand the upheavals which affected cavalry during this period. The adoption of firepower by cavalry constitutes the main, but by no means the only factor that led to changes in the field of both offensive and defensive armaments. Hence in the first part of this book the focus will be on the use of firearms. Thereafter we will move onto deal with swords and finally defensive armour.

Firearms were not unknown at the beginning of the sixteenth century. But the size of these weapons and the means of firing them made adoption by cavalry difficult. The riders equipped with such weapons were rather horse-mounted infantry or units dedicated to skirmishing and raiding, not the heavy armoured cavalry armed with lance and sword. The development of the wheel-lock and of the pistol mark a real turning point, allowing mounted units equipped with firearms to play a key role on the battlefield.

Improvements in weapons favoured cavalry armed with firearms. The most widespread portable firearm at the end of the fifteenth century was the arquebus. Until the very beginning of the sixteenth century, they were fired using a slow match; a cord soaked with saltpetre, which was used to ignite the powder in the flash pan of the weapon. The arquebusier held the match in the right hand and the arquebus in the left. The invention of the matchlock allowed for an improvement in the precision of shooting an arquebus. The matchlock is a mechanism fixed to the weapon. The arquebusier no longer needed to hold the slow match in his right hand, as it was now held between the jaws of the lock (the serpentine). Pulling the trigger causes the lock to come into contact with the priming charge, igniting it and thus firing the main charge in the barrel of the weapon.[1]

Arquebus balls were capable of penetrating armour and caused 'dirtier' and more harmful wounds than arrows. But above all bows and crossbows required in-depth and frequent training – especially the bow – necessitating a lengthy and almost daily training regimen. The arquebus on the contrary, could be served by a man having only a few days of training. It was thus possible to equip large numbers of soldiers and to compensate for the defects of the weapon by the volume of fire. These defects were important. The difficulty in keeping the match lit – even worse in bad weather – was not a minor inconvenience.[2] It should also not be forgotten that, from the point of view of the rate of fire and the limited range, the 'traditional' weapons were more effective.[3]

These significant evolutions for foot soldiers became almost impossible ones for cavalry to adopt. Although marking real progress, the matchlock required both hands to operate; not easy when on the back of a horse. If we also consider the weight and length of the weapon – the difficulties faced when reloading and with handling the match – it is easy to understand why the use of such weapons was somewhat limited when mounted.

This situation changed radically when a small and lighter weapon was developed which was more suited to use on horseback: the wheel-lock pistol. The decisive element of this innovation was not the length or weight of the weapon, but in the firing mechanism; the wheel-lock, introduced between second and third decades of the sixteenth century. The basic principle can be seen in modern-day cigarette lighters. In the wheel-lock system, the shooter used a key to wind a spring connected to a wheel until it was locked under tension. The firer then pulled the trigger, freeing the wheel to rasp against a piece of pyrite which generated sparks, igniting the priming powder and discharging the weapon. These wheel-locks were delicate and complex, and to use a modern term, barely 'soldier proof'. The spring could break or be overtightened, thus risking the weapon becoming inoperable.[4] The spring mechanism and the trigger were designed with the precision of a clock. This sensitivity in construction presented numerous reasons for it to fail when on active service, probably at precisely the wrong moment for the user![5] Consequently, as the wheel-lock was more delicate and expensive than the matchlock, its use was generally limited to cavalrymen and sporting weapons.

---

1 Thomas F. Arnold, *Les guerres de la Renaissance*, collection 'Atlas des guerre' (French translation: Paris: éditions Autrement, 2002), p.73. Also read Dominique Venner, *Les armes de combat individuelles* (Paris: Jacques Grancher, 1976), p.92.
2 Franco Cardini, *La culture de la guerre, Xe–XVIIIe siècle* (Paris: Gallimard, 1992), p.87.
3 Philippe Contamine reminds us that an archer could fire 10 arrows per minute with an acceptable level of accuracy up to a range of 650 feet, whilst the reloading of an arquebus of the beginning of the sixteenth century required several minutes, and it was only accurate up to 260 feet. Contamine, *La guerre au moyen âge* (Paris: PUF, Nouvelle Clio, 1999), pp.248–250.
4 Bert S. Hall, *Weapons and Warfare in Renaissance Europe* (London: Johns Hopkins University Press, 1997), p.191.
5 Hall, *Weapons and Warfare*, p.191.

Firing mechanisms developed further with the introduction of the flintlock, whereby a flint is used to create the spark necessary to ignite the priming powder. The flintlock allowed for a much quicker rate of fire – two to three times as fast as a matchlock – with fewer misfires and the design was more robust than a wheel-lock.[6]

As we have already seen it was the wheel-lock mechanism that allowed the development of the pistol. Thanks to the wheel-lock, the pistol, once loaded, could be kept at hand until needed, without impeding the rider in controlling his mount. Unlike the mounted arquebusier, the pistoleer was not forced to stop before firing and could move at the trot whilst still discharging his pistols. Pistoleers carried a pair or more of pistols, allowing for a higher rate of fire before having to withdraw and reload,[7] whereas, according to the author Tavannes, arquebusiers firing from horseback 'do nothing worthwhile'.[8]

Wheel-lock pistols had their limits – as mentioned earlier – and required regular maintenance to remain in good condition. 'Whoever is willing to help such weapons, he must be curious about it [careful] as we are with a horse, but it is very difficult to subject to it the nations which consider this activity as a low and slavish one'.[9] It is the reason why, according to La Noue, French gendarmes were reluctant to use pistols or used them badly, leaving the loading and maintenance in the hands of their servants.

Pistols also suffered from issues of short range and inaccuracy. La Noue expresses this very clearly, 'the pistole makes almost no effect if it is not fired at three steps'.[10] This obliged horsemen to get close the enemy before firing. So close according to Basta, that the flame from the discharge must touch the enemy. 'Some approach so close that they put their pistol on the thigh or other part of the opponent'.[11] Montgommery also states that the gendarmes 'will fire only rested on the stomach of their opponent, below the edge of the breastplate in the first or second plate of the tasset (if it is possible); or to the shoulder of the horse'.[12] When facing cuirassiers protected by their heavy

---

6 François Bonnefoy, *Les armes de guerre portatives en France du début du règne de Louis XIV à la veille de la Révolution*, thèse de doctorat sous la direction d'A. Corvisier (Paris: Librairie de l'Inde éditeur, 1991), Tome 1, p.45.
7 It would be necessary that soldiers carry three pistols, one in the hand and two others hung on the saddle. Gaspard de Saulx, Seigneur de Tavannes, *Nouvelle collection des mémoires pour servir à l'histoire de France, par MM. Michaud et Poujoulat*, Tome VIII (Paris, 1838), p.192.
8 Tavannes, *Mémoires*, p.192.
9 François de La Noue, *Discours politiques et militaires* (Geneva: F.E. Sutcliffe, 1967), pp.361–362.
10 La Noue, *Discours*, p.360.
11 Giorgio Basta, *Le gouvernement de la cavalerie légère,* French translation by Théodor de Bry, *Il governo della cavalleria leggiera dal conte Giorgio Basta*, Venice: 1612 (Rouen: J. Berthelin, 1627), p.20. This is also the view of Johann Jacobi von Wallhausen, *Art militaire à cheval, instruction des principes et fondements de la cavalerie et des quatre espèces, ascavoir lances, corrasses, arquebus et drageons, avec tout ce qui est de leur charge et exercice … par J.J. de Wallhausen, principal capitaine des gardes de la louable ville de Dantzig (Francfort, imprimé par Paul Jacques aux frais de Théodor de Bry, 1616)*. Original edition: *Kriegskunst zu Pferd* (Frankfurt: privately published, 1616), p.30.
12 Louis de Montgommery, Seigneur de Courbouson, *La milice Françoise, contenant plusieurs belles et notables instructions sur ce qui doit être observé à bien ordonné des batailles, dresser des bataillons* (Paris: Corrozet, 1636), pp.138–139.

Pistoleers vs. lancers, French Wars of Religion. Jean Perrissin, 1570. (Rijksmuseum)

armour, it was necessary to aim at the weak points. Wallhausen recommends not even to try to hit the rider but to aim directly at the horse 'As it could not damage the man, it is necessary to aim at the heart of the horse of the enemy'. He advises 'to present the pistol on the throat of the horse, with a downward blow so that the bullet penetrates to the heart. Against an enemy who will be less protected, we can place the blow on the area that we find the most advantageous'.[13] It is finally necessary to remember that reloading a weapon on horseback was not an easy task, while controlling his horse and trying hard to keep formed in ranks; all this in the middle of jostling riders plus the dust and noise of battle.

Despite these obvious limits, contemporary authors recognised the power of the pistol. La Noue evokes thus the 'pistolle', 'espouvantable et offensible'. Tavannes reminds us that the pistoleer 'carries the death and the fear' with him.[14] He also summarises lucidly one of the main reasons which explains the success of this weapon: 'the weakest of men, if they have courage can well use it, even on poor horses'.[15]

---

13 Wallhausen, *Art militaire*, p.10.
14 Tavannes, *Mémoires*, p.192.
15 Tavannes, *Mémoires*, p.192.

THE MEN, THEIR ARMS AND TACTICS

The manufacture of the weapon and its reloading was no doubt complex, but it was simple to use, as all the riders had to do is to stretch out their arm, aim – or point it in the general direction of the enemy as aiming with any hope of accuracy from a moving horse was a challenge – and pull the trigger.

Pistols were not the only firearms used by cavalrymen. The wheel-lock was used with longer weapons of higher calibres. Montgommery mentions the possibility for the gendarmes of the second rank to use 'escopettes' during the fights.[16] The advantage of these new weapons was twofold; they gave increased range and had heavier stopping power. From this point of view a rifled barrel possibly constituted the most effective missile weapon in a cavalryman's arsenal. The principle of rifling in the barrel goes back most probably to the second half of the fifteenth century. The bullet was loaded into the barrel by means of a rammer and perhaps a mallet. The main effect of the rifling grooves was to make the bullet spin as it left the barrel, allowing for greater range and accuracy; far superior to a smoothbore weapon.[17] The rifled pistol or arquebus suffered however from a slower loading time and could not be easily unloaded or have the charge withdrawn in inclement weather. As a result, the development and use of rifled weapons was limited and their use was generally as sporting weapons rather than as a standard issue weapon for any troops, mounted or otherwise, although there were exceptions.[18]

However, the firearm most used in the cavalry – apart from the pistol – was undoubtedly the carbine; suspended on the rider's right side by a shoulder strap and hook arrangement, whence we get the term 'carabiner' used in mountaineering terms. The main difficulty for the employment of firearms on horseback lies in the need to always keep control of the horse. The carbine or shortened musket was more compact and often of smaller calibre than the infantryman's musket. It was suspended on the right-hand side and could be fired and let go of once it had been discharged. Puységur provides a testimony on the way the riders used this arrangement. He describes a confrontation (doubtless during the War of the Spanish Succession), between French squadrons and their opponents, without specifying the nationality of the latter. When the French were around seven feet distant from their enemies, those who had their carbines hanging on the shoulder strap 'took them in the right hand, and with only this hand aimed, each choosing the one that he wanted to fire, and as soon as the shot had left, they dropped the weapon which was attached to the shoulder strap and grasped their swords'.[19] Any

---

16 'The second rank will pull its 'escopettes' (pistols) between the riders of the first rank, and if the third rank cannot fire and that the enemy persists in fighting, they can pass from hand-to-hand escopettes and pistols.' Montgommery, *La milice Françoise*, p.137.
17 Bonnefoy, *Les armes de guerre*, p.77.
18 In France, an order of 1679 required the adding of two men armed with rifled carbines per company of cavalry. Those men were then combined in specialist companies, then, in 1693, constituted into a regiment of exceptional size. This elite corps of carabiniers distinguished itself, in particular at Fontenoy.
19 Jacques-François de Chastenet, Marquis de Puységur, *L'Art de la guerre par principes et par règles, ouvrage de M. le maréchal de Puységur, mis au jour par M. le Mis de Puységur, son fils* (Paris: Jombert, 1748), Tome I, p.121.

Italian lancer, 1577. Abraham de Bruyn. (Rijksmuseum)

kind of accuracy was limited. Even so the carbine hook became standard issue to French cavalry in 1676.[20]

The adoption of firearms by the cavalry did not lead to the disappearance of bladed weapons. These remained the prime weapon for cavalry. The lance is the weapon which symbolises heavy cavalry as seen at the beginning of the sixteenth century. After having considerably increased in length by the end of the Middle Ages, by the start of the sixteenth century the length of the lance could be between 10 and 16½ feet. Its weight often required a lance rest (*arrêt de cuirasse*), to relieve the man-at-arms of some of the burden. However, it seems that the length of the lance increased again by the second half of the sixteenth century. Wallhausen mentions for example, long weapons of 18, 20 and 21 feet![21] Such a change is doubtless rooted in the need of the cavalryman to have a greater reach and thus be in a better position to contend with his two main types of adversaries; the pistoleer and the pikeman. The strengthening of armour – to better resist the power of firearms – also led to an additional problem for lance-armed cavalry. It is significant that the lance reached its maximum size at the very moment it began to disappear from the cavalry of Western Europe.

From the Middle Ages to the early modern period, all authors agree that the lance – a simple weapon in its conception – is more complex to use and requires much training. To his physical strength, the cavalryman had to be agile and able to react quickly and seize the moment to overcome his opponent.[22] Only the nobility had access to the means and to the leisure necessary for the acquisition of a 'so delicious science'.[23]

The man-at-arms of the beginning of the sixteenth century is no longer braced against the high cantle at the rear of the saddle but is sat well into the bottom of his saddle,[24] legs forward, feet pushed into the stirrups. This position assures the maximum stability thanks to the design of the saddle. This allowed the rider to resist the shock of the lance striking the enemy and to help maintain a solid seat on the horse. The left hand holds reins, the right is folded up to bring under the armpit the foot of the lance and put it on the lance rest. The rest proved to be extremely useful as it relieved the rider of much of the weight of the lance, allowing him to control it more effectively when aiming at

---

20 Order of 9 March 1676.
21 Wallhausen, *Art militaire*, p.6.
22 Cardini, *La culture de la guerre*, p.45.
23 Wallhausen, *Art militaire*, p.3.
24 Marcel Dugué Mac Carthy, *La cavalerie française et son harnachement* (Paris: Maloine, 1985), p.96.

the enemy; the ideal being to aim at the neck or the head of his opponent.[25]

At the beginning of the seventeenth century, Wallhausen describes in his *Art de la guerre à cheval* some details on the use of the lance. Although towards the end of our period, the author's account is nevertheless instructive. Even if the lance was made a little lighter, the principles dictating its use probably remained unchanged since the first half of the sixteenth century. Wallhausen reduces these principles to three movements. The first is made by bringing the lance into the couched position described earlier. The second consists in maintaining the lance straight, useful against the cavalry by striking them on the torso to knock the rider off his saddle. Finally, the third movement is made against the enemy rider's horse, by aiming the lance against its breast or against a man on foot.[26]

However, by the end of the sixteenth century the use of the lance in Western Europe had declined significantly while pistols were in the ascendency. A very lively debate took place on the merits of the lance as a weapon. La Noue asserted in 1587 that it is 'a miracle when somebody is killed by the lance'.[27] Later than La Noue, it is the Frenchman Tavannes who underlines the weaknesses and the constraints of using the lance as follows. Both man and horse must be very well trained and the flatter the ground the better. The lance itself must be neither too strong nor too fragile. A poorly trained man-at-arms is afraid of receiving more wounds than he would inflict on the enemy, so he prefers to let the lance strike the ground and so break it. It would appear that 'five or six blows often do not pierce (the armour), and do no harm, except to the horses, where significant damage could be done whilst putting the enemy horseman out of action (since the invention of shot proof armour this was a wise option to choose)'.[28]

The lance still had its defenders. Roger Williams – veteran of the wars in France and in the Netherlands – reminds us that the effect of a cavalry charge is largely psychological. From this perspective the lance is found to be a most appropriate weapon as the detrimental effect a body of lance-armed men-at-arms has on enemy morale cannot be underestimated, especially as it thunders forward. This author is convinced that the lancer would have the will to come into contact rather than wheeling away as would be the case with pistol-armed horse.[29] Bernardino Mendoza, the most prominent

Bernardino Mendoza (1540–1604), author of *Theórica y práctica de la guerra*

---

25 Arnold, *Les guerres de la Renaissance*, p.92.
26 Wallhausen, *Art militaire*, p.7.
27 La Noue, *Discours*, p.360.
28 Tavannes, *Mémoires*, p.192.
29 John X. Evans (ed.), *The works of Sir Roger William* (Oxford: Clarendon Press, 1972), p.34.

Multiple branches guard
Maurice Maindron, *Les armes*, Paris, 1890

A : Quillons
B: Ecusson
C: Knuckle guard
D. Pas d'âne
E: Welding of the rings guard
H and H' : Rings guard
V and V' : Counter guards

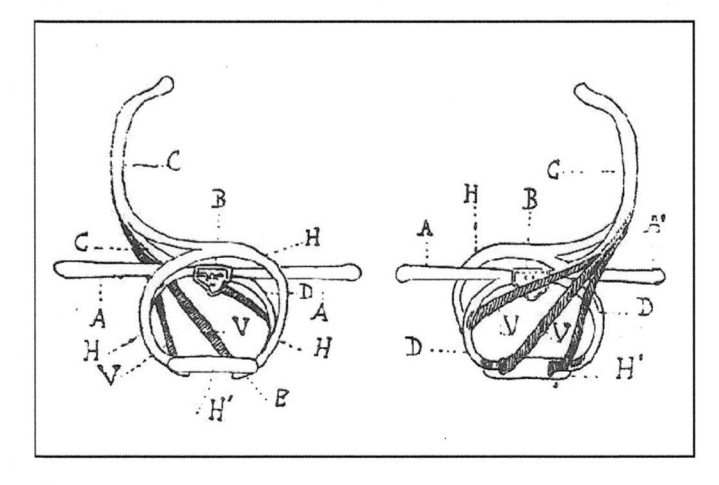

Multiple branches guard. From Maurice Maindron, *Les armes*, Paris, 1890.

Spanish military author of the second half of the sixteenth century was also a supporter of the lance. He took a pragmatic view however, recognising that its use is less and less in favour. He asserts that the reason for this is that cavalrymen preferred firearms – ideally pistols – as they were less bulky and their use required less strength and skill.[30] But whatever the reasons, the use of the lance decreased relentlessly as the end of the century approached, particularly in France and the Netherlands.

This debate did not end however, with the century. Two works, by Basta and Wallhausen, maintain the argument until the second decade of the seventeenth century. The first, in 1612, found that the conditions required for the employment of lancers were no longer met.[31] Wallhausen answered him very vigorously in 1616. His rebuttal, however, was more incendiary than the basis for a sound argument. His aristocratic prejudices and nostalgia for days gone by constituted a prism that distorted his perception of the art of war, linking it to an obsolete ideal of how warfare was conducted. He did not deny that the 'lance for the present is hardly esteemed even by soldiers of great experience. … It is not used even by the greatest warlords of our time '.[32]

Unlike the lance, although it evolved significantly during the period under review, the sword has never ceased to be used in combat. The symbolic dimension attached to the sword must not make us forget that it is also a weapon, a 'fatal object'.[33] It is one of the essential weapons of the cavalryman and one cannot properly understand the process of the mounted charge if one does not also study its technological and technical aspects.

---

30 Bernardino Mendoza, *Theorica y practica de la guerra* (1577, 1595, 1596). Quoted by Hans Delbrück, *History of the Art of War* (Lincoln and London: University of Nebraska Press, 1990), volume III, p.132.
31 Basta, *Le gouvernement de la cavalerie légère*, pp.71–73.
32 Wallhausen, *Art militaire*, p.4.
33 Pascal Brioist, Hervé Drévillon, Pierre Serna, *Croiser le fer, violence et culture de l'épée dans la France moderne (XVIe–XVIIIe siècle)* (Paris: Champ Vallon, 2002), p.10.

From the fourteenth to the fifteenth centuries the first notable changes appear. Some swords embodied new designs, such as the *pas d'ane*; a bar in a semi-circle placed vertically under the quillons. In addition to the *pas d'ane*, added protection in the form of a horizontal guard ring was placed on the guard at the same level as the quillons, or a little lower. These transformations were sometimes accompanied by modifications to the blade. The upper part of it, near the hilt, thickens for a few inches to give space to place the fingers, called the *ricasso*.

These evolutions highlight the importance of thrusting or giving point. *Pas d'ane,* guard ring and *ricasso* permitted the bearer to hold the sword with the index and middle finger around the quillons without hurting themselves and remaining relatively well protected. This grip gives much more force to the thrusts. Such an evolution is the result of the improvements in armour in the fifteenth century. It was necessary to find weapons able to overcome the improved protection offered by full armour. It was this reason that saw the development of the *estoc* (thrust), whose name underlines the function well enough. The square or triangular section of this blade allowed the attacker to better pierce the steel of full armour.[34] This necessity led men-at-arms to have two swords. In the middle of the sixteenth century, Fourquevaux said that the gendarme had to have '*l'épée d'arme*' to the side' and '*l'estoc* to the saddle tree'.[35] The *estoc* could also be attached to the wrist of the rider by a strap. *L'épée d'arme*, suspended on the shoulder belt, was distinguished by a wider blade and was longer than the *estoc*. It was designed to cut as well as to thrust with the point, while the *estoc*, shorter and pointed, was particularly effective for thrusting.

Fourquevaux is very brief in his description and does not mention *pas d'ane* or other guard rings. Neither do Montgommery nor Tavannes at the turn of the next century. It is true that in the second half of the sixteenth century the evolution of the military sword is slower than the civilian weapon. This is mainly because of the influence of new fencing techniques from Italy.[36] These two authors leave no doubt that by the time of writing, the riders – even gendarmes – are equipped with a single sword. The rapid introduction of pistols is responsible for this, in part at least. The use of a pistol in close combat makes a second sword redundant. Pistols were generally carried in cases attached to the pommel, and the riders had at least two. However, it remains a little difficult to get an exact understanding of these heavy cavalry swords in the early seventeenth century. In 1612 Basta is hardly more descriptive than Montgommery. The sword, he says, 'will be neither too broad nor too narrow, and in length a little shorter than a measure of Spain, with the point rather round and sharp'.[37] Wallhausen, describing the sword of the cuirassier,

---

34 Brioist et al., *Croiser le fer*, p.27.
35 Raymond de Beccarie de Pavie, Seigneur de Fourquevaux, *Instruction sur le fait de la guerre* (Paris: Galiot du Pré, 1548), p.24.
36 In the second half of the sixteenth century Italian fencing masters spread throughout all the great courts of Europe. 'The superiority of Italian fencing, as much with the sword alone as with the sword and rapier, benefits, at the end of the sixteenth century, of universal recognition'. Brioist et al., *Croiser le fer*, p.64.
37 Basta, *Le gouvernement de la cavalerie légère*, p.18.

Unarmoured horsemen with pistols, Battle of Rocroi in 1643. Solmon Savery. (Rijksmuseum)

mentions a sword 'short and sharp with a sharp point and as effective with the edge as the point'.[38] Thus, the single sword of the cavalrymen enabled cutting and thrusting. The plates of Wallhausen make it possible to imagine the main features of this weapon.[39] Models appear a little shorter than the civilian sword, making them easier to handle on horseback. They were also probably wider to be able to better deal with blocking enemy attacks. The guard was often much simpler. Quillons were generally symmetrical and straight. We do not see any *pas d'ane* or *ricasso*. They may however have included guard rings at the level of the quillons and sometimes a knuckle guard to reinforce the protection of the hand. There were some swords with more elaborate guards, including several branches, but most often these were the property of generals and other officers.

Not every army saw their cavalry develop as already described. A good example of this is Gustavus Adolphus' Swedish cavalry. The most common sword among Swedish horsemen was the so-called 'Swedish style', imported from the United Provinces.[40] It was characterised by its great simplicity; the quillons forming an 'S', sometimes with the addition of a small horizontal guard. The blade was wider than seen in civilian swords and had two cutting edges. Officers tended to prefer more elaborate weapons like the so-called 'Pappenheim' swords.[41] These appeared around 1620 and included a *pas d'ane*, a knuckle guard, rings of guards and two pierced shell guards which covered the hand. The appearance of the 'Pappenheim' was quite significant to the evolution of swords. It was characterised by the increased protection offered to the hand. During the Thirty Years' War another new model emerged: the

---

38 Wallhausen, *Art militaire*, p.30.
39 Wallhausen, *Art de chevalerie, comprenant, après un advertissement nécessaire touchant l'estat douloureux de la chrestienté, l'instruction de touts avantages et dextérités nécessaire à chascun chevalier* (Frankfurt: Paul Jacques, 1616). Especially the boards showing individual fights, n°6, 8, 10, 11.
40 Brzezinski, *The Army of Gustavus Adolphus*, p.12.
41 Gottfried Heinrich von Pappenheim (1594–1632), one of the most famous cavalry generals of the Emperor during the Thirty Years' War, died at Lützen.

'Walloon'. The hilt was formed by a double shell guard, or *pontat*, pierced and fixed on both sides of the guard quillons. One of the quillons elongated into a knuckle guard. This style is devoid of a *pas d'ane* but has a thumb ring attached to the side of the guard. The blades were usually flat, with one or two cutting edges and a good point. They were also wider than other swords – especially civilian ones – which due to the development of fencing and the practice of duels, were made increasingly lighter and thinner to be more suitable to thrusting exclusively.[42] Weapons with a wider blade, capable of cutting as well as thrusting – from around this time –were called sabres or 'strong-swords' (*fortes épées*) to distinguish them from the other types of swords.

The 'Walloon' was considered an excellent weapon for cavalry, and it probably served as a model for the first French regulation issue weapon in 1679. Until then the choice of weapons was left to the captains.[43] These gentlemen probably showed a preference for cheaper swords with a blade less wide and less sharp than say the 'Pappenheim' or 'Walloon'; using the 'Swedish' style for example.[44] Those in use during the war in the United Provinces were not up to the job as they were either too delicate or too short.[45] The soldiers wanted a strong weapon, capable of cutting as well as thrusting. Louis XIV therefore ordered a large quantity of the new model from Solingen; a design that had all the characteristics of the 'Walloon'.[46] The blade was flat broad and double-edged. They were 35 in (95 cm) long, with a 'fuller' (median gutter) on each side of the blade to lighten it. The guard had a knuckle guard screwed to the pommel and two heart-shaped shell-guards. According to Dominique Venner it was a weapon of excellence, superior to all swords that would succeed it.

The early modern period under review saw the disappearance of the fully armoured man-at-arms. Why was this? It was not a linear development across time as Olivier Chaline recalls; the cuirassiers at the Battle of White Mountain (1620), being still very similar in appearance and role to the medieval knight.[47]

Contradictions existed in the developments seen in the sixteenth century. At the beginning of the sixteenth century the complete armour, the 'white harness', completely covered the knight's body with metal plates. Its design reached its peak. Its efficiency, strength, and its weight (it could weigh as much as 55–66 lb), forced the knights to abandon the use of the shield.

When do we see the first changes? Fourquevaux gives us a glimpse of changes taking place in the middle of the century. He castigates 'these

---

42 Dominique Venner, *Les armes blanches, sabres et épées* (Paris: Jacques Grancher, 1986), p.85.
43 The Order of 1676, however, already imposed some basic criteria concerning cavalry weapons. Pierre de Briquet, *Code militaire ou compilation des ordonnances des rois de France concernant les gens de guerre* (Paris: Prault père, 1761), p.7.
44 What Birac suggests, for example. Sieur de Birac, *Les fonctions du capitaine de cavalerie, et les principales de ses officiers subalternes ... par le sieur de B* (Paris: Quinet, 1669), p.33.
45 Louvois' letter of 22 February 1679, underlines the turning point of the adoption of the new weapon: 'the King wants all his cavalry to be now armed with sabres instead of the swords our riders have had so far'. Quoted by Venner, *Les armes blanches*, p.103.
46 Christian Ariès, *Armes blanches militaires françaises*, 1er fascicule (Paris: Librairie Petitot, 1968). Quoted by Venner, *Les armes blanches*, p.103.
47 Olivier Chaline, *La bataille de la Montagne Blanche (8 Novembre 1620), un mystique chez les guerriers* (Paris: Noêsis, 1999), p.159.

THE NEW KNIGHTS

Fully armoured cuirassier, 1577. Abraham de Bruyn. (Rijksmuseum)

men-at-arms, who want to be man-at-arms, yet nevertheless desired to be armed and equipped the same as the light horse'.[48]

In the army assembled by King Henry II of France for the expedition of 1552, the light horse was already as numerous as the men-at-arms.[49] They served as light cavalry. However, even though their duties were more diverse than men-at-arms, we can now begin to consider them as a form of semi-heavy cavalry. They are moreover, 'light' only in relation to the complete armour of knights. The main difference was the minimal leg protection. Cuisses (or cuissots), and 'faulds' were replaced by long tassets that extended down to below the knee. Greaves or shin guards were replaced by tall and stout buff leather boots. Some men-at-arms began to lighten their armour by getting rid of some unnecessary elements, especially that protecting the legs.

Are these the first signs of the disappearance of armour? Things are more complicated than they seem. According to Father Daniel, after the lightening of armour under Henry, armour returned to 'the old manner' under Charles IX and Henry III.[50] The testimonies of authors in the second half of the century seem to support the change in direction, highlighting a significant increase in the weight of the armour. The reasons for this phenomenon seem quite clear: it is the wider use of more efficient firearms which explains the increase in defensive armour. This is also what La Noue records. The gendarmes 'had good reason' he said, 'because of the violence of the arquebuses and pistoles, to make their harnesses more massive and better tested than before'.[51] Tavannes insists this is particularly the consequences of the appearance of reiters or pistoleers, armed with wheel-lock pistols. So long as battles took place with the lance and sword, the traditional armour was sufficient to protect the men-at-arms. But the development of firearms and these 'big pistols', made such armour useless.[52]

These concerns are commensurate with the danger now facing all soldiers. Those who had adopted firearms were just as much vulnerable as men-at-arms. To be able to use their own firepower they had to expose themselves to the fire of their enemies. The short range of the pistols forced them to get very close to the opposing troops and they would not engage in this mutual exchange of

---

48 Fourquevaux, *Instructions*, p.24.
49 6,000 men in both armies. Général Louis Susane, *Histoire de la cavalerie française*, Tome I (Paris: J. Hetzel et Cie, 1874), p.47.
50 Père G. Daniel, *Histoire de la milice française et des changements qui s'y sont faits depuis l'établissement de la monarchie dans les Gaules jusqu'à la fin du règne de Louis le Grand* (Paris: Delespine et Coignard, 1721), Tome I, p.399.
51 La Noue, *Discours*, p.330.
52 Tavannes, *Mémoires*, p.191.

fire if they did not feel sufficiently protected by their armour.

The horsemen were therefore drawn into a race for improved protection. If La Noue recognised that the men-at-arms were right to reinforce their armour, it is regretful that they went too far in this direction. 'They have gone so far, that most of them have loaded anvils instead of armour.'[53] The 'beauty of the horseman' is diminished, all these defensive weapons have 'converted into deformity'. But it is the weight of the armour which now posed a problem. During the reign of Henry II of France, the gendarmes and light-horsemen 'had none of their heavy weapons which prevented them from wearing them for twenty-four hours. But those of today are so bad that a gentleman at thirty-five is crippled by such a burden'.[54] Tavannes makes the same observation. The penetrating power of firearms worried the riders. To protect themselves, they added new pieces of armour, sacrificing speed and agility for improved security. 'Those who do not want to risk anything to their fortune have reinforced their breastplates, made plastrons lined with blades, their musket-proof helmet, unable to serve in combat, being fought, chained and bound by the gravity of their weapons: they become like an anvil, motionless, charging the horses so much that the slightest accidents they succumb under'.[55] The relation between the evolution of arms and armour and the development of cavalry tactics is clear. Armed with pistols and heavy armour, charges were necessarily slower, and the original shock principle lost its importance.

Dutch cuirassier, 1618. Paulus van Hillegaert.

These increases were the reason why the abandonment of defensive armour on the legs took place. It is probable that attempts were made to compensate for the increases observed in the breastplate or helmet by reducing protection to the legs. 'La milice Françoise' of Louis de Montgomery depicts gendarmes wearing high boots by the beginning of the seventeenth century.[56]

Olivier Chaline noted the armour weight at the beginning of the Thirty Years' War, preserved in the museums of Vienna and Graz. His observations confirm that they were at least as heavy, if not more, than those of the men-at-arms of the first half of the sixteenth century. In Graz is a suit of armour weighing between 70 and 77 lb; the heaviest is 92 lb! Montecuccoli echoes Tavannes when he observes that the complete armour 'embarrasses the

---

53 La Noue, *Discours*, p.331.
54 La Noue, *Discours*, p.331.
55 Tavannes, *Mémoires*, p.191.
56 Montgommery, *La milice Françoise*, p.135.

person so much that the horse having fallen, the rider cannot help himself'.[57]

In these conditions it is easy to understand the intervention of Gustavus Adolphus. For P. Lacombe, the King of Sweden was 'the man of modern times, the enemy of the old defensive weapons which deprived the soldier of the freedom of his movements'.[58] It is true that the Swedish national cavalry was largely composed of regiments which, according to the norms of the time, were classified as light cavalry.[59] More specifically, they were – according to contemporary terminology – arquebusiers. They wore only a front and back plate, and tall boots covering their knees. Instead of the heavy and cumbersome helmet of the cuirassiers they donned a lighter helmet, generally of 'Polish' or 'Hungarian' type, covering the neck, the temples and had nasal protection. Part of the face was exposed, but the field of vision was considerably enlarged. But to what extent does the lightness of the armament of the Swedish cavalry result from a tactical choice, or by the will of the sovereign?

Gustavus Adolphus undoubtedly gave considerable impetus to the lightening of defensive armour when he himself decided not to wear a breastplate, which was impractical as a consequence of a musket ball taken at Dirschau in 1627.[60] Many officers then followed his example, whether they wanted to imitate their sovereign and make themselves known to him, or that they intended to take advantage of this opportunity to lighten defensive armour that they considered impractical. Gustavus allegedly at times had to order them to protect themselves.[61] But external factors of an economic and logistical nature undoubtedly played a significant role. At the time, Sweden was suffering from a significant technological delay from the point of view of their capacity to manufacture weapons. The Swedish workshops were unable to mass produce the essential elements of the 'modern' rider's armament and accoutrements. Until about the year 1640, most, including armour, had to be imported from Germany or Holland. For example, the manufacturer Louis De Geer was one of the main suppliers of the Swedish army. In addition, supply was sometimes difficult in times of war. Gustavus was thus faced with a lack of armour for his cavalry from the early days of the German campaign in November 1630.

Swedish King Gustav II Adolf (1594–1632). Copy of portrait by Michiel Jansz van Mierevelt, after 1633. (Rijksmuseum)

---

57 Raimondo Montecuccoli (1609–1680), *Mémoires de Montecuculi, généralissime des troupes de l'Empereur* (Amsterdam: Wetstein, 1752), p.19.
58 Paul Lacombe, *Les armes et les armures* (Paris: Hachette, 1886), pp.153, 154.
59 There were cuirassier units in the Swedish army, but they were almost exclusively non-Swedish in their make-up, being raised in Germany and the Baltic provinces.
60 Brzezinski, *The Army of Gustavus Adolphus*, p.6.
61 Brzezinski, *The Army of Gustavus Adolphus*, p.10.

This forced him to equip only a proportion of men of some regiments.

Finally, these external factors were combined with a real awareness of the inconvenience resulting from defensive armament that was too heavy. This was undoubtedly true when Gustavus Adolphus began his great reforms in 1620, and it became even more so when he engaged in the war against the Habsburgs. This evolution is particularly clear after Breitenfeld. This battle confirmed the idea that with the firepower now acquired by the infantry and the artillery, the heavy cavalry of the cuirassiers could not render more services than a cavalryman more lightly protected but less expensive, faster and more manoeuvrable.

Significantly, when the breastplates ordered from De Geer in January 1631 finally arrived in September 1632, Gustavus cancelled the delivery. The poor quality of the items was highlighted, but it appears that the equipment of the armoured cavalryman was no longer a priority.[62] A new manifestation of this is noticeable after Nördlingen. Defeated by the Habsburg army, the Swedish army was forced to make numerous and tiring marches, for which defensive armament proved to be an unnecessary luxury. Oxenstierna wrote from the theatre of operation that 'no harness or pot [helmet] for riders or soldiers needs to be sent here, because they would be of little use, most would even be rejected because of the long marches in which one is engaged'.[63] This was not a temporary decision but a new stage in the lightening of battle cavalry, where armour was worn less than before.

The first half of the 1630s was therefore decisive for Swedish cavalry and led to the almost complete abandonment of back and breastplates. Was this change also seen in other major European armies? Some had probably already made the same observations about the weight and usefulness of the armour as the King of Sweden. In the Imperial army the move to lighten heavy cavalry is visible from the middle of the 1630s. The last significant order for complete armour for cuirassiers dates from 1635. From then on, if some officers continued to wear it, the simple cuirassiers – very happy no doubt, to be able to lighten their burden – reduced theirs sensibly, and it now consisted simply of a musket-proof breastplate for the front and a thinner one to protect the back.

A transformation so radical and so rapid could not fail to arouse the interest of contemporary writers. James Turner, a veteran of the Swedish army, summarises very well the technical and tactical 'slip' then underway before his eyes: 'instead of cuirassiers we have arquebusiers, and instead of arquebusiers

Spanish trumpeters, siege of Jülich, 1622. Mattheus Melijn, 1636. (Rijksmuseum)

---

62 Brzezinski, *The Army of Gustavus Adolphus*, p.10.
63 Brzezinski, *The Army of Gustavus Adolphus*, p.11.

THE NEW KNIGHTS

we have riders, armed only offensively'.[64] This is a relatively important change that affects all mounted troops. Its main consequence is the disappearance of the most heavily armed cavalrymen and their replacement by a type of horseman hitherto regarded as light troops. Montecuccoli gives a rather precise description of what will be the complete defensive armour of Imperial heavy cavalry until past the end of the seventeenth century. 'The cavalry regiments are now armed with half cuirasses, which have the front and the back, Burgonet [open helmet on the front] composed of several iron blades fastened together behind and on the sides to cover the neck and the ears; and gauntlets, which cover the hand up to the elbow. The front of cuirasses must be musket-proof, and the other pieces must be pistol-proof and sabre-proof'.[65]

Even if one thinks that this evolution should not be credited solely to Gustavus Adolphus, it appears that the changes in the Swedish army carried some a considerable influence. Thus, the same Montecuccoli, giving in 1643 his opinion to the Duke of Modena on how to equip the cuirassiers, refers directly to the model of the Swedish cavalry: 'Cuirassiers must be equipped with a cuirass in front and behind, a helmet … That is the way Swedish cuirassiers are armed'.[66] Those whom Montecuccoli calls 'Swedish cuirassiers' were still considered light cavalry 10 years earlier, and the changes to the equipment of Swedish cavalry had been copied throughout much of Europe.

According to P. Lacombe, France did not adopt the changes implemented by the Swedes. French cavalry was still wearing armour at the beginning of the reign of Louis XIV, he says. The tassets were only abandoned around 1660.[67] *Le Parfait capitaine*, published in 1636, agrees. The Duc de Rohan still distinguished the two main categories of riders: the 'heavily armed' cavalry first – gendarmes and chevau-légers – which must have as defensive weapons 'cuirass, salad [helmet], armbands, tassets, knee-pad and loin-guards [kidney protector]'.[68] Then there was light cavalry – using a carbine – protected only by a 'pot' (simple helmet) and a breastplate.[69] So we find the cuirassiers and the

French officer, Saint Martin na Île de Ré, 1627, Jacques Callot, 1629–1631. (Rijksmuseum)

---

64 James Turner, *Pallas Armata* (London: 1683). Quoted by Brzezinski, *The Army of Gustavus Adolphus*, p.11.
65 Montecuccoli, *Mémoires*, p.18.
66 Quoted by Brzezinski, *The Army of Gustavus Adolphus*, p.11.
67 Lacombe, *Les armes et les armures*, p.155.
68 Henri, Duc de Rohan, *Le parfait capitaine. Autrement, l'abrégé des guerres de Gaule des commentaires de Cesar, suivy d'un recueil de l'ordre de guerre des Anciens, ensemble d'un traité particulier de la guerre.*(Paris: Houze, 1636), p.229.
69 The Duc de Rohan distinguishes between carabineers, using the rifled carbine, a wheel-lock weapon, and the arquebusiers proper, using the arquebus with a matchlock. The latter are hardly used any more according to him. The armies of Central Europe seem to use both terms indiscriminately.

THE MEN, THEIR ARMS AND TACTICS

equivalent of arquebusiers as they appeared at the beginning of the Thirty Years' War. However, it is not certain that in practice all French cavalrymen complied with these regulations. Thus, the Duc regrets that soldiers 'are reluctant to wear their armour, arguing that it is lacking in courage to go armoured'. For the individual horseman it was only a question of comfort, the absence of which was harmful to both combat effectiveness and discipline.[70] This attitude was probably not just held by a minority, it could be the expression of a wider movement towards the rejection of armour. For example, the requirement made in 1638 for all cavalrymen to arm themselves with defensive armour, on pain of disgrace, was reiterated in 1639.[71]

It seems in any case that the armament described by the Duc of Rohan in the mid 1630s quickly evolved. The examples kept at the Army Museum show that around 1640 most of the newer regiments of the so-called light cavalry – the former chevau-légers – have considerably lightened their armour. There are only a few pieces left, such as the breastplate, the colletin, the Burgonet. This in turn is also often replaced by an iron hat, even a felt one.[72] Although it is true that fuller armour was still worn at the start of the reign of Louis XIV, it only applied to the gendarmerie and some cavalry units. Indeed, from 1660 there was only one regiment, the Cuirassiers du Roi, who wore any armour.[73]

The period of the Thirty Years' War seems to be a real breakwater in the development and use of protective armour. The 'Swedish phase' of the conflict could be seen as a decisive moment. One can however also think that Gustavus Adolphus accelerated changes which without doubt would have taken place without him. This phenomenon ultimately holds less in the action of a man than in breaking the status quo. Every weapon system is maintained only because its advantages are greater than its disadvantages. But it became apparent to all from the mid 1630s, that the cuirassier was no longer fit for purpose. Cuirassiers' protection was undeniably effective, but it no longer outweighed the negative aspects of its use: by its cost and the complexity of its manufacture, but also its weight that made it a burden during campaigns and battle. More so since the general evolution of the art of war tended more and more to pit horsemen against horsemen. It was known that the weapons used by the cavalry – namely pistols, carbines and swords – were less powerful and effective than the infantry musket. Lighter protection, consisting of a simple breastplate, strong boots and an open helmet, offered a cost against quality effectiveness ratio higher than that of the heavy armour of the cuirassier. When it was realised that armies could operate on the battlefield with riders equipped at less expense and with additional mobility, agility and speed than when wearing heavier protection, the fate of cuirassiers was sealed.

---

70 Rohan, *Le parfait capitaine*, p.235.
71 Père Daniel, *La milice françoise*, p.401.
72 Marcel Dugué Mac Carthy, *Soldats du roi, les armées de l'Ancien Régime, 1610–1789* (Paris: Collections historiques du Musée de l'Armée-Preal, 1984), p.19.
73 *Ibid.*, p.56. All chevau-légers officers, however, are required to wear a breastplate in war.

2

Man and Horse

What were the qualities of effective cavalry? After discussing the evolution of armour and weapons, it is necessary to focus on a study of the main participants in the charge, namely the riders and their mounts. They are the ones who risk their lives on the battlefield, but for the officers and generals, these were fundamental factors to consider in the great game of war. Success or failure of a charge – a battle – may depend on the cavalrymen's behaviour, their qualities, and their faults. This is obviously equally valid for the infantry, but with horsemen the behaviour of an animal must also be considered. 'It is the horse that makes the rider'[1] said d'Auvergne. Specialists know very well that a bad horse is very dangerous in a troop. Xenophon observed that a horse inclined to kick out was to be eliminated, 'these horses are more dangerous than the enemy'.[2]

Our analysis will seek to identify, for the man and the horse, the criteria that governed recruitment and selection, observing the extent to which the demands of the cavalry charge weighed when it came to making choices. In both cases for example, it is useful to question the physical and moral qualities, the geographical origin, but also the study of the horses will have to consider the problems related to supply (*la remonte*).

The soldiers of the army of the King of France have been the subject of many studies, but it is nevertheless relevant to reflect on what the cavalry was doing. In other words, was it considered that the cavalry recruit had to possess characteristics and have these characteristics varied over time and with evolution of the art of war? By characteristics it is meant the physical (size), moral (courage, obedience …) and social criteria which, according to contemporaries, made a soldier fit to fight on horseback and to carry out a cavalry charge. The question arises particularly for our period, where the cavalry undergoes very important transformations which affect its makeup. Whilst not exhaustive, we will try to construct a 'pen portrait' of the heavy

---

1 *Service Historique de la Défense/Direction de l'Armée de Terre (SHD/DAT)*, 1MR 1732 f°89, 'Observations sur l'équitation', par d'Auvergne, février 1769. Jacques Amable d'Auvergne was riding master in of the riding school of the Royal Military School of Paris from 1756 to 1788.
2 Xenophon, *Le commandant de la cavalerie* (Paris: Les Belles lettres, 1973), p.34.

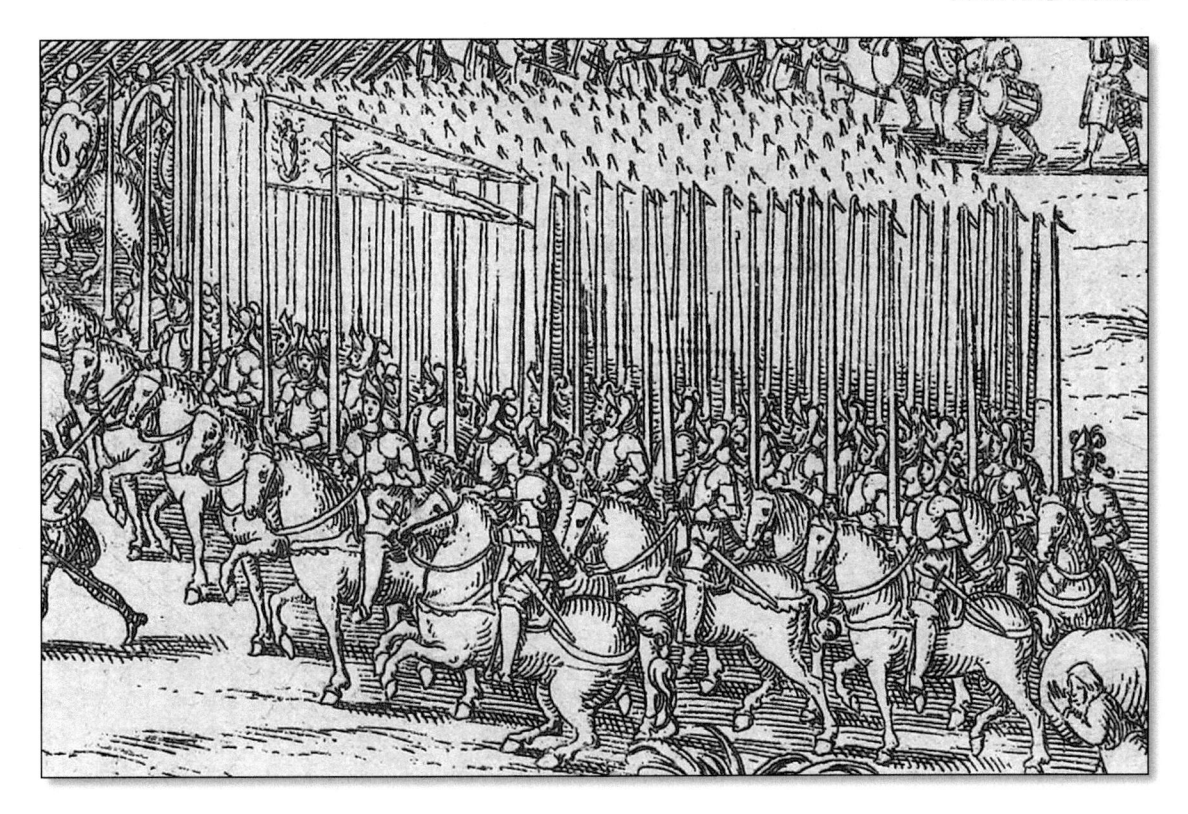

Imperial lancers, Tunis campaign. Frans Hogenberg, after Jan Cornelisz. Vermeyen. (Rijksmuseum)

cavalry fighter and then ask questions regarding the geographical criteria for his recruitment.

From the sixteenth to the seventeenth centuries, the physical criteria become clearer. The common soldier was of no concern to sixteenth century authors. When addressing this subject, it is usually without drawing any distinction between infantry and cavalry. It is clear that, at least in the first half of the century, the dominant figure of combat and the cavalry charge is still the gendarme. The lack of interest in the question of physique is evident from the writings of Machiavelli. For example, he would take soldiers for 17 to 40 years, 'nervous neck, broad chest, muscular arms, long fingers, little belly, rounded kidneys, legs and dry feet'.[3] The portrait thus drawn seems to illustrate the 'image' of the ideal infantryman and does not particularly represent cavalrymen. The same goes for Tavannes at the beginning of the seventeenth century. His observations on the physical qualities necessary to the soldiers are again limited to pikemen, arquebusiers and musketeers.[4] Fourquevaux nevertheless mentions the minimum age required – according to him – to accept young men into a mounted company. He said that they should not be less than 17 years old, and yet they could not immediately become a man-at-arms. They would have to wait at least six years and serve first in the mounted arquebusiers, the Stradiots and the light horse.

---

3   Machiavelli, *L'Art de la guerre*, p.746.
4   Tavannes, *Mémoires*, p.72.

French lancer, 1577. Abraham de Bruyn. (Rijksmuseum)

This apprenticeship by the less noble categories of the mounted troops seemed necessary to Fourquevaux, in order to acquire the wisdom indispensable to the man-at-arms.[5] It was not then the policy of the Royal Army (of France), but one might think that this dimension was somehow taken into account since the 1549 Ordinance sets the minimum age for recruitment at 17–18 years old for the archers – who were the 'light cavalry' of the *companies d'ordonnance* – and 19–20 years for the men-at-arms. Even if the authors of the first half of the sixteenth century do not bother to be specific, it seems obvious that the weapons used for the charge of heavy cavalry required robust and tireless combatants.

This becomes more apparent during the seventeenth century. Birac, captain of cavalry, is closely interested in the physical appearance of the rider. The captain must be 'a little physiognomist,' this facilitates his recruitment because 'almost all men carry on the forehead certain characters, by means of which one easily knows their behaviour and their inclinations'. The physical qualities required are broadly agreed; the rider must be of 'strong and robust' constitution, with a great deal of stamina, and must have the body 'dry and nervous'. Birac also says that he must have the 'proud look'. A pride no doubt based on the belief of belonging to a 'superior' arm, and on the need also to impress the enemy with a fearless face.[6] As for the age it was necessary to choose the horsemen between 18 and 35 years, beyond which the men usually have 'incorrigible defects and do not fold so well with the discipline'.[7]

Birac's remarks agree with those of Manesson-Mallet about the fitness of cavalry recruits, who he says must be 'robust' and says of the age that men were to be recruited aged between 20 and 30 years. The latter author, however, draws our attention to the question of size. The rider he says, 'must be of a mediocre size, both for the ease of riding and not to inconvenience him'.[8] Also the author of works of geometry and geography, Manesson-Mallet is not a specialist in the cavalry, yet his opinion should probably not be dismissed too quickly. It may suggest that the favourability towards large riders was not as strong, unlike in the following century.

The eighteenth century was obsessed with size, and it is this century which undeniably gives the most attention to the physical qualities of cavalrymen. This is especially true from the end of the War of the Spanish

---

5   Fourquevaux, *Instruction*, p.22.
6   Birac, *Les fonctions du capitaine de cavalerie* (1669), p.30.
7   Birac, *Les fonctions du capitaine de cavalerie* (1669), p.31.
8   Alain Manesson-Mallet, *Les travaux de Mars ou l'Art de la guerre* (Amsterdam: Janson, 1684–1685 [1st edition 1671]), vol. 3, p.94.

Succession. As we know, the tactical inertia observed during this conflict led officers and theorists to consider a number of lessons. Because the time was for reflection and the questioning of the 'routine', they did not neglect any element that could have contributed to improving the art of war. The choice of cavalrymen, if it was not of primary importance, could be one of those. This is for example what Langeais seems to think. There are three things to watch for in good and imposing troops, says the cavalry officer. The first is 'to have beautiful and good riders'. His definition of the handsome and good rider begins with the size, which must be 'reasonable'; five feet and a few inches. He must also be over 20 years of age, broad shouldered, be 'nervous and in force'. The qualities required certainly correspond to the physical constraints that a rider must be able to bear, but Langeais also emphasises that a tall rider, strong and proud, is advantageous because of his impression on the enemy.

We can probably find this idea in Birac's works, but it is only implied; Langeais does it much more clearly: one must choose such men because 'mediocre riders' do not impose 'a certain daring, which prints the attention and the fear'. This remark can be related to a widespread idea at that time that the outcome of the fight is decided in part before the melee takes place. The moral force of one of the two adversaries, manifested by his assurance and his audacious attitude, must assure him a certain superiority. De Saxe, who wrote in 1732 a few years after Langeais, argued something slightly different. Leaving aside the sturdy stature advocated by Langeais, he rather wants men 'slim, slender, and not ventrus (pot-bellied or paunchy)'. He is more assertive about his requirements regarding the size of the ideal cavalryman. He stated that they must be five feet six to seven inches for the horse regiments, as opposed to five feet or five feet one inch for the dragoons.[9]

Although it is exaggerating to state that they were the same throughout our period, the physical criteria for recruiting the new cavalryman seem to follow some recurring rules. He must generally be strong, robust, wide shouldered and tall; the importance of this last element having particularly increased in the eighteenth century. This 'profile' of the soldier of the heavy cavalry is dictated at the same time by military imperatives of general orders – the fatigues of the campaigns and by the constraints peculiar to the employment of this category of mounted troops. Used primarily as shock cavalry, the squadron must be made up of men strong enough and vigorous enough to face the enemy directly, repelling them by their mass and their strength; impressing them enough to make them feel beaten even before contact. This is not the case for the dragoons, who performed more reconnaissance missions and were required to fight on foot if necessary. The hussars also skirmished and concentrated on the 'little war', and were required to be quick and light, like their horses. We must not forget, however, that there was certainly a significant margin between the characteristics of the ideal rider as desired by the officers and the realities of recruitment. This

---

9   Maurice de Saxe, *Mes Rêveries* (Paris: Economica, 2002 [édition de l'abbé Pérrau, 1757]), p.125. The *Rêveries* were written in December 1732. It was for de Saxe's father, and only him, that the manuscript was intended for. It was published only after de Saxe's death in 1750.

difference varied greatly according to the frequency of wars, the intervening peace and the duration of the conflicts.

Should a cavalryman be braver than the infantryman? Some writers think that he must be of a more daring and resolute nature in combat. 'As it is the fact of the cavalry to go looking for and insult, and not to wait for them,' explains Birac, 'this is also why the captain must choose his bold and determined horsemen …, a lively and resolute spirit, passionate about good glory and fearing nothing but shame'.[10] Birac emphasises here a detail that will assert itself over time. Indeed, the gradual increase in the firepower of the infantry, which is accompanied by the final disappearance of the pikes by the late seventeenth and early eighteenth centuries, increased the possibility of remote combat between infantry decided by firepower. On the contrary, the mode of combat of the heavy cavalry, which rested on the charge, suggests at least theoretically the necessity of actual contact and close combat, even if firepower was used in the charge by many armies at least until the middle of the eighteenth century. The horseman must be brave; he is brave because he is a horseman; a horseman because he is brave. This link is one of the principles most present in the collective accounts concerning cavalry. The bravery and madness of the rider are the foundations of the *esprit cavalier*.[11]

Does the rider know no fear? The subject is obviously not the one that the military approach with the greatest of ease. However, courage and fear are two elements too intimately bound so that the authors did not – more or less directly – express themselves on the second. La Noue, whom we know had a pragmatic and lucid perspective, does not hesitate to evoke its manifestations. Thus, when a troop is arranged in formation, it may happen that men of valour and courage, usually the least numerous, rush wildly forwards while 'others who have little desire to fight (who pretend to bleed from their nose, have a broken stirrup, or their horse has cast a shoe), lag behind, so that in two hundred paces we see this long line becoming clearer, and big gaps appear in it … and often of 100 horses that started there will not be 25 of them who charge on'.[12]

The charge of cavalry, it cannot be forgotten, is the moment in battle at which anguish, and fear reach their maximum level.[13] The rider must therefore dominate his fear and overcome it. This is what true courage is, as defined by many authors. 'There are two kinds of bravery,' explains Courtilz de Sandras, 'one who does not know the danger and the other who knows and despises it; the first is recklessness and the other true value'.[14] The officers, especially the noble ones, seem particularly adept with this kind of courage. 'An officer whose birth has been aided by a happy education,' says Langeais,

---

10 Birac, *Les fonctions du capitaine* (1669).
11 Gilbert Bodinier in A. Corvisier (ed.), *Dictionnaire d'art et d'histoire militaire* (Paris: PUF, 1988), p.159.
12 François de La Noue, *Discours politiques et militaires*, ed. F.E. Sutcliffe (Geneva: Droz, 1967), p.337.
13 'The cavalry fights are terrible; the value alone always decides the victory, because one fights from man to man and with the sword', says d'Authville, *Essai sur la cavalerie tant ancienne que moderne* (Paris: Jombert, 1756), p.307.
14 Anonymous (Gratien Courtilz de Sandras), *Les devoirs de l'homme de guerre* (La Haye: Van Bulderen, 1693), p. 111.

'must know how to feel in himself that the most real value is not to ignore the danger, but it is duty to his country, the oath he has made to his prince to serve him, which makes him expose his life to support his interests'.[15]

Duty and honour thus appear as the main sources of courage. The second element, as we know, is not to be neglected. It is the 'demands of honour' that drive officers to face the danger because peer judgment was ruthless. Courtilz de Sandras mentions the case of a cavalry officer of noble blood who testified to weaknesses so 'inconceivable that he was obliged to change his status so as not to suffer further the mockery of others'.[16]

But is the simple cavalryman capable of feeling courage? In several works we find the idea that soldiers have some form of warlike state of mind, but this is most often considered as 'recklessness'. It would thus be only 'the ardour of the blood,'[17] the unconsciousness of danger in short, which would lead the horseman of rank into the charge.

Self-control and discipline were also necessary. The importance of the '*esprit cavalier*', the image of his legendary courage, must not hide from us the fact that fear was also the lot of the cavalryman. But the other moral qualities required for recruitment sometimes also deviate from the rider's image of Epinal. Thus, if Fourquevaux refused to incorporate too young recruits into the gendarmerie, it is also because they must first abandon 'the fury and fire of their youth' to become 'cold and moderate to know how to govern themselves wisely among the men-at-arms'.[18] This idea is not so surprising. It agrees as we have seen, with the image that was true courage, which, since the days of chivalry, was distinguished from the ancient and wild furore of the Frankish warrior.[19] At the beginning of the eighteenth century, Langeais again reminds us of this: 'courage is not associated with a tumultuous and angry mood, the characteristic of courage is a simple friend of reason'.[20]

In the same way, the horseman must be able to obey orders and comply with discipline. This concern is not new. To subdue the men-at-arms who were too impetuous, in the sixteenth century La Noe gave the necessary authority to

François de La Noue (1531–1591), author of *Discours politiques et militaires*

---

15 Monsieur de Langeais, *Des fonctions et du principal devoir d'un officier de cavalerie, augmentées de réflexions sur l'Art militaire* (Paris: Ganeau, 1726), p.151.
16 Anonymous (Courtilz de Sandras), *Les devoirs*, p.17.
17 Langeais, *Des fonctions et du principal devoir d'un officier de cavalerie*, p.152.
18 Fourquevaux, *Instruction*, p.22.
19 Cardini, *La culture de la guerre*, p.49.
20 Langeais, *Des fonctions et du principal devoir d'un officier de cavalerie*, p.150.

the captain who, in a compagnie d'ordonnance, 'must be obeyed with love or force'.[21] However, it is known how difficult it was for captains to be obeyed by young men-at-arms of their company. Above all, it seems that from the second half of the seventeenth century the demand for discipline was increasing. Louis XIV himself sets the example and boasts, in his memoirs, of the discipline of his armies.[22] Even if, as Pierre Goubert thinks, the King's point of view may sometimes seem viewed through rose-tinted glasses, the fact remains that never had such strict discipline been applied in the King of France's army.[23] The cavalry is not immune to this general movement and the criterion for recruiting riders encapsulates these new factors. Birac, as we have seen, wants to take recruits between the ages of 18 and 35 to make them 'agile, obedient and flexible, because older men … do not bend so well to discipline'.[24] Manesson-Mallet also states that they should not be too young, 'to be more adaptable to discipline'.[25] This issue does not change much in the following century. Maurice de Saxe sums up a widely held opinion that 'after the creation of the troops, discipline is the first thing to come. She is the soul of the whole military genre'.[26]

Where could we find the recruits who best matched the expectations of the officers? One can of course ask the question in terms of geography. In a very general way, it can appear that certain regions lend themselves better than others to the recruitment of soldiers. The preference for one or another may be influenced by certain prejudices. The role of the climate, for example, was not neglected. Jean de Tavannes, at the beginning of the seventeenth century, remarked that 'cold countries are the birth of great bodies and great forces, which increase courage … In hot countries the spirits dilated by the whole body, make men more ingenious and cunning in the face of danger'.[27] It is therefore logically in the 'temperate regions', such as France, Germany, Italy and Spain, that we find the best soldiers. But some more pragmatic men of war who were thinking about it also knew how to distance themselves from this theory. Fourquevaux, half a century before Tavannes, reminds princes that they can use their subjects regardless of the climate since we can clearly see by the ancient examples 'that in all places, cold or hot, there may be very good soldiers by means of exercise and good diligence'.[28]

Reflection on the regions most conducive to recruitment seems rather undeveloped in our period. The question of whether the simple rider should be recruited in the city or country is a recurring theme. Machiavelli, whose ideas on the criteria for recruiting riders is quite limited, establishes

---

21 La Noue, *Discours*, p.338.
22 Louis XIV, *Mémoires pour l'instruction du Dauphin*, présentation par Pierre Goubert (Paris: Imprimerie nationale, 1992), p.206.
23 To impose on the military of every rank the presence in the army, to establish a strict subordination, to advance the uniformity in the troops, these were the main objectives of Le Tellier and Louvois. André Corvisier, *Histoire militaire de la France* (Paris, PUF, 1992), Tome 1, p.401–404.
24 Birac, *Les fonctions du capitaine de cavalerie*, p.31.
25 Manesson-Mallet, *Les travaux de Mars*, vol. 3, p.94.
26 De Saxe, *Mes Rêveries*, p.154.
27 Tavannes, *Mémoires*, p.72.
28 Fourquevaux, *Instruction*, p.3.

a difference between the infantrymen and the mounted troops. The first must be chosen in the countryside and the second in the cities. He does not explain himself more precisely on the justification for this, but one can think that it is linked to his affirmed will to take the horsemen preferably from 'among the rich'.[29] These men must have had their own horse to be able to claim to be accepted in the cavalry. Machiavelli's preference for urban recruitment will not however, stand up. In the second half of the seventeenth century, the predilection for riders from the countryside is clearly affirmed. Manesson-Mallet reminds us that the rider must be of a robust constitution and naturally love horses.'That is why country riders are preferable to those in cities, where there is more delicacy'.[30]

Birac is more explicit and increasingly severe towards the city suggestion. Horsemen born in the fields, in the mountains and barren places must be taken as far as possible, 'accustomed if it is possible to go on horseback, fed on hunting and all sorts of fatigues. For those of the big cities are usually more delicate, nourished in the shade and the delights, and the most incapable of discipline, finding the sufferings of the war intolerable and exposing themselves less willingly to danger'.[31]

Spanish arquebusier, 1577. Abraham de Bruyn. (Rijksmuseum)

As we can see, two factors influence this idea. First, the physical constraints, since the peasant was supposed to have a stronger constitution and a stronger endurance, which makes him more able to bear the conditions of the military life than the delicate and softened city dweller. To this explanation, not devoid of prejudices, is added a second characteristic of the cavalry; the potential recruit must not only ride horses, but he must also know how to look after them and provide his mount with the necessary care so that, in view of the harshness of the conditions of life in campaign, his horse does not become quickly unusable, which would be tantamount to putting him out of the fight as well. But does this ideal drawn up by the authors correspond to the reality of recruitment? It is difficult to establish, and we need to jump out of our period to get an idea. The Chevalier de Chabo writing in the mid eighteenth century, was hardly optimistic and he estimates that two-thirds of recruits were city dwellers or peasants unaccustomed to horses.[32]

Because of its links with ancient chivalry, cavalry is traditionally considered a more 'noble' weapon than infantry. As part of research into the social origin

---

29 Machiavelli, *L'art de la guerre*, p.754.
30 Manesson-Mallet, *Les travaux de Mars*, p.94.
31 Birac, *Les fonctions du capitaine de cavalerie*, p.31.
32 SHD/DAT, 1M1730, '*Mémoire sur la cavalerie*' par le chevalier de Chabo, 1755–1756(?).

THE NEW KNIGHTS

Unarmoured arquebusier, 1577. Abraham de Bruyn. (Rijksmuseum)

of cavalrymen, the question on the numbers of the nobility within the composition of the troops can be asked. It does not arise much in the first half of the sixteenth century, since the cavalry is still confused in the minds of contemporaries, with the *compagnies d'ordonnance* and they are very largely composed of nobles.[33] It becomes more obvious from the moment the considerable growth of the numbers of the heavy cavalry renders inapplicable any idea of recruiting most of the combatants from the nobility.

The social criterion may have appeared problematic to some from the beginning of this movement of widening the recruitment target groups. Thus, at the Estates General (*Etats généraux*) of 1588, the recent intrusion of commoners within the gendarmerie may seem abnormal to the deputies of Paris. This social dilution was likely to alter a corps' discipline.[34] But above all, from the middle of the sixteenth century and especially with the beginning of the French Wars of Religion, new units of heavy cavalry appeared – even if they bore for a long time the denomination of 'light cavalry' – whose social composition was much more open: reiters and pistoleers, also known as cuirassiers or 'corasses'. These are not, of course, the first mounted troops to be made up of commoners, but they were then only mounted arquebusiers or stradiots, who apparently did not deserve the name of cavalry. With reiters and pistoleers it was a question of heavily armed units, whose mission was to directly oppose the gentlemen of the *compagnies d'ordonnance* and light horse companies, and who did it successfully.

This social characteristic of the reiter troops was noticed by contemporaries. Tavannes called to mind for example 'these reiters who make 'their valets their companions'.[35] Wallhausen was without doubt one of the most severe regarding these new cavalry troops. He very clearly opposed the lancers, gentlemen of quality, to the 'inelegance' that one asks for the cuirassiers.[36] He regrets that one recruiting party may have mainly sought the required numbers, at the expense of quality, and that the majority of cavalry units are now composed of 'poor servants or villainous scoundrels amassed from all sides to reach the target number'.[37] This is one of the major consequences of the wide adoption of pistols. As we have seen, these weapons are characterised by their ease of use.

---

33 Even if, as Louis Tuetey remarks, the companies did not recruit so easily among the nobility as one progressed through the century. *L'officier sous l'ancien régime, nobles et roturiers* (Paris: Plon, 1908), p.43.
34 Chagniot, *Guerre et Société*, p.20. Louis Tuetey observes in the same way that measures were taken as early as 1579 'to stop, or at least moderate, this threatening invasion of the commoners', *L'officier*, p.54.
35 Tavannes, *Mémoires*, p.73.
36 Wallhausen, *Art militaire*, p.17.
37 Wallhausen, *Art militaire*, p.47.

Thus, any man, if he knows how to ride a horse, can quickly learn how to use them. It was then possible to equip many simple soldiers quickly, the defects of the weapon being compensated by the mass effect.

In France, the development of the units of pistoleers testifies to the process of 'democratisation' which appeared during the Wars of Religion. The noblemen 'have been definitively robbed of the monopoly of the profession of arms, even the heavy cavalry is no longer for them an area'.[38] Louis XIII tried, however, to maintain a minimal number of nobles in his companies of light cavalry, as shown by the ordinance of 1629.[39] But these attempts were illusory, because from now on the need for men became too important. On the other hand, according to Louis Tuetey, 'the state of simple cavalier had become too humiliating for the nobility to be content with it'.[40]

One could then think that, failing to preserve the status of the rank and file, one could at least secure the social integrity of the corps of officers. However, at the end of the reign of Louis XIV, Hervé Drévillon showed that the proportion of officers promoted from out of the ranks was greater in the cavalry than in the infantry.[41] Of course, all these officers were not commoners, but their proportion was probably not insignificant, other than those from the lowest ranks. This phenomenon emphasises in any case that the cavalry 'reputed more aristocratic, was more open to the advancement of men out of the ranks'.[42] There was a greater share of experience gained from 'the bum on the saddle', because finally, 'the noble status of the cavalry was not so much the social character of its recruits, but rather the intrinsic dignity of the arm'.[43]

The qualities of the war horse predicate much of the success or not of cavalry, especially during a charge. But is it possible to get a clear idea of the warhorse and the characteristics that are specific to it? Nicole de Blomac first reminds us of the importance of applying the size criterion, measured from the hoof to the withers.[44] The coat colour, teeth and age of each horse were also important elements. But to judge the overall quality of the animal, men-at-arms and officers also observed other essential parts of the horse's anatomy: the rump, chest and joints. They could see immediately if the rump was full enough, the chest wide and the joints sound. There is an obvious difficulty facing the researcher here. The adjectives used to describe the condition of the horses would be quite significant to the ears of specialists, but much less so to a non-expert. They also suggest the importance of the aesthetics used in defining a 'good' horse. Despite this, we will try to determine

---

38 Jean Bérenger, 'Les armées françaises et les guerres de Religion', *RIHM*, n°155, 1983, p.26.
39 'He had expressed the wish to see the companies of cavalry and infantry filled with children of the nobility, so that in each there is at least the fourth part'. Tuetey, *L'officier*, p.55.
40 Tuetey, *L'officier*, p.55.
41 Hervé Drévillon, *L'impôt du sang, le métier des armes sous Louis XIV* (Paris: Taillandier, 2005), p.235.
42 Drévillon, *L'impôt du sang*.
43 Drévillon, *L'impôt du sang*, p.294.
44 Nicole de Blomac, 'Le cheval de guerre entre le dire et le faire. Quelques variations sur le discours équestre adapté à la guerre', in Daniel Roche (ed.), *Le cheval et la guerre, du XVe au XXe* (Paris: Association pour l'Académie d'art équestre de Versailles, 2002), p.57.

THE NEW KNIGHTS

Francis I captured at Pavia in 1525. Dirck Volckertsz. Coornhert, after Marteen van Heemskerck, 1555–1556. (Rijksmuseum)

the assumed or expected characteristics of a warhorse, highlighting areas where they might generate debate, and then give an account of the system of supplying and resupplying horses for the army.

What horse was in use at the beginning of our period? For the heavy cavalry, it was still the steed inherited from the end of the Middle Ages. One can imagine a breed of massive draft horses, like the Percheron of today. This image is of course wrong. One must not take too literally the beautifully stylised horses in the paintings of Uccello, nor their height and mass.[45] In fact, it seems that one should rather visualise an animal somewhat akin to a strong hunting horse. Gervase Phillips reminds us that the warhorse was the result of selective breeding; its size and characteristics corresponding to the role on the battlefield.[46] It was the result of a carefully operated selection process, which aimed at bringing together the best qualities of Arab horses and those of heavier European breeds.[47] The steed that was used at the beginning of the Italian Wars first emerged in the fourteenth century. Its size is subject to debate. R.H.C. Davis suggests that he could reach 17 or 18 hands, Andrew Ayton thinks more plausible the figures of 15 or 16 hands.[48]

---

45   Paolo Uccello (1397–1475), *The Battle of San Romano*, oil on wood, *c.*1456–1460.
46   Gervase Phillips, '"of nimble service": Technology, Equestrianism and the Cavalry of Early Modern Western European Armies', *War and Society*, XX, 2 (October 2002), p.16.
47   Liliane and Fred Funcken, *Le costume, l'armure et les armes au temps de la chevalerie* (Tournai: Casterman, 1977), vol. I, p.102.
48   R.H.C. Davis, *The Medieval Warhorse: Origin, Development and Redevelopment* (London: Thames & Hudson Ltd, 1989), p.69; Andrew Ayton, *Knights and Warhorses* (Woodbridge: Boydell, 1994), p.23. Works quoted by Phillips, 'of nimble service', p.16.

MAN AND HORSE

Yet the crucial point is probably more the horse's build. From the study of two sets of barding from the beginning of the Tudor period, Ann Hyland concluded that although they were able to carry significant weight, these horses were of moderate size but robust build.[49] Charles Gladitz says there is 'no doubt that they were generally quite big compared to other horses … the steed was a powerful and very strong animal, which could carry its own harness, the armour and the lance of its rider'. Speed and agility were then less important than strength and power.[50] Although they were not the enormous size sometimes attributed to them, the horses of the men-at-arms were still impressive animals. Those of Charles VIII of France made a good impression on Paolo Giovio when they entered Rome: 'Their horses, excellent in power and size, were more terrible because they cut off their hair and ears'.[51]

According to Phillips, it seems that during the sixteenth century horse breeders for the most part favoured a medium-sized warhorse, still robust but faster and more agile. The breeding programmes of Henry VIII and the Duke of Mantua could be an early example of this development.[52] However, although their size may have gradually decreased, the fact remains that the horses destined for the gendarmes and other 'shock' cavalry continued to be generally heavier and more powerful. The Lord of Fourquevaux, writing in the middle of the sixteenth century, insists that notice be taken of the specialisation of tasks to be undertaken by the horses in question. The difference between the arms, armour and tactics attributed to men-at-arms and those of the light horse do not permit them to be equipped with the same class of mounts. The former, preserved to undertake charges and close combat, do not have the same concerns for mobility as light horse. Their armour is accordingly full and heavy, and 'to bear such a burden they must have strong and large horses', especially as these are also in barding.[53]

The reflections of Fourquevaux are however rather brief. It was not until the end of the sixteenth century and the beginning of the next that a more detailed analysis was made of both squires and men-at-arms. This is hardly surprising for the former. The lessons of the Italian Riding Masters were sufficiently integrated in France for the French to develop their own styles. Although it is true that there was not yet a defined concept of military horsemanship, the authors still address the question of the warhorse. This is the case for example, of Salomon de La Broue, author of the first French horse-riding book.[54]

---

49 Ann Hyland, *The Warhorse, 1200–1600* (Stroud: Sutton, 1998), p.9.
50 Charles Gladitz, *Horse Breeding in the Medieval World* (Dublin/Portland: Four Court Press, 1997), p.157. Work quoted by Phillips, 'of nimble service', p.16.
51 Paolo Giovio, *Histoire de Paolo Govio sur les choses faites et advenues de son temps en toutes les parties du monde, traduite en français par Denis Sauvage, Historiographe du roi* (Paris: Olivier de Harsy, 1570), p.145.
52 John Tincey, *Ironsides. English Cavalry 1588–1688* (Oxford: Osprey Publishing, 2005), p.20. Dominique Fratani, 'Les chevaux des Gonzague à la bataille de Fornoue', in Roche (ed.), *Le cheval et la guerre*, p.48.
53 Fourquevaux, *Instruction*, p.24.
54 Salomon of La Broue (second half of the sixteenth century). Gascon Gentleman, page of Count d'Aubijoux, he travelled to Italy where he was a pupil of Pignatelli. He returned to France as squire of the Duke of Epernon and ordinary squire of the Great stable of the King. At the end of

THE NEW KNIGHTS

Fully armoured cuirassier. Workshop of Jacob de Gheyn II, 1599. (Rijksmuseum)

La Broue deals with the choice of fighting horse. He considers first the age of the horse. Here he qualifies the rather widespread judgment that 'old' horses would be more useful for war. Their age would make them more docile and easier to control, which is not without its uses in a charge or a melee. This is probably true, but for the author the necessities of war considerably alter the reasoning behind it. Let the lords who prefer these mounts for a day of combat thus make them fit for 'three months of marches, cavalcades and other fatiguing movements that one makes with the armies', they will regret then, when the day of battle comes, that they are not riding a younger horse.[55] La Broue was also a man of war, and this allowed him to consider some of the realities of the practice of war.

It appears from these observations that the choice of a warhorse cannot be considered solely from the point of view of shock tactics, even if as with heavy cavalry, it is its main mission. This does not mean of course, that La Broue ignores the characteristics of cavalry charges and combat. This is seen in the way he deals with the question of size; the second element in determining the effectiveness of a warhorse. At that time there were different opinions on the subject. He is inclined to favour big horses, 'better able to sustain a great shock and get out of a melee'. He did not think as some do, that small horses could compensate by their speed and determination, the defects of their size and strength. 'They will not be able to overthrow a bigger one even', he says, 'in shocking him in the middle of the race.'[56] These reflections highlight two important elements; first of all at the end of the sixteenth century, there seems to be a real debate about the size and stature of warhorses, as evidenced by the arguments of supporters of smaller mounts.[57] But on the other hand, the defenders of the 'great horse' – which includes La Broue – refused to compromise.

Finally, the last criterion of choice; the author examines the behaviour and temperament of the horse. From this point of view, he attacks the opinion of those who want their warhorses to be particularly fierce. On the contrary, they must be easy and peaceful in nature because the angry and fiery horse is not able to restrain himself and will tire quickly. A less active and excitable horse will be able to maintain his speed and strength to meet the needs of the rider. He will also be more manageable and obedient in melee. One

---

his life, when he was 'deprived of health, old and almost useless', he wrote *Le Cavalerice françois* in 1593.

55 Salomon de La Broue, *Le cavalerice c* (Paris: Charles du Mesnil, 1646), p.133. According to him 'the horses are in their best strength between seven and fourteen years'.
56 'In a charge', says La Broue, 'the bigger the shock is, the greater the horse has to bear a big return'. *Le cavalerice françois*, p.134.
57 La Broue, *Le cavalerice françois*, p.134.

cannot forget that, in the heart of a melee, the cavalryman who fights for his life does not have the leisure to also have to restrain and calm his mount.[58] Pluvinel, who was probably the most famous French rider of the seventeenth century, says no more than La Broue on this subject. We must therefore turn to others; that is officers and military theorists.

The publication of three books marks the beginning of the seventeenth century. In France, Jean de Saulx-Tavannes – who describes the thoughts of his father, Gaspard – reminds us, as will d'Auvergne a century and a half later 'that a part … of the value of the rider lies in the goodness of his horse'.[59] However, he does not focus much on the qualities he would require of a warhorse. The ideal mount, he explains, should not be tricky. She must not have any imperfections. He tolerates a strong mouth, because that can be corrected; it is better to be strong than tender. This observation about the mouth is not unimportant as it implies that Tavannes had real experience of horses. The horse's mouth is indeed the most sensitive part on which a rider interacts. If one doesn't take care of it, the mouth can become the main cause of resistance and lack of understanding by the horse.[60]

Dutch officer, 1618. Paulus van Hillegaert. (Rijksmuseum)

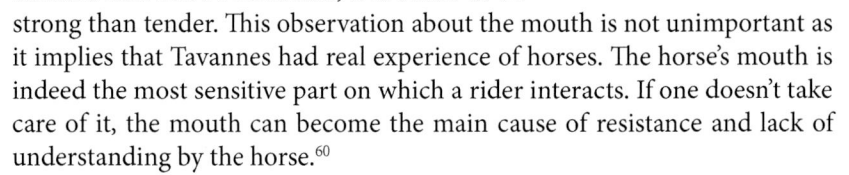

Finally, it is important for the author that the horses are strong and fit enough to remain in a melee, so that the rider can maintain a good seat and is not jostled or overthrown: 'the whole thing is that they are so strong that one can remain for longer in the fighting'.[61] Tavannes does not go much further in the description of the ideal horse. But his thinking still extends to emphasise the specificity of the mounts of the various mounted troops. He reminds us that the lancers, who are almost no longer employed at the time he wrote, must have strong and good horses, able to gallop to allow the lance its full effect. On the contrary, the cuirassiers who use pistols, do not need high quality mounts, they can be content with 'bad horses' without this preventing them from doing their service.

This remark is not specific to Tavannes, and it is even more widely developed by Basta and Wallhausen. For Basta – the Italian general – it is one of the main reasons he gives for the gradual disappearance of lancers and their inferiority compared to 'corasses'. The constraints related to the use of the lance – already underlined by Tavannes – forced them to have very good

---

58 La Broue, *Le cavalerice françois*, p.136.
59 Tavannes, *Mémoires*, p.209.
60 The means of communication through which a dialogue is established between the horse and the rider. They are the plate, the legs, the hands, the stick or the whip, the tone of the voice. M. Henriquet, A. Prévost, *L'équitation, un art, une passion* (Paris: Seuil, 1972), p.15, 64.
61 Tavannes, *Mémoires*, p.192.

THE NEW KNIGHTS

horses; mounts of 'price'.[62] This is not the case for the pistoleers. These men fight mainly with their firearms, so they do not need to gallop. On the other hand, the use of fire tactics also forces them to wear heavy, bulletproof armour. They clearly needed a 'strong and heavy horse'.[63] These characteristics made it possible to mount the corasses (cuirassiers or pistoleers) at a lower cost, and thus be able to recruit them in greater numbers because they need only 'mediocre horses which are everywhere sufficient'.

By using a modern analogy, one could say that Basta tackles the problem in terms of cost-effectiveness. What advantages then, can the lancer mounted on a high price horse expect when faced with armoured 'corasses' on horses of lesser value? 'They risk a significant loss without hoping for a small profit or even none.'[64] The analysis is tainted with much acrimony by Wallhausen. The decline of the lance and the increasing success of the 'corasses' is for him, militarily questionable and socially unacceptable. The question of mounts is another way of emphasising the contempt he feels for these pistoleers. These men would end up being nothing more than a bastardised form of lancer: 'Remove him [the lancer] with his lance, his good horse, giving him a smaller, heavy and useless for a sudden violence and it will then be a corassier.'[65] Unlike Basta, the mediocre mounts of the pistoleers did not in his opinion give an advantage; on the contrary, they are a sign of inferiority and weakness. In general, Wallhausen seems not to understand, or want to understand the principle upon which Basta's argument is based. It fails to understand the war in terms of economy, in the sense of getting the best effect at the least cost. It is precisely because the lancer's horse is so expensive – too expensive compared to the benefits it brings – that it becomes used less frequently and that this category of heavy cavalry is almost abandoned.

After La Broue, Basta and Wallhausen, we get a clearer idea of the horse of heavy cavalry at the end of the sixteenth and start of the seventeenth centuries. The evolution highlighted by G. Phillips towards medium-sized frames and faster and more agile mounts is certainly valid, but it should not be exaggerated. In particular, the tactical context must be considered. It is now the time of the reiters and other cuirassiers who rely mainly on firearms. Their way of fighting is no longer the same as that of the lancers and knights. Their horses are also different, but not quite in the sense envisioned by G. Phillips.

Fully armoured lancer. Workshop of Jacob de Gheyn II, 1599. (Rijksmuseum)

---

62 Basta, *Le gouvernement de la cavalerie légère*, p.72.
63 Basta, *Le gouvernement de la cavalerie légère*, p.20.
64 Basta, *Le gouvernement de la cavalerie légère*, p.72.
65 Wallhausen, *Art militaire*, p.28.

It is not their speed and agility that characterise the mounts of the cuirassiers of this period. The physical qualities expected of these horses depended heavily on their tactical use and the constraints of weapons and armour. Their riders were heavy and used the pistol which dispensed with the need to gallop. Horses therefore did not need to be of high quality. On the contrary, they must be easy to find, strong and heavy enough to support the man and his armour to be able to play a role during a charge or a melee. 'It may be possible,' says Wallhausen, 'to have common horses, provided that they are strong and obedient to the bridle'. The horses of the officers and of the aristocracy, carefully raised and selected, certainly support the idea of a progression towards more agility and speed and not those of the simple horsemen, which constitute the greater part of the mounted troops.

What of the choice between size and agility? These questions are still valid at the beginning of the Thirty Years' War. The tactics had not changed, and the armour of the cuirassiers was still heavy. In the second half of the conflict however, the conditions that dictated the choice of warhorses evolved. The influence of the Swedes was felt in two areas; the speed of the charge first, which Gustavus wanted to be carried out at the gallop. These evolutions made the heavy horses less necessary and implied on the contrary that horses needed to be a little more agile and fast. G. Phillips observes that the authors of the seventeenth-century push more for the requirement of agility and lightness.

The horse must have a 'good footing'. John Vernon, an officer of the Parliamentarian cavalry during the English Civil War recommends in 1644 a 'skilful and agile horse, of a suitable stature, of 15 hands of height'.[66] A few years later, Charles V, Duke of Lorraine, asserts that the ideal warhorse must be powerful and well-proportioned rather than large and heavy. It is important that he has strong legs and a 'good footing'.[67] It is now the ideal that the mount be lighter and livelier than the heavy horses of the cuirassiers. However, there

Cuirassier (top) and unarmoured arquebusier, both 1600. Paulus van Hillegaert. (Rijksmuseum)

---

66   John Vernon, *The Young Horse-Man, or the Honest Plain-Dealing Cavalier* (London: printed by Andrew Coe, 1644), p.1. Book written during the winter 1643–1644. Fifteen hands was also the size advocated by John Cruso in 1632, *Militarie Instructions for the Cavallrie* (Cambridge: printed by the printers of the University of Cambridge, 1632).
67   Phillips, 'of nimble service', p.17.

THE NEW KNIGHTS

was no question of sacrificing the size or the build of the horse. Vernon still advocates a height of 15 hands, which was already the case in the previous century. Charles V, meanwhile, wanted his horses to be powerful. The horse of the heavy cavalry must be able to look the part in melee and not to cause any problems with the riders during charges.

French military writers of the second half of the century are not very concerned about the subject. Birac, who nevertheless devotes a work to cavalry officers, is rather vague. The captain, he says, 'will buy the best horses he can find, whoever they may be, provided they are good and clean, that is, they are neither too old nor too young, nor too small or too tall, taking them rather larger than smaller, good legs, fit for fatigue'.[68] It can hardly be less precise. Perhaps we see here less a lack of interest in the question rather than a great deal of pragmatism. Unlike Charles V, Birac is probably not trying to describe the ideal warhorse, but rather the type that the captain would be likely to find and must be content with. It should be noted however, that it makes two recommendations. These correspond to the two constraints which weigh the most on the use of the warhorse. Birac wants his horses big, fit to fight, and endowed with 'good legs', to better handle the fatigue of campaigning. The author reminds us in passing one of the most constant realities of the war on horseback. Fighting occupies only a small part of the time, the rest is given over to marches and counter marches, which exhausts men and horses alike. La Broue, as we have seen, had already arrived at this conclusion at the end of the preceding century.

French officer, Saint Martin na Île de Ré, 1627, Jacques Callot, 1629–1631. (Rijksmuseum)

A contemporary – La Touche – brings a somewhat different vision. His is one of the only ones to evoke horse fencing, so his concept of what makes a 'good' horse is instructive. 'The horse has to be strong and big,' he says. 'Everyone knows that the strength of the horse increases that of the rider. Indeed, it is certain that it will open a press more easily, that it will overthrow the horse of the enemy by its weight, and that the blows that will be given from top to bottom will have much more force'.[69] La Touche speaks as a man experienced in combat. His point of view is unambiguous, stating that a high stature and the power of the horse remain fundamental criteria.

---

68 Birac, *Les fonctions du capitaine de cavalerie*, p.33.
69 Philibert de La Touche, *Les vrays principes de l'épée seule* (Paris: F. Muguet, 1676), p.95.

His words, however, suggest as Gervase Phillips does, that there is a debate between the supporters of the great horses and those of the smaller. Some consider the latter, La Touche explained, 'because they have more skill and lightness, and it is true,' he concedes, 'that barbs can serve in a pass or particular fight'. However, one can also find great horses that have the agility and lightness, and especially as this type of combat does not compare to the close combat of cavalry squadrons and does not possess the same requirements. Large size horses have so many advantages 'when you fight in troops and in battles that I think they should be preferred'. A limit appears, however, in his presentation of the perfect warhorse. Unlike Birac, it focuses only on the demands of combat itself, and ignores the other aspects of military campaigns.

The comparison of these writings with those of Vernon or Charles V, reveals two important lines of thought. Firstly, they make it possible to assert that the strength of the horse, its strong stature, and its large size, remain characteristics to which the officers attach a great importance because of the very nature of the combat between heavy cavalry units. On the other hand, they also testify to the real interest in the agility and the lightness of a warhorse. Consequently, they highlight some authors' opinions who call into question the usefulness of large horses. Size is therefore one of the fundamental criteria for selecting the ideal among warhorses.

This concern for size is clearly reflected in the texts of the French monarchy. They suggest a worry caused by the issue and try to fix it by ordinance. The ordinance of 25 September 1680 requires horses of about four feet seven inches (1.48 m). They must in all cases not exceed four feet eight inches (1.51 m), and not be less than four feet six inches (1.4 m).[70] As can be seen, the maximum size prescribed is not far from the 15 hands recommended by Vernon. Yet the cavalry faced some constraints that led to a downgrading of the desirable size. The King was informed that 'the horses of the size of the order of 1680 were extremely expensive, and that those of smaller size survived more easily and withstood the fatigue better'.[71]

This observation reflects the difficulty that the kingdom faced in equipping mounted troops. But it also shows that the authorities had to consider the absolute logistical requirements, especially the upkeep of horses such as the provision of fodder, replacement horseshoes and saddlery. Finally, we note concerns about stamina. This is now new but emphasises the fact that heavy cavalry should not be confined to shock actions, but also takes part in marches, foraging and scouting. The ordinance of 25 October 1689 therefore provides for a slight loosening of requirements, as well as establishing the difference between the horses of the gendarmerie and the regiments of the line cavalry, by then largely referred to as chevau-légers.[72] Those of the gendarmerie must be between four feet seven inches (1.47 m) and four feet five inches, the second

---

70 Ordinance of 25 September 1680. Pierre de Briquet, *Code militaire ou compilation des ordonnances des rois de France concernant les gens de guerre* (Paris: Prault père, 1761), Tome 2, p.32.
71 Briquet, *Code militaire*, Tome 2, p.33.
72 The gendarmerie, which constituted the 'heavy cavalry', was composed of the units of the king's household and of the gendarmerie companies, heirs to the old *compagnies d'ordonnance*.

between four feet six (1.44 m) and four feet four inches. Two years later, there was another new ordinance which concerned only the horses of light cavalry and dragoons. For the former, the height should not exceed four feet four inches (1.39 m), nor less than four feet two inches (1.3 m).[73]

We have seen a succession of ordinances over just a few years. Their frequency probably reflects the difficulties in the supply of horses for the cavalry, but it also quite clearly indicates a tendency to decrease the size of warhorses. Those of the gendarmerie were not covered by the last ordinance. But the suggested size of mounts for the light cavalry goes from four feet eight inches to four feet four inches at the most, a substantial decrease of four inches. The need to have well-built horses to take part in melee seems to decline at the end of the century, given the logistical constraints and the concern for mounts having a degree of versatility.

The debate about the need for large mounts still appears to be relevant in the early eighteenth century. That is what Marshal Villars believed. In a memoir of 1701, he considers it indispensable not to order the captains to have large horses. He wrote that he would like the King to give 'orders like those he once received'.[74] This sentence probably refers to the orders of the end of the previous century and suggests that on the eve of the War of the Spanish Succession, the French had returned to a predilection for larger mounts. His arguments are in line with the ideas already mentioned in these ordinances. 'Firstly because of the high price, being more difficult to support a cavalry which costs three times more than our enemies. Secondly, big horses cannot provide a race or graze easily'. Horses of mediocre size seem to him easier to maintain and to keep in the field than the big ones.[75] Very pragmatic reasons, which recognise the constraints of economy, subsistence, and versatility.

At the end of the War of the Spanish Succession the debate always seems open. Not all cavalry officers seem to share the opinion expressed by Villars at the beginning of the century. This is true in the case of Langeais. This officer explains that the most suitable size is a height of four feet nine inches (1.53 m), that is significantly bigger than the orders apparently referred to by Villars. Not that he ignores the realities of being on campaign, but his preference is based more on the requirements of cavalry charges.

The horses, he explains, must be 'wide and well crossed, strong enough to withstand the press, and if it is still possible, light, to do the races that are necessary, because a heavy horse gets tired easily'.[76] Stamina takes second place, and it is the ability of the horse to meet the challenges of shock action that prevails. Langeais insists on this necessity: 'by the size which I fix with the horses it is to follow the opinion where I am to believe that a small horse not having the strength of a big, when it is a question of entering a squadron, it cannot cause the same effect, by the shock and the wrinkling of the shoulder'.[77]

---

73 Ordinance of 24 Novembre 1691, Briquet, *Code militaire*, Tome 2, p.32.
74 SHD/DAT, 1M 1725, f°1, 'Mémoire de Villars', 30 Octobre 1701.
75 SHD/DAT, 1M 1725, f°1, 'Mémoire de Villars', 30 Octobre 1701.
76 Langeais, *Des fonctions et du principal devoir d'un officier de cavalerie*, p.126.
77 Langeais, *Des fonctions et du principal devoir d'un officier de cavalerie*, p.126.

The author therefore claims horses of the same size as those that equipped the heavy cavalry in the sixteenth century. Would he be an officer with too traditional, even anachronistic views? The answer is not obvious because it appears that his observations echo the writings of Maurice de Saxe.

In his *Reveries*, de Saxe does not argue for versatility. On the contrary, the cavalry must preserve itself for what constitutes its raison d'être, according to de Saxe; shock action. The size prescribed by the count remains particularly high (at least five feet two inches or about 1.65m).[78] Even if he wants only a smaller number of them, it seems difficult to understand how a kingdom like France could really consider supplying all its regiments with big and expensive horses.

It seems in any case that Langeais and de Saxe were not alone in their views. A year after the latter wrote his *Reveries*, the ordinance of 28 May 1733 highlights the preference of officers for large horses. 'Although the size of the horses has been regulated by different ordinances', the latter states, 'nevertheless the captains buy horses much higher than what is prescribed by the said ordinances.' Consequently, the monarchy was forced to legislate to limit abuses, but knew also to consider the realities of horse supply. From now on there will be 'no horses received for the remount of the light cavalry above four feet eight inches or four inches at most'.[79] This size is found to be well above that prescribed in the ordinance of 1689, and especially in that of 1691 (four feet four inches). The heavy cavalry mount of the first half of the eighteenth century remained of a size very close to that of its predecessor of the previous century.

How to acquire horses meeting the criteria we have just determined? Before answering this question, it would be useful to try to take stock of the needs of the cavalry and the army. This requires a brief consideration of the numbers required, but also to try to understand the likely losses incurred. We can then question the officers and men to determine what, according to them, were the most suitable regions or countries to produce horses necessary for heavy cavalry.

Regiments of heavy cavalry were not the only ones needing remounts. The considerable increase of the strength of armies had resulted in at least a proportional increase in overall horseflesh requirements. Of course, it is equally necessary to take account of the desire of the nobility to show off, which is particularly evident among officers and their servants, and

Claude Louis Hector de Villars (1563–1743). Martin Bernigeroth, 1704. (Rijksmuseum)

---

78 De Saxe, *Mes Rêveries*, pp.125–126.
79 Ordinance of 28 May 1733, Briquet, *Code militaire*, Tome 2, p.12.

includes a number of horses that cannot be negligible. As to the numbers of the heavy cavalry, strictly speaking, it is certain that there must be lots of them. Remember however, that the practice of dismissing some regiments at the end of the conflicts was still prevalent, to relieve the royal coffers. The number of horses needed could therefore fluctuate considerably. In the seventeenth century for example, the end of the long war with Spain (1659) gave rise to a general reform of almost all the regiments of 'light cavalry'. Only four complete regiments and about 60 free companies were kept. By 1665 the number of regiments was increased to 41, then 45 in 1667 and 95 the following year. On the eve of the peace of Nijmegen in 1678, the 'light cavalry' had 99 regiments, theoretically representing 47,100 horses.[80] The Nine Years War and the War of the Spanish Succession led to more regiments being mobilised, and the number of regiments of cavalry and dragoons reached 147 and 135 respectively; a significant proportion of the army.

These are of course theoretical numbers. The losses in combat on one hand and those caused by exhaustion or diseases on the other, reduced the number of horses in a sometimes very critical way, thereby forcing an increase in numbers for the next campaign. There is some evidence to estimate the number of horses of cavalry lost in battle. The main battles could give us more or less accurate figures. We must be careful because we know that, as for their riders, some of the wounded animals would die in the hours or days following the battle. On the other hand, it is not necessarily sufficient to try to establish proportions of losses for the entire cavalry of an army. A seemingly unimportant overall figure can mask very high loss rates for regiments that have been particularly engaged. At Poltava (1709), Peter Englund observes that a unit like the Vologodska regiment lost 24 men killed and missing against 127 horses lost. The Kropotov regiment, hurt hard in the battle, suffered the loss of 56 men while 244 horses perished (nearly a quarter of their strength).[81]

If battles are the source of a great many deaths and injuries for horses, the next cause of losses is not negligible. The afflictions suffered by horses in armies were not fundamentally different from those which they could experience in civil life. But the peculiarities of military life – such as large concentrations of animals or often stressful living conditions – could and did worsen the scale and consequences of these losses. As Pol Jeanjot-Emery observes, there are few contemporary testimonies on this subject. It was not until the second half of the eighteenth century that it was possible to see a thorough analysis of the causes of mortality among horses.[82] Nasal discharges were one of the main calamities affecting mounted troops, as it makes the horse gradually unfit for any service, before in many cases leading to death.

---

80 Susane, *Histoire de la cavalerie française*, vol. I, p.126.
81 Peter Englund, *Poltava, Chronique d'un désastre,* translated from Swedish by by Erik Harder (Paris: Esprit ouvert, 1999), p.251.
82 Pol Jeanjot-Emery, 'Les maladies, les accidents et les blessures du cheval de guerre', in Roche (ed.) *Le cheval et la guerre, du XVe au XXe siècle* (Paris: Association pour l'académie d'art équestre de Versailles, 2002), pp.299–300.

Can we now quantify the needs of the cavalry each year, in times of peace and war? The exercise is difficult for the period covered by this book, but the estimate proposed by the Chevalier de Chabo in the middle of the eighteenth century can at least provide us with some benchmarks. In fact, it fixes the numbers of remounts to one sixth of the cavalry strength each year in time of war.[83] This figure, applied for example to the Dutch War, suggests that the cavalry of the King of France would need every year about 8,000 horses.

Who was responsible for the supply of horses? Based on the system of the farm-company (*compagnie-ferme*), the organisation of the French cavalry made the captain the owner of his company, so it was up to him to find and buy the horses necessary for the mounting of his troop. Captains operated individually or collectively, as they did for recruits. They made their purchases with the funds that the King gave them in addition to their salaries; funds which often proved insufficient. The cost of the horses thus represented one of the principal expenses of the captain; an expense which increased considerably under the reign of Louis XIV.[84] To relieve him of this burden however, the King could intervene and contribute to the purchase of horses. This was sometimes the case when new regiments were created, or when some companies had been destroyed by an epidemic or by enemy action. In these cases, the King was trading with suppliers such as the Hogguers, who in 1704 committed to supply 6,660 horses for the cavalry and 3,340 for the dragoons.[85]

Whether it be the responsibility of the captain or the King, the provision of remounts remained essential to allow the cavalry to properly perform its tasks. Providing poor horses as remounts, or those unsuited to the demands of combat, could have considerable consequences on the battlefield. From the seventeenth century, contemporary authors and cavalry officers seem to include this issue more often in their reflections. Birac shows that the task of providing remounts, though not glorious, was taken seriously by the leaders concerned with the conduct of their company.

The captain had to first sell the 'ruined' horses and buy better ones instead, then supply horses to those of his men who were on foot by the end of the campaign. The author insists particularly on the need to provide remounts without delay. 'This is,' he says, 'a very important thing that must occupy the captain as soon as he enters winter quarters'. This priority is mainly due to the need to train and discipline the horse, to exercise it to withstand the fatigue it will face when on campaign; 'If the riders had not been mounted until the start of the campaign, most of the horses would not be fit for service, especially if they were too young or had not been wintered well; and the least work could put them out of action'. In addition, horses are generally cheaper at the beginning of winter than when entering the army.[86]

---

83 SHD/DAT, 1M1730, 'Mémoire sur la cavalerie', par le chevalier de Chabo, 1755 ou 1756.
84 In 1690 it took about 250 livres for a mount. During the War of the Spanish Succession, prices exceeded 350 livres. But the King only gave the captains of cavalry a sum of 150 livres for purchase of each horse and his equipment. Drévillon, *L'impôt du sang*, pp.123–124.
85 Jacques Mulliez, *Les chevaux du royaume, aux origines des haras nationaux* (Paris: Belin, 2004) p.169. The funds were then taken from the royal treasury, for example they amounted to over a million livres in 1704.
86 Birac, *Les fonctions du capitaine de cavalerie*, pp.155–156.

THE NEW KNIGHTS

Lancer from Netherlands, 1577. Abraham de Bruyn. (Rijksmuseum)

Most authors who dwell on the issue of horses usually give some thought to the regions and countries that provide the best animals. If it is difficult to ascertain what was meant then by a 'good horse', the previous pages allow us to glimpse some of the characteristics sought for horses fighting in line: tall, wide, robust and resistant to fatigue. What, in the eyes of contemporaries, were the privileged sources of the production of such horses?

Several countries may be mentioned, but for a variety of reasons only a small number seem appropriate. Thus, from the most distant, the horses of Turkey may have seemed excellent, especially in the eyes of Pluvinel, but as the author acknowledges 'we have too little of them to talk about it'.[87] Closer to home, the good horses of Italy, North Africa or the horses of Spain are also praised. The latter are even the most esteemed horse for La Guérinière, because of their courage, their docility, and their obedience when conducting 'a day of business'.[88] Jean de Tavannes, however, criticises these three sources of mounts to be too rare. Finally, the same Tavannes seems to sum up the opinion of most cavalry officers of our period when he asserts that the source of the best are the horses of France and Germany; the latter being included in a broad geographical sense.[89]

These are for many authors, the two main sources for supplying horses to the French heavy cavalry, even if all the regions of Germany were not accessible or suitable. In France too, some regions seemed better at producing heavy cavalry horses. At the forefront of these was Normandy, Brittany and perhaps Limousin. The horses of Limousin are sometimes mentioned first, but it is probably appropriate to qualify their importance. Then there is Brittany. Two bishoprics were in fact particularly concerned by the production of horses of the type wanted for the cavalry: Leon and Tréguier. But some of the Breton horses, especially those of Leon, were found in Normandy. This province was in fact, both a 'foaler' country (Cotentin) and a 'breeder' country, able to raise and train foals bought in other provinces. The plain of Caen is in the second category, and it specialised in the feeding and training of the young foals fit for the cavalry. Jacques Mulliez asked himself 'to what extent most of the Norman horses fit for the cavalry are not in fact Breton foals 'Normandisés'.[90] He also mentions Poitou, and this last region also seems to be able to produce suitable mounts. Phillipe Chabert remarks

---

87 Antoine de Pluvinel, *L'instruction du roi en l'exercice de monter à cheval* (Amsterdam: Schipper, 1666 [1625]), p.18.
88 François Robichon de la Guérinière, *L'Ecole de cavalerie* (Paris: Jacques Collombat, 1733), p.30. About the Turkish horse, La Guérinière is more nuanced than Pluvinel.
89 Tavannes, *Mémoires*, p.192.
90 Mulliez, *Les chevaux du royaume*, p.58.

in 1788 that, despite some shortcomings, some elections of this géneralité[91] provide horses 'very good, very strong and very nervous', useful for the cavalry and the dragoons.[92] Other regions also produced horses for the army, such as Boulonnais and Franche-Comté, or the Pyrenees and Auvergne. But the former provided stronger horses, used for pulling gun carriages, and the latter mounted the dragoons and hussars.[93]

The main changes from the sixteenth and seventeenth centuries are undoubtedly the evolution of the composition of the heavy cavalry. The spread of firepower allowed it to increase its numbers and expand its recruitment, both from the point of view of riders and horses. The criteria that dictated the choice of recruits became increasingly apparent during the modern era. Some of these related to the military life or the nature of the equestrian arm in general. But other criteria were more directly related to what remains – in the opinion of the greatest number – the main mission of the heavy cavalry, the cold steel charge. This is because, at least in theory, in a direct confrontation with the enemy, the man and his horse are required to control their fear. It is because the charge must be conducted in the most orderly manner possible that they must also be disciplined and attentive to orders. Finally, the very nature of this type of combat, based on the shock factor, led the officers to want to recruit riders and horses of robust stature and tall, even if this last point is not admitted by all.

---

91 Main administrative circumscription in early modern France.
92 Chabert, director general of veterinary schools, left valuable reports following these inspections in the west between May and October 1788. Blomac, 'Le cheval de guerre entre le dire et le faire', p.60.
93 Jacques Mulliez, 'Le cheval d'arme en France au XVIIIe, un fantôme?', in Roche (ed.), Le cheval et la guerre, pp.70–71.

3

Organisation and Training

It is not enough for riders to be recruited, mounted and armed. They must be able to fight on horseback. This implies first of all the existence of an organisation that will shape them; a pyramid organisation that will ensure that the soldiers are not left to fend for themselves;that will facilitate unit cohesion and guarantee the general that his orders will be followed. It seems impossible to envisage any approach to war and combat without a thorough knowledge of these basic assumptions that shape the army. The organic structure of the French cavalry was set around the middle of the seventeenth century. Each rider was then only a tiny part of a whole, and was successively integrated into a company, a squadron, a regiment and an army brigade. These structures differ in their size and functions, which are characterised administratively or tactically. It should also be remembered that what is being described here could vary from one country to another.

Riders must be trained and exercised. 'Whatever the choice and the weapons of a soldier, his exercises must be the main object of your care, otherwise you will not draw any useful part.'[1] Machiavelli's assertion is significantly aware of the importance of the training of men in the new art of war. However, this seems to have mainly been within the context of the infantry, with the cavalry seeming neglected. The issue is nevertheless essential because there is a substantial link between cavalry combat and instruction. The number of elements involved in the successful conduct of a cavalry charge implies the existence of a minimum degree of formation training, without which it would be doomed to failure. Riders must master their mounts, use their weapons, keep their place within the unit, manoeuvre and all whilst under enemy fire. Training is one of the elements that can make a difference on the battlefield.

Our analysis will focus exclusively on the organic structures of the company and the squadron, these being the structures that provide the most relevant framework for studying cavalry combat. Initially a sub-unit of a larger body of cavalry, the company then becomes primarily an administrative entity. The squadron, which emerged later, represents the basic tactical unit on

---

1 Machiavelli, *L'Art de la guerre*, p.766.

ORGANISATION AND TRAINING

the battlefield throughout the seventeenth and eighteenth centuries. As the company became less important, the squadron formed the unit of reference for cavalry in most narratives and theoretical discussion; an indication of their importance; it is by the number of squadrons that one judges the strength of the cavalry of an army.

Although the tactical importance of the company declined from the end of the sixteenth century, it remains an important topic of study for the entire period. First of all, from the perspective of battle, it is the number of companies and the size of each of them on which the strength of a squadron depends. From an administrative point of view, the implications for combat, though indirect, are nonetheless very important. Finally, it undoubtedly has the strongest identity, because of its limited staff and its status, which makes it the 'property' of the captain. This strong link between the captain and his men, reinforced by the way of recruitment, is not found so clearly at the level of the squadron. We will first consider the size and management of the companies, then discuss the central issue of the 'farm-company' system.

Cuirassier captain. Workshop of Jacob de Gheyn II, 1599. (Rijksmuseum)

The origin of the companies can be found partly in the famous *companies d'ordonnance* of the fifteenth century, consisting of 100 'lances' each. The 'lance' was made up of a man-at-arms, three archers, a coustillier and a page. The archers and coustilliers did not fight with the men-at-arms, but they fought alongside them as auxiliaries. Then, under Louis XII, General Susanne says that the archers began to cease operating as closely with the gendarmes. They grouped themselves into specialist companies, which were recorded as 'light cavalry'.[2] At the end of the French Wars of Religion this process had come to an end, and the men-at-arms remained the only combatants found in their companies. This phenomenon explains why companies are for the most part reduced to a relatively low strength, often just 50 men. Light cavalry companies experienced similar reductions, and by the end of the sixteenth century the strength of a light cavalry company averaged 80 horses.[3]

These strengths then increased during the reign of Henry IV. The strength of companies increased to about 100 men. This threshold, however, seems to have been difficult to maintain. The troubles which accompanied the regency of Marie de Medici in France favoured the creation of numerous companies,

---

2   Susane, *Histoire de la cavalerie Française*, Tome I, pp.44, 72. Some see it as the origin of chevau-légers companies. This is not the opinion of James Wood, who thinks rather that these units were initially composed of volunteer gentlemen who accompanied the army or noble who chose to serve rather than to contribute financially when the *ban* or *arrière-ban* were called. James Wood, *The King's Army, Warfare, soldiers and society during the Wars of Religion in France, 1562–1576* (Cambridge: Cambridge University Press, 2002), p.130.
3   Susane, *Histoire de la cavalerie Française*, p.75.

THE NEW KNIGHTS

which the captains did not always have the means to maintain on such a footing.[4] France's entry into the war in 1635, could only increase the distortion between the theoretical numbers and actual numbers, even as they continued to decrease. The companies were thus reduced from 80 men in 1639 to 34 in 1655. However, the actual average strength of a company is at this date only 17 horsemen.[5]

The considerable increase in the number of companies (700 in 1659), resulted in an equally significant reduction of the strength in each unit. The Crown had resigned itself, explains André Corvisier, to the existence of such a large gap between theoretical and actual numbers. The social reasons behind this are also recognised. Maintaining a high number of small-scale companies, for example, gave employment to the nobility, and thus limited unrest among the aristocracy.[6]

The return of peace led to the dismissal of most cavalry companies and allowed the strength of those who were maintained to be increased to 50 men. The number and size of companies fluctuated considerably however, according to the mobilisations and reforms that featured in the long reign of Louis XIV. The theoretical numbers vary most often between 50 and 70 men until the end of the century. During the last two wars of Louis XIV's reign, the cavalry encountered the same difficulties to maintain their strength as those seen during the Thirty Years' War, especially during the War of the Spanish Succession, where the problems of desertion, diseases and losses in combat, combined to make the reconstitution of the troops particularly difficult. After the Treaties of Utrecht and Rastadt, the return to peace was marked by new reforms to the strengths of the companies. But the new peacetime strength was this time particularly low, falling to 35, then a mere 25 men.[7]

In the sixteenth century, the companies of gendarmes were commanded by a captain, who had under him a lieutenant, an ensign, a guidon bearer and a sergeant. The ensign carried the banner of the men-at-arms and the guidon bearer that of the archers.[8] In imitation of this, the first companies of light cavalry, when they were constituted together as independent from the men-at-arms, adopted the same structure. They also had two standards: the cornet

Spanish arquebusier, 1577. Abraham de Bruyn. (Rijksmuseum)

---

4   Susane, *Histoire de la cavalerie Française*, p.83.
5   Bernhard Kroener, *Les routes et les étapes, Die versorgung der französicher armeen in Nordostfrankreich, 1635–1661* (Münster: Aschendorff, 1980). Quoted by André Corvisier, *Histoire militaire*, Tome I, p.363.
6   Corvisier, *Histoire militaire*, Tome I, p.347.
7   Susane, *Histoire de la cavalerie*, p.152.
8   Susane, *Histoire de la cavalerie*, p.132.

and the guidon. The question of standards – a matter dear to the heart of captains – arose again with the development of the dragoons. Their companies were given the guidon whilst the cornet remained the distinguishing mark of light cavalry companies. An even more important evolution was perceptible under the reign of Henry IV. Montgommery mentions that in the companies of gendarmes, there existed 'brigade chiefs'. These men, under the authority of one of the four main company officers, were responsible for one of the four brigades (or platoons or squads in modern-day parlance), that formed a company.[9]

Under the reign of Louis XIV, the management of light cavalry companies seems to have changed little at the top. In addition to the captain and the lieutenant, there is a cornet, sometimes a second lieutenant, and a sergeant. The real novelty lies in the creation of the brigadier role, which perpetuates and formalises the function of a brigade leader evoked by Montgommery at the beginning of the century. These men were responsible for every 12 to 16 other ranks; a company of 60 riders thus had four.[10] Susane emphasises the very important role these brigadiers played in the company, much better than that of their successors in modern armies.[11] In 1684 the rank of cornet was abolished and officially replaced by that of second lieutenant.[12] This decision, however, does not seem to have been applied across the army in the long term and the rank of cornet could still be found in the following century.

The main dividing line between officers who commanded the company was 'low officers' and 'the others'. The former being so called because they were directly appointed by their captain and their colonel held a patent granted by the king.[13] There is also the special situation of 'reformed' (discharged) officers. We know that the monarchy used to make major reforms, such as reductions in the army, with the men discharged at the end of each conflict. Although the officers were also victims of these reforms, it was understood that there was a need to preserve the experienced officer cadres. By the regulation of 27 May 1668, Louis XIV created the status of reformed officer. These officers who had lost their posts were henceforth maintained by the King while waiting for a position to be vacated, for which they had priority. This is, according to Hervé Drévillon, one of the key elements leading to the professionalisation of the officer's function and of 'the creation of a career'.[14]

The number of officers did not increase significantly over the whole of our period, but the general downward trend of the strength found in France as in most European cavalry, led to an increase in the proportion of officers to men. At the end of the reign of Louis XIV, the number of men in a company on a war footing was no more than 40 men, while the senior officers were

---

9   Montgommery, *La milice Françoise*, p.135.
10 George Guillet, *Les arts de l'homme d'épée ou le dictionnaire du gentilhomme* (Paris: Clousier, 1678), p.40.
11 Susane, *Histoire de la cavalerie*, p.131.
12 Susane, *Histoire de la cavalerie*, p.147.
13 Guillaume Le Blond, 'Bas-officiers', in Denis Diderot and Jean le Rond d'Alembert, *Encyclopédie ou Dictionnaire raisonné des sciences, des arts et des métiers* (Paris: Briasson, David, Le Breton, 1751), Tome II, p.114.
14 Drévillon, *L'impôt du sang*, pp.218–220.

more numerous than at the beginning of the century, when the companies numbered 100 men. The officer-to-men proportion had thus been more than doubled. This change could have been the result of a deliberate policy. The increase in the number of officers – particularly the junior officers – was an essential factor in the modernisation of the European armies. The tactical requirements, in terms of manoeuvring abilities and of discipline, made a high level of management essential. Non-commissioned officers were fundamental to the increasingly complex mechanics of modern tactical structures.[15] This is evidenced for example, by the creation of the rank of brigadier; this is not a general officer rank but one more akin to a corporal or sergeant. French companies seem to have benefited from a higher officer-to-men ratio than that of other Western European cavalry. Tactical arguments undoubtedly play an important role in this state of affairs. Many officers thought, like Belle Isle in 1733, that 'the strength of our cavalry consists in the quality and quantity of our officers'.[16]

Now we must turn to the so-called farm-company system. Historiography has sometimes been very severe with regard to this form of administration of the company, which represents for some a symbol of the problems within the cavalry under the *Ancien Régime*. E. Desbrières condemns it without recourse, 'the owner captain', he says, 'administers his company like a farm and only seeks to benefit from it'.[17] Does this system deserve such a harsh judgment? Was it really intended for the officers to make a financial profit from their company?

What gives the system its 'entrepreneurial' dimension is undoubtedly due to its contractual aspects.[18] The captain received a commission from the king to raise and command a company which he is obliged to keep in the best possible state, in order to best serve the interests of the sovereign. The salary and the lump sum paid to him served both to remunerate him and to assure the maintenance of his troops. So, he has to look after himself – with appropriate clothes, horses and arms – and of course, to recruit his men. We find here what could be the first advantage to the company farm. The captain, during his leave, returns to his home or his lands to recruit his staff. It is in this network of knowledge, peers or dependents, that he will first take his recruits. The social and geographical as well as military logic come together, giving rise to the idea that a common origin is the guarantee of a better level of cohesion within the troop or company.[19]

But there is no doubt another explanation to better understand the longevity of the farm-company. In simple terms it could be said that the monarchy relied on this mode of administration to discharge the responsibility to the officer, a greater part of the extraordinary burden of waging war. This

---

15 That is why, according to J.R. Hale, the linear tactical model had difficulty developing until the years 1620–1630. The theory, favourable to the lengthening of the units, then encountered an insurmountable difficulty: the insufficient number of subordinate officers. *War and Society in Renaissance Europe 1450–1620* (Montreal: McGill-Queen's University Press, 1998), p.60.
16 Quoted by Corvisier, *Histoire militaire*, Tome II, p.41.
17 Edouard Desbrières, Maurice Sautai, *La cavalerie de 1740 à 1789* (Paris: Berger-Levrault, 1906), p.8.
18 Drévillon, *L'impôt du sang*, p.101.
19 Corvisier, *Histoire militaire*, Tome I, p.349.

is particularly apparent from the work of David Parrott when he describes the Richelieu government.[20] For financial and political reasons, France had not followed the model of military enterprise developed on a very large scale in other European states.[21] First, the high cost and constraints of hiring foreign mercenaries limited their use. On the other hand, the memory of the Wars of Religion and of the taking up of arms by the nobles under the regency of Marie de Medici, made the idea of leaving the 'ownership' of whole bodies of men to great nobles – even if they were of royal blood – unacceptable. The royal authority could not allow such a delegation of power, always aware of the potential for threats to the equilibrium of the monarchy to appear.[22] The Duke of Saxe-Weimar, a German general, was the only major mercenary contractor maintained by the monarchy. Prevented at the highest level, the system of military enterprise resurfaced, but in a lessened and more acceptable form for the Crown, at the company level.

The King and his ministers knew how to count on the desires of the aristocracy of the kingdom, to be given a commission as a captain, chiefly of cavalry, in the Royal army. Even if the majority of nobles did not embrace a military career, the fact remains that it ensured their awareness of something of considerable value.[23] The number of companies available being lower than that of gentlemen or bourgeois wishing to serve, the temptation was great for royalty to take advantage of this 'competition' to delegate onto captains the responsibility for part of the cost of the maintenance of the army. It was not uncommon for captains to be forced to advance money to their men in order to make up for the very great irregularity of the payment, to prevent desertion. The monarchy was able to take advantage of the financial capabilities of these officers, forcing them to use their personal wealth and credit to provide a significant portion of the cash required to raise and maintain their company.[24]

The works of Hervé Drévillon make it possible to see something quite similar during the reign of Louis XIV.[25] It is clear that the captains are on their own. The sums paid by the king are indeed far from enough to meet the real needs of the captain, especially when a company is raised. The company's ongoing maintenance costs were lower than the initial investment required to raise it. This was probably not a financially insurmountable problem in times

---

20   David Parrott, *Richelieu's army: War, Government and Society in France, 1624–1642* (Cambridge: Cambridge University Press), 2006.
21   Parrott, *Richelieu's Army*, chapters 5 and 6.
22   Especially in troubled times. The revolt of Soissons, which raised its own troops and joined the enemies of France is from this point of view exemplary. It was this army, aided by Imperial contingents, which defeated the royal troops of Chatillon at La Marfee in 1641. A defeat which, without the death of Soissons on the day of the battle, could have had very serious consequences for the kingdom.
23   Parrott, *Richelieu's Army*, pp.316–317.
24   Parrott, *Richelieu's Army*, pp.329–331.
25   Drévillon, *L'impôt du sang*, chapter 3. However, Guy Rowlands underlines a difference between the *ministériats* of Richelieu and Mazarin and the personal reign of Louis XIV. Conscious of the essential role played by the officer corps, the King understands that he should rather support them and do so that they are not crushed by their loads and their spending. Guy Rowlands, *The Dynastic State and the Army under Louis XIV* (Cambridge: Cambridge University Press, 2002), chapters 6, 7 and 8.

of peace, but during times of war, when a company might have suffered from a difficult campaign or costly battle, the financial situation became much more fragile. Cases of captains forced to go into debt or to appeal to family generosity are far from rare.

We are very far from the idea of owner captains enriching themselves by the 'exploitation' of their company. The term 'owner' may also appear somewhat tenuous if one considers the theoretical rights of captains. The military officer, unlike the financial or judicial officers, held his office by way of a commission. This was revocable, and a captain was therefore not safe from seeing his company reformed or dismissed.

This policy, which relieved the treasury, had however, a certain number of constraints and unfortunate consequences. The first concerned the choice of captains. The monarchy was very aware of the financial capacity of the of those seeking a commission. Hervé Drévillon noted that the officers' service records that were held during the War of the Spanish Succession mentioned this information, particularly in respect of the cavalry, because the financial burden was heavier than in the infantry.[26] Another consequence was to force captains to use illegal practices to prevent their company from being under strength – 'false soldiers' or 'flying guns' – and to divert some of the money from pay into their pockets. Finally, an indirect consequence with very serious implications, concerns the quality of the training of the troops. Since the captains knew that the equipment and horses were provided at their own expense and that each rider or lost horse will incur expenses that the King's allowance would not cover, they have every interest in limiting desertions and the cost of training in order to spare their 'capital'.

These abuses were of course well known to contemporaries and the monarchy. They were regularly denounced, without any success in ending the practice; this despite the progress made under Le Tellier and Louvois. The effectiveness of any monitoring or sanctions for those found guilty of these abuses was poor, but this explanation is not enough. Even if he had had the means, would the King have wanted, even if he could have, to sanction all such action? He could not ignore that it was actually the policy of the monarchy which was in part responsible for this profiteering. The system in place of financing war, meant that the King sometimes knew how to turn a blind eye to illegal recruitment practices.

Even more so than the company, the squadron was the basic tactical unit in cavalry combat. To understand this, we must first go back to the origins of cavalry organisation and to trace its evolution. There are then two essential points that need clarification in order to better understand the conditions of employment of the squadron: the number of ranks it would form up in and the placement on which the riders were placed and the disposition of officers and non-commissioned officers.

Before the appearance of the squadron, the tactical disposition of men-at-arms for battle was very simple. They arranged themselves in almost a single

---

26　Drévillon, *L'impôt du sang*, p.140. Read also Emile G. Léonard, *L'armée et ses problémes au XVIIIe siècle* (Paris: Plon, 1958), especially pp.166–168.

line. Of course, the ground or the number of men sometimes necessitated the formation of two or more lines, which were arranged one behind the other, forty paces apart.[27] The thin line formation was partly adopted due to the use of the lance, which they would be free to use without interference, and also makes the use of a second rank of little use.[28] Another important factor is the so-called chivalrous code: 'I believe too,' explains La Noue, 'that this order was chosen, because this gendarmerie is all composed of nobility, everyone wanted to charge headlong towards the enemy and not remain in the last rank.'[29]

This order, La Noue tells us, was followed 'with many happy successes' until the middle of the reign of Henry II. Towards the end of his reign however, the gendarmes suffered major setbacks. These failures were, according to him, directly attributable to the traditional formations of the gendarmerie, which were inferior to that of the Imperialists. 'For then the squadrons of lances entered into reputation, which were thus arranged by the Emperor Charles, which having clashed with our gendarmerie hedges, easily overthrew them. This has also been done sometimes by squadrons of reiters.'[30] La Noue mentions the men-at-arms, the 'lancers', as being the first to have formed squadrons, while the reiters are often credited with this innovation. It is rather what Tavannes suggests, that the German gentlemen who composed the first reiters units 'were the first to be squadroned.'[31] It was from Germany that the new formation came, and the French began to recognise its strength at the end of the reign of Henry II. The French cavalry were quite progressive in adopting the squadron as the main battle formation; the single line 'hedge' did not disappear abruptly. The simultaneous use of both formations is observed in most of the French Wars of Religion. Protestants seem to have adopted it more quickly, especially under the leadership of Gaspard de Coligny and La Noue. Henry IV, influenced by his experienced commanders, then extended the use of the squadron for all French cavalry.

In the aftermath of the Wars of Religion, the squadron had thus supplanted the 'hedge' as the basic tactical unit for heavy cavalry. This organisation however, remained informal and quite flexible. The squadrons were formed only before battle – or at best for the duration of the campaign – and the companies remained administratively independent of each other. It was necessary to overcome the reluctance of the captains who were anxious to

Arquebusier from Netherlands, 1577. Abraham de Bruyn (Rijksmuseum)

---

27 Montgommery, *La milice Françoise*, p.133.
28 Daniel, *Histoire de la milice françoise*, Tome I, p.312.
29 La Noue, *Discours*, p.333.
30 La Noue, *Discours*, pp.333–334.
31 Tavannes, *Mémoires*, p.267.

THE NEW KNIGHTS

Spanish unarmoured lancers, 1607. Adam Wilaerts, 1617. (Rijksmuseum)

preserve their privileges and their autonomy. This was the work of Richelieu, who managed to make the squadron a permanent tactical structure, commanded by the oldest captain.

The composition and the strength of French squadrons were initially rather fluid, unlike the reiters, who were among the first to adopt this formation, making up some very important units, which could be up to 1,500 or 2,000 men strong.[32] Tavannes and La Noue, however, judge this strength as excessive. In fact, the squadrons deployed by Henri IV at Coutras (1587) and Ivry (1590) were between 300 to 600 men strong. After the Wars of Religion, we do not find squadrons as massive as those of the reiters; too slow and difficult to manoeuvre and their disproportionate size being their weakness. The difficulty faced by captains trying to complete recruiting to their company also led to much weaker squadrons under the reign of Louis XIII. Even when the number of companies per squadron was increased to three in 1636, the theoretical strength of a French squadron – 300 riders – was still lower than that of the Swedes.[33] With the continuation of the war the theoretical strength of the French companies was reduced considerably. In 1642, the number of riders for a complete company fell to 60. A squadron of two companies thus represented only 120 men. At the same time, during the English Civil War the Parliamentarian squadrons ranged between 170 and 250 riders and officers.[34] In 1658, most of the squadrons were made up of two companies, so a squadron on a war footing was only a mere 68 men without officers.

---

32 Tavannes, *Mémoires*, pp.190 and 299.
33 Richard Brzezinski, *Lützen 1632, Climax of the Thirty Years War* (Westport-London: Praeger, 2005), pp.21–22, 49.
34 Tincey, *Ironsides*, p.22.

Such a low strength did not last into the second half of the century. The strength of the companies increased somewhat, but insufficiently, and it was then necessary to increase the number of companies per squadron. According to Puységur, the squadrons had three companies during the War of Devolution and the Nine Years War. But on the eve of the last conflict of the reign, when the company's strength had been reduced to 35, a fourth was added.[35] Langeais however considers this increase insufficient to overcome the weakness of French squadrons compared to their foreign counterparts.[36] Here we find one of the consequences of the company-farm system. Captains could not maintain large companies without risking ruin. On the other hand, the wish of the monarchy to offer commissions to the nobility led to a preference for numerous, albeit small companies. This explains the relative weaknesses of the French squadrons when compared to their European counterparts.

In addition to the actual numbers, there is also the question of the internal structure of the squadrons and how they deployed and manoeuvred. This was important to ensure the balance of the unit and its ability to move while preserving combat effectiveness.

The first squadrons of reiters deployed themselves with an impressive depth of up to 15 or 20 ranks. Henry IV moved away from these massive units and aligned his own squadrons in five or six ranks, a practice that became common in France. On a European scale, the Swedish cavalry of Gustavus Adolphus was organised into squadrons in three or four ranks and 80 or 100 files and was without a doubt the most influential of practices. Gustavus helped reduce the depth of the squadrons during the second half of the Thirty Years' War, resulting in units deployed in three to six ranks at the end of the conflict. In France, the weakness in numbers of each company meant that the Swedish model was followed. To do so, it was necessary to reduce the number of ranks in order to present a front equal to that of the enemy.[37] The structure of the squadron stabilised and became a standard by the second half of the seventeenth century. At the beginning of the eighteenth century, cavalry was deployed in three ranks with a width of 40 to 60 files. Such formations offered more flexibility and manoeuvrability. Their frontage and depth were thought to be sufficient to ensure the squadron's 'resistance' and to avoid being enveloped. Facing the enemy, ranks were generally quite close together and the riders placed 'knees against knees' to get the most out of the formation.

There was a consensus emerging at the beginning of the seventeenth century about how to dispose officers in the squadron. The principles on which it was based constitute a compromise between the two functions of the officer. These were first of all, to train the men, and then to control the squadron and watch over its discipline and order. Both are essential to ensure success in combat. However, the captain's courage was not enough

---

35 Puységur, *L'Art de la guerre*, p.17.
36 De Langeais, *Des fonctions et du principal devoir d'un officier de cavalerie*, pp.77–78.
37 Antoine de Pas, Marquis de Feuquières, *Mémoires du marquis de Feuquière, contenant ses maximes sur la guerre* (Paris: Rollin, 1740), Tome I, p.184.

Johann Jacobi von Wallhausen (1580–1627), author of Kriegskunst zu Pferd

if the rear ranks could pull up before contact with the enemy. The captain of each company was thus in the first rank, the other officers distributed throughout the ranks; on the wings and in the rear. Basta comments on the key role of the lieutenants 'The lieutenant will follow at the tail with the sword in his hand, to quickly punish the soldier who will commit some cowardice, or even kill him; a single villain being enough to shame, even to rout an entire army and not being like people worthy of life.'[38] This unambiguous statement emphasises the essential role of officers in maintaining discipline.

One of the main difficulties in approaching this question is that the rules regulating the exercise and training of cavalry are generally not earlier than the eighteenth century. For the preceding years it is necessary to be content with theoretical works, which we know are sometimes far removed from practices in the field.[39] We must therefore try to determine the place occupied by instruction during these three centuries, in theory as well as in practice, and attempt to specify also what were the principles that governed training and instruction; the reason for such training and the results obtained.

To do this we will follow the path traced by Wallhausen, Director of the school of Siegen since its creation in 1616 – at the initiative of Jean de Nassau – until its closure in 1623. It distinguished two things necessary to lead the cavalry well: at an individual and squadron basis; 'The individual means are address, institution and science of each man or member of the body in his particular. The common means are well-armed, well-disciplined and well-governed companies, which stretch over all regiments and squadrons of the whole body.'[40]

Firstly, we shall consider equestrian instruction. At the time when the only equestrian arm worthy of the name consisted of the gendarmes of the *compagnies d'ordonnance*, the problem of equestrian instruction doubtless did not arise, or at least not in a major way. It behoved the gentlemen who composed these *compagnies* to learn their equestrian skills. They did so from their earliest youth, and this was therefore more of an aristocratic culture than a strictly military one. It is therefore not very surprising to find that the works dealing with the art of war give almost no space for this question throughout the sixteenth century.

---

38 Basta, *Le gouvernement de la cavalerie légère*, p.68.
39 David Parrott emphasises that the theoretical works of the first half of the seventeenth century, often very much inspired by the Dutch school, probably had only a marginal influence on the training of soldiers as it was practiced in the infantry units. *Richelieu's Army*, pp.38–42.
40 Wallhausen, *Art militaire*, p.44.

It may seem more surprising that the need for equestrian instruction does not appear much more at the beginning of the seventeenth century, because the make-up of the cavalry arm had changed considerably over the course of the previous half century. The so-called 'light' cavalry companies had multiplied, and their recruitment was very different from that of the *compagnies d'ordonnance*, and which were forced to open its ranks to the lower social orders. Of course, the works of La Broue or Pluvinel were intended to teach the riders but it is horse riding for gentlemen and had no military character. The first books dealing exclusively with the cavalry – those of Melzo, Basta and Wallhausen – although having a certain pedagogical dimension, almost ignore this.

One can then wonder about the actual level of equestrian training required of the riders. It is obviously very doubtful that they were already good riders. Melzo and Wallhausen, in a different source, suggest that some did not know how to ride up or rode badly or incorrectly.[41] The question arises particularly for cuirassiers and pistoleers. One might think that the fighting methods developed by the latter – notably the caracole – implied the existence of a high level of riding. However, it does not make it clear from the writings of authors at the beginning of the century that the charge of the cuirassiers required any particular skill in riding. At no point do they insist on this point. On the contrary, Basta asserts that 'every man armed in this manner [armour, pistols and mediocre horse] can, with a little exercise, serve as a cuirassier'.[42] It is also the opinion of Melzo for whom 'any man can easily acquire the skill necessary for this weapon'.[43]

These observations run counter to the idea that the development of the use of cuirassiers was made possible by an incremental increase in the level of equestrian skills. The horse-riding skills developed in the Italian academies around the middle of the sixteenth century could be very innovative and was probably not intended for the German reiters and the units who copied them. Pistoleers and other cuirassiers, some of whom were probably engaged without knowing how to ride, were likely to practise a more elementary level of horse riding than the gentlemen of the *compagnies d'ordonnance*. The latter had to be skilled enough to steer their horses at a gallop (at least in the last 50 or 60 steps) while focusing on the difficult handling of the lance and preserving at least a minimum level of cohesion in their linear formation. It would be an exaggeration to say that manoeuvres such as the caracole were easy to carry out, but it is not certain that they required high individual mastery of horse riding, especially as according to some authors, the caracole was actually little used on the battlefield. The pistoleers had to know how to control their mount at trot, shoot (aiming and accuracy being an issue), and then turn away to the left with their comrades.

---

41 Wallhausen mentions the 'heavies' that made up the companies of cuirassiers. *Art militaire*, p.17.
42 Basta, *Le gouvernement de la cavalerie*, p.73.
43 Lodovico Melzo, *Les reigles militaires du chevalier frère Luis Melzo de l'Ordre de Malte pour le gouvernement et service particulier et propre de la cavallerie, traduictes d'Italien en françois par Paul Varroy* (Anvers: Verdussen, 1615), p.45.

THE NEW KNIGHTS

Giorgio Basta (1550–1607), author of *Il maestro di campo generale* and *Il governo della cavalleria leggiera*

It was ultimately less about horse-riding proper and the initial instruction of each rider, than the collective instruction of the squadron. This may be where the main advances took place. In any case, it would probably be necessary to qualify the assertion that 'the practice of such horse-riding [the equestrian science inherited from the Italians], now reserved for rare specialists, was then part of the combat training of the riders of rank.'[44] It was probably not within the abilities of these horsemen, any more than of their horses, which all agree were mediocre and of little value.

Tavannes also testifies to a rather low level of discipline applied towards the 'horsemen of the rank'. 'The soldiers, he says, can be encouraged and disciplined in a short time: the curvets are useless, just trot and turn the horses in the charges. … An apprentice rider and a horse can be trained in three months for the war, the rest is superfluous.'[45] Du Praissac, even if these remarks are very general, seems to agree.[46] That the initial equestrian training is almost completely absent from the works devoted to the cavalry does not mean of course that it was ignored. The absence of any standardisation on the subject left the commanders of units to do as they saw fit. It may even be that those who were training their men properly did not want to share their experience, preferring to keep it for themselves, much as the masters of trades kept their secrets. Wallhausen reproached some officers who, when they have some knowledge, 'do not want to communicate, and even hate those who push the love of this noble science, of a laudable desire to advance'.[47]

The rest of the seventeenth century offers no more thoughts on the individual instruction of the riders. It is certain however, that some cavalry commanders demanded a fairly high level of horsemanship. Gustavus Adolphus was very interested in the training of his troops and it is difficult to think that this was limited to just the infantry. The King must no doubt have been much more attentive to the equestrian training of his soldiers, since Sweden – with the exception of the Finnish light cavalry – had never been a nation of horsemen.[48] The effectiveness of this training can probably be measured by the ability of Swedish riders to take on a faster charging pace than hitherto practiced. It was thus possible that they could gallop the

---

44 Marcel Dugué Mac Carthy, *La cavalerie Française et son harnachement* (Paris: Maloine, 1985), p.111.
45 Tavannes, *Mémoires*, pp.73, 194.
46 Jean du Praissac, *Les discours militaires du sieur du Praissac* (Paris: Guillemot et Thiboust, 1623, 1st edition 1612), p.18.
47 Wallhausen, *Art militaire*, preface.
48 Brzezinski, *The Army of Gustavus Adolphus*, pp.4, 6.

last yards separating them from the enemy, whereas the ordinary practice at that time was still to trot into contact. The unusually high level of discipline prevailing in the Swedish troops certainly helped to make this possible and allowed for a better mastery of horse-riding. The same level of instruction may also have been achieved in some units composed of veterans or elite troops forming the guard of a sovereign. Examples include the cuirassiers of Pappenheim or the Weimariens and the *Maison du Roi*.

This situation was obviously different for the ordinary troops and the freshly raised units. The brutal increase in numbers to which the French cavalry faced in the 'open war' in 1635 undoubtedly posed a real problem from this point of view. In this case the equestrian qualities of the riders were probably more limited, which put a stop to considerations to undertake the charge at a speed faster than trotting. The idea that the instruction of the riders was less demanding than that of the infantrymen, which prevailed for example, to a certain extent in France, could only accentuate this state of affairs.[49] Finally, there was no systematic approach to answering this question. The practice of training remained based mainly on the variable level commitment and willpower of the leaders and the quality of their troops.

The early eighteenth century is marked by the figures of two great commanders who valued the use of horsemen: John Churchill, Duke of Marlborough and Charles XII of Sweden. It is generally agreed that these two men were very much concerned with the training of their troops. It is probable that the latter went even further. His expectations surpassed what was then demanded from the riders: they must be able to overcome all the obstacles on the ground and drive their horses in the gallop over a longer distance. In France one finds only Maurice de Saxe much concerned with training. De Saxe was aware of the difficulties involved in equestrian instruction and the time needed to complete it perfectly; 'it takes ten years to train a rider', he wrote. This required frequent and testing exercises; 'the cavalry must ... gallop and run to break horses, as well as men'.[50] This view was not shared by any of his French contemporaries. The instruction and the level of riding seemed to be sufficient in the eyes of the officers of the French cavalry. It was not until the War of the Austrian Succession that interest in this subject increased.

'The handling of the sword for the rider is as necessary as the handling of the musket to the soldier. I have never been able to understand why it was neglected so much in the cavalry.'[51] This observation of an officer of the mid eighteenth century pretty much sums up the problem faced with instruction and the exercise of arms in the cavalry and is barely mentioned in contemporary reflections on training.

---

49 'It was always necessary during the peace to keep much more infantry than cavalry, because five or six years were necessary to make an infantry regiment and it took only a year for a good regiment of cavalry.' *Mémoires of the Marquis de Chamlay*, quoted by Jean Bérenger, *Turenne* (Paris: Fayard, 1987), pp.383–384.
50 De Saxe, *Mes rêveries*, introduction of Jean-Pierre Bois, p.133.
51 Service Historique de la Défense/Direction de l'Armée de Terre (SHD/DAT), 1MR1731, f°29, 'Observation sur l'instruction des exercices de juin 1753', anonyme, 1753.

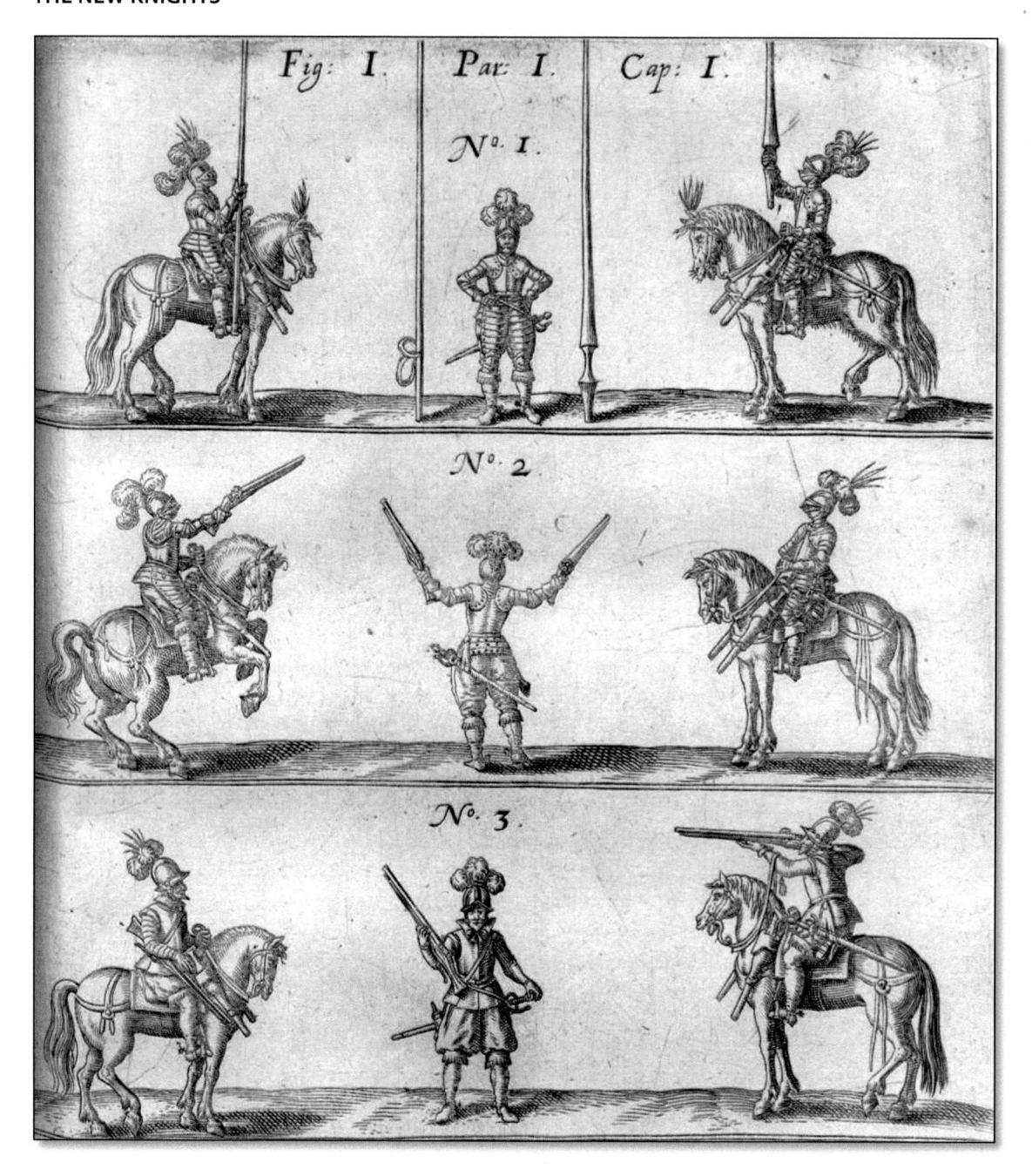

From top: lancer, cuirassier and arquebusier, from J J. Wallhausen's *Kriegskunst zu Pferd*. (Michał Paradowski's archive)

ORGANISATION AND TRAINING

The only exercises on which Fourquevaux makes reference to are in the middle of the sixteenth century – as far as the gendarmerie is concerned at any rate – are those which aim at accustoming the gendarmes to bear the weight of their heavy armour.[52] We know however, that the handling of the lance required constant and rigorous training. The nobility devoted a large amount of time to this, more often through games and tournaments. For some authors, it is precisely because 'the feasts and exercises of nobility, such as breaking lances, running the ring, jousting, and other similar games have passed away' that the use of the lance almost disappeared as a weapon for heavy cavalry in the early seventeenth century. The disappearance of the lance rendered some exercises redundant. 'The form of war is changed from useless lance to pistols, says Tavannes, instead of [the race of] rings, one would have to adjust to shoot with pistols, and to the sword fight.'[53]

This does not prevent Wallhausen, who was very attached to the lance, to show in detail the manner of practising the three main movements.[54] However, the director of the school of Siegen, aware of emerging new technology, also proposed exercises for the pistol and the sword. For pistols it was by practising shooting 'on some targets, at the walk or gallop, or in the middle of the gallop, fixing the target to a stake at the same three levels as used when practising with the lance'. For the sword 'one will make three marks in a stake or a tree, and as with the pistol, at different speeds, using an old sword ... or other which is not too good'.[55] Even if one questions the real usefulness of shooting while at a gallop, the exercises proposed by Wallhausen seem likely to have taken place. It may be that this was the way in which cavalry companies could operate. This instruction was under the responsibility of the captain but was undoubtedly under the actual direction of the junior officers, sergeants, corporals and more experienced cavalrymen.

In the seventeenth century, there are hardly any other written works which make much mention of the exercise of arms.[56] The contrast is glaring when compared with the infantry. It is true that the manipulation of the pike or the musket – which can be reduced to a given number of precise gestures – lends itself more to being documented step-by-step than for the sword; the use of which was subject to all the vagaries of the charge and hand-to-hand combat. The lack of interest shown in books covering the exercise of cavalry weapons can be explained by the difficulty to record in writing in such a way as to be easily understood by a recruit, and the complexity of the situations likely to be experienced in combat. La Touche is one of the few to consider swordsmanship whilst on horseback, but his work was not well known.[57] Moving to the exercise of the pistol or carbine, these are generally mentioned only in the context of unit training, most often to train the riders to shoot

---

52 Fourquevaux, *Instruction*, p.26.
53 Tavannes, *Mémoires*, p.98.
54 Wallhausen, *Art militaire*, p.7.
55 Wallhausen, *Art militaire*, pp.10–11.
56 Of course, we could mention John Cruso's *Militarie Instructions for the Cavallery*, but he is largely inspired by Wallhausen for this question.
57 La Touche, *Les vrays principes de l'espée seule*.

by ranks and by files. This subject was therefore left to the initiative of junior officers and veterans, who tried to teach recruits the basics of shooting and swordsmanship on horseback.

The importance of unit training and the beginnings of some written exercises of arms found in the sixteenth century, do not spend much time discussing the question of collective rather than individual instruction. It was probably rarely encountered amongst the heavy cavalry during a time where the gendarmes were content to charge in a line. It is likely that this became more important from the middle of the sixteenth century, with the emergence of more massive formations of combined squadrons. The strength of these new units was in their ability to manoeuvre and fight by preserving their cohesion and unity. It is on this point for example, that, according to La Noue, lies the superiority of the German reiters.

The Germans surpassed all the other nations, because they remained tight and stuck with each other, which proceeds from an ordinary acceptance that they must always hold themselves together in good order … And what makes good testimony that they do not fail in this, is that when they are broken, they withdraw and flee without separating; being all together.[58]

This flexibility did not necessarily depend solely on the equestrian skill of each of the riders that made up the squadron. As we have suggested, the equestrian skills of reiters and pistoleers were not necessarily higher than those of gendarmes. It is essential that these men be trained to move together as a unit. It is perhaps here, in this collective dimension of training and instruction, and discipline – which holds everything together – that lies the true concept which characterises the passage from knights and chivalry to an altogether different type of cavalry. From this point of view, although apparently not much used on the battlefield, the famous caracole, or 'snail' manoeuvre traditionally associated with the tactics of reiters, represents without doubt, a very good exercise for a squadron to partake in. It is also a reasonable measure of how much progression had been made in the instruction of cavalry.

It is clear, writes Delbrück, that a cavalry captain who managed to train his company to execute a perfect caracole had their men under control and also had a truly disciplined unit.[59] This could not be achieved without considerable effort and work, both from riders and horses. The company then became a real 'tactical corps in which each rider was integrated as a simple part of the company and whose head and soul resided in his leader; the captain.[60] The affirmation of collective training is a symbol of the passing of the individualist 'warrior' in favour of type of warfare based more on the discipline and cohesion of the group.

This new dimension is something else that is not much written about in the second half of the sixteenth century. However, it is difficult to think that it did not occupy an important position in the practice of war. The captains of reiters and pistoleers knew that this was key in making their troops

---

58   La Noue, *Discours*, pp.358–359.
59   Delbrück, *History of the art of war*, vol. IV, p.124.
60   Delbrück, *History of the art of war*, vol. IV, p.124.

fit for battle, and it was up to them and their subordinates to take charge of this training. This of course meant that the form and quality of such training varied considerably from one unit to another, since no standards or instructions had yet to be an influence.

The need for more in-depth thought starts to emerge from the beginning of the seventeenth century. However, it progressed very slowly. For example, in France and England, the military authors continued to favour the infantry in the area of training and manoeuvres. Most recognised the need to instruct men in groups and teach them to evolve into squadron, but they seemed reluctant to go into the details of this matter. This attitude is particularly clear in Du Chastelet: 'I do not speak either of developments that will be made during the fight is a lesson in tactics that would be difficult here to give surely. Officers who know their craft must resolve as opportunities arise.'[61] Although probably not himself an officer, the theorist's reluctance probably also illustrates the difficulty of debating this element of the art of war. The learning of evolutions and combat manoeuvres seemed to remain an aspect dealt with in a pragmatic and empirical way. It is through observation and experience that officers learn this subject and it is with the same method that they must teach their men.

The Sieur de Birac's book is therefore an exception. He reminds us of course of the main manoeuvres that the riders must know how to perform: about turn, doubling the ranks, marching past and the caracole.[62] But he does not stop at this simple explanation and begins to explain a little more in detail to the captain on how to exercise his company. This is the first and probably the only French work of the seventeenth century to propose the beginning of the theory of collective military instruction. Based on the repetition of simple exercises, the objectives seem rather limited and there is no question of being able to conduct complex manoeuvres and unnecessary parades. It is noteworthy that experienced riders undoubtedly played a significant role in the training of recruits. As a result, they had an important place in newly raised companies, which numbered a considerable proportion of the whole.

The weakness of instruction in France at the beginning of the Thirty Years' War – although in practice the training of the units was more advanced than what most of the works proposed, it seems that the French cavalry sometimes suffered from a real lack of instruction. This is particularly true in the early years of French intervention in the Thirty Years' War. The farm-company system of course, partly explains this weakness. The captain, who often had to invest his own money, sought to keep costs and expenses to a minimum. But frequent and strenuous training was probably in his eyes one of the best means to exhaust and damage costly horses.

However, these troops also paid the price of the disaffection of which troubled the ranks of the cavalry. The manner in which the French monarchy

---

61 Paul Hay du Chastelet, *Politique militaire ou traité de la guerre*, nouvelle édition revue, corrigée et augmentée de notes et de citations (Paris: Jombert, 1757 [1st edition 1667]), p.137.
62 Birac, *Les fonctions du capitaine de cavalerie*, p.14. The caracole no longer refers here to the 'snail' of the reiters. In addition, the last two manoeuvres must not be confused. The two aim to make a half turn, but in the first is the rank that makes the movement, while in the second is the line.

THE NEW KNIGHTS

Quarter-wheel. Troop making a quarter-wheel on the left. ABCD: starting position; AEFG: arrival position. From Encyclopédie ou dictionnaire raisonné des sciences, des arts et des métiers … *par M. Diderot et d'Alembert, Paris, Briasson, David, Le Breton, 1751–1765. (Bibliothèque de l'Université de Nantes)*

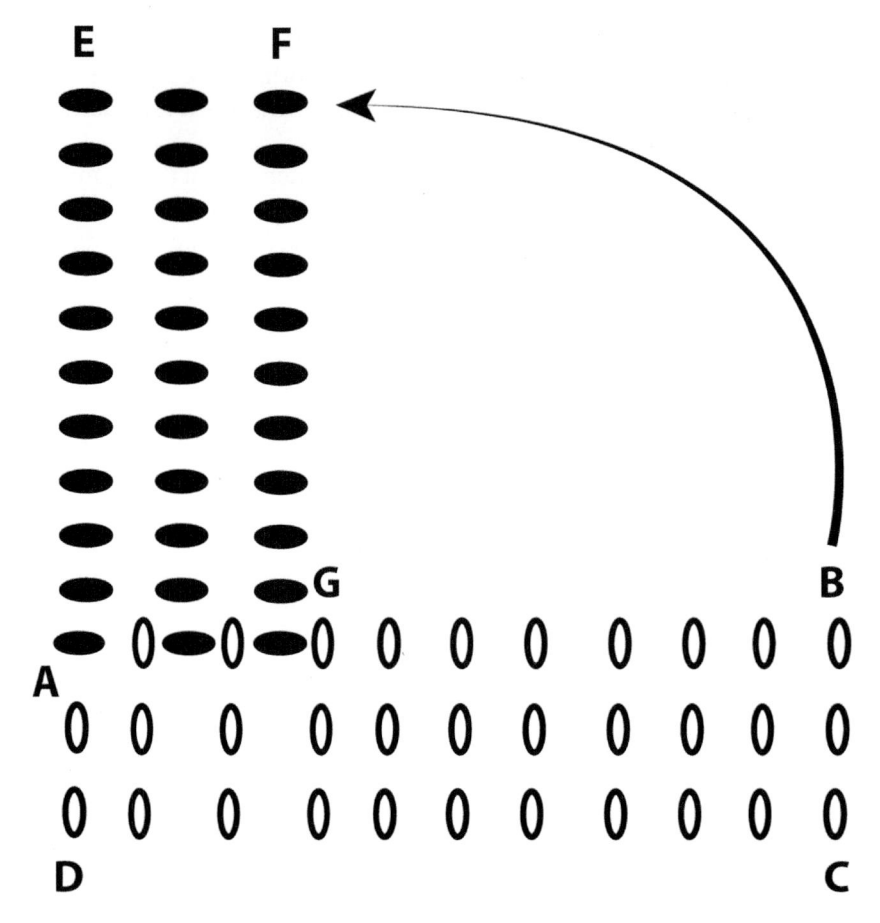

A, B, C, D starting position
A, E, F, G arrival position

pursued the art of warfare (essentially as a war of sieges), had made mounted arm of secondary importance.[63] According to H. Choppin the whole exercise was limited to caracole.[64] Foreign veterans and experienced officers like Gassion were all the more in demand.[65] In the first years of the war in any case, the weakness of the national cavalry regiments was known in the French high command. The Cardinal de La Valette confirms this in a letter to Richelieu in 1636: 'the French cavalry is still weak; we must resolve to raise Germans when we can.'[66]

---

63 Parrott, *Richelieu's Army*, pp.59–65.
64 Henri Choppin, *Les origines de la cavalerie française* (Paris: Berger-Levrault, 1905), p.277.
65 Gassion served several years with the Swedes before joining, in 1635, the army of the King of France. He had an important part in the recovery of the French cavalry. Hervé Drévillon, 'L'héroïsme à l'épreuve de l'absolutisme, l'exemple du maréchal de Gassion (1609–1647)', in *Cahiers du CEHD, Nouvelle Histoire Bataille (II)*, n°23 (2004), pp.149–169.
66 Quoted by Choppin, *Les origines de la cavalerie française*, p.278.

ORGANISATION AND TRAINING

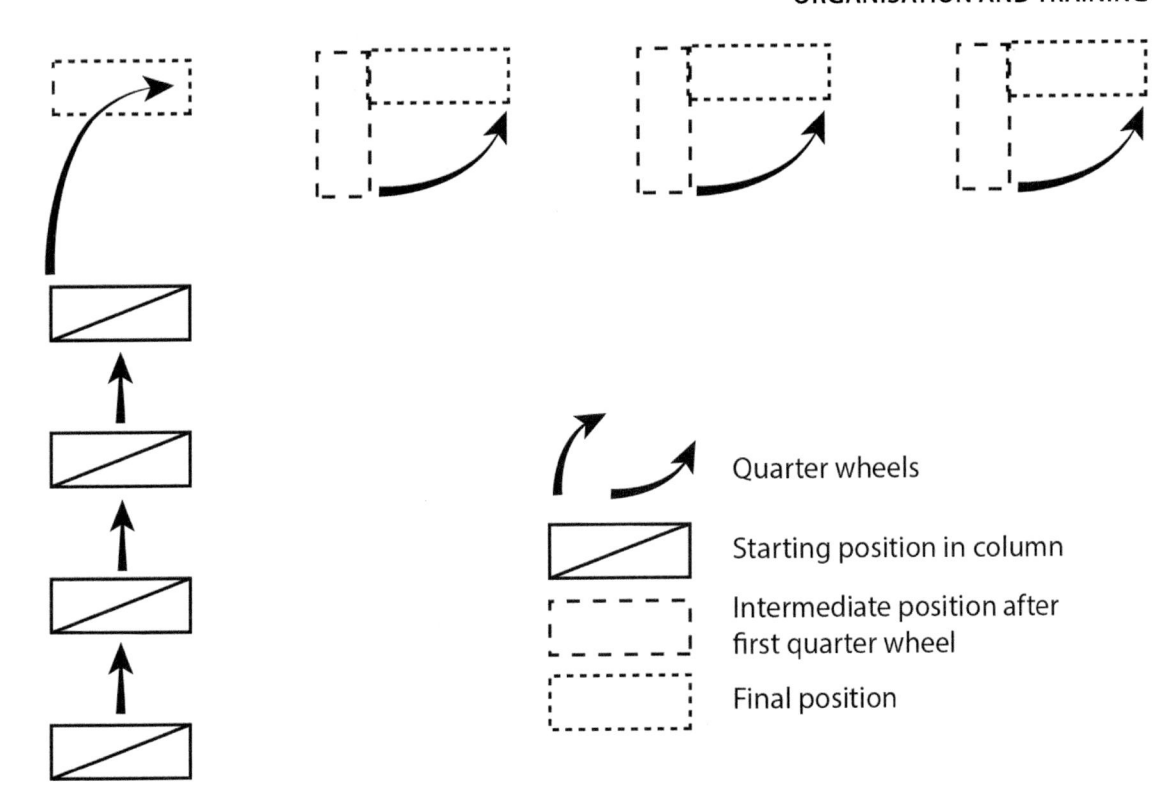

Deployment of a column of squadrons in battle line. 'Processionary' deployment on the right by two successive quarter-wheels. (author's diagram)

Rocroi (1643), however, shows that the recovery had started in the early 1640s. Indeed, we can only note a real improvement when comparing the squadrons of Feuquières, unable to manoeuvre against the enemy in Thionville (1639), and those of Enghien and Gassion on the right wing of the King's army four years later. The latter placed themselves in one line, then manoeuvred to allow the seven squadrons of Gassion attack the enemy flank while the eight squadrons of Enghien charged him to the front. They were able to rally to overthrow the second line of the Spaniards and exploit their success by attacking the enemy centre.[67] The defeat of La Ferté's squadrons on the left wing, carried away by an impetuous charge, remind us of the limits of these advances.

Progress in the first decades of the eighteenth century was however uneven. The main players at the beginning of the century were arguably the Duke of Marlborough and Charles XII. They gave the training and exercising at unit level as much attention as that of the individual men. This is the first time that the supreme commanders developed and standardised their instruction practices on such a scale. Charles XII himself supervised the training of his cavalry, which he used to manoeuvre at a gallop. The high degree of instruction enjoyed by the Swedish cavalry, can be seen in the very peculiar order the King gave to his squadrons. The riders were not there 'knee to knee' as it was everywhere else, but 'knee behind knee', forming a

---

67 Henri d'Orléans, Duc d'Aumale, *Histoire des Princes de Condé aux XVI et XVIIe siècles* (Paris: Calmann Levy, 1886), Tome IV, p.101 and following.

chevron or wedge.[68] No contemporary book considers the question of the training of companies and squadrons in a systematic way. From the 1720s however, there are some interesting observations by Lecoq-Madeleine and Langeais, both of whom were cavalry officers.[69]

The 1730s marked a change in France. The high command seems to have understood the importance of setting the evolutions peculiar to cavalry. Such action was much slower in being introduced for the infantry. If never fully implemented, the *Instruction on the evolutions and exercises of the cavalry*, written around 1732, at least reflects this new thinking.[70] It was also in the 1730s that Puységur wrote the main parts of his *Art de la guerre*.[71] While his approach to the issue is perhaps a novelty, his innovations remained fairly limited in substance. They restricted themselves to improvements. In a more general way Puységur does not go further than his predecessors on instruction and training itself. The nature and the frequency of the exercises to be done to the riders to manage and control the evolutions of the squadron are not covered. It should also be born in mind that in the absence of organic texts – in France in particular – the individual commanders had great autonomy to regulate the instruction of their men.[72] It may be that the training of cavalry, as it was actually practiced in the squadrons, was mainly aimed at learning to open, tighten and double the lines and ranks, to form a line and especially to perform the quarter wheeling (which is also now sometimes called, with a risk of confusing things, caracole).

This evolution was indeed the basis of what was then one of the essential manoeuvres of the cavalry: the deployment of the squadron columns into battle line and vice versa. Thus, a column of five squadrons wishing to deploy in battle on the right – the leading squadron, arriving at the limit of the deployment area – makes a first quarter wheel on its right and advances to the end of this line and takes its position by conducting a new quarter wheel to the left. The three squadrons that follow it successively, make the same moves and align with it. The last one goes straight ahead to take position on the far left of the line. This processional movement took time, of course, and made the squadrons vulnerable to an enemy already deployed and ready to charge.

The two essential factors that are organisation and instruction do not appear to have evolved at the same rate. At the beginning of the eighteenth century the main tactical and administrative frameworks that structure the French cavalry are in place. They are not free from defects, especially with respect to foreign cavalry, but their permanence and the relative stability of their organisation create the necessary conditions for the conduct of modern cavalry combat. The same is not true of instruction, where we have seen that

---

68 David Chandler, *The Art of Warfare in the Age of Marlborough* (Staplehurst and New York: Spellmount, Sarpedon, 1997), p.57.
69 Lecoq-Madeleine, *Le service ordinaire et journalier de la cavalerie en abrégé* (Paris: Delatour et Simon, 1720), p.155. Langeais, *Des fonctions et du principal devoir d'un officier de cavalerie*, pp.81–83.
70 SHD/DAT, 1MR1731, f°83, 'Projet d'instruction sur les évolutions et exercices de la cavalerie', par M. de Mortaigne, vers 1732.
71 Puységur, *L'Art de la guerre*, Tome I, p.76.
72 Louis Drummond de Melfort, *Traité sur la cavalerie* (Paris: Desprez, 1776), p.217.

written works on the subject are incomplete; both in the field of equestrian instruction and manoeuvres. This field is still largely left to the pragmatism and the know-how of the low-ranking officers and the good will of the unit commanders. The overall level of instruction of the riders can be questioned. At the end of the eighteenth century, some officers shared a very critical view, such as Drummond de Melfort: 'The exercises of the cavalry were based only on the lights of some colonels or the arbitrariness of the large number. Provided it was actually exercised, since it was known that a regiment that had spent three years in a row in winter quarters might not have mounted a horse once to practise.'[73]

---

73   Drummond de Melfort, *Traité sur la cavalerie*, p.217.

Part II

How Did the Charge Change?

4

The Triumph of Firepower

It is enough to consider all the consequences of the introduction of firepower in heavy cavalry to understand the changes that took place on the battlefield. The appearance of the pistol (and through it, firepower), is the key aspect of this transformation. The constraints of using pistols, forced for example – to make the most of their effect – a reduction in the speed of the charge. But the desire to develop firepower also led to a questioning of cavalry tactics. The hedge – a thin formation adopted to get the most out of the lance – was no longer suitable for a charge based on firepower rather than shock. No more the idea of a frontal and brutal attack as conceived by the gendarmes at the beginning of the period.

It is therefore necessary to consider precisely how these new principles of cavalry combat became widespread in the second half of the century. First, because their development ultimately condemned to the history books the chivalrous charge and a weapon system dating back to the twelfth century; that of the armoured man-at-arms, armed with the lance and fighting on horseback. The charge of heavy cavalry as practiced in the early seventeenth century was nothing like that of the Italian Wars. A look at the French Wars of Religion will allow us to understand the way in which these dramatic changes took place.

Reiters and their new mode of combat questions the principles that were the basis of the traditional charge of men-at-arms for several centuries. The use of lance-armed gendarmes galloping in a line towards the enemy at high speed begins to disappear and are replaced with new principles based on firepower – delivered in deep formations by each squadron at the trot. 'It pierces, it kills, it carries death and fear with him'[1]: this is the pistol, the main challenger of the lance.

Some historians have not given much attention to the use of pistols. Denison for example, thought the primary problem was the drastic reduction in shock action.[2] Michael Roberts even thinks that the cavalry thus armed had become a 'debilitated' troop.[3] Yet more recently, D. Eltis saw

---
1 Tavannes, *Mémoires*, p.192.
2 Georges T. Denison, *A History of Cavalry from the Earliest Time* (London: Macmillan, 1913).
3 Quoted by Philipps, 'of nimble service', p.8.

THE NEW KNIGHTS

Charging lancer. Workshop of Jacob de Gheyn II, 1599. (Rijksmuseum)

in it a formidable weapon.[4] And we must admit, as we have seen, the pistol had some significant advantages. The adoption of the pistol proves in any case the surprising adaptability of a weapon that some consider a hotbed of conservatism – unable to integrate the rapid transformation of warfare.[5]

It was probably in the beginning an attempt to find a new solution to an old problem: the very rapid and effective strengthening of the defensive capacity of infantry. Proponents of the cavalry could see in their new firearms a means of counteracting the massive 'hedgehogs' of pikes of the Swiss and Landsknechts. The problem of course, was that the infantry itself was able to quickly make good use of its own improving firearms. It was not necessarily easy to imagine tactics making it possible to fight pikemen and arquebusiers together.[6] These two weapons could be engaged separately, which then made an attack with pistols quite formidable when fighting the isolated pikemen. However, in the face of combinations of sleeves of musketeers supporting solid squares of pikemen, the task proved much more difficult. For Denison the use of the pistol in these conditions was absurd and went against the 'genius of this weapon'. Mounted on animals that made them easy targets and relying mainly on firearms that required a stable and careful aim (against infantry who used similar and more powerful weapons), the tactics of the reiters and their fellows defied logic.[7]

---

4 Quoted by Philipps, 'of nimble service', p.8.
5 Robert O'Connell, in *Of Arms and Men: A History of War, Weapons, and Aggression* (Oxford: Oxford University Press, 1989) evokes the knight as 'the human equivalent of some overspecialised reptile'. Quoted by Phillips, 'of nimble service', p.2.
6 The observations of Tavannes at Ceresole (1544) prove that it was not common in the middle of the sixteenth century. Tavannes, *Mémoires*, p.111.
7 Denison, *A History of Cavalry*, p.119. This is also the opinion of many historians, such as Susane, *Histoire de la cavalerie Française*, p.76.

THE TRIUMPH OF FIREPOWER

Cavalry clash during Battle of Jarnac in 1569. Jean Perrissin, 1570. (Rijksmuseum)

If we agree with Denison and recognise that the charges of pistoleers against battalions of pikemen and arquebusiers must target the former, we can nevertheless wonder why they did not stop to use their pistols. To understand this, it would first be necessary to accept the fact that this weapon was not exclusively intended for charges against infantry. It must not be forgotten that the reiters obtained their greatest successes against the *Gendarmerie*, at Saint-Quentin (1557) or Dreux (1562) for example. This type of the cavalry combat, directly opposing firepower to armour – the pistol to the lance – was recognised by contemporaries. La Noue writes at length on this subject, in a chapter entitled 'That a squadron of reiters must beat a squadron of lances.'[8]

He reminds us that one of the keys to the superiority of the reiters is in the use of their pistols. 'It must be confessed that the pistoles, although daughters of these devilish instruments invented to depopulate the kingdoms, are very dangerous when one knows how to use it; for which the Germans pay the price.'[9] While the gendarme only used his lance once, the reiter, who carried several pistols, could fire six or seven shots. These could penetrate the armour of the gendarme more than the lance could damage that of the reiter, and it follows that the latter is equal for defensive purposes but is superior for the offensive.[10]

---

8   La Noue, *Discours*, p.355.
9   La Noue, *Discours*, p.356.
10 La Noue, *Discours*, p.357.

Armed in this way, the reiters could therefore challenge lancers, provided they gave up some bad habits that countered their superiority. La Noue is speaking here about the caracole, whose movement, the most dangerous, is for the reiters to turn their backs to the enemy in order to reload weapons, which cannot fail to benefit a determined opponent.[11] Thus, the pistol could not do everything, and the impact of their firepower can be cancelled if it was not used correctly, for example if the reiters refused to contact the enemy. They did not have much to fear from the lance because, says La Noue, 'if it can hurt horses, there is a miracle when it manages to kill a man'.[12] On the contrary, at the moment of clashing with an opponent, pistols fired at close range were very effective, with experienced pistoleers aiming always at the thighs and the face. It is at this moment also that the second rank would also fire, the power of shot thus released would put half of the leading ranks of a squadron of gendarmes out of action. The reiters could gain the advantage even before coming directly to hand-to-hand combat, for experience confirms that 'the reiters are never as dangerous as when one is mixed up with them'.[13]

Thus, when they use their firepower correctly, the result is generally a foregone conclusion: 'if we want to look at the reiters who have attacked as they should, we will find that they have done murder and routed the lancers'.[14] Despite the arguments of Roger Williams[15] and other writers even later, such as Wallhausen, we can see the abandonment of the lance. Its disappearance, which gradually took place throughout Western Europe, was probably witnessed earlier in the Kingdom of France and in the Netherlands.[16]

The French gendarmes themselves gradually modified their attitude towards the pistol. La Noue remarks in the 1580s 'the gendarme also wears a pistol', which he uses when his lance is broken. Admittedly, the men-at-arms still appear to use them only with a great reticence, and delegate the task of loading and maintaining them to their valets.[17] Yet this observation is significant to understanding the importance of firepower in cavalry fights, since even the gendarmes, overcoming their contempt and their prejudices, were forced to adopt it.

This trend will assert itself further at the end of the century. The gendarmes were no longer content to use the pistol as well as their lance and they gradually abandoned the latter. The movement took shape first of all on the Protestant side. The difficulty the Huguenots faced in obtaining lances, no doubt contributed to their abandonment. The Battle of Saint-Denis is an example of the problems they encountered attempting to equip their heavy cavalry. In this battle Tavannes notes, the Huguenots did not have

---

11 La Noue, *Discours*, pp.359–360.
12 La Noue, *Discours*, p.361.
13 La Noue, *Discours*.
14 La Noue, *Discours*, p.360.
15 Roger Williams, *A briefe Discourse of Warre* (1590), quoted in Evans, *The works of Sir Roger Williams*, pp.34–35.
16 Maurice d'Orange was one of the first to abandon the lance. Wallhausen, *Art militaire*, p.5.
17 La Noue, *Discours*, p.356.

many lances, but 'it is by default, not by design'.[18] However, they then became aware of their 'little usefulness' and gradually abandoned them. The King of Navarre, then also the King of France, Henry IV, assumed and led this evolution into the Protestant ranks. At Coutras, while the Catholic gendarmes sported lances 'so full of taffeta that they wore shade',[19] those led by Henry already fought with only swords and pistols. Of course, there was strong resistance to change. Some hoped to thwart the effectiveness of firepower by improving the protective capability of their armour. Others, the Catholic gendarmes in particular, continued to rely mainly on their lances, as shown by the last great battles of the Wars of Religion (Coutras 1587, Arques 1589, and Ivry 1590). But the lessons of these battles will be remembered, and the analysis of Jean de Tavannes at the end of the reign of Henry IV removes any ambiguity. It is no longer necessary to discuss which of the lance or pistol should prevail. Although he does not deny the disadvantages of the latter, it is clear to Tavannes that 'the pistol takes the prize; it pierces, it kills, it carries death and fear with it.'[20] The time is no longer for half-measures and the lance, with the axe and a mass of other weapons, were part of the weapons 'of our ancestors'.

French King Henry IV (1553–1610). Hendrick Goltzius. (Rijksmuseum)

Here we can measure the progress made since the middle of the century. Not only was the French nobility forced to equip themselves with firearms, but it also had to abandon the lance; the weapon that founded its reputation and prestige. Economic and social explanations certainly are important factors in this upheaval (difficulty finding good horses, and the end of tournaments being other examples). But the gentlemen must above all adapt to the new threat posed by firearms, mainly the pistol. It is necessary to change or die. 'The form of war is changed', concludes the Vicomte de Tavannes pragmatically 'from the useless spear to pistols.'[21] For Claude Gaïer, while it was clear that firepower was the main cause of this transformation, it seems equally obvious that it is not that of infantrymen that is decisive. 'It is not the infantry but the mounted pistoleers who put an end to the long reign of the heavy rider armed with the lance.'[22]

New technology and tactics favourable to trotting were emerging. The use of firearms in heavy cavalry and particularly the pistol, would have

---

18 'Especially since they had not yet experienced the useless of lances and were poorly armed', Tavannes, *Mémoires*, p.296.
19 Agrippa D'Aubigné, *Histoire Universelle* (Geneva: Droz, 1993), p.137.
20 Tavannes, *Mémoires*, p.191.
21 Tavannes, *Mémoires*, p.98.
22 Claude Gaier, 'L'opinion des chefs de guerre Français du XVIe siècle sur les progrès de l'art militaire', *R.I.H.M.*, 29 (1970), p.744.

significant influence on the pace of the charge. Lancers used to gallop to get the best possible effect from their lances, but riders who used the pistol were no longer compelled to keep such a pace, especially as their weapon imposed new constraints. Indeed, if the pistol was held with one hand, its use has certain limits. Thus, adjusting his aim on a galloping horse – with weapons whose accuracy is not their strong point – turns out to be a very uncertain exercise. On the other hand, we must not forget that the transformation of the mounts also accompanied that of the weapons. Reiters and pistoleers had horses of a quality much lower than those possessed by gendarmes. 'Heavy and badly trained'[23] horses are an increasing part of the battle cavalry mounts. Finally, the inappropriateness of the gallop appears particularly in the context of the caracole. Ideally, the squadron would get closer to the enemy to fire a shot or two, then turn around to reload weapons. This manoeuvre, which relies exclusively on the use of firepower, cannot be executed at a gallop. The unit would lose its cohesion and the salvo would be ineffective. This last element adds to the previous ones and makes it possible to understand that it was probably quite difficult for this new heavy cavalry to charge at a very fast pace, which Giorgio Basta once again expresses very clearly: 'the corasse [the cuirassier] will not meet faster movement than the trot and will flees the runaway gallop'.[24]

Technical and tactical logics are not the only things at stake and the recruitment of new riders must also be considered. We have seen that the use of pistols allows generals to raise larger numbers of cuirassiers. However new recruits are not always the best with the quantity of men being recruited often at the expense of social 'quality'. In this respect, Basta and Wallhausen make remarks which are at times harsh and full of aristocratic prejudices,[25] which bear witness – in their own way – to a very real phenomenon whose consequences in combat can easily be apprehended. As long as the heavy cavalry units consisted mainly of gentlemen, the concern for glory and honour – or at least that of avoiding dishonour – often carried them along and often guaranteed if not success, at least the good conduct of the charge. Since the ranks were becoming mainly composed of commoners and people of low quality, the 'motivation' of the men to go on and complete the charge was questionable. Because the social and psychological frameworks that allowed aristocrats to overcome their fears are much less important in these men, officers became suspicious of their motivation to fight.[26]

This phenomenon is recurrent in the writings of Tavannes. The latter, like some of his contemporaries, does not deny an interest in the gallop for which he has perfectly identified the advantages: 'the momentum of the race increases the force, carries and serves especially the cavalry, the spurs put

---

23   Wallhausen, *Art militaire*, p.16.
24   Basta, *Le gouvernement de la cavalerie légère*, p.22. The trot also allows the cuirassier to take advantage of a soft and disunited ground; Basta, p.73.
25   Basta, *Le gouvernement de la cavalerie légère*, p.18; Wallhausen, *Art militaire*, pp.3, 17.
26   These men would not have, in the words of Franco Cardini, 'a mental and bodily technique of overcoming fear' (*La culture de la guerre*, p.48).

THE TRIUMPH OF FIREPOWER

Half-armoured horsemen, with full helmet. Workshop of Jacob de Gheyn II, 1599. (Rijksmuseum)

the horses out consideration of danger.'[27] He is however very reluctant to advise this pace, because of the reliability of the troops. Riders did not have the equestrian instruction or the training of the mounts of the old knights, and they seemed unable to advance quickly while keeping the cohesion of the squadron. A captain who sped up the pace of his squadron too quickly would only lead disordered people into combat. As for the final phase of the charge – when the squadrons were supposed to gallop full out – Tavannes is even more circumspect. His preference is quite clear, that is, for a slower pace.

The reason is once again the quality of the men, whom the captain pushes more than he leads, and which prevents him from considering an attack at a full gallop. Indeed, if the gallop increases the power of men and horses, it also gives 'much more means to those who have no desire to mingle among this momentum to stop, to hold bridle, and to get out of the charge.'[28] 'The cowards pull up their charges [at a gallop], holding a bridle at six paces from the enemy, and let their companions to break through the enemy; but charges at the trot, make them known as they are, and make them lose the artifice; the last ranks push them in spite of themselves.'[29] It is in any case the pace that was to be most frequently adopted in action: 'the charges of today are trotting', he observes by way of conclusion.[30]

The observations of Tavannes make it possible to understand the limits which touch and constrain the cavalry of this time. The galloping charge has a twofold advantage – both physical and moral – but it cannot be conducted because of the lack of instruction received by the riders and the lack of

---

27 Tavannes, *Mémoires*, p.193.
28 Tavannes, *Mémoires.*, p.117.
29 Tavannes, *Mémoires.*, p.193.
30 Tavannes, *Mémoires.*, p.194.

THE NEW KNIGHTS

Clash between lancers, French Wars of Religion. Jean Perrissin, 1570. (Rijksmuseum)

confidence that the captains had towards some of them. It is no longer those gentlemen of whom La Noue said, not without pride, 'it is difficult to make such an order [the squadron] in our nation, [.] everyone wants to be the first to walk and fight.'[31] Some however, like Montgommery, want to preserve the gallop, at least in the last strides, as did the King of Navarre in Coutras (1587). His words are neither false nor unreasonable.[32] However, it is one thing for Henry IV – an exceptional captain – to lead his Huguenot gendarmes at the gallop, and quite another to lead ordinary cavalry.[33] Charging at the gallop was not officially rejected but it did not seem to be adopted any longer.

From the end of the reign of Henry II, the gendarmes faced a new tactical formation from Germany, popularised by the reiters: the squadron. Despite the defeats of Saint-Quentin (1557) and Gravelines (1558), the gendarmerie did not rush to adopt the new formation. The first engagements of the civil wars thus saw the French men-at-arms confronted by squadrons of the German reiters. At Dreux (1562) in particular, Tavannes clearly describes the defeat of the gendarmes of Damville and the Constable de Montmorency; defeated by the large squadrons of German reiters in the service of the Protestants.[34]

The lesson of Dreux however, did not pay off quickly, and the use of squadrons met with sustained resistance. This is undoubtedly one of the main issues of the famous fifteenth *Discours* of La Noue: 'That the old form of arranging the cavalry in hedge or line is now of little use, and that it is necessary that it take use of squadrons.' Some men of war, very attached to the 'old custom', still remained convinced of the necessity of not changing. It was for the author to overcome their resistances, and to convince them 'that the way we observed until this time to arrange it must be left to take the one that reason admonishes us to follow as the best.'[35] 'One must not be much amazed', in fact, of the defeats experienced by the hedges, 'because the natural reason demonstrates it, who wants the strong to have the upper hand

---

31 La Noue, *Discours*, p.354.
32 Montgommery, *La milice Françoise*, pp.137, 141.
33 Moreover, in the Battle of Bonneval (May 1589), Chatillon, if he followed the precepts of Henri by forming his gendarmes into squadrons, charged the enemy only at trot. Ronald S. Love, "'All the King's Horsemen': The Equestrian Army of Henry IV 1588–1598', *The Sixteenth Century Journal*, 22, n°3–4 (1992), p.518.
34 Tavannes, *Mémoires*, p.266.
35 La Noue, *Discours*, p.332.

on the weak, and that six or seven ranks of cavalry joined together overthrow only one'. The strength of the famous reiters lies at least as much in their deep formation as in their firearms. Their squadrons 'are so thick that there is no way to get through'.[36] It was left to Henry IV to complete the transformation of the tactical structure of the reformed cavalry, and then extend it to all French mounted troops. The King was personally convinced of the necessity of charging in squadron rather than in hedge. This is also a point emphasised by the propaganda texts, such as the *Discours véritable, récit de la bataille d'Ivry*: 'His majesty who has experienced in other battles and fights that it was more advantageous to make the cavalry fight in squadron than in hedge (even his own, which has no spear), has organised all his cavalry in seven regiments, arranged in as many squadrons.'[37] But beyond his own experience, his action in this area was also influenced by some great captains. The forerunner was probably Gaspard de Coligny. In 1570, at Arnay-le-duc, he decided to place his riders in six squadrons instead of arranging them traditionally in line.[38] Henri was also no doubt familiar with the theories of La Noue, an ardent supporter of the abandonment of the charge in hedge. Thus, the King was not the first to advocate the establishment of the squadron, his efforts were no less decisive. He systematised the use of this formation and imposed it on the cavalry.

The reiters' units were originally very strong. Franco Cardini speaks of squadrons of a frontage of 25 riders in 15 or 20 ranks, or between 375 and 500 men.[39] Their size, however, could be even greater. According to Tavannes, the strength of a 'big squadron' of reiters could reach 1,500 to 2,000 men.[40] It is apparently a formation of this size (about 2,000), that faced the hedges of French gendarmes and light horse at Renty (1554).[41] Such numbers induced large formations. Tavannes mentions 15 to 16 ranks deep and a front of 100 to 130 men. The squadrons of reiters thus constituted massive blocks of horsemen, slow to move and manoeuvre. Objective reasons could have determined such large squadrons. The desire for example to produce a rolling fire, or to present a sufficiently compact body against the enemy. It soon became apparent however, that these advantages sacrificed manoeuvrability. Their exaggerated depth rendered many of the riders impotent, as they could not take part in the fight.[42]

It therefore seemed necessary to reduce the number of men and to seek a new balance between ranks and lines. La Noue, from the 1580s, planned to reduce the depth of the squadron to seven ranks only.[43] Henri IV, familiar with the reflections of La Noue, seems to have retained this idea. He thus

---

36 La Noue, *Discours*, p.335.
37 Anon., *Discours véritable de la victoire obtenue par le roi, en la bataille donnée près le village d'Ivry, le quatorzième de mars, 1590* (Lyon: Ancelin, 1594), p.10.
38 D'Aubigné, quoted by Love, 'All the King's Horsemen', p.515.
39 Cardini, *La culture de la guerre*, p.114.
40 Tavannes, *Mémoires*, p.300.
41 Tavannes, *Mémoires*, p.190.
42 Tavannes, *Mémoires*, p.299.
43 La Noue, *Discours*, p.336.

THE NEW KNIGHTS

Cavalry charging an infantry square, French Wars of Religion. Jean Perrissin, 1570. (Rijksmuseum)

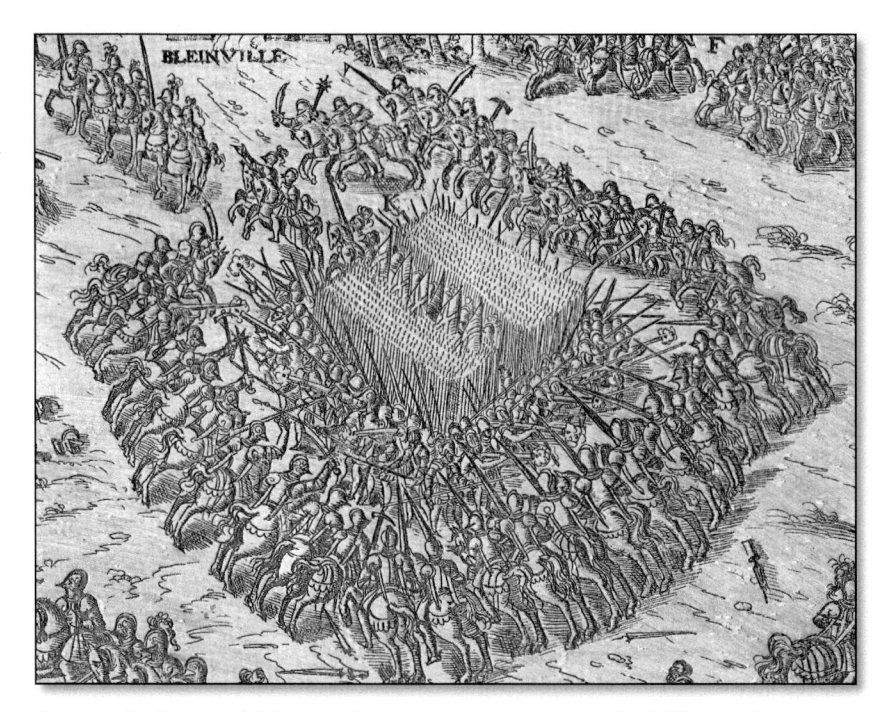

frequently deployed his squadrons in six or seven ranks.[44] This is the case at Coutras (1587), where he arranges the riders of his two main squadrons in six ranks and a frontage of 50. He goes even further at Ivry (1590). During this battle, in order to face the large numbers of his opponent – Mayenne – he did not hesitate to organise his squadrons on 120-man frontages and in just five ranks.[45]

The decrease in the depth of the squadron cannot simply be seen as a response to the numerical superiority of the Catholic League troops. Certainly, reducing the number of ranks allowed the King to keep an extended front and thus avoid being enveloped by the enemy. But there is no doubt that this decision is also the result of a real tactical choice, the result of his experience and practice of war. These new squadrons proved their effectiveness in combat. They proved particularly flexible and could easily adapt to circumstances. At Ivry, Henry asked his horsemen to keep their lines and ranks tight, in order to produce a greater effect against the uneven and disorderly lines of the cavalry of the League.[46] At Amiens (1597), the King ordered his men to leave between them a large space, so that the shock of the Spanish lances was absorbed in part by the gaps in the squadron's ranks and files.[47] As a pragmatic warrior, Henri IV was able to change the internal arrangement of the squadron to obtain more flexible and manoeuvrable units. Henry IV's singularity, wrote R.S. Love, is the way

---

44 Love, 'All the King's Horsemen', p.514.
45 Anon., *Discours véritable de la victoire obtenue par le roi*, p.11.
46 Baptiste Legrain, *Décade contenant la vie et gestes de Henri le Grand Roy de France et de Navarre IIIIe du nom* (Paris: 1614), p.428, quoted by Love, 'All the King's Horsemen', p.517.
47 Love, 'All the King's Horsemen', p.517.

he organised and trained his squadrons, combining the power and mass of the reiters' formation with the speed and strength of shock of men-at-arms.[48]

The principles gradually imposed from the middle of the sixteenth century suggest a way of charging that has nothing to do with that of earlier men-at-arms. The objective was to exploit the maximum firepower of the riders. For this reason, the reiters developed the famous tactic of the caracole, which theoretically allows them to generate continuous fire. Although it is often mentioned by historians, it is helpful to analyse in detail this tactic; first because the term caracole in fact covers several variants and secondly because the effectiveness of this tactic was frequently questioned. However, whatever the degree of efficiency of the caracole, it is still true that the new modes of charges based on firepower became widespread during the Wars of Religion. Skilful and pragmatic captains, like Henri of Navarre, knew how to take advantage of the principles of charge introduced by the reiters while accommodating their disadvantages.

The caracole is described by Tavannes; 'After firing the first rank turns to the left, revealing the second rank that shoots, and then the third rank, one after the other, moving at a snail's pace, and moving away to left to reload.'[49] One can imagine this big squadron of 1,000 or 1,500 horsemen, armoured to the knee, advancing at the trot. The men control their horses with their left hands, the right holds the wheel-lock pistol; loaded and primed. It is necessary to ride very close to the enemy considering the short range of the weapon. Less than 10 metres away, the first rank fires. One can easily imagine the accuracy of shooting from a trotting horse. The jolts produced by this pace hardly allow for any adjustments when taking aim. In any case the manoeuvre must be done quickly because the riders must give way to the second rank by riding off the left. They then quickly come back to the tail of the squadron to reload their weapons.

There are some variations on the traditional tactic. Sometimes the rank that is to fire is detached from the squadron to go along the flank of the enemy, delivering its salvo only at this moment. It would then join the back of the formation to reload. Brent Nosworthy also mentions another way of proceeding. The squadron comes up on the flank of the enemy and keeps this position during all the manoeuvring. Each rank in turn comes up, stands in front of the opposing front and shoots before returning to the tail of the squadron. This practice would preserve the following ranks that would remain safe from enemy fire while waiting for their turn.[50] The principle of these variants, however, remains the same. The ranks fire one after the other to produce a continuous fire and then come back to their place at the tail of the formation by two half turns. The riders usually broke away to the left, the majority firing with their right hand, but the constraints of the

---

48 Love, 'All the King's Horsemen'.
49 Tavannes, *Mémoires*, p.267. The first part of Plate n°20 of Wallhausen's *Art militaire* closely depicts this evolution, with the proviso that the figured horsemen are arquebusiers on horseback, and that they therefore emerge from the right.
50 Brent Nosworthy, *The Anatomy of Victory, Battle Tactics 1689–1763* (New York: Hippocrene Books, 1990), p.11.

THE NEW KNIGHTS

German horseman with pistol, 1577. Abraham de Bruyn. (Rijksmuseum)

ground sometimes required that they broke off to the right. The broad and regular turns described by the manoeuvring of the ranks of riders gave this manoeuvre its name, deriving from the Spanish caracole; a term equivalent to the French 'snail' or the German *schnecke*.[51]

It seems, however, that this processionary system was not the only way to execute the caracole. At least that is what the testimony of La Noue suggests. Referring to the first of the characteristics of the reiters' tactics, he explains thus that 'being at twenty paces enemies they turn flank & unload on them their salvo of pistols, for (say they) that more people can shoot than if they clashed head-on with enemies. And if these enemies are amazed and turn their backs, no doubt they accost them and make them harm. But if they stand firm, they will remake a great circuit to recharge or resume new pistols.'[52] La Noue explicitly evokes the 'grand circuit' that the reiters make to reload their pistol after firing, as in the manoeuvre presented above. However, there is no mention here of detaching the ranks one by one and sending them in succession to fire on the enemy. It appears rather that the caracole is carried out in one movement by the entire squadron. It should then be understood that it is the whole squadron that reaches the flanks of the opponent, and that then it is not a single rank which fires, but all the riders who can, that is to say the first two or three ranks, at the same time. Another observation from La Noue reinforces this impression. 'Another custom they observe', he adds, 'is that when the front ranks of the squadron start firing, all the rest also fire, and most of them in the air.'[53]

Finally, to judge the diversity of practices, one can consider the second description of Tavannes. 'The first rank fires and turns to the left, revealing the second which does the same; the rest follows, turning away, and get safe behind the others who have fired, and take a great wheel to go all together and reload their pistol in safety.'[54] This testimony differs from the first in that the ranks that come to the rear of the squadron after firing do not reload their weapons immediately. They wait until everyone else has fired their pistols, and only then does the entire squadron withdraw to reload safely. This system, although processionary, does not provide a continuous fire. It may have been used when the squadron did not have the depth needed to allow the riders time to reload.

---

51 Cardini, *La culture de la guerre*, pp.114–115.
52 La Noue, *Discours*, p.359.
53 La Noue, *Discours*, p.360.
54 Tavannes, *Mémoires*, p.347.

THE TRIUMPH OF FIREPOWER

The caracole by squadron.
(Author's diagram)

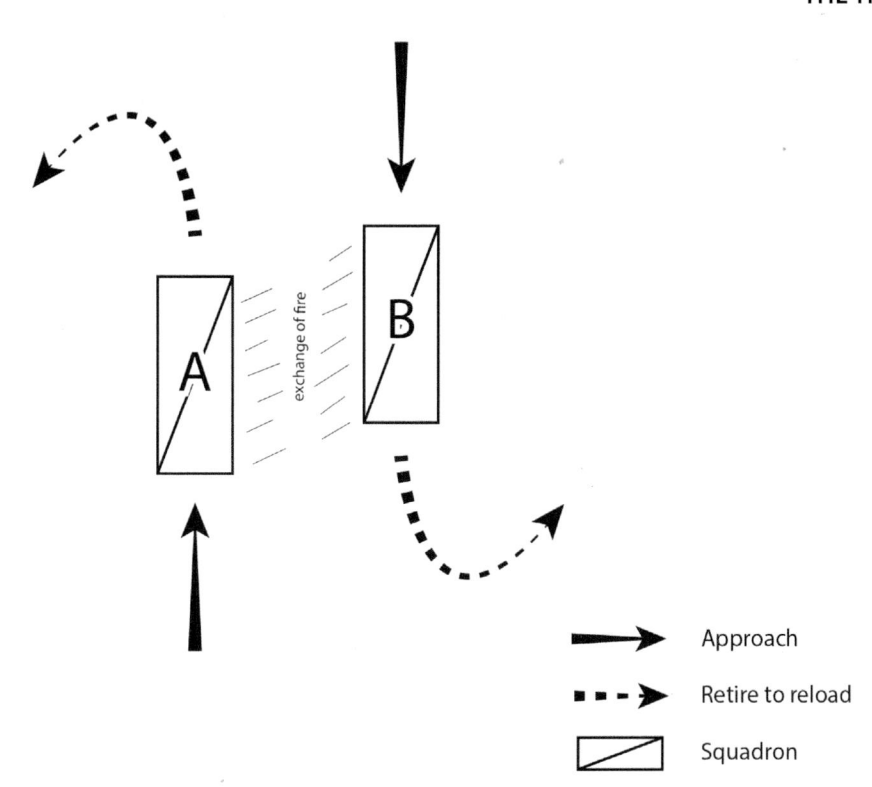

Approach
Retire to reload
Squadron

The effectiveness of the caracole has, however, often been questioned. This tactic could be effective against squares of pikemen unprotected by arquebusiers. The range of the riders' firearms was enough to protect them from pikes, and the succession of ranks produced a continuous volume of fire that could shake the infantrymen. The firepower of the reiters impressed contemporaries. Monluc judges them thus 'terrible to the war, because one sees nothing but fire and iron'.[55] In the case of infantry with arquebusiers, the range of arquebuses was beyond that of pistols, and the task became more difficult. In addition, the riders advanced at a fairly slow pace, making them easy targets. They were also particularly vulnerable immediately after firing, during the time they have to go along the front of the enemy to let the next rank take their place. However, what really disqualifies the caracole in the eyes of the French men of war is the refusal to charge into contact. The reiters 'do not push in', says Tavannes.[56] 'If the squadron meets resistance,' explains La Noue, 'if the first salvo was not enough, they fall back to reload.'[57] But for these men, the shock tactics and a direct confrontation with the opponent was the only way to win. In addition, facing a determined opponent, the turn made by the squadron such a short distance away could be disastrous. Even in the case of a traditional caracole, where the ranks fired successively,

---

55 Blaise de Monluc, *Commentaires de Messire Blaise de Montluc, mareschal de France*, Nouvelle collection des mémoires pour servir à l'histoire de France, Par Michaud et Poujalat, Tome VII (Paris: chez l'éditeur du commentaire analytique du code civile, 1838), p.327.
56 Tavannes, *Mémoires.*, p.347.
57 La Noue, *Discours*, pp.359–360.

THE NEW KNIGHTS

the squadron was not immune to being disordered. One can imagine that the enemy ignored the discharge of the first rank and counter-attacked immediately afterwards. The first rank had no time to disengage completely, and it was caught between the advancing enemy and the second rank that came to take its place. Riders who had not had time to escape, were surprised, their pistols unloaded, and turned around and try to ride through their comrades, creating confusion and disorder.

Finally, as Delbrück remarks, it is against an adversary also using this tactic that the caracole is the most suitable. In this case victory would go to the one of the two who is able to manoeuvre and shoot the longest with the most cohesion and accuracy. That is to say the one that was best trained and had the most reliable and best maintained weapons.[58] The other would necessarily give way, either because the accumulation of losses led to a collapse of morale, or because the exchanging of ranks ended up disorganising the squadron. In any case the unit would begin to disintegrate, and the enemy had only to take advantage of the disorder and the panic caused. They would then interrupt their caracole and advance to complete their victory.

The tactics of the reiters were not limited to the caracole. They could also charge in a much simpler way, using their two main assets: the fire and depth of the units. These elements were enough to rout a formation of gendarmes, without having to resort to the complex manoeuvre. 'The reiters of Dreux', explains Tavannes, 'in a big squadron, and being only faced with lines of lancers, did not need to make this turn to the left, and they carried them off easily'.[59] The caracole was far from useless in front of men-at-arms charging in line. Even if the only first two ranks opened fire, each gendarme would be the target of two shooters. Those who had not been injured or dismounted, could not stop the advance of the massive formation of the reiters. Their lances and speed were of little help against the fire of the squadron perhaps 15 ranks deep. It is true that the gendarmes may have a had a wide front than the squadron of reiters, so in this case they would only overthrow part of the gendarmes' line. However, 'it will be at the place where the standard is, and where the captains and the best men are placed; and that being carried away, everything is shaken.'[60] The risk of envelopment is also largely irrelevant; 'and even if what has not been shocked gives on the flanks of the squadron, it does little harm, for it cannot force into the men who are thus amassed and united, which also strike them as they did for the first

Blaise de Monluc (1500/1502–1577), author of *Commentaires*

---

58 Delbrück, *History of the art of war*, vol. IV, p.125.
59 Tavannes, *Mémoires*, p.267.
60 La Noue, *Discours*, p.334.

Armoured arquebusier, shooting from horseback. Workshop of Jacob de Gheyn II, 1599. (Rijksmuseum)

one.'[61] Many lines of gendarmes attacking in succession would not be any more successful. The squadron of reiters would overthrow them all, 'almost as easily as a ball would make several rows of bowling pins'.[62] Even if the lancers were deployed in a deeper formation, they would still get the worst of the exchange if their opponents charged intelligently. That is to say according to La Noue, using their firepower at close range, without trying to avoid the shock of contact. The effectiveness of the lance is particularly questionable. It rarely killed and only the first rank gendarmes could use it during the initial contact 'And the other ranks that follow cannot do the same but are forced (at least the second and the third) to throw it away and to use their swords.'[63]

Leaving aside the caracole whose limits contemporary writers had perceived, the new modes of combat thus had enough advantages for their employment to become generalised, at least in part. Henry IV, who was a great cavalry leader, was particularly successful in profiting from it. The examples and reflections of his elders, such as Coligny and La Noue, as well as his own experience, led him to take the best of innovations coming from Germany. He abandoned two basic aspects of the medieval charge – lance and

---

61 La Noue, *Discours*.
62 La Noue, *Discours*.
63 La Noue, *Discours*, p.361.

hedge formation – and instead adopted the pistol and the deeper squadron formation. These radical moves should not however lead us to believe that Henri was content to copy the fighting methods of the reiters; it was not a question of simply reproducing the caracole. One notable difference was with the size of the squadron, which he decreased substantially the depth. Henri did not intend to sacrifice the benefits of shock, which remained one of the fundamental elements of the charge. Speed was therefore a factor that could not be neglected. However, it is difficult to produce a brisk enough pace with squadrons in 15 or 20 ranks. From this point of view, it seems that he managed to constitute tactical units combining strength and mobility while still preserving the ability of riders to gallop.[64]

The question of the adaptation of such tactical novelties also arose with regard to the use of firepower. In general, the gendarmes were intended to strike the enemy, to break them by hand-to-hand combat, and they could not be used like pistoleers or mounted arquebusiers. Thus, if Henri recognised the usefulness of firepower in mounted combat, he could not go too far without risking losing the underlying advantages inherent in heavy cavalry: speed and shock. Henri relied on the infantry, thus systematising an idea of Coligny. At Moncontour (1569), reiters were accompanied by Huguenot arquebusiers, who ran by their side while holding the stirrups.[65] This innovation of Coligny is then resumed and improved by the King, who was also present at Moncontour. At Coutras, each of the five squadrons of Huguenot cavalry is supported by a small platoon of 25 arquebusiers on foot in five ranks, placed at its sides to 'fill its stirrups'. The volume of fire is thus shared between the riders and the infantrymen who accompany them. This combination allowed Henri to have a significant level without giving up the benefits of both shock action and mobility.

---

[64] Simon Goulart, *Mémoires de la Ligue* (n.p., 1602), vol. 2, p.265.
[65] Edouard Hardy de Périni, *Batailles françaises* (Paris: Flammarion, 1894–1906), volume II, p.80.

5

Enter Gustavus Adolphus

By the dawn of the seventeenth century the heavy cavalry had completed its metamorphosis, and the time of great tactical upheavals seemed over. We are often reminded that the seventeenth century is one that saw armies move from deep to linear formations with the infantry asserting themselves as the queen of battles. This is, for Michael Roberts, the prime aspect of this 'military revolution'. The infantry appears to be the main subject of the work of most theorists who, like Maurice de Nassau,[1] seem to sideline the role of mounted troops. The works devoted to cavalry are few in number, as if the subject was thought to be not very interesting or too difficult to understand. Real changes are however noticeable during the seventeenth century and historiography has tried to evaluate them. The study of the evolution of the cavalry during the seventeenth century is thus generally centred on the chaos that represents the Thirty Years' War, and more particularly on Gustavus' innovations; Gustavus Adolphus (1611–1632) would indeed embody a radical turning point in mounted combat, abandoning the caracole and changing the speed of the charge and the use of weapons. However, while it is legitimate to question the role actually played by the King of Sweden in this field, such an analysis requires a consideration of cavalry practices before the Swedish intervention.

What mounted tactics were inherited from the sixteenth century at the beginning of the Thirty Years' War? We know quite well the main characteristics of heavy cavalry at the beginning of the century: the man-at-arms equipped with the lance and using the shock of the charge, gave way to riders often as heavily armed but relying mainly on firepower and using a slower pace. However, beyond these main traits, is it possible to have a precise understanding of the tactics practiced by heavy cavalry when the longest war of the seventeenth century begins? The question arises particularly in respect of the caracole, which we have seen was the subject of criticism in France from the end of the sixteenth century. Theoretical works written shortly before the conflict are disappointing. Fortunately, the tactics of the cavalry charge at the beginning of the war owe much to the changes put in

---

1 Maurice de Nassau (1567–1625), Prince of Orange, Stadtholder of the United Provinces, was with his cousin Guillaume-Louis one of the greatest reformers and tacticians of his time.

THE NEW KNIGHTS

Cavalry skirmish, both armoured and unarmoured horsemen can be seen. Jan Mortszen the Younger, between 1619 and 1649. (Rijksmuseum)

place from the second half of the sixteenth century. It is therefore possible, by cross-referencing different sources, to identify the main characteristics of German cavalry during the first years of the Thirty Years' War.

One can get an idea of the shape of the charge at the beginning of the Thirty Years' War. It is possible to revisit some of the earlier observations made about the French cavalry. This was characterised by an apparent dichotomy, rather unbalanced, between the elite (constituted by the gendarmes), on the one hand and most of the companies of light cavalry on the other. The main difference, as we have seen, was undoubtedly in the pace adopted for the charge and in the way of balancing the shock to fire ratio. It seems however, that in general, the course of the charges should be more in keeping with Tavannes' observations than with Montgommery's wishes. Jean de Billon, who wrote at the very beginning of the reign of Louis XIII, partly confirms this idea. He does not distinguish the gendarmes from the light horse, but simply the 'horsemen', armoured from head to knees. His recommendations for the pace of the charge are particularly significant. The cavalry must begin the charge at a walking speed, then when within 60 or 80 paces of the enemy, must speed up to a fast trot or gallop. 'But still, it is not good to gallop because those in first ranks walk while the other ranks open and stay behind.'[2]

Were the cavalry tactics of the Empire close to those of the French? Some respected authors from the second decade of the century provide important answers. Basta and Wallhausen speak of two methods. The first is that adopted by lancers. They charged in small, shallow squadrons, galloping when within 60 paces of the enemy, to push them back and break them. The second is that of corasses, or cuirassiers. The latter seem to have had a more defensive function, to 'support and stop'[3] the enemy. They were thus

---

2   Jean de Billon, *Les principes de l'art militaire* (Rouen: Berthelin, 1641[1st edition 1613]), p.254.
3   Wallhausen, *Art militaire*, p.50.

Lancer vs pistoleer, from J.J. Wallhausen's Kriegskunst zu Pferd. (Michał Paradowski's archive)

arranged in much more massive formations, since their solidity and mass were the guarantors of their success. They relied mainly on firepower and used the sword only in the melee. The shock of impact is still an important factor, at least for Basta, who gives them the ability to 'break' the enemy. Its effectiveness is nevertheless limited by the reduced speed of the cuirassiers. The need to preserve their cohesion and the poor quality of their horses meant the squadrons could not exceed the trot.[4]

Beyond these facts relating to the main principles of the charge, the two authors do not give an overall description of the elements of the charge. Wallhausen develops some of the combat tactics of the lancer and cuirassier companies, but his manoeuvres do not always seem very realistic. He proposes for example, a way for a company of 60 lances to successfully

---

4   Basta, *Le gouvernement de la cavalerie légère*, p.23.

charge a company of 100 cuirassiers. The 60 lancers must be divided into eight groups. One group was sent to each flank of the enemy squadron and a third to its rear: 'So, the corasses have to face three sides, which would undoubtedly disturb their order. Then if one, two, or the three groups should fail, they could be replaced gradually by the five others held in reserve. Thus, the corasses attacked unceasingly on their three faces will eventually bend.'[5]

One can wonder about the real chances of success of such a thin line of lancers facing the fire of pistols. It is not a certainty that attacking on three sides could compensate for this weakness, especially since it was quite difficult to imagine the execution of such an attack on the battlefield. The cuirassiers will hardly allow the lancers to be placed on their flanks as if on parade. Would they not be hampered by the presence of infantry corps or other squadrons?

Wallhausen's suggestions for the charge of cuirassiers seem even less feasible. This is for example the case of what he calls 'caracole' (different to the snail of the Reiters), which is: 'a detour from the place where you were standing to let pass the fury of the enemy who thought charge you. Seeing that the enemy advances to charge you, you will make your company turn as unified as possible, to the right or left of the place where it stood so that the enemy is caught in the empty place. And seeing you have given him enough room to pass, you will reject, turning your company suddenly against the flank of the enemy.'[6]

This suggests that the plan was to avoid the charge trajectory of the enemy unit to let it pass, and then to fall on its flank. Certainly, the reduced pace of charging cuirassiers probably left time to consider some manoeuvring before contact. But, as we have already pointed out, this slowness also gave the enemy time to see what was being attempted, and to try to counter it. Would the enemy really continue on his way as if nothing was happening and let himself be flanked? On the other hand, to have a squadron of 300 or 400 horsemen promptly execute such a manoeuvre while preserving order and cohesion of the unit seems uncertain.

These observations also apply to another even more surprising tactical proposition. Seeing the enemy coming, the company would open up in their centre and charge the enemy on both sides. This is a manoeuvre that undoubtedly is represented very well on Wallhausen's rich engravings but is much more difficult to execute on the battlefield. John Cruso, who is largely inspired by Wallhausen, is not mistaken. He considers this tactic 'doubtful.'[7] It implies, if one follows its author, that they open their files, turning each rider to the right or to the left, and once the new position taken, everyone makes a complete half-turn to be able to be in a position to charge. All these operations are very dangerous in the midst of battle, and a wise enemy could not fail to take advantage of them. Wallhausen's writings reveal a too-theoretical representation of the cavalry charge. It can hardly be likely that such tactics

---

5   Wallhausen, *Art militaire*, p.72.
6   Wallhausen, *Art militaire*, p.62.
7   Cruso, *Militarie Instructions for the Cavallerie*, quoted by John Tincey, *Soldiers of the English Civil War, vol. 2: Cavalry* (Oxford: Osprey Publishing, 2004), p.6.

were adopted – successfully or not – in real combat conditions. We cannot therefore restrict ourselves to this work when considering the tactics of the charge. The vision presented by Wallhausen is all the more truncated as lance-armed gendarmes had almost completely disappeared by this time, a fact which he recognises and regrets. In fact, as in France and in the United Provinces, there is only one category of heavy cavalry: cuirassiers or 'corasses'. We should also remember that, as in France and in the United Provinces, charges by German cavalry generally relied on a slower pace and a very heavy use of firepower.

With the exception of those armies noted above, it is safe to assume that the conditions and tactics of a cavalry charge are quite close to those described as by Tavannes, or even to a certain extent, La Noue. Can this similarity of practices be extended to the caracole? Tavannes, like La Noue, does not favour this tactic, but can we hypothesise that it was perpetuated until the 1620s, and in what forms?

Imperial or Spanish horseman in buff coat, Battle of Nördlingen 1634. Pieter Snayers. (Nationalmuseum, Stockholm)

The caracole is not mentioned by Wallhausen when he speaks of a charge by cuirassiers, and only mounted arquebusiers seemed to practice it. Would that mean that the old tactics of the reiters would already have disappeared in Germany – at least for heavy cavalry – on the eve of the Thirty Years' War? Once again Wallhausen's writings must be considered with caution. The best proof is the testimony of one of the losing commanders at the Battle of White Mountain (1620), the Prince of Anhalt: 'One of our greatest imperfections was that most of our cavalry troops did not want to mix with the enemy, as I have often preached to them, rejecting the bad custom of caracole … and I put this expressly here, so that it is necessary to hate as the plague this custom to go to the charge without mingle well.'[8] And, even though Anhalt suggests, it is very probable that the Imperial cavalry, which was not particularly different from that of Bohemia, also practiced the caracole. Even if it cannot be said for certain that the Prince is referring to the 'processionary' caracole, it seems clear that this tactic was still used at the beginning of the war.

Inspired by the observations of La Noue and complemented by those of Tavannes, one can imagine then the way in which a charge between two squadrons of opposing cuirassiers was conducted in the first years of the war. The two units are quite massive, larger probably than contemporary French squadrons, eight or 10 ranks deep on a frontage of sometimes 40 or 50 files. They advance towards each other at the walk, then speeding up to the trot. This pace would not be the most comfortable, because the riders are heavily armoured, from their head to their knees. They must therefore withstand

---

8   Account of the Prince of Anhalt, quoted by Olivier Chaline, *La bataille de la Montagne Blanche*, p.158.

the movements of their mount and the restrictions of their armour. As they get closer, the first ranks at least would lower their visors and the pistols are out of their holsters, ready to fire. However, there would be no question of contacting the enemy and coming to blows with him. The two units would instead change their approach, so as not to be completely face-to-face. Only half, or even a corner of each formation would be directly opposed to their opponent. The riders in the front are close enough to clearly see the men who face them, at least as much as the dust kicked up by the advance of so many horses would permit. Then, on the orders of their officers, they would fire a salvo at a range of twenty paces. Only the first ranks of the squadrons would have a chance of hitting their target, but it is not impossible given the tension of the moment, that the riders located further back also fired their weapons, even if largely above the heads of their comrades. At twenty paces on a trotting horse, the shooting of a wheel-lock pistol was not very precise. Men would not know for sure if they had hit their target, or anything else. The smoke released by the black powder, the dust already mentioned, and the reduced vision caused by their lowered visors only permitted a poor view of their surroundings. In addition, the squadrons do not carry on into contact. Neither are looking to close into melee. If they had been on the receiving end of a volley as well there would have been losses, and they would then move to their left to reload their weapons or fire again with the additional pistol or pistols they would be carrying.

If the officers held their men under control, they could then launch a new charge, if indeed one can call this type of attack a charge. It would unfold in the same way as before. However, this time one of the two squadrons could refuse the confrontation and turn back. The second discharge could also be effective. The men of the following ranks, seeing (or guessing) the gaps created by the enemy fire, would see they were facing a determined enemy; often breaking ranks and fleeing. Thus, the manoeuvre to the rear after firing could easily transform into a real rout. The winners would then be left to pursue the fleeing fugitives.

There is no doubt a number of possible variants to this scenario. Instead of facing each other more or less partially head on, the squadrons could also move towards the enemy on their own right hand. They would approach closer without getting into hand-to-hand contact and, like two ships of the line, release their salvos as they passed. Under these circumstances they could also adopt a different formation; very deep, with a narrow front, which allowed more riders to shoot. Again, according to the general principle of the caracole, the squadrons would then break off to reload their pistols and prepare for a possible second round.[9]

However, there were other ways to carry out a charge, which notably avoided the about-turn to reload weapons which is a characteristic of the caracole. The story of the young Anhalt, colonel of a regiment of mounted arquebusiers, and his sons, who also took part in the Battle of White Mountain, gives us an example:

---

9   A pattern quite close to the caracole by squadron described by La Noue.

At this moment in the battle, he boldly attacked the Imperial cuirassiers. Löben [his lieutenant-colonel] reminded me to stop regularly until my three other companies, which had been separated from the others, could join me. When we were re-united, we attacked the enemy full of assurance …When we faced the cuirassiers, they were stunned and waited our attack calmly, open helmets …While waiting for the three companies of which I spoke, I had shouted to my soldiers not to shoot at all as long as I did not take out my pistols or before they could aim. Then came the cuirassiers, those of Don Balthasar or Colonel Kratz. … But it turned out that they had received the same orders [as our unit] to hold their fire, so that we remained a moment staring at each other, astonished, as if we were good friends. This lasted until my lieutenant-colonel, no longer bear it, opened fire and it occurred as usual in such circumstances. My riders had a great advantage of which I noticed later because they had been able to take aim during the moment of silence and to have more easily their man then. When the enemy saw so much resolution and all the powder that came into his eyes, some of them coming off worst, he could not bear it any longer and fell back into great disorder.[10]

The cuirassiers retreated without being vigorously pursued. The lieutenant-colonel judged it more prudent to pursue them only 'gently and in better order'.

This testimony sees a unit of mounted arquebusiers opposing cuirassiers, which was probably not very common (hence the surprise of the enemy). It is nonetheless revealing enough how the charges could pan out. 'It happened as usual in such circumstances', adds Anhalt, which suggests that this scenario was not uncommon. We are no longer looking at the configuration of the caracole. It is clear however, that the squadrons did not intend to 'mingle well', as the Prince of Anhalt regrets. They had to approach each other at a trot then stop to face each other. The distance is not specified. It cannot be too far given the range of weapons. It is nevertheless important enough for the cuirassiers to be able to retreat without the arquebusiers rushing upon them immediately after the salvo. In any case, it is not at all certain that the latter had any particular desire to do so.

The peculiarity of this confrontation obviously lies in the fact that the two adversaries were instructed to preserve their fire. There followed a period during which the two parties observed each other. The order to let the enemy fire first is probably because it was thought that this salvo, taken a little hastily by far, would not be as effective. The squadron that was able to hold its fire then benefited from the fact that its opponent had wasted his own shot and would then advance and perform a better aimed volley. This effect would be amplified by the moral ascendancy that would have been won by the squadron which managed to stand firm under fire. This scenario is however still rather theoretical. As we can see, Anhalt's squadron fired first, but its salvo was precise since the riders took advantage of the wait facing the enemy to aim properly. It is uncertain that it was a very deadly volley,

---

10   Quoted by Chaline, *La bataille de la Montagne Blanche*, p.177.

THE NEW KNIGHTS

Mounted officer, 1577.
Abraham de Bruyn.
(Rijksmuseum)

but the smoke and noise that accompanied it, and the determination it demonstrated, were enough to discourage the cuirassiers.

In most cases, one of the two squadrons would break contact rather quickly, without having to exchange actual blows. When neither side wanted to give in, the fighting would intensify. Since there was no question of turning back to reload, as is the case in the caracole, the two sides remained face-to-face. Riders carried several loaded pistols with them, which allowed them to maintain a fairly continuous fire for a little while. The rear ranks could also pass their own guns to the men in front. If the exchange of pistol fire lasted, it was not impossible that one side would move into contact, or that the two squadrons broke off, as if with a tacit agreement to do so. But the most common alternative was probably that one of them ended up 'cracking'. Again, it was usually the rear ranks that faltered first. The riders of the last ranks were not in direct contact with the enemy and had only a partial view of what was happening in the front ranks. But it was precisely these elements that weighed on the minds of the men. They saw of the enemy only what was visible through the thick powder smoke. On the other hand, they would be able to make out their front-rank companions killed, wounded or unhorsed and see those of the second or third rank advancing to replace them. As the fight went on, they could then believe the determination of the opponent to be unshakable. The wait became too difficult in the face of the increasingly doubtful outcome (they think), of the fight. It may have been enough for just a few horsemen to fall out of the ranks and move back, thus precipitating an irreversible scramble away from the enemy by the entire squadron.

Of course, not all squadrons charged in this way. Elite units undoubtedly had the experience and confidence to continue into contact, but they did not constitute the majority of the troops engaged. According to Anhalt, during the Battle of White Mountain, 'most' cavalry troops refused to move into close combat. Squadrons did not systematically look to carry out shock tactics – one of the more essential elements of a successful charge in the past – this no longer being in practice. Whether they executed the caracole or shot each other face-to-face, it is on firepower they must rely. Thus, the great principles of the middle of the sixteenth century became the foundations of the charge at the beginning of the Thirty Years' War; it usually being conducted at a trot and the dynamics of the offensive movement reduced to only a little. Riders of one side or the other would gain a decisive advantage from their fire and would not moving to contact until one was beginning to crumble.

History often presents Gustavus Adolphus' involvement in the Thirty Years' War as a key moment in the evolution of the art of war. From the point of view of cavalry, the practices initiated by the King of Sweden mark a real break, correcting the errors of the sixteenth century and bringing cavalry into a new era. By having his riders charge with sword and at the gallop – focussing on shock tactics – he led the cavalry of other European nations to abandon the caracole. The delicate balance between firepower and cold steel was changed in favour of the latter, this change being almost like the swing of the pendulum after the previous period which had been characterised by the general adoption of fire tactics.

Such a rapid and fundamental transformation raises questions. As Richard Brzezinski remarks, the contemporaries of the King of Sweden did not seem to have been particularly impressed by the exploits of his cavalry.[11] On the other hand, the innovations which are attributed to him in cavalry tactics are scarcely mentioned in the military manuals of the seventeenth century. It therefore seems appropriate to take stock of the changes really initiated by Gustavus Adolphus, and their innovative character and limits. To measure the real influence of Gustavus on the history of cavalry combat we must analyse the genesis and the context of the reforms undertaken in order to better understand the nature of them. It is then easier to undertake a detailed analysis of what was attributed to the King. These bring into play the three main principles on which the charge is based; the charge itself, the weapons used, and the speed and shock, that considerably changed the look of cavalry combat.

Firstly, it should be remembered that the Swedish cavalry which presented itself in 1630 during the Thirty Years' War was the result of a unique situation. It is without doubt that the cavalry inherited by Gustavus Adolphus upon his accession to the throne did not constitute a particularly powerful military tool. Due to weaknesses in national military procurement, Swedish cavalry appeared poorly equipped compared to Western European standards. The local breeding stock also gave them only mediocre and small horses, which were derided by their opponents. The tactic of charge was modelled on that of the cuirassiers of the continent, and it included the use of the caracole. However, the Swedes had neither the armour nor the firepower, nor even the mounts of their counterparts in Germany or France, and it is easy to believe that the efficiency of their cavalry in action was not high. These limitations appeared with a vengeance during conflicts with their Polish neighbours.

The Polish armies possessed a large proportion of cavalry, composed of heavy and light units. Among the first, the famous 'winged hussars' formed an elite. If their defensive armament was similar to the western cuirassiers, they were distinguished by the use of the lance, about five metres long. Handled with skill these lances proved formidable.[12] Their use also implied correctly that the charge was conducted at a gallop and that it focussed entirely on shock. The hussars charged in deep formations – the 'huf' – much more difficult to disperse than the simple shallow ranks of men-at-arms. They had inflicted more than one setback on the squadrons of Charles IX, the father of Gustavus Adolphus. In particular, his cavalry was slaughtered at

---

11   Brzezinski, *The Army of Gustavus Adolphus*, p.3.
12   Brzezinski, *Polish Winged Hussar, 1576–1775* (Oxford: Osprey Publishing, 2006), pp.8, 46–47.

Kokenhusen (1601), Weissenstein (1604) and Kircholm (1605). A drawing (a nineteenth century copy of a J. Lauro engraving of 1603), depicting the Battle of Kokenhusen, clearly shows the inferiority of the Swedes.[13] One can see there a formation of Polish lancers about to break a squadron of Swedish cavalry. The hussars are shown charging without any concern for the fire of the arquebuses and pistols. The moment of contact has not yet occurred but already the Swedish squadron can be seen disintegrating from the rear ranks.

Gustavus' wars with Poland (between 1616 and 1629) were instructive for the new King, who faced the same difficulties as his father. During the first clashes with the Poles, Gustavus was soon confronted with the limits of tactics based mainly on giving fire while moving at the trot. The inefficiency of the caracole was evident in the face of the terrible charges by the Polish hussars. But the King was also able to learn from these failures and he began to reform his cavalry.

He could have chosen to strengthen the protection of his riders and increasing their armament by adding more firearms. This would have led to increased firepower and a closer alignment with the Western model. It is the opposite that occurred. Not only was there no question of turning the arquebusiers into cuirassiers, but they also had to abandon their arquebuses as early as 1621. After that date they were only equipped with a pair of pistols and a sword. The supply difficulties of the Swedish army were certainly not irrelevant when this development began.[14] However Gustavus Adolphus also understood that forging ahead towards an ever greater reliance on firepower – a principle that led to the complete transformation of his infantry – was probably not what the cavalry needed. Although still equipped with pistols, riders now had to rely more on their swords: relatively light weapons more easily handled. They became, according to Michael Roberts, their main weapon.[15]

The fighting method of the cavalry was no longer based on the delivery of salvos of pistols at close range, but on the confrontation of man on man. Since the charge was no longer based on firepower, it was no longer necessary to operate in deep squadrons. Gustavus therefore reduced the number of ranks which had the benefit of increasing their manoeuvrability. In short, the cavalry learned from the Poles to make more use of its natural assets, 'mass, speed and shock'.[16] But to solve the problem posed by the formidable hussars, the King of Sweden also relied on his infantry. He detached groups of musketeers to accompany the squadrons and thus allow them to benefit from additional firepower, and from 1627 the Swedish cavalry began to gain more successes against the Polish hussars.[17]

Thus, the Swedish cavalry of the 1630s owes much to what it learnt in the Polish wars. It is necessary however, to better characterise the 'Swedish' charge, and to focus on three essential points: the question relating to the abandoning

---

13 Drawing reproduced in Brzezinski, *Polish Winged Hussar*, p.47.
14 Gustavus Adolphus certainly copied the Polish methods, says Brzezinski, 'but he may also have been influenced by the lack of pistols in his own cavalry'. *Polish Winged Hussar*, p.24.
15 Michael Roberts, *Gustavus Adolphus* (London and New York: Longman, 1992), pp.102, 104.
16 Roberts, *Gustavus Adolphus*, p.104.
17 Nosworthy, *The Anatomy of Victory*, p.23.

ENTER GUSTAVUS ADOLPHUS

of fire tactics, the reintroduction of the gallop to contact, and finally the shock of close combat.

The reborn Swedish cavalry that landed in Germany in 1630 contrasts with those of its Imperial and Catholic League adversaries, for whom firepower remained essential. However, this break in the Swedish doctrine is somewhat nuanced. It should be noted that the King of Sweden did not go so far as to completely suppress the firing of pistols during the charge. Reporting on Gustavus' instructions to his riders, von Chemnitz writes that only the first or at most the first two ranks, when they were close enough to see the whites of the eyes of their enemies, had to shoot, then draw their swords. The riders of the last rank, however, had to attack without firing but with the sword held high, and keep their pistols for the melee.[18]

The testimony of Robert Monro, a Scottish officer fighting alongside the Swedes says much the same: 'The horsemen of the two wings furiously charged each other, our riders with the resolution not to fire on the enemy until he made his salvo first, then, at short distance, our musketeers greeted them with a salvo, at that time our horsemen fired their pistols and charged with the sword.'[19]

These extracts are very significant. It is clear the use of pistols by the Swedish cavalry was still an option. The initial objective was to disrupt the enemy with a 'preparation' salvo and then to take advantage of the confusion created to break the enemy squadron with the sword. Gustavus did not suddenly decide that firepower would no longer play any role in a cavalry charge, rather he changed the way it was used. Given the small range of pistols, it was more effective to shoot at a short range. But there was only time for one salvo, and the rest of the time was to be used to draw swords and charge into contact with cold steel. Gustavus forbade the soldiers of the rear ranks to fire, judging their shots would be ineffective, and could probably even cause cohesion difficulties for the squadron.

After Breitenfeld (1631), the King again limited the use of firepower by proscribing that his horsemen would not be permitted to fire until they had received the fire of the enemy.[20] This leaves us thinking that Gustavus had little fear of the pistol volleys of the enemy because they were fired from too long a range, or with too much apprehension and too little control. The Swedes, who knew that the enemy had wasted his fire, could then advance more resolutely,

A cuirassier and his equipment, from J.J. Wallhausen's *Kriegskunst zu Pferd*. (Michał Paradowski's archive)

---

18 Bogislav Philipp von Chemnitz, *Königlichen Schwedischen in Teutschland geführten Krieg*, vol. I (Stockholm: 1648). Quoted by Brzezinski, *The Army of Gustavus Adolphus*, p.23.
19 Robert Monro, *Monro, His Expedition with the Worthy Scots Regiment* (London: 1637), p.65. Quoted by Nosworthy, *The Anatomy of Victory*, p.33.
20 Nosworthy, *The Anatomy of Victory*, p.23.

no longer worrying about avoiding enemy bullets. Finally, the firepower of the cavalry was diminished, but this was only because Gustavus Adolphus entrusted this role to small groups of supporting 'commanded' musketeers, who stood between the cavalry squadrons.

Thus, Gustavus did not totally give up the use of firepower, as one reads on occasion. He was also not the only one to bring in innovations in this area. Richard Brzezinski reminds us that since the beginning of the Thirty Years' War, practices had changed somewhat even in the German cavalry. Large numbers of units continued to think of the charge as a series of salvos of arquebuses or pistols, fired point-blank, until one of the adversaries gave up the ground, in the manner of the caracole, and as we have seen at the Battle of White Mountain.[21] But other regiments, representing the elite of the armies or trained by bold leaders like Piccolomini or Pappenheim, had already adopted modifications in line with the reforms of Gustavus Adolphus. The cuirassiers of the former only used the first two ranks to shoot, seeking only to produce sufficient fire to create disorder in the enemy ranks before going into contact.[22]

Finally, we can see that the improvements put in place by Gustavus are close to the practices experimented with by Henri IV of France. The desire to restrict the importance of firepower is similar, yet sufficient firepower was maintained to disrupt the enemy ranks. Gustavus had therefore diminished the role of firepower in the charge, relying on the shock of cold steel. It remains, however, to determine the speed at which it must be conducted.

The misadventures of the Swedish cavalry in Poland led Gustavus to modify their tactics relating to the speed of the charge as well as in the tactical use of weapons.[23] Gustavus no doubt considered that it would be best to reproduce these tactics to his benefit in Germany – against the heavy cuirassiers – to prevent a repeat of the pattern of defeats suffered by his cavalry in Poland. However, other considerations – more specific to the theatre of the wars in Germany –were also factors to motivate the adoption of a faster pace in the charge. For example, the use of firearms has to be considered, since it is on the effect of firepower that the success of the charge was generally based. From the moment when the King made the decision to reduce the importance of firepower in favour of cold steel, he had to accept that his riders would be subjected to a volley greater than that which they themselves could deliver; a consideration further reinforced by the fact that Swedes often only wore light armour, such as a helmet and a cuirass over a stout leather buff coat.

From this point of view, the idea of speeding up the pace of the charge makes perfect sense. The best way to limit the losses caused by the opponent's fire is to move quickly. The sooner the Swedes closed with the enemy, the less time they had to endure his pistol salvos; it is also more difficult for the

---

21 The mercenary regiments. Brzezinski, *The Army of Gustavus Adolphus*, p.23.
22 Brzezinski, *The Army of Gustavus Adolphus*, p.23.
23 Michael Roberts reminds us that the Poles taught Gustavus to use speed, one of the natural advantages of cavalry. *Gustavus Adolphus*, p.104.

enemy to aim at a fast-moving target.[24] The principle of speed is also essential if one considers that the King intended to base the success of the charge on the shock factor of fast-moving cavalry. It is true as has been said earlier that Gustavus had not completely abandoned the use of firepower, but a speedy pace like the gallop would then also affect the effectiveness of his own troops' shooting. However, this disadvantage was largely counterbalanced by the fact that only part of the men in the Swedish squadron were allowed to shoot. In addition, their salvo was delivered at very short range, which would clearly improve the chances of hitting the enemy. Finally, it must not be forgotten that the King was the first to significantly reduce the depth of his squadrons, which was a definite advantage when maintaining a gallop. It is easier, or perhaps less difficult, to form a squadron of three or four ranks than one of eight, and the impact on their order and cohesion would be less.

However, this analysis is but one of many, and other authors consider it unlikely that Swedish cavalry really charged at the gallop. That this is the opinion of Michael Roberts: 'the final approach of the cavalry … was closer to trotting than galloping'.[25] Colonel Gyllenstierna also thinks that the cavalry attack did not reach this pace and did not try to charge as fast as the horses could gallop. Admittedly, the Vicomte de Turenne had dubbed his method of charge 'Swedish attack'. But, according to the colonel, it was in fact the Duke Bernard of Saxe-Weimar who had taught his cavalry to charge at a gallop, and who would have influenced the Vicomte, and not the example of Gustavus' Swedes.[26]

Maintaining a gallop over a long distance requires training, because the risk of disorganising the squadron before even being within firing range of the enemy was greater. But above all, this question cannot be considered in isolation of the tactical guidance put in place by Gustavus. Michael Roberts and Colonel Gyllenstierna also underline the constraints of the use of the small groups of 'commanded' musketeers arranged between the squadrons. This tactic implied that the musketeers and the cavalry would march together at the same pace, at least until the infantry had come within firing range.

It is hardly imaginable that a squadron accompanied by a group of musketeers would start to gallop at 200 paces from the enemy. Not only would the musketeers be obviously left behind and no longer be able to support the riders, but they themselves would be left at the mercy of an enemy attack.

These points suggest that the Swedish cavalry could at best gallop only in the last moments of the charge. According to E. Gyllenstierna and M. Roberts,

---

24 Jean Roemer, *Cavalry: its history, management and uses* (New York: D. Van Nostrand, 1863), p.324. Quoted by Nosworthy, *The Anatomy of Victory*, p.23.
25 Roberts, *Gustavus Adolphus*, p.107.
26 Colonel Ebbe Gyllenstierna, 'Henri de Turenne et Charles-Gustave Wrangel. Stratégie et tactique pendant les dernièr esannées de la guerre de Trente Ans', *Turenne et l'Art militaire*, Actes du colloque International sur Turenne et l'Art militaire, 1975 (Paris: Les Belles lettres, 1978), pp.204–205. Bernard, Duke of Saxe-Weimar served in Protestant armies in Germany (1621–1623, 1625–1627) and in the United Provinces Army (1623–1625, 1627–1630) before joining the Swedish army, of which he became one of the principal officers. He spent 1635 in the service of France. After his death in 1639 his army, including his elite cavalry, was incorporated into the French army.

it trotted to a distance of 50 metres from the enemy.[27] The testimony of Robert Monro on the Battle of Breitenfeld is once again useful and supports these observations: 'The horsemen of the two wings furiously charged each other … and then, at short distance, our musketeers greeted them with a salvo, at that time our horsemen fired their pistols and charged with the sword.'[28]

His account is devoid of any explicit mention of the speed of the cavalry, but it allows us to understand the elements of the charge, in particular the role of the infantry, and to understand why it was impossible for Swedish cavalry to break into a gallop early in the charge. The term 'furiously' must be interpreted with caution, as it does not mean that the two lines rode at full gallop towards each other right from the beginning of the attack. How could the Swedes have done so, marching as they were with musketeers at their side? Monro probably wishes to point out that the two adversaries were advancing towards each other with firm resolve, without appearing to want to avoid contact or delay.

According to Munro's description, the riders were only able to make their approach at a slow speed, and perhaps they even had to stop to let the musketeers execute their salvo. It was only then that they had the opportunity to leave the protection of the infantry and to free themselves from their slow march to finally charge at a gallop. But they could only do so for a short distance, since the musketeers gave their volley at about twenty paces range, and it took further than this for the squadrons to increase their speed to the gallop.[29]

The starting point of a charge was not always especially close to the enemy. Nevertheless, it remains obvious that so long as the two arms were thus combined, it was difficult to envisage the cavalry actually galloping, or it could only do so at the end of the manoeuvre. This perspective should not be dismissed since if going into the trot about 50 metres from the enemy, it was still possible for the riders to reach at least a slow gallop for the last metres of the charge, after the first rank had fired their pistols.

It is possible to observe a certain degree of similarity between the practices of Gustavus and those of Henry IV, who we saw galloping from 10 steps away from the enemy at Coutras. There is also a question about whether Gustavus was able to employ his cavalry without adding to it the groups of musketeers. This configuration is found at Lützen (1632). According to Brézé, the musketeers accompanying the squadrons led by the King of Sweden would have stayed behind to let the horsemen cross a ditch and would then have continued their own advance alone. This hypothesis is confirmed by R. Brzezinski.[30] The latter shows that Bernard of Saxe-Weimar, who commanded the Swedish left, also separated the cavalry from his supporting musketeers, as they were required to attack the village of Lützen. In such conditions, the obstacle represented by the attachment of the musketeers

---

27 Gyllenstierna, 'Henri de Turenne et Charles-Gustave Wrangel', p.204. Roberts, *Gustavus Adolphus*, p.106.
28 Monro, *Expedition*, p.65. Quoted by Nosworthy, *The Anatomy of Victory*, p.33.
29 Gioacchino Bonaventura Argentero, Marquis de Brézé, *Observations historiques et critiques sur les commentaires de Folard et sur la cavalerie* (Turin: les freres Reycends, 1772), Tome II, p.148.
30 Brzezinski, *Lützen 1632*.

was lifted and the riders could then ride at the gallop. The increase in speed was a significant alternative for squadrons deprived of their fire support.

This marked a radical break from the Swedish doctrine. The changes made by Gustavus Adolphus in the field of firepower and speed lead us to infer that the place of shock tactics in the charge went through a profound renewal. At the beginning of the Polish wars, Swedish tactics were mainly based on avoiding hand to hand combat The Swedes hoped, according to Western custom, to win the advantage by the sole effect of their firearms. But it is very unlikely that the fire of a rank, or even the first ranks of the squadron, could be enough to break a formation of hussars charging at the gallop. The determination of the latter would be even stronger in the knowledge that their opponents did not intend to move in but wished to avoid contact at all costs.

Gustavus therefore opted for a more offensive and aggressive doctrine, obliging his cavalry to close into hand-to-hand combat with the enemy. It is in this context that we need to understand the emphasis placed on swords and charging at a faster pace. Remember also that Gustavus decided to rely on detachments of musketeers interspersed with the cavalry whose fire intended to contribute to disordering the enemy. This choice highlights the ambiguity of the relationship between shock and fire tactics. The use of firepower by the heavy cavalry had indeed led to a reducing the role of shock tactics, or even banished altogether since the use of the lance had almost disappeared. However, the King of Sweden went beyond the conflict between these two tactical principles. He knew that the power of shock tactics was indispensable, but that it would not be enough in the face of the Polish Winged Hussars. The fire of the musketeers and the – albeit very limited – shooting from the riders, was intended to prepare the way for a cold steel charge and improve the chance of success. It was somehow by a combination of fire and shock that the King planned to defeat his formidable enemies. But we must not lose sight of the fact that he gave primacy to shock over fire. As M. Roberts explains, firepower alone could no longer be expected to win but to open the way to the benefits of shock tactics and melee, which alone would decide the victor.[31]

Gustavus Adolphus had realised that victory could only be won by charging the enemy, not by avoiding him. His personal authority and the discipline prevailing in the Swedish army no doubt enabled him to gain obedience from his cavalry so that they stopped relying exclusively on their firearms and on avoiding contact. It was more difficult for the German mercenary regiments to conform, as they sometimes had trouble complying with Swedish standards of military discipline. But the King was totally convinced of the necessity of such a fundamental reform, and they had to comply. They had to review their tactics and adopt the Swedish way, supervised by Swedish officers. Israel Hoppe recounts for example, that in September 1628, the recently arrived Beaudissin regiment showed 'only a feeble desire (as is the custom in the Germans) to fight'. Gustavus Adolphus addressed this by ordering them to charge right into contact.[32]

---

31 Roberts, *Gustavus Adolphus*, p.105.
32 Israël Hoppe, *Geschichte des erstenschwediscen-polnischenkrieges in Preussen* (Leipzig: M. Toeppen, 1887), quoted by Brzezinski, *The Army of Gustavus Adolphus*, p.24.

If this break was radical in the Swedish cavalry, can we say that it was the same in the other European armies, starting with the German opponents of Gustavus Adolphus? R. Brzezinski nuances this idea by arguing that the caracole was, by the early 1630s, an outmoded tactic. True, as proved by the words of the Prince of Anhalt after the Battle of White Mountain, some captains did not wait for Gustavus to benefit from the employment of such a tactic. In fact, some German squadrons – like those of Tilly or Piccolomini – did not refuse to move into contact. Faced with these elite units, unafraid of the prospect of shock action, the Swedes would find victory difficult to achieve.

But do these examples allow us to generalise? Does the fact that Piccolomini or Pappenheim were aware that victory could only be won through the use of shock tactics and cold steel, mean that all the regiments of the Imperial and Catholic League cavalry followed this doctrine. The injunctions of the Prince of Anhalt do not seem to have prevented the majority of his squadrons from 'going to the charge without mixing'. As R. Brzezinski points out, it is likely that only the best regiments sought to move into contact. For many German mercenaries – who possessed a valuable horse and career prospects – there was no question of risking shock tactics and close combat without some serious consideration. They were content to fire their pistol in the direction of the enemy and 'considering their duty accomplished, turned back, leaving the next rank running the risk. Charges often degenerated into a caracole.'[33]

Against such enemies, the cavalry of Gustavus Adolphus had a considerable advantage, reproducing the pattern that prevailed at the beginning of the Polish wars. The Swedes knew that these adversaries did not intend to carry out their charge to the end; the most probable idea being that they would turn around after firing their pistols or come to an almost complete halt to execute a salvo which they hoped would be enough to disorder or discourage them. The German horsemen saw the Swedish front ranks holding their fire, shrugging off their own, and approaching at a speed sufficiently fast to clearly indicate their intention to move into contact. The Swedish cavalry were sufficiently well trained and instructed – sure of themselves – to benefit from the superiority acquired by the units which, even without firing, made it into contact while still maintaining their good order. They dominated 'by the fear of the contact the enemy feel toward their unshakable appearance.'[34] Success was even more certain when the Swedish squadrons fell on cuirassiers caught in the act of caracole, that is while they were turning to go to the rear.

Thus, while it is undoubtedly an exaggeration to say that the King of Sweden put an end to the practice of the caracole and its variants, it is fair to think that he hastened their disappearance. This is recorded in a memoir sent by Wallenstein to his lieutenants in January 1633. He draws lessons from Lützen, proposing for example to prohibit the German riders from using their firearms, because 'after shooting they turn around, which causes a lot of disorder'.[35] It should be noted that Gustavus Adolphus had introduced the same innovation within his own cavalry from 1621. Wallenstein therefore

---

33 Brzezinski, *The Army of Gustavus Adolphus*, p.24.
34 Alain Joxe, *Voyage aux sources de la guerre* (Paris: PUF, 1991), p.263.
35 Brzezinski, *Lützen*, p.90.

intended to eliminate by this order any of the practices inherited from the use of the caracole.[36]

One could argue that Gustavus's actions are the origin of a return to shock tactics in a cavalry charge but only the elite units took the charge to contact with the enemy, the greater number relied exclusively on firepower and practiced – in one way or another – avoidance tactics. Some generals were very aware of the shortcomings of this tactic, but to engage in real change involved a great deal of restraint, discipline and instruction. This was an effort which they judged unnecessary, since all the cavalry in Western Europe acted in the same way, and none held any real superiority over the other. The change came from the imbalance brought about by the arrival of Gustavus. By systematising the adoption of shock tactics in his cavalry he forced his opponents to also practice this tactic with most of their squadrons, on pain of placing them in a dangerous position of inferiority. Even if one cannot speak of a real revolution, the reforms introduced by the King (whether they were due to technical constraints or tactical choices), constituted a real change compared to the most accepted practices of the time. They represented at least an acceleration; a general adoption of trends already in progress. Thus, cavalry tactics could no longer be considered quite the same after Gustavus Adolphus.

If we take for granted the importance of the reforms initiated by Gustavus Adolphus, then it becomes legitimate to question the way in which they were received in the armies of Western Europe. It is easy to understand that the German horsemen, because they were his direct adversaries or fought alongside him, quickly adopted Gustavus' innovations. But what about armies whose countries were allies but more distant like France and England? It is known that some foreign officers (Prince Rupert, Gassion), fought alongside the Swedes then played a considerable role in the modernisation of the cavalry of their country of origin. The battlefields of the British Civil Wars and those of the last years of the Thirty Years' War provide an opportunity to measure the impact of Swedish reforms in the field of cavalry tactics.

The Imperial cavalry learnt directly from Gustavus Adolphus' battles. It soon appears that caracole and similar practices were no longer used in the face of an enemy systematically charging – vigorously – and seeking to make contact. We have seen that after Lützen, Wallenstein proposed to forbid the use of the carbine for his German cavalry. Montecuccoli stated however, after Nördlingen (1634), two years after the death of Gustavus, the prevalence of these practices still among some cavalry. 'Although the Spanish cavalry, which refused the fight after a manner of caracole, was driven by Gambarcota, a soldier of reputation, it was more mocked than praised because it was unable to collide with the enemy.'[37] It is true that the Spanish cavalry had a different tradition from that of the German cavalry. It is in the Kingdom of

---

36 The caracole was also condemned by Montecuccoli in his *Sulle Battaglie*, an analysis of the battles of the first half of the 1630s. Thomas M. Barker, *The Military Intellectual and Battle. Raimondo Montecuccoli and the Thirty Years War* (Albany-New York: State University of New York Press, 1975), pp.108–110.
37 Keith Roberts, *Cromwell's War Machine, the New Model Army 1645-1660* (Barnsley: Pen & Sword, 2005), p.154.

THE NEW KNIGHTS

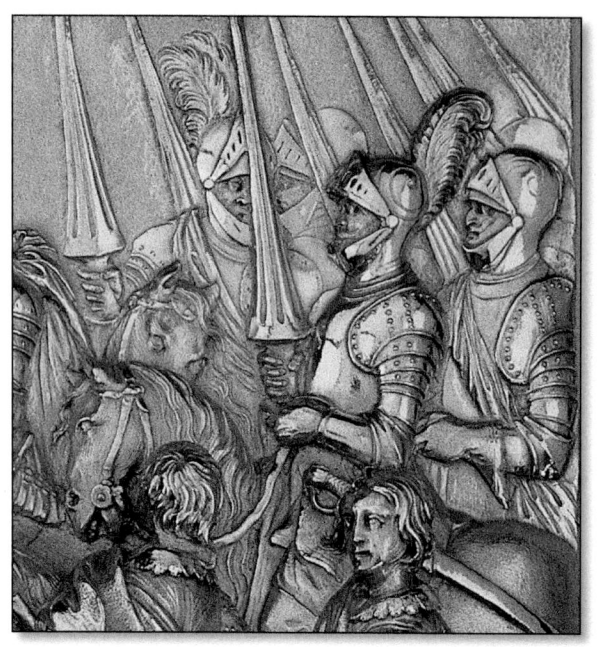

Spanish lancers, siege of Jülich, 1622. Mattheus Melijn, 1636. (Rijksmuseum)

Spain that was born for example the *jineta* way of fighting, using speed and manoeuvrability in combat.[38] However, troops closer to the German model, like those in France, also had difficulties adopting the Swedish standard.

We know for example the state of the French cavalry at the beginning of their intervention in the Thirty Years' War. The rout of Thionville (1639), symbolises the situation of mounted troops, hitherto neglected, insufficiently instructed and prepared. A change of tactics would therefore be difficult. Hervé Drévillon emphasises the role played in this revival by Gassion, who served alongside Gustavus Adolphus. His 'experience and expertise' was a considerable asset, and his regiment was one of the hardened cadres from which the French cavalry arm was rebuilt.[39] Four years later, at Rocroi, Thionville was avenged, highlighting the progress made. There are actually a number of actions at Rocroi which highlight the changes being undertaken with their approach to mounted combat. The fighting on the French left wing showed for example that charges were now being conducted at a gallop. It was no longer a question of using the caracole or tactics based exclusively on firepower. The sword found its place, and the idea that charges must be conducted until contact is made in order to win the melee was put into practice.

However, the limits of these tactical advances are also apparent, in respect of the speed of the charge. On the enemy's right wing, the cavalry of Alsace was facing the French squadrons of La Ferté and had also learned the lessons of Gustavus' reforms. It was galloping into contact using shock tactics and the sword that the Alsatian cavalry attacked the French. They only began to gallop for a short distance prior to contact, to exploit their speed without reducing their cohesion. The French got it wrong, breaking into a gallop too early, and La Ferté caused his formation to become disordered; his mounts were blown. Consequently, he and his men were swept away. This kind of speed was therefore difficult to implement and manage properly and only the most experienced units would probably risk it. The Duc d'Aumale sums up the lessons of Rocroi quite well: 'In short, it was a glorious day for the French cavalry, a rehabilitation, a continual charge or, rather, a succession of scrums, of rapid engagements where trot and pistols were more used than gallop and swords. However, there were violent shocks where the sword played its role.'[40]

The Battle of Lens (1648) is also very significant moment in the scope of the transformation that had taken place since the beginning of the Thirty Years' War. Condé's instructions before the battle are enlightening. The Prince

---

38 Riding in the *jineta* way was adopted in Spain during the reconquest from the Arabs.
39 Drévillon, '*L'héroïsme à l'épreuve de l'absolutisme*, pp.157–160.
40 D'Aumale, *Histoire des princes de Condé*, Tome IV, p.122.

ordered his men 'to let the enemies shoot first, to begin the charge only at a walking pace.'[41] We can clearly see the importance of the use of firepower, and the inherent caution with regard speed of movement. Condé wanted to prevent the charge from starting too fast and too early, which would leave the horses out of breath and repeat the misfortune of La Ferté at Rocroi. The account, by the Duc d'Aumale, of Condé's charge on the French right wing clarifies these points:

> The two troops are walking against each other. Arrived at a hundred paces the enemy take trot to charge: the French stop. The enemy, astonished, stops in his turn; we are ten paces away, the pistol high. Our horsemen remain motionless, all have their eyes fixed on Monsieur le Prince, who is in front of the line between two squadrons of 'Villette'. He can count on this regiment, it was Gassion's. M. de Salm is in front of him. After a few moments of hesitation, the enemies send a general salvo. Many of our people are on the ground; but Condé's sword is out of the scabbard and shining in the sun: this is the signal 'remember Rocroi', he cries to the old soldiers of Gassion. With swords and pistols, our horsemen collide with those of the Prince of Salm; the first line of enemies is crushed.[42]

Here we can measure the developments which took place concerning the course of a charge. The squadrons carried it out at a slower pace, and firing still plays its part, but the outcome of the combat is decided by the shock of hand-to-hand combat. We can also note that if the enemy interrupted their charge, it was mainly because they were surprised by the French halting. Condé's tactic is much closer to that of Gustavus' than the type of charge carried out by Anhalt at White Mountain. It is based on an attitude that is both defensive and aggressive. He waits for the enemy and then lets him open fire first before rushing at him. It is not certain that the Prince took the trouble to order his men to fire before launching his attack, and d'Aumale is not clear. However, it appears that the success of the charge did not rest on the salvo of the pistols of one side or the other but is found in the shock of contact and melee. It relied as much on the psychological impact as on the physical effect. At 10 paces, the riders were only able to accelerate moderately without gaining much momentum, but they arrived with the moral force of those who had endured the enemy fire without flinching and displayed their will to engage in close combat. It was necessary, however, that the Prince be sure of his men to adopt such a tactic, one that was probably beyond the ability of most units.

What of the English experience? The English – or more accurately British – Civil Wars reveal similar trends. However, these wars were distinguished by the speed and sharpness with which they manifested themselves.

The changes which had taken place on the continent in the 1630s had not yet reached Britain on the eve of conflict breaking out. The cavalry tactics were therefore very similar to that practiced by Western European horsemen at the beginning of the Thirty Years' War, especially the tactics of the Dutch, who

---

41 D'Aumale, *Histoire des princes de Condé*, Tome V, p.232.
42 D'Aumale, *Histoire des princes de Condé*, Tome V, p.247.

many English officers had served. Indeed, at the beginning of the seventeenth century, service in the United Provinces' army offered many possibilities for those who wanted to pursue a military career. It also gave the opportunity for certain English gentlemen to perfect their military education by serving only for a summer or a particular siege.[43] This influence largely explains how mounted tactics changed. The squadrons were deep, up to six ranks, the pace was slow, and the firing of pistols and carbines was an important factor and allowed for squadrons to avoid or mitigate the effects of shock tactics. In theory the squadron approached at a walking pace and then stopped when it reached pistol range. The ranks then moved forward one by one in front of the squadron to fire on the enemy. The salvos came one after another until they had caused enough losses and disorder in the opposing ranks. The entire squadron then attacked at trot to complete their victory. Like their comrades on the continent however, the English riders had also significantly lightened their defensive armour. With the exception of the personal guards of some commanders, there was only a single regiment equipped as cuirassiers.

On the Royalist side however, this tactic was changed at the beginning of the war through the innovations of Prince Rupert of the Rhine. The nephew of the King was the main agent of change. To the experience gained with the Swedes he added his own reflections matured during the three years of his captivity in Linz and Vienna.[44] Like Gustavus Adolphus, he thought that firing should be minimised. He was also determined to charge into contact, convinced that it was necessary to attack the enemy directly to be sure of winning victory. His orders given before the Battle of Edgehill (1642), are particularly revealing. 'Prince Rupert', says Sir Richard Bulstrode, 'passed from one wing to the other, giving positive orders to the horse, to march as close as possible, keeping their ranks, with sword in hand, to receive the Enemy's shot, without firing either Carbine or Pistol, till we broke in amongst the Enemy, and then to make use our firearms as need should require.'[45]

The pace of the charge was necessarily faster than that of the Parliamentarians, especially since the Royalists charged in three ranks, although we do not know for certain that Rupert routinely conducted all charges at the gallop. Concern to preserve the cohesion of the squadron must encourage us to be cautious in this respect. Rupert ordered his men not to shoot at all before the two bodies of horse clashed together. This instruction was not always applied, as shown by the example of Roundway Down (1643).[46] It emphasises however, that Rupert had gone further than Gustavus in his desire to lessen the importance of fire. His idea of the charge was therefore based on aggressive tactics, giving precedence to the sword and the shock of impact. It was in sharp contrast to most English commanders' actions. He made his mark from the outset of the war. The charge at Powick Bridge (1642) in particular, gave his riders increased

---

43 Roberts, *Cromwell's War Machine*, p.43.
44 Rupert was taken prisoner at Lemgo in 1638, after a heroic charge of cavalry. John Tincey, *Marston Moor 1644. The beginning of the end* (Oxford: Osprey Publishing, 2003), pp.14–15.
45 Memoirs of Sir Richard Bulstrode quoted by Tincey, *Marston Moor*, p.34.
46 John Tincey, *Ironsides: English cavalry, 1588–1688* (Oxford: Osprey Publishing, 2002), p.31.

confidence and considerable moral ascendancy.[47] Edgehill gives a good example of the effect that such charges could have on inexperienced and untrained troops. The Parliamentarian troops saw determined squadrons coming forward, advancing at an unusual speed, charging right at them sword in hand, without even taking the time to stop for a salvo. The result was certain: 'The horsemen did discharge their long pieces [carbines] afar off and without distance [that is, out of effective range] and immediately thereafter wheeled all about and ran disorderly.'[48]

Although sometimes seriously under pressure, the Parliamentarian cavalry took some time to react to the Royalist tactics. It is true that the problems of recruiting, equipping and training troops – and the provision of replacements after battle – made it difficult to adopt such considerably different, tactical innovations. At the instigation of Cromwell however, they set themselves in step with Rupert's reforms. The work of John Vernon, written in the winter of 1643-1644, sums up quite well the new doctrines of the cavalry of Parliament:

> Each squadron being not above three deepe ... Those troops are to be at their close order, every left man's right knee must be close locked under his right hand man's left ham ... In this order they have to advance towards the enemy with an easy pace, firing their carbine at a convenient distance, always aiming at the breast of the enemy or lower, because the powder is of an elevating nature, then drawing near the enemy, they are with their right hands to take forth one of their pistols out of their holsters ... and firing as before, always reserving one pistol ready charged, spann'd and primed in their holsters, in case of a retreat as I have shown before, having thus fired the troops are to charge the enemy in full career, but in good order, with their sword fastened with a riband or the like unto their wrists, for fear of losing out of their hand, if they should chance to misse their blow, placing the pommel on their thigh, keeping still in their close order, locked as before.[49]

Prince Rupert of the Rhine (1619–1682). Anthony van Dyck.

It appears that the Parliamentary cavalry relied even more on firepower than Rupert did. The first salvo, with the carbine, still forced them to interrupt their advance. This pause in the charge reduced momentum and impetus. Nevertheless, some progress is obvious, and it was no longer a question of waiting for the enemy and be content to shoot at him from a distance. The

---

47 Powick Bridge was a simple cavalry fight. The losses were modest and the strategic consequences none, however the Royalist propaganda knew very well how to exploit this first success.
48 Tincey, *Soldiers of the English Civil War*, pp.16–17.
49 Quoted by Tincey, *Marston Moor*, pp.35–36.

purpose of both discharges (first with the carbine and second with the pistol), was to prepare the way for charging into contact, which was considered the whole point of a charge. Henceforth the Parliamentary cavalry, at least the most experienced and determined such as Cromwell's men, no longer hesitated to confront the Royalists in hand-to-hand combat.

Ludlow, a parliamentary officer, tells the story of a cavalry fight, 'The horse of both sides behaved with the greatest bravery, for having discharged their pistols and flung them at each other's heads they fell to it with their sword.'[50] This example shows, given the small distance that separates the two adversaries, that the momentum could be much reduced at the moment of the contact. The desire to preserve cohesion probably outweighed speed. Ludlow stressed however, that the determination to join in hand-to-hand combat with the enemy was very apparent on both sides. The fighting thus become much more contested; transformed into fierce melees. So, at Marston Moor: 'Cromwell's own squadron had a hard pull of it: for they were charged by Rupert's bravest men, both in front and flanks: they stood at the swords point a pretty while...; but at last (it so pleased God) he [Cromwell] brake through them, scattering them before him like a little dust.'[51]

Thus, the English example confirms the significant evolution of the charge observed during the Thirty Years' War. First, the pace of the advance is a little faster, although galloping is not the most common practice. On the other hand, firing, while still important, no longer seems to be conceived as anything more than a preparatory element before contact. The riders often took their swords after firing the last salvo. As a result, the resolution of the charge was based, in theory at least, on the concept of shock rather than avoidance tactics.

Gustavus Adolphus' part in all of this is not easy to determine. He probably did not introduce any real innovations, in the sense that the evolutions were for the most part already in use. But they were only developed in a limited way, and the King standardised their introduction in all his cavalry, some of whom were more adept at the new tactics than others. We can only really say that the key elements of the new doctrine of the charge to contact and shock tactics was put in place by Gustavus and were then adopted by the cavalry of most of Western Europe.

---

50   Tincey, *Ironsides*, p.32.
51   Quoted by Tincey, *Marston Moor*, p.64.

6

The Relative Stability of Cavalry Tactics

The end of the Thirty Years' War saw a general adoption of some of the developments introduced by Gustavus Adolphus. The question now arises as to whether these may have undergone further major changes during the period from the mid seventeenth century to the beginning of the eighteenth. This question concerns France first and foremost. It had prestigious cavalry leaders (Turenne, Condé, Luxembourg), but we also know of the interest Louis XIV had in siege warfare; not something heavy cavalry was much use for. Some seemingly contradictory elements make the evolution of French cavalry a little difficult to follow. The question also affects the troops of the Emperor, who was involved in every conflict against France during this period. This is all the more interesting as the Empire was engaged in wars of a totally different kind on its eastern borders. The Imperial cavalry was confronted with different modes of fighting, all of which influenced its employment and tactics. This chapter is divided into three parts. The first concerns the second half of the century. Then we will focus on the beginning of the eighteenth century – a shorter period but very rich in content marked by the great figures of Marlborough and Charles XII plus the War of the Spanish Succession. Finally, we will look at the years following this great conflict.

The years of wars that marked the second half of the seventeenth century saw the emergence of new cavalry tactics. It is true that the diversity of battlefields increases our understanding of combat. From Flanders to the Danube, from Italy to Germany, cavalry charged, and counter charged. They were led by generals with recognised talents such as Condé, Turenne, Luxembourg or Montecuccoli. All this may seem conducive to a further evolution of tactics, or at least to a certain degree of diversification of tactics. Thus, the French cavalry, under the leadership of its great leaders, was to further the practices initiated by Gustavus Adolphus. The Emperor's cavalry, for their part, were able to take advantage of their dual experience in Western and Eastern theatres to produce original and innovative tactics.

In France, continuity prevailed. We are not lacking sources when it comes to understanding the wars of Louis XIV, yet it is quickly apparent that it is

THE NEW KNIGHTS

quite difficult to get a precise idea of how cavalry doctrine evolved. Beyond the figures of Turenne and Condé – exceptional horsemen who often led their men at the gallop sword in hand – it seems that the reality is more complex. It would be wrong for example, to accept that the cavalry of the line followed the same principles as those followed by the King's household troops – the Maison du Roi – a large body of elite units. For the majority of ordinary line regiments, no real change seemed to appear before the end of the century.

Despite the influence of Turenne and Condé, trot and fire tactics prevailed until the end of the 1670s. Turenne and Condé were exceptional leaders; officers of cavalry by education and spirit, they demonstrated throughout their careers, great skill in the use and conduct of this arm. If any changes were initiated in the third quarter of the century, it is in the practice of these two generals that we must look for their origins. Puységur suggests that a turning point occurred for the French cavalry in the early 1670s:

Henri de La Tour d'Auvergne, Vicomte de Turenne (1611–1675). Christiaan Hagen. (Rijksmuseum)

> At the beginning of the war of 1670 [Dutch War, 1672–1678], when the squadrons charged each other, it was still the more often with snap hooks, they made a caracole and, after turning, returned to the charge, either to shoot again, or to charge the sword in the hand; but since that time, what has been most practiced, is that when cavalry troops march against each other, the squadrons shock the enemy head on, and with sword strikes try to overthrow him, and there are very few who shoot.[1]

The charges of Condé's cavalry at Seneffe (1674) correspond very closely to this observation. At the beginning of the fighting, the Maison du Roi crossed the stream that separated them from the enemy. Condé put himself at the head of the first two squadrons; 'At the sight of 20 enemy squadrons,' says Le Pippre, 'he walked straight to them, took their opponent's first volley and then charged them vigorously. While the Marquis de Rochefort, at the head of two other squadrons of the Guards, sword in hand, charged the enemy in the flank, breaking all in their path.'[2] In the same way Turenne at Sintzheim (1674), 'ordered on all things to his cavalry to sustain the fire of the enemy without firing and to charge only with the sword in his hand.'[3]

---

1   Puységur, *L'Art de la guerre*, Livre I, p.120.
2   Simon Lamoral Le Pippre de Noeufville, *Abrégé chronologique et historique de l'origine, du progrès et de l'état actuel de la maison du roi et de toute les troupes de France* (Liège: Kints, 1734), Tome I, p.372.
3   Leroy de Bosroger, *Eléments de la guerre* (Paris: Costard, 1773), p.197.

We can see some marked developments, particularly in the increased speed and almost exclusive use of swords during the charge. However, it was not as simple as this. Firstly, Puységur's remarks about practices before 1670 are undoubtedly exaggerated. We have seen that at the end of the Thirty Years' War the caracole was no longer the preferred tactic of the French. In the same way, he makes some sweeping statements regarding the changes that occurred from the Dutch War.

Of course, Condé charged at the gallop and sword in hand at Seneffe, but the Gardes du Corps (one of the Maison du Roi regiments), that he led were the elite of the French cavalry, and their practice an exception. Their example shows at least that, although Louis XIV favoured siege warfare, he was also greatly concerned for the cavalry troops: the Maison du Roi cavalry. However, the high quality of these troops cannot be extended to include ordinary line regiments, which did not benefit from the same level of training or the same standard of mounts.[4] As for Turenne, if his preference was for cold steel, it is doubtful even he could have imposed their tactics on all his other squadrons.[5] The use of infantry platoons between squadrons in some battles does not sit well with the argument of a noticeable acceleration of the speed of the charge. We can finally add the statement of his nephew, the Maréchal de Duras, who saw him 'use all the ways'. The conduct of the charge in these years was probably closer to the writings of d'Aurignac than the work of Puységur.

D'Aurignac is generally presented as one of Turenne's pupils. However, if it involved contact with the enemy, his concept remains marked by the use of firepower and a speed that probably did not exceed the trot:

> The general must point out that by marching to the enemy, from 50 steps, we stop to give time to the squadrons … to draw up their lines as well as their ranks and their files. And for the last command he must order [them] to go to the charge only at a walking pace, the lines very tight, knees to knees, and the ranks at a distance of one from each other. And to fire only pistol, and especially to do the discharge only after that of the enemies; and after having strongly exhorted everybody to do his duty, he must at the same time get the signal given by his trumpet, which sounds the charge, to which all the others … must unanimously answer, and the thing must be done afterwards.[6]

Changes at the end of the seventeenth century tended to be in favour of swords. The recommendations of d'Aurignac are in line with the practices observed at the end of the Thirty Years' War. His writings are valid for the 1660s, but they could also apply to the following decades, which do not seem to have experienced any major upheavals. The examples of the charges led

---

4   Frédéric Chauviré, 'La Maison du roi sous Louis XIV, une troupe d'élite, étude organique', *Revue Historique des Armées*, n°242, 2006.
5   His German regiments, for example, had not given up the use of the pistol. Bérenger, *Turenne*, p.520.
6   Paul Azan, *Un tacticien du XVIIe siècle, D'Aurignac* (Paris: Chapelot, 1904), p.65. The manuscript of d'Aurignac is dated 1663.

by Condé or Turenne were not necessarily the norm, and the practices or preferences of these generals did not conflict with the fundamental principles of the charge.

The famous letter of Duras to Louvois (1689), if it is to be considered with some caution due to its controversial context, reflects this situation well.[7] Centred on the problem of the choice between swords and pistols it is very revealing of the practices of the time. Duras poses as an essential principle: if elite troops, such as the Gardes du Corps, can charge sword in hand, 'head-to-head to the enemies', was it not the same for most line cavalry regiments. It is very difficult for the maréchal to prevent 'a man who is certain of being shot when he cannot use his sword, to take his pistol or his carabiner to give a little respect to his enemy'.[8] Apprehension of the imminent fight is therefore common, inducing the shaping of substantially different practices from those of the elite units. The fear of enemy fire – of the melee – and the lack of training explains why the riders preferred to deliver one or two salvos before contacting the enemy at an often-slow speed. The use of fire and the constant concern for the cohesion and control of the squadron, made the actual impact far from violent. That is of course if it occurred at all, because most of the time one of the two squadrons turned back or disintegrated before contact was made.

Duras reminded the minister that the greatest freedom has always prevailed when it came to the conduct of the charge: 'Ever since I was in the world, I had always seen give all those who commanded a troop the freedom to make it use the weapons they wanted'. The wide variety of opportunities and circumstances encountered on the battlefield explains that 'this cannot be solved by anybody, whatever great captain he is' (especially a minister from Versailles).

Duras' observations make it possible to see the beginning of the changes evolving in the use of firepower: 'I found old officers here who are of my opinion. I found young people who had never talked about using their guns, only their swords'.[9] The new generation of officers would thus have learned to do without firing, and to base the success of the charge only on shock tactics. It seems that Louvois interfered, much to the chagrin of the Maréchal, that he wanted to make the charge with the sword the 'official' doctrine to be adopted by the French cavalry. According to Victor Belhomme, the instructions given in 1690 – and maintained in the following years – required squadrons to charge home with the sword, without firing. It is difficult to say whether ministerial wishes translated into a general change of practices. The testimony of Villars at the beginning of the War of the Spanish Succession, suggests that the habit of charging the 'sword in hand' had gradually been accepted:

---

7 Perhaps even more than the nephew answering his uncle's old enemy, this is the general who answers to the minister, piqued on the haughty incursion of an armchair general into an area he still considers reserved for actual battlefield commanders. Letter from Duras to Louvois, reproduced by Yves Durand, *La Maison de Durfort à l'époque moderne* (Fontenay-le-Comte: Lussaud, 1975).
8 Durand, *Ibid.*, p.89.
9 Durand, *Ibid.*, p.89.

Then I would pass on the necessity of walking to the enemy with the sword in one hand and without firing ... Let one troop march with the sword in one hand and the other with the carabiner, whoever wants to use his carabiner, is it not true, monseigneur, that it must stop to shoot fifteen paces from its enemy, which is very dangerous because nothing is more certain when you lead the squadrons to the charge than to make them go very slowly up to thirty paces of the enemy, then to take a trot a little sharp, firstly in a troop thus shaken the horse sometimes leads the cavalier in spite of himself, whereas the man who, marching to the enemy, stops, appears in an approaching disposition to turn and flee. Moreover, this troop that wants to shoot, it is necessary that it is closely to hope some effect. Does it have time to leave the carabiner to take back the sword, that is dangerous. ... I have heard from the Emperor's generals that henceforth their cavalry would no longer fire. And, indeed, one has seen them all this campaign only with the sword in their hand. If then, this cavalry, which we have always beaten before, and, I believe, because it fired, changes its manner of fighting, we must certainly preserve ours.[10]

Apart from Villars' clear preference for the sword, the way to conduct a charge was like that which had prevailed at the beginning of the Nine Years War. Charging at a gallop was still not recommended as the normal pace to adopt, with the exception probably of the best troops like those of the Maison du Roi. These shock tactics are therefore based more on the need for cohesion and the 'morale effect', than on the physical outcome of the charge.

Then we have the Empire and the influence on them of the wars against the Turk. Villars' remarks about the Emperor's cavalry give important information about the practices of the Habsburg squadrons who, until the beginning of the eighteenth century, still used fire tactics. The practices of the Habsburg cavalry were probably different from those of the French cavalry during the second half of the seventeenth century. It is important to remember that the Imperialists' experience of fighting was not limited to the war with their old French enemies, but it was also shaped by contact with very different opponents. The wars against the traditional Ottoman enemy saw the Turks mobilise considerable forces during this period. Brent Nosworthy emphasised the influence these conflicts had on the development of the tactical Habsburg Army.[11]

The Turkish horsemen fought in a way sharply contrasting that of Western cavalry. Excellent horsemen, they also handled their swords with formidable dexterity. Using lances, bows, maces, sabres or scimitars, they put all their trust in bladed weapons and melee combat, where they excelled.[12]

---

10 Service Historique de la Défense/Direction de l'Armée de Terre (SHD/DAT), 1MR 1725, f°1, '*Mémoire relatif à l'organisation de la cavalerie par M. de Villars*', 1701.
11 Nosworthy, *The Anatomy of Victory*, pp.36–38
12 Robert Mantran (ed.), *Histoire de l'empire ottoman* (Paris: Fayard, 1989), p.200; Jean Bérenger, '*l'influence des peuples de la steppe (Huns, Mongols, Tatares, Turcs) sur la conception européenne de la guerre de mouvement et l'emploi de la cavalerie*', *RHIM*, n°49, 1980, p.37; Nosworthy, *The Anatomy of Victory*, p.37.

THE NEW KNIGHTS

Their charge generally avoided a frontal attack, favouring a more oriental approach, based all on speed and evasion.

The Turkish horseman attacks, and then retires, or runs away. He comes and goes to excite the enemy to follow him and leads him there in double and triple ambushes where he has many people; and when he sees our people open and disbanded, he takes his time, turns around, and uttering loud cries, he returns to the charge, and envelops them. He presents himself with large front squadrons; but when he finds an interval, he makes in a moment of his flank a new forehead with an agility which is natural to him, and he penetrates there.[13]

The ensuing melee then degenerated into a multitude of single one-on-one battles in which the Turks had an advantage.

We have seen that the Polish wars led Gustavus Adolphus to adopt certain practices of his enemy. The situation was different. The Polish heavy cavalry practiced a mode of war which was still part of the western model. This was not the case for Ottoman *Sipâhîs*. Their tactical doctrine was far too different from that of the Habsburgs so that their tactics would not evolve in that direction. How could they have achieved such a degree of agility on horseback, and of rapidity in manoeuvring? It was a mistake to attempt to compete with the Turks on their terms. The Habsburg cavalry instead had to rely on their own strengths and seek to exploit the weaknesses of their enemy. The Turks:

> are prompt to run in front and behind, to prance on the flanks and tail, to harass, to invest, to retreat and to ambush the enemy, but they cannot sustain resolutely and without to open themselves the shock of a squadron well proportioned, well tightened and heavily armed.[14]

This only encouraged the Habsburgs to give more importance to the cohesion and the stamina of their squadrons. It was necessary 'to form a solid body, so firm and so impenetrable, that wherever he may be, wherever he goes, he will stop the enemy as a mobile bastion'.[15]

They also exploited their firepower, which was feared by the more lightly armed Ottomans. As Montecuccoli remarked, their dislike of firearms was commensurate with their predilection for edged weapons. The use of the former went too much against the ideal of the individual valour and skill at

Turkish 'sipahi' cavalryman, 1577. Abraham de Bruyn. (Rijksmuseum)

---

13 Montecuccoli, *Mémoires*, pp.355–356.
14 Montecuccoli, *Mémoires*, p.235.
15 Montecuccoli, *Mémoires*, p.238.

arms of Turkish horsemen.[16] Since it was at once too risky to confront the Turks with swords but possible to exploit their weakness or even their fear in respect of firearms,[17] the logical solution was to reinforce the firepower of cavalrymen and rely on it to destabilise the Ottoman cavalry before the two formations made contact. The squadrons approached the enemy, halted and began to deliver a steady and sustained fire, which was generally enough to disconcert and disorganise the Ottomans.[18]

Such characteristics inevitably led to sacrificing speed and momentum. Of course, the Habsburgs did adapt their practices when they were opposed by their Western opponents, but this did not much effect their charge doctrine, based on advancing at a moderate pace. To preserve their order, the squadrons advanced towards the enemy at a walking pace, or a slow trot. Arriving at a range of about twenty paces they delivered their first volley with their carbines, which caused them to momentarily stop. They then resumed their march forward, fired with their pistols and seized their swords, throwing their pistols if they did not have time to return them to their holsters to further disrupt the enemy. Again, there were variants. Pistol discharges were not always preceded by a carbine salvo, and the pace could sometimes be faster, especially for elite troops. However, most charges conformed to this practice.[19] Even though the Turkish wars did not lead the Habsburgs to question the need to close into contact with the enemy, they undoubtedly influenced them in adopting a moderate speed and the increased use of firepower.

Turkish 'deli' cavalryman, 1577. Abraham de Bruyn. (Rijksmuseum)

The sources available do not make it possible to establish with any certainty the exact method adopted for cavalry charges in the second half of the seventeenth century. In France, as in elsewhere across Europe, the officers still had a freedom of choice. On the other hand, it is known that elite corps – better equipped, better mounted and better trained – distinguished themselves from ordinary troops and newly raised regiments.

For most of this period the principles put in place at the end of the Thirty Years' War did not really change. The pace was limited to the trot, whether slow or extended. The use of firearms also remained a constant, although there may have been further changes on this point by the end of the century in France. These elements had consequences upon shock tactics. Moderate speed and the use of firearms, including carbines, reduced it to a collision

---

16 Bérenger, 'l'influence des peuples de la steppe', pp.36, 43.
17 Nosworthy, *The Anatomy of Victory*, p.38.
18 Nosworthy, *The Anatomy of Victory*, p.224.
19 Nosworthy, *The Anatomy of Victory*, p.6.

in which the maintenance of the squadron's cohesion counted more than its kinetic impact on the enemy.

It is therefore possible to represent the overall course of a charge between two squadrons in the second half of the seventeenth century. However, since it appears that different practices coexisted, we will propose for our narrative that one of the two squadrons will consist of elite troops and the other of inexperienced or poorly trained soldiers. We will construct this narrative from the point of view of the latter.

The army has completed its deployment and is facing the enemy at 250 or 300 paces distance. The squadron is arranged in three ranks, lined up boot to boot, and they check their alignment while keeping the appropriate distance between the ranks. Then the trumpet signals them to walk towards the enemy. The squadron stops after 50 paces to restore its order. It then moves forward again, always at a walking pace. Officers and NCOs strive to be heard, they shout and threaten, to maintain alignment and cohesion. Despite the reduced pace, some riders find it difficult to steer their horses who are frightened by the sounds of the battle. The left hand alone holds the bridle, as the right is holding the carbine. The front line slowly begins to imperceptibly turn into a crescent.

The enemy is now clearly visible. They have already begun to trot, but that does not disrupt their order and there are no gaps in their files. They appear confident, seem determined, and only the first rank carries their pistols, and the others have drawn their swords. By contrast, the nervousness is palpable in many soldiers of our squadron, who are taking part in their first charge. The captain commanding the squadron knows the poor quality of his troops. He believes that the time has come to execute the first salvo, which will, he hopes, strengthen the confidence of his men. At 20 or 25 paces the squadron stops to fire. The shots are not very precise. Some horses tumble, some men fall, but the advance of the enemy – which has not responded – is not stopped. Very quickly, it is then necessary to drop the carbines, which hang on their shoulder straps, and to seize their pistols; the sword is suspended on the wrist by a strap. At the captain's command the horsemen trot.

The increase in speed increases the disruption visible earlier to the front of the squadron. The officers are no longer able to preserve the order. The men on both wings, despite the efforts of their officers, begin to deviate outwards towards the flanks of the squadron. Gaps appear in the centre of the line, which threatens to open up. There are many errors in which the experienced adversary can see the promise of success. The latter also increase their speed and extends their trot. Their determination impresses. Now just a dozen paces from the enemy, our commander gives the order to fire the second salvo. But only a small part of the first two ranks fires with any precision. The men are nervous and are in a hurry to shoot. The discharge is ineffective but has the effect of increasing disorder in the squadron.

This is the moment chosen by the enemy to execute their own salvo. Although it is also relatively bloodless and fired by the first rank alone, it leads to the collapse of morale amongst our squadron. Some men in the front rank are holding their horses back, causing them to knock into their comrades in the following ranks. Others, on the wings and in the rear, are already turning to escape the shock and melee. The riders of the first enemy rank discard their pistols, most likely simply throwing them to the ground, and draw their swords, and the last metres are travelled at a gallop. They hit a squadron already three quarters routed. It is easy for them to catch the fugitives, slashing or stabbing them. The officers know their job and do not let their men get carried away in the pursuit. Indeed, behind the squadron they have just dispersed, can be seen another squadron, of the second line. The victorious squadron halts and reforms ready to face the new opponent.

The differences between the two squadrons used in this example may seem extreme at first sight. However, practices varied between elite and ordinary units, between Imperial cavalry and French cavalry and for the French, between the middle and the end of the century. But beyond the glorious charges of the Maison du Roi (whose over-exposure may have led to a distortion of the picture), one is struck by a certain homogeneity in the principles of cavalry tactical doctrine. For example, evidence shows that to advance into actual contact with the enemy is now accepted universally. The slow speed of the charge is another point of note. No more in France than in the Empire, ordinary squadrons ran a risk when faced with a galloping enemy. Finally, the relative persistence of the use of firepower must be underlined. Whether a squadron was content with a single discharge of pistols or believed it was preferable to precede it with a volley of carbines, the place of firearms in the charge remains quite important. If one can perceive an evolution in the French cavalry towards the end of the century, it is impossible to say that this practice could be applied to all units. It thus appears that the development of the charge as it was conceived from the 1630s, helped to create a tactical framework that neither the multiplication of conflicts nor the quality of the generals could upset.

This relative immobility in tactics is explained by factors at once technical, psychological and cultural, such as the lack of instruction for the men or the comfort of the following the old routine, which led some commanders to limit these tactical innovations.

The impact of Marlborough and Charles XII on the scene brought more change. We were able to identify the main principles of the charge as they were applied at the end of the seventeenth century. If we exclude elite units, the form of the charge is characterised by a relatively slow pace, and the concept of shock tactics is based more on the unit's solidity rather than its speed. The use of firepower and swords may have been of greater concern, at least in France, where the exclusive use of cold steel seemed to be increasing. Did the long War of the Spanish Succession – which involved so many different armies, practices, and experiences – lead to a change in this routine; to innovation in a particular field; the adoption of galloping or abandoning firepower? If Turenne, Condé or Montecuccoli are no longer alive, the armies were still commanded by some great generals, with recognised tactical talents like Villars, Eugene, or Marlborough. Finally, we must also consider that even beyond this conflict, other wars ravaged the continent. That is why Sweden, engaged in the Great Northern War (1700–1721), must again be the subject of all our attention, as it was then ruled by arguably one of the greatest cavalry commanders of the time, Charles XII (1697–1718).

THE NEW KNIGHTS

The Battle of Höchstädt in 1704. Romeyn de Hooghe, 1704. (Rijksmuseum)

In France the two doctrines coexisted, and we have seen that this situation was complicated at the end of the seventeenth century. If the pace of the charge was still relatively moderate, if shock tactics were based more on unit cohesion than on speed, the importance of the sword was strong. This evolution, confirmed by Villars, was not across the board.[20] Not all officers shared the Marshal's preference for the sword. The Battle of Höchstädt in 1704 (or the Battle of Blenheim as it is more properly known to a British reader), gives us examples of prestigious units – the squadrons of the Gendarmerie de France – using fire before the contact. 'They fired instead of charging sword in hand', condemns Saint-Simon.[21] This is notably the case of eight such squadrons, in an attack against five English squadrons. These have just crossed the Nebel and were therefore quite disorganised. In addition, they had the disadvantage of the slope against them. The eight squadrons of the

---

20 SHD/DAT, 1MR 1725, f°1, *'Mémoire relatif à l'organisation de la cavalerie par M. de Villars'*, 1701.
21 Louis de Rouvroy, Duc de Saint-Simon, *Mémoires de Saint-Simon, nouvelle édition augmentée des additions de Saint-Simon au journal de Dangeau et de notes appendices par A. de Boislisle*, Tome XII (Paris: Hachette, 1879–1831), p.182.

Gendarmerie then advance as if they were going to charge them. However, to the surprise of the English, they stop at pistol range and then fired a poor salvo. This was largely ineffective, and worse, it interrupted the momentum of the charge, cancelling their advantage of the ground.[22]

It is of course possible to find examples of the opposite approach. Thus, at Friedlingen, two years earlier, Quincy mentions the charge led by M. de Magnac on the French right wing. The latter saw the enemy coming to him, and he let them get three quarters of the way across the gap which separated the two armies:

> He took the head of the first line – leaving the second to M. de St. Maurice – and started only a hundred steps; he sustained, without firing a single shot, the discharge of the enemy at fifteen paces; but in the moment he charged them with his sword in his hand, with so much vigour and order, that after a rather stubborn resistance on their part, he broke down their first line, which fell into confusion over the second, and all two fled.[23]

There is also the example of Tessé's dragoons, charging Imperial cuirassiers with boldness and only with their sword:

> When M. le Comte de Tessé arrived, the enemy were already close to Carpi; he found in his hand Albert's dragoons. Although the enemy arrived by large columns, cavalry, and infantry, the Comte de Tessé resolved to charge with the three squadrons of this regiment, putting their muskets on their back and their sword in their hand ... This charge was so strong, sire, that they each overthrew their squadron of the cuirassiers of the Emperor.[24]

These examples strongly suggest that the two doctrines coexisted at that time in the French cavalry. One still relied on firepower to prepare the way for the shock of contact, which forces a very measured pace. The other relied exclusively on the sword and shock, giving slightly more importance to the speed of the charge.

Other European cavalry seemed less affected by this diversity of practices. However, it should be noted that all of the great cavalry throughout history is distinguished by its own doctrine, and there were no two exactly alike. Differences were also formed on basic principles. With the allies, opposing France, we know that the Imperialists usually fired once or twice before closing with the enemy at a reduced pace. Villars had noticed at the beginning of the war that tactics were evolving in the direction of abandoning firepower altogether. However, it is hard to believe that they actually gave up this practice, one deeply rooted in their military tradition. This is also a characteristic common to other German cavalry, as the Bavarians, though allied with the French, also followed it as well. Villars testified that at the

---

22 Nosworthy, *The Anatomy of Victory*, pp.128–129.
23 Quincy, quoted by Louis de Boussanelle, *Commentaires sur la cavalerie* (Paris: Guillin, 1758), p.366.
24 SHD/DAT, A1 1515, f°20, quoted by Drévillon, *L'impôt du sang*, p.386.

THE NEW KNIGHTS

first Battle of Höchstädt (1703), with the Franco-Bavarians facing the Imperialists, the Bavarian squadrons – which occupied the first line on the left wing – and their Imperial counterparts also made use of firepower: 'At the first charge, the enemies fired and turned. The Bavarian cavalry fired and did likewise'.[25]

This brief observation also tells us the course of the charge when neither of the two adversaries had the desire to come to blows. Each gave a salvo and withdrew. There was of course no prior consultation, but they were both convinced that they could not win. They were also unable to take advantage of the withdrawal of their opponent, especially as they were partly obscured by the smoke. We cannot imagine the manoeuvre to wheel about would be as precise as that seen on the exercise grounds. It is rather a reaction, started as usual by the men at the rear and flanks. Despite the oddness of such an unusual situation, one could believe that what has been described was not a truly exceptional event. The example where at least one of the two opponents wheel about before contact is not a rarity. It is however, perhaps a little tenuous to say that this was a particularly common event. La Colonie reports that at Enzenkirchen (1703) and Schmidmittel (1703), the same Bavarians and Imperials fought a fierce melee.[26] It does appear that it would have been very difficult to lead into contact a squadron that did not have the will to do so. When trust was lacking – trust usually brought by experience and training – the fear of hand-to-hand combat probably outweighed any other consideration, even insults and death threats from the officers and NCOs. If we add to this the characteristics that we know were peculiar to Austrian and Imperial cavalry, it is not surprising that in spite of his convictions, Prince Eugene did not order his men to the charge at a gallop with cold steel.

A testimony of Puységur makes it possible to illustrate these observations on Imperial cavalry. He referred to a charge he witnessed during the War of the Spanish Succession.[27] He did not specify the nationality of the opponents

Prince Eugene Francis of Savoy–Carignano (1663–1736). Adolf van der Laan. (Rijksmuseum)

---

25 Louis-Hector, Duc de Villars, *Mémoires du maréchal de Villars, Nouvelle collection des mémoires pour servir à l'histoire de France, par MM. Michaud et Poujalat* (Paris: chez l'éditeur du Commentaire analytique du Code civil, 1839), Tome 9, p.130.
26 Jean-François Martin de La Colonie, *Mémoires de monsieur de La Colonie, maréchal de camp des armées de l'Electeur de Bavière [éd. Présentée et annotée par Anne-Marie Cocula]* (Paris: Mercure de France, 1992), pp.204, 212.
27 That is at least Nosworthy's opinion, *The Anatomy of Victory*, p.122.

THE RELATIVE STABILITY OF CAVALRY TACTICS

of the French squadrons but, given the characteristics of the English cavalry, there is every reason to think that these were Imperial troops.

> The line of enemy squadrons saw our line of cavalry march at walking pace towards it with sword in hand, without using any firearms. When our line was about at eight toises, this cavalry had its sword hung on the wrist; Officers and riders had their carbine hanging on the shoulder strap. The officers and riders took them in the right and aimed, each one choosing the one he wanted to shoot. And as soon as the shot was gone, they dropped the carbine ... and grabbed their swords and received our cavalry with their swords in their hands. By this close fire many of our people fell; nevertheless, in spite of this, as our cavalry corps was composed of all that is best, that of the enemy, although it was even more numerous than ours, was beaten.[28]

The course of the fight suggests that these French squadrons clashed with experienced riders. They were not overawed by facing a determined charge by enemy willing to move into contact. This story from Puységur is quite revealing of the diversity of practices in Western Europe.

The tactics followed by the English cavalry seem to be significantly different. At the end of the seventeenth century, the current practices were still those of the New Model Army, forged during the years of civil war under the direction of Oliver Cromwell. The squadron approached to within range of the enemy, discharged their pistols and then charged at their opponents, sword in hand.[29]

The main elements of a charge did not undergo any major upheaval. Admittedly, the choice of the exclusive use of the sword allowed for the momentum to be maintained without a break for shooting. However, Marlborough still ordered the squadrons not to exceed the extended trot. This limit relates directly to his concept of shock tactics, based more on the weight of the squadron and on its ability to maintain cohesion and good order, than on speed and impact. These practices did not make Marlborough a revolutionary. His desire for innovation was real in the choice of weapons. It created a break with the earlier practices of English cavalry, and probably most of the cavalry of Western Europe as well. He was not the only one implementing such changes. We have seen that at least some French officers thought it best not to fire during the charge. In this he was matching the tactical thinking of his time, but with his audacity and his conservatism added. His representation of the charge was finally very close to that adopted by Villars, who considered an 'indispensable necessity' to charge with sword in hand, but only planned to contact the enemy at the 'trot a bit lively'.[30] It is Charles XII of Sweden who would most fundamentally change the principles of the charge.

It could be said that the history of Swedish cavalry begins with Gustavus Adolphus. The decades after his death, however, saw no further changes. It remained fixed in the doctrine that the winner of Breitenfeld had set for them.

---

28 Puységur, *L'Art de la guerre*, Livre I, p.121.
29 John Tincey, *The British Army 1660–1704* (Oxford: Osprey Publishing, 2005), p.9.
30 SHD/DAT, 1MR 1725, f°1, 'Mémoire relatif à l'organisation de la cavalerie par M. de Villars', 1701.

John Churchill, 1st Duke of Marlborough (1650–1722). Jan de Leeuw. (Rijksmuseum)

It is likely that Gustavus' doctrines even experienced a small decline, at least from the point of view of the use of firepower.[31]

These concepts did not suit Charles XII, however. A 'Soldier King' with his own vision of war in general – and of cavalry in particular – he tended towards the primacy of the offensive. For Peter Englund the Swedish army was, like its sovereign, controlled by an omnipresent offensive spirit: 'Armament as well as the way of fighting, the dominance of the bladed weapon, the bayonet attack and the cavalry shock demonstrate an almost fanatical faith in attack it as a universal means of winning'.[32] It was not enough, therefore, for the King to have his cavalry charge with the sword, but they must also do so at a gallop. Charles XII considered speed as the main factor of success in charge. It gave a superior shock upon impact with the enemy; made your men forget the danger and it unnerved their opponent. There was no question, however, of letting a squadron attack in a disorderly manner, and the men had to maintain their good order as they galloped.

The King's example of flawless discipline and a very high level of instruction gave Swedish cavalry the capacity and moral strength to attack effectively in this manner. Never had anyone charged in this manner in Europe. The doctrine was a complete break with the then practices of Western cavalry. It stands out even more compared to the tactics of the Russians, Sweden's main rival. Their way of fighting had some archaic aspects, as evidenced for example by an English officer at the Battle of Holowczyn (1708): 'Never in the course of the action did they come to blows with the Swedes, but they usually discharged their weapons at 30 or 40 paces, then ran to reload, rally and fire again.'[33] The Russian dragoons, which made up the bulk of Peter the Great's cavalry, relied on fire to oppose the Swedes. They hoped their salvos would cause enough casualties or disruption to break the enemy's momentum, allowing them to cross swords in a more advantageous situation. However, given the experience and skill of the cavalry of Charles XII, this goal was rarely if ever achieved.

To imagine a charge between a Russian squadron and its Swedish counterpart one must imagine the two units arranged in three ranks. However, the arrangement of the Swedish squadron is different from usual practices. The riders form-up not 'knee-to-knee' as usual, but 'knee behind knee'. The squadron thus forms a chevron or wedge with the cornet, located in the middle

---

31 Velimir Vuksic, Z. Grbasic, L'âge d'or de la cavalerie (Paris–Lausanne: La Bibliothèque des arts, 1989), p.31.
32 Englund, Poltava, p.131.
33 Ragnhild Hatton (ed.), Captain Jefferye's letters from the Swedish army, 1707–1709 (Stockholm: P.A. Norstedt and Söner, 1954), quoted by Angus Konstam, Peter the Great's Army, vol. 2: Cavalry (Oxford: Osprey Publishing, 1993), p.12.

of the first rank, constituting the point. When the order came, they began their advance at walking pace, then quickly moved to an extended trot. At 150 paces from the enemy the Swedish riders would go at the gallop and rush on the enemy without worrying about his fire. Most of the time there was no proper shock, as the Russian riders had already turned around at the sight of 'this wall of hoof and swords' rushing towards them.[34] If their squadron stood, it was very likely to be scattered. Even if the Swedes instinctively slowed their speed before contact, the shock force induced by their speed was enough to allow them to physically force and exploit gaps in the Russian squadron, without having to fear such disorder in their own ranks. The melee that followed could be deadly. Charles XII ordered his riders to thrust, and he was one of the first commanders to show a clear preference for thrusting. This type of blow is probably more difficult to perform, but also caused much more serious injuries, especially as Russian dragoons were unprotected by armour or buff coats.

Swedish King Charles XII (1682–1718). David von Krafft. (Rijksmuseum)

The King of Sweden thus occupied a unique place at the beginning of this century. Going far beyond the principles of Gustavus Adolphus he introduced a considerable break in the development of the cavalry tactics. More than just in the prohibition of the firing, the real innovation of Charles XII lay in the speed of the charge, and in the concept of 'shock such speed induces'. No other cavalry commander before him, Marlborough included, had conceived such a bold doctrine.

The long War of the Spanish Succession raised many tactical questions and challenges. The end of the conflict saw an intense period of reflection and disputes. The discussions primarily focused on the infantry, but we must not forget that the cavalry – hitherto often kept out of the debate – also became the subject of emerging ideas. The evolutions recorded in the doctrines of French or English cavalry, and the radical innovations of Charles XII, give us something to reflect upon. Admittedly this was not as radical as might have been thought. More than the speed or necessity of shock tactics, it was in fact the equilibrium of iron and fire that gave rise to the most important questions, revealing a certain dichotomy between a 'conservative' trend and authors more open to changes. It is also important to measure the influence that these theoretical debates had on the development of an official doctrine, the earliest beginnings of which are perceptible in France in the 1730s.

Certain principles of charges were clearly embedded even before the start of the War of the Spanish Succession. Thus, the necessity to move into contact with the enemy to ensure success had long been recognised. All

---

34 Englund, *Poltava*, p.116.

authors agree with this, and the question therefore is not whether the charge must be resolved by the shock but whether it was necessary to precede it with a salvo. A form of doctrinal diversity had appeared on this point at the turn of the century. Once the war was over, the lessons of the conflict seemed likely to change the focus of the debate. The French failures, the examples of Marlborough or Charles XII, plus the debate on the efficiency of infantry firepower, are all factors that led to a real challenge to the old school tactics. Yet the traditional or more conservative perspectives still seemed to carry a certain weight in the reflections and doctrines of the cavalry.

The Chevalier de Quincy, author of *L'Histoire militaire du règne de Louis XIV*, published in the last volume in 1726, his *Maximes et instruction sur l'art militaire*, which were intended as a reflection of the art of the war.[35] The book was well enough placed to testify to a possible change of tactics, but it also admitted to a lingering attachment to the use of the firepower. 'There are usually twenty masters commanded at each wing of the squadron, which the commander can use when he deems it appropriate … The commanded cavalrymen have the snap hook [carbine] high; those of the first rank can use it while charging, the others have their sword in the hand'.[36] Even if the wording of this last sentence is not very clear, one can think that 'those of the first rank' designates the horsemen of the first rank of the squadron, and not those 'commanded' or detached on each wing. The position of the author is ambiguous. He did not formally advise shooting, but it is possible that the first rank alone used their carbines. One can question the real impact of such a choice. What effects would the discharge of a single rank have? Would this not be just shooting for the sake of it? Quincy was of the view that more reliance was placed on the effects of smoke and noise than on actual losses to the opponent.

Could Quincy's position, which is not very explicit and well argued, be considered marginal? Probably not, because another great classic of military literature strongly supports it: Puységur spoke at length in this regard.[37] If he condemned the caracole, he fully admitted that two squadrons that are walking towards each other can use their firearms before contacting each other. He did not seem to view this practice as an error or a destabilising factor for the squadron; quite the contrary. Some – protests the Maréchal – claimed that squadrons were beaten because they had stopped to fire. But 'if they had not fired, they would have been beaten anyway', because 'it is often an excuse rather than to admit that one fought badly'.[38] He even regretted that the lack of training and the excessive increase in the calibre of the carbine impeded the use of fire in cavalry. He also rejected the idea that the noise of firearms would frighten horses: 'if you do not shoot but the enemy pulls up,

---

35 Charles Sevin, Marquis de Quincy, *L'histoire militaire du règne de Louis Le Grand, contenant L'art de la guerre ou maximes et instructions sur l'art militaire* (Paris: Coignart, 1726).
36 Quincy, *L'histoire militaire du règne de Louis Le Grand*, p.63.
37 Puységur, *L'Art de la guerre*, pp.253–254. The work was certainly published in 1748, but we know that the main elements were written from 1720–1730, which makes its reflections contemporary with those of Quincy.
38 Puységur, *L'Art de la guerre*, p.253

your horses will probably still be afraid because the fire goes straight to their eyes, and they hear the whistling of bullets'.[39]

Bardet de Villeneuve, who published shortly before Puységur, was hardly more innovative. According to him, it was quite conceivable to order the squadron to fire before joining in melee with the enemy with the sword in hand, using their carbine as well as pistols.[40] How could his reflections also claim to be innovative, since they are inspired by the words of La Fontaine,[41] which took over from the work of the Sieur de Birac dated 1668?[42] If these pages have a place in a work of the third quarter of the seventeenth century, does it always make sense when considering cavalry combat towards the middle of the following century? The fact remains that these remarks inevitably echo those of Puységur and show that if the use of firearms was debated by theorists when writing about infantry, it was of significant importance to the cavalry.

Where were the defenders of the sword, such as those who, like Villars or Saint-Simon, judged firearms inappropriate for use in the charge? Let us first note that Puységur's belief – 'we say that squadrons have been beaten for firing' – implies that critics are then strong enough for the author to focus on answering them in a methodical and well-argued manner. However, if such works exist, they are not numerous, and only one has been found dated before the War of the Austrian Succession.

This book is *Des fonctions et du principal devoir d'un officier de cavalerie*, published by the Seigneur de Langeais in 1726.[43] The author argues that the sword should be used in preference to firearms, and his arguments in part contradict those of Puységur. If the latter clearly stated that the use of carbines or pistols was not contraindicated for mounted troops, especially for the horses, Langeais thinks the opposite is the case with as much certainty. The pistols terrify the horses, and the reaction of the horses, already strained by all the noises of battle, did not allow for shooting with any degree of accuracy.[44]

But he went further. It was the weapon that is not suitable to the cavalry charge. Its short range was the main limitation: 'the fire shotted from a great distance is useless, and when it is done very close, the squadron is in danger of breaking'.[45] No matter how it is used, it will only produce mediocre effects on the enemy and disunite the squadron. Moreover, the simple act of shooting is already in itself disadvantageous, since it forced the squadron to pause its advance:

---

39 Puységur, *L'Art de la guerre*, pp.253–254.
40 Bardet de Villeneuve, *Cours de la science militaire, à l'usage de l'infanterie, de la cavalerie, du génie et de l'artillerie*, Tome I. *Les fonctions et les devoirs des officiers tant d'infanterie que de cavalerie* (La Haye, Van Duren, 1740), pp.299, 306.
41 Sieur de La Fontaine, *Les devoirs militaires des officiers*.
42 Birac, *Les fonctions du capitaine de cavalerie*. This type of use should not be judged by our current practices and ethics of literary creation.
43 Langeais, *Des fonctions et du principal devoir d'un officier de cavalerie, augmentées de réflexions sur l'Art militaire* (Paris: Ganeau, 1726).
44 Langeais, *Des fonctions et du principal devoir d'un officier de cavalerie*, p.69.
45 Langeais, *Des fonctions et du principal devoir d'un officier de cavalerie*.

An empty time, which suspends the action, which the enemy benefits more easily than the rider who has shot with his carbine is instantly surprised by the one who falls on him with blows of sword, which therefore has a certain advantage against the one who finds himself disarmed, defenceless, not having the leisure to use his sword, perhaps still astonished by the charge he receives.[46]

Langeais finally 'tolerates' the pistol only in a very obstinate melee, or when the enemy has turned away to precipitate his escape.

Of course, we cannot reduce military thinking to just printed works. Officers could for example, go directly to their superiors through technical memoirs, which were becoming more and more numerous from the beginning of the eighteenth century. In this case it was a Dutch cavalry captain, Gruys, who said in 1733 that a rider should never shoot when on horseback but must keep his fire for the pursuit.[47] There are also works that were not intended to be made public, such as the *Rêveries* of the Maréchal de Saxe. The first edition dates from 1756, but the original manuscript, written for his father, was written in 1732 and gives us the Maréchal's thoughts in this debate. As with Gruys – who wrote at the same time – the Maréchal condemns the use of the fire: 'Where there is a preference for fire, that cavalry is not very formidable; and I have always heard that everyone who tried to shoot was beaten'. Riders therefore did not need to use pistols which 'are only good for making weight'. Taking this logic further he even advised trying to encourage the enemy to shoot, which would be a mistake on their part.[48] Once the salvo was done, the riders who endured it would throw themselves on the enemy. Protected by a sword-proof cuirass and animated by the desire to avenge themselves for the firing they had endured, they would be now certain of finding their adversary unarmed and open to defeat.[49]

All these reflections allow us for the first time to identify some specific arguments against firearms. First there is the harmful effect it has on the mounts, followed by the poor efficiency of these weapons, both carbines and pistols. The first argument is not unfounded, although Puységur thinks the opposite. The need to accustom the horse to the noise of firearms is a recurring concern among writers since the sixteenth century. For the second, the short effective range is a fact often recognised. In the sixteenth century,

Prince Maurice de Saxe (1696–1750). Jean-Étienne Liotard. (Rijksmuseum)

---

46 Langeais, *Des fonctions et du principal devoir d'un officier de cavalerie*, p.70.
47 SHD/DAT, 1MR 1702, f° 1, 'Traité de la tactique ou pensées sur tous les mouvements des troupes, soit escadrons et bataillons, et tous les mouvements d'une armée', par Gruys, capitaine de cavalerie Hollandais, 1733.
48 De Saxe, *Mes rêveries*, p.126.
49 De Saxe, *Mes rêveries*, p.127.

La Noue specified that 'the pistole does no effect if it is not fired from three paces'.[50] Although firearms had certainly improved since then, De Brack reminds us that at the beginning of the nineteenth century, the most effective pistol shots were still those fired at point blank.[51] As for the quality of the shooting, it is enough to imagine what it would be like to shoot from the back of a horse, even if stationary, in the middle of a battle with weapons whose precision left something to be desired.[52] 'Not very formidable' for Maurice de Saxe, 'very mediocre' for Langeais,[53] these weapons seem very ineffective.

How do we measure the influence of these theorists (or 'armchair generals')? We have been able to distinguish throughout this period, as many defenders as critics of the firearm. Are their differing views balanced? It is necessary to measure of the real importance of each of these authors, and how representative these are in relation to the practices of time. In terms of notoriety and influence, the camp favouring the sword appears not the equal of the other. The influence of Langeais – not to mention Gruys – is not that of Quincy and his *Histoire militaire*. As for the Maréchal de Saxe, his *Rêveries* were published only after his death. In 1732 he was still only a German in the service of the King of France, certainly a Maréchal de Camp, but better known for his misadventures in Courland than for his feats of arms. His authority in military matters did not equal that of Puységur. Consulted by Louis XIV for the campaign plans of the War of the Spanish Succession, he also sat on the Council of Regency and was promoted in 1734, to be a Maréchal de France. It seems certain, therefore, that in the eyes of the enlightened public and readers interested in the art of war, the opinion of a Quincy or a Puységur weighed much more heavily than those who thought differently.

However, to make them marginal theoreticians – cut off from the realities of war – would be a step too far, because there is a significant difference between them, and the two great writers mentioned above. As well recognised as they were in their understanding of the military art, Quincy and Puységur were not cavalry officers, like Langeais or Gruys.[54] De Saxe meanwhile had a very good knowledge of this arm; his father, the King of Poland, consulted him in the same year, 1732, on the advisability of creating a regiment of light cavalry in Saxony.[55] More aware of the tactical details, the reality of the cavalry fights and their evolution, these officers would undoubtedly benefit from a certain level of interest among their contemporaries. Less known and read than Quincy and Puységur, they were perhaps more listened to by other cavalry officers. In any case, their observations are more in line with what is known from the reflections of the highest military authorities on the subject.

There is by now more interest in the basic principles governing the conduct of the charge. This interest manifested itself during manoeuvres, but also

---

50 La Noue, *Discours*, p.355.
51 Antoine Fortuné de Brack, *Avant-postes de cavalerie légère* (Paris: Anselin, 1831), p.64.
52 As for the carbine, though a better weapon than what preceded it, a document of 1672 recommended shooting at only four metres range.
53 Langeais, *Des fonctions et du principal devoir d'un officier de cavalerie*, p.69.
54 Puységur, for example, revealed his greatest talents in the function of maréchal général des logis, for the organisation of forage, marches and camps.
55 Jean-Pierre Bois, *Maurice de Saxe* (Paris: Fayard, 1992), p.180.

through studying text on the subject. In 1732 manoeuvres and exercises were organised at the camp of Richemont. On this occasion the high command seems to have solved the question of whether shock must be preceded by fire. The Comte de Belle Isle, exercising the squadrons, ordered that one rank would make use of the carbine and the others the sword, and that the first after having discharged 'will be supposed to be beaten and forced to turn around'.[56] This way of conducting the exercise, although stereotypical, is quite revealing. For the Comte and undoubtedly a number of officers, it now appeared that the use of sword was preferred over that of firearms, where the use of the latter inevitably led to the failure of the charge.

But the military authorities seemed to want to go further. This can be seen by the *Projet d'instruction sur les évolutions et exercices de la cavalerie*, written in 1732 or 1733 by Mortaigne, major of the Royal Allemand cavalry regiment:

> One day of battle the officers must be in the same line as the riders. It is necessary to be very careful to keep the files tight and not to allow the delicacy of the rider on this. A squadron is strong only so long as it is tight and close and cannot manoeuvre without this. When it comes to fighting, each squadron will be placed in three ranks, the first will be composed of four captains, four lieutenants and two cornets. To these officers will be added 40 brave horsemen. The other two ranks of 50 riders. The squadron being 160 men, there will remain 20 of them, including four trumpets. We will then make two small troops of eight horsemen, each including a brigadier. These two small troops will march to the right and to the left of the squadron in such a way it does not open any distance with it. The three ranks and the files will march as tightly as possible, the strength of a squadron being in its mass and in its weight. In this state and sword in hand, when the squadron will be 50 paces from the enemy, the commander will make them go at a little trot, and at 15 paces he will put him at a great trot but not allowing them to gallop which would disorder the squadron. The commander, putting his squadron at a great trot, will make a signal to detach the two small troops. They will go with the pistol in their hands and the sword hung to the wrist and they will swoop on the flanks of the enemy squadron. … The mixture of officers and riders makes the shock [sic] more abrupt than when the rank is not full and spares a lot of officers, the enemy cannot distinguish them in advance among the riders.[57]

This regulatory text is by its very existence, an undoubted sign of change. Even if it did not lead to an ordinance (probably because of the War of the Polish Succession, 1732–1738), it was the first real attempt to standardise the charge in its entirety. From officer dispositions to the pace and approach, almost every aspect of the charge is addressed. But these lines are especially significant in the context of the doctrine favoured by commanders of cavalry.

At first, we see that the use of carbines and pistols was abandoned, and only the charge with sword in hand was envisaged. Two small troops were kept in

---

56 Desbrières and Sautai, *La cavalerie de 1740 à 1789*, p.9.
57 SHD/DAT, 1 MR 1734, f°83. 'Projet d'instruction pour sur les évolutions et les exercices de la cavalerie', par M. de Mortaigne.

reserve at the rear of the squadron to take the enemy in flank, and they alone would have their carbine or pistol in hand, with their swords hanging from their wrists. Thus, and despite their reputation, the opinions of Quincy and Puységur did not prevail. These two authors must undoubtedly be regarded (for this question at least) more as the defenders of practices of an earlier era than as being truly representative authors of their time. Even if it is not yet written in stone, a turning point was reached within the cavalry. Here, unlike the infantry where the debates were more profound, the supporters of the sword gradually took and held an advantage over the supporters of the firearm.

There is nothing truly revolutionary in this text on the question of pace. The abandonment of firepower tactics, however, removes the obstacle represented by the firing of salvos during the charge. Riders no longer had to stop or slow their pace to shoot more efficiently and were now free to increase their speed. This was obvious even for the few authors who addressed the issue. The Comte de Saxe clearly advocated the gallop in his *Rêveries*.[58] He considered it essential to exercise cavalry at a gallop and asserted that 'any squadron that cannot go two thousand paces at full speed, without breaking, is never fit for war'.[59] Langeais meanwhile defended the idea that when the squadron reached half pistol range it was more important to close with the enemy quickly rather than to seek to preserve the order of the squadron.[60]

But these audacious precursors are not followed, any more than were the examples of Charles XII. Mortaigne took care to establish real progress in the movements of cavalry squadrons, which made acceleration easier for the unit and for the whole line (it is more difficult for example to speed up without some upward transition from walking to a large trot). There was nothing fundamentally new in substance, however. Once again, the 'maximum' speed was only reached in the last 10 or 15 metres. Remember, Gustavus Adolphus allowed his cavalry to trot from 50 metres and that Villars advocated a fast trot, 'a little sharp' from 30 paces.

The concern for maintaining cohesion over momentum again prevailed. Shock tactics were a matter of order and union, of 'mass' and 'weight'. Above all, it was important that files and ranks remained as tight as possible at the time of contact. This is explained by a certain tactical rigidity without doubt, but more pragmatic considerations cannot be excluded. For example, the level of expertise of most cavalrymen did not permit them to take gallop without the risk of disordering the squadron.

One last thing testifies to the conservatism which still permeated French doctrine: the two small troops which were placed at the flanks of the squadron and were expected to detach themselves from it to take the enemy in the flank during the final phase of the charge. This in fact does not constitute a tactical innovation. The earlier writings of Montgommery, and even more of Tavannes, suggest similar tactics. In his *Histoire militaire*, Quincy also mentions such a tactic, advocated in a royal regulation of 1692. Finding mention of these 'commanded troops' in the Mortaigne project,

---

58 De Saxe, *Mes Rêveries*, p.135.
59 De Saxe, *Mes Rêveries*, p.136.
60 Langeais, *Des fonctions et du principal devoir d'un officier de cavalerie*, pp.86–87.

suggests that this is an established tactic in the cavalry. To what extent it was practiced on the battlefield in the first half of the eighteenth century is open to question, as there is no evidence of such attacks during the War of the Spanish Succession. On the other hand, neither de Saxe, Langeais nor Lecoq-Madeleine, who all wrote in the years 1720–1730, did not refer to it either.

On the eve of the War of the Austrian Succession, the conduct of the charge was hardly different from that of Villars at the beginning of the previous war, almost 30 years earlier. It appears that the example of Charles XII of Sweden was not adopted as the norm for French cavalry. His innovations were never mentioned in the writings of military authors. The exclusive use of the sword was by now institutionalised, but a certain level of change was already perceptible in France before the War. On the other hand, if external influence can be believed, it was more probably Marlborough than Charles XII who must be credited with it. The abandonment of tactics based upon firepower was the only significant post war development, for the rest the French cavalry remained faithful to its routine. This is also valid for the main European powers' cavalry. The conduct of the charge did not undergo any real modifications in England or Austria, the cavalry of these two armies continuing to charge as they did during the War of the Spanish Succession. As dazzling as the epic of Charles XII was, it is not him that must be regarded as the origin of the upheaval in the practices of cavalry charges that occurred in the 1740s, at least not directly.

7

A Question of Shock

Since the time of La Noue, who reminded us that 'the squadrons break from the violent shock they receive' and until Guibert asserted that cavalry was 'undoubtedly a shock force', this question seems to be one of the recurrent and essential issues when reflecting on the development of cavalry combat. It is nevertheless surprising that there is an absence of in-depth analyses of this phenomenon and is notable that contemporary writers do not reflect much on the description of shock tactics.

Shock appears as a subject as difficult to understand as it is unavoidable. It is certainly possible to remember that it is part of the final stage of the charge, the moment when two opposing units contacted. The shock manifested itself at the moment of contact, but this attempt to define shock is unsatisfactory, because we face the problem of the duration of this final element of the charge. What kind of 'contact' are we talking about? The semantic analysis of the term 'shock' could give us some indication. There is a relatively practical image of what it might entail because it implies the vivacity and brutality particular to what is imagined at the moment of contact. It also lends itself well to the epic 'Hollywood' vision that has long dominated the perception of the charge. To want to understand the exact moment that is the 'shock' requires the answers to several essential questions: does the shock factor really exist? Then, if it does, how should this contact between two moving lines of cavalry be envisaged? It is therefore the nature of the shock that is the focus here, which can be enriched by logically addressing the issue of melee and combat.

The notion of shock tactics is therefore much more complex than it might first seem. It is enough to deepen this analysis to realise that this approach is weak. The first obstacle is simply the very existence of the 'shock' or impact. Was it really a common phenomenon; was it really possible? This question arouses the interest of some present-day historians, such as Gavin Robinson, who tries to put into perspective the place of the cavalry shock in the context of the English Civil War.[1] The problem is even more justified because some nineteenth century authors did not hesitate to question the realities of shock.

---

1   Gavin Robinson, 'Equine Battering Rams? A Reassessment of cavalry Charges in the English Civil War', *The Journal of Military History*, n°75 (2011), pp.719–731.

We will question differing points of view, focusing in the first place on the arguments of the authors who downplay this subject and then will try to understand what the expression 'cavalry shock' can mean in the early modern period. To answer the question of the reality of shock tactics, it is necessary to question its very nature. What should we see and hear when we consider the thought of the shock factor as two lines of gendarmes or two squadrons of horse collide? Should it be considered only as the brutal collision of two compact masses, or something else?

The idea of two lines of gendarmes or two squadrons of horse rushing forward towards each other as portrayed in many a Hollywood epic, and crashing into each other at full speed and with all their strength arouses some sharp criticisms. For example, Seydlitz gives a pictorial representation of the Prussian charge *en muraille* (like a wall): 'When the big wall suddenly and impetuously hits the enemy, it is not possible to offer resistance.'[2] The authors of the late nineteenth and early twentieth centuries are among those who are the most circumspect in relation to this traditional vision of cavalry combat. Hans Delbrück noted some quite significant testimonies of officers. In particular, he agreed with a study by General Wenninger stating that the situation where two squadrons collided with one another with all their weight in a tightly packed formation never happened. In such a situation, said the officer, 'the two squadrons would be destroyed.'[3] An observation by General Pusyrewski further illuminates this point of view:

> There is no real shock. The moral primacy of one of the opponents overthrows the other a little earlier or a little later, even if they are separated by the length of a nose. Before the first sabre blow, one of the camps is already beaten and fled. In a real shock both sides would be destroyed. In practice, the winner loses few men.[4]

What these two officers emphasise is the physical impossibility of galloping cavalry hitting each other head on. Such a thing is unthinkable because the two units that would advance towards each other at full speed would simply be committing suicide. The shock effect produced by such a charge would be such that everyone would quickly end up as a pile of men and horses. It is this same conviction which makes Ardant du Picq say that the hurricanes of cavalry which are found in fiction belong to 'poetry', 'the shock at full speed, men and horses would break there, but neither ones nor others want it.'[5] From the end of the eighteenth century, the Prince de Ligne raised this. 'We always misjudged the shock', he said. It seemed to him impossible to imagine 'whole tumbles of squadrons', or to see 'a troop going at a gallop to overthrow another':[6]

---

2 Delbrück, *History of the art of war*, vol. IV, p.282.
3 *Kavalleristische Monatshefte* (1908), p.908. Quoted by Delbrück, p.283.
4 *Untersuchung über den Kampf* (Warsaw: 1893). Quoted by Delbrück, p.283.
5 Charles Ardant du Picq, *Études sur le combat* (Paris: Economica, 2004), p.76.
6 Charles-Joseph Lamoral, Prince de Ligne, *Préjugés militaires* (Paris: Champion, 1914), p.14.

> I never understood how we imagined the shock. It was believed that it was chest against chest: it is of all impossibility, what would become the heads of horses if they collided? It would be a very uncertain movement, and what would depend on the hard head of the horse could too be as fatal to the one who attacks, as to the one who is attacked. If they fit together and get stuck between the two shoulders of the enemy rider's horse, that would be another disadvantage.[7]

The shock effect did not exist. Would all the writers and officers who evoke it throughout the early modern period have only built a myth? It would be impossible for two cavalry units launched against each other to collide head on. These observations appear stamped with the seal of common sense, and we can hardly fault them. Yet is it appropriate to generalise their conclusions and make them the general rule for the whole early modern period? The sixteenth century, for example, seems to have to escaped in part. Indeed, gendarmes charging in line and colliding directly with the enemy, would strike them brutally with their lances; this is the only way to use their weapon. However, they were not in the formation envisaged by Wenninger or Pusyrewski, and the contact of these lines of gendarmes should not be considered as the shock of two masses colliding, but rather as a set of individual collisions, with each gendarme seeking to knock his counterpart over.

Furthermore, the reflections of these officers all start from a presupposition: the squadrons charge at a gallop. As we have seen, such a pace is far from the norm between the middle of the sixteenth and the beginning of the eighteenth century. Until the Seven Years' War the Prussians were probably the only ones to really charge at a full gallop. We are still outside of the pattern criticised by the authors of the nineteenth and twentieth centuries. The squadrons were for the most part unable to charge at a gallop and in the best-case scenario only one of the two adversaries would be able to reach such a speed, and most often the two parties could only advance towards each other at a moderate pace.

The shock of impact should be possible, but how to envisage it in a more concrete way? Burnez, who also wrote at the end of the nineteenth century, proposed an original idea that allows us to move on a little in our analysis.[8] Like his contemporaries, he begins to remind us of the absurdity of imagining two lines *en muraille* meeting at full speed. The theorists who were proponents of this idea should have drawn from their works the only useful conclusion: 'to know that two lines thus approaching would be annihilated, crushing both.'

Something like that may have taken place in a general melee between some horsemen who would be overthrown, both men and horses, but this could never occur between two formed lines. However, Burnez's statement is not limited to this impossibility. If the meeting of two lines of cavalry under the conditions mentioned above is not possible, it does not mean that contact is impossible between them:

---

7   Ligne, *Préjugés militaires*, p.15.
8   Pierre-Marie Burnez, *Notes pour le cours de tactique appliqué à la cavalerie*, monographie, 1888–1889, Ecole de Cavalerie de Saumur.

> What can happen is the meeting of two cavalry when they are equally well conducted, equally confident in their means and in their chief, equally brave. There is then boarding, but not shock. At the moment of approaching there is an instinctive restraint in the horse, in the rider, who feels very well that it would break unnecessarily by hitting the enemy at full speed. In this slowdown, there are unequal speeds which lead to openings through which the bravest riders rush forward.[9]

We note the choice of semantics, the shift from 'shock' to 'boarding' (hand-to-hand combat). Burnez does not exclude the possibility of direct contact between the two squadrons, but he refuses to describe it with the term 'shock'. Does this imply on the part of the author the will to establish a scale in the violence of contact? It is a highly improbable phenomenon, inducing a gallop and producing the maximum violence, while the alternative approach is made at a more moderate pace and produces a lesser level of violence. The horsemen of our period only very rarely galloped, so we find ourselves considering the second configuration the most plausible, and we should abandon the use of the term 'shock'. It would be to neglect the custom of the seventeenth and eighteenth centuries where cavalry would hardly imagine anything but charging at a trot, so we must review and adapt the scale measuring the violence of the contact implied by Burnez. Although the violence of such a charge seems minimal to the officer of the nineteenth century, it is the maximum level that could be envisaged by two ordinary squadrons of the seventeenth century. It was however real to them. Beyond the battle of words, the observations of Burnez at least confirm that all out shock tactics were quite possible from the sixteenth to the eighteenth centuries. The challenges of nineteenth and twentieth century writers, such as the Prince de Ligne, are valid only for the period when going at the gallop had again become the norm, greatly increasing the violence of contact.

De Ligne also allows us to understand more precisely the way in which the cavalry units charged each other; or 'boarded each other' according to Burnez's terminology. It is a question of 'openings' in the ranks and files and that horses would aim for these, and it evokes the 'cracks' through which the riders infiltrate.[10] This description is quite transferable to our period. Given the failures in the instruction of men, and despite the moderate speed, it was extremely difficult for one squadron to maintain perfect cohesion to the end. Gaps appeared between the ranks and files, that enemy riders were trying to widen. They penetrated these so to increase the disorder within the enemy unit, even to break it, to shatter it so that it was reduced to a set of individuals or small isolated groups, which would have no salvation but fleeing. Tavannes mentions the strength of the French gendarmes who 'shock head-to-head, split the squadrons, pierce through them and make gaps in them.'[11] Under these conditions it was important to force a passage, to shove themselves into the enemy ranks, to penetrate the unit and break its order without losing theirs.

---

9   Burnez, *Notes pour le cours de tactique*, pp.379–380.
10 Burnez, *Notes pour le cours de tactique*, p.382.
11 Tavannes, *Mémoires*, p.73.

In this perspective the words of the Prince de Ligne take on another meaning. As the Prince points out, it is indeed difficult to imagine horses at a gallop colliding head on. Such speed would at the very least put the two animals out of action. But this becomes possible at a slower pace, at a trot. Moreover, the Prince de Ligne himself, if he does not envisage a charge at full speed, does not absolutely rule out the possibility of a brutal physical confrontation between riders and horses. It would happen when one of the two adversaries, poorly exercised, finds his formation too open, 'when he gives daylight between the files to the enemy, who then fall into the openings, where the sword and the shock are used.'[12]

It is partly to cope with the physical challenge of shock that the horses of the line cavalry were often chosen from among the largest. At the end of the sixteenth century, Salomon de La Broue displays his preference for great horses, which 'are better able to sustain a great shock and go out of a melee', 'to invest the enemy troop'.[13] More than a century later, Langeais joins him in this opinion: 'By the size that I fix to the horses, it is to follow the opinion where I am to believe that a small horse, not having the strength of a great one, when it enter in a squadron, it cannot cause the same effect, by the shock and the wrinkling of the shoulder.'[14] It is the same phenomenon that Grandmaison describes when he reminds us that the horses of the light cavalry 'are too small to hit with the chest against those of ordinary cavalry'.

The physical dimension of the shock factor is very noticeable here. The collision of horses is a common subject in theoretical and technical writings, particularly in the eighteenth century. General de Vault suggests lines of squadrons fighting 'with swords and with a blow of chests'.[15] The draft Instruction of 1753 also specifies that the first rank should in combat rely on 'either of the sword or by the chest.'[16] In the following decade Boussanelle still insisted on the commanders' attention not to mount their men on horses too fine and too low, which are 'less suitable … for the blow of the chest and for the essential friction of the fighting.'[17] There is no man of war, he explains, 'who does not grant superiority in a shock at the height of the waist, as well as at the thickness of the shoulders, the chest and the kidney of a horse, and more again of a set of horses.'[18]

In these brutal 'collisions' that are the cavalry charges, it is as much for the rider to violently move his enemy aside as to kill him. A squadron is not beaten because its fighters have all been knocked out, killed, or wounded, but because it has lost all cohesion, because it has broken as the result of the collision. It is the most open of the two, the most 'porous' that would lose the game. The squadron that finds itself broken, explains d'Authville, will be 'because he walks limply, he is open, disunited, or even because being

---

12 Ligne, *Préjugés militaires*, p.16.
13 La Broue, *Le Cavalerice françois*, p.134.
14 Langeais, *Des fonctions et du principal devoir d'un officier de cavalerie*, p.125.
15 Service Historique de la Défense/ Direction de l'Armée de Terre (SHD/DAT), 1MR 1731, f°8: 'Mémoire sur la cavalerie', par le général de Vault, 1750
16 SHD/DAT, 1MR 1731, f°24: '*Projet d'instruction pour le service de la cavalerie*', 1753.
17 Louis de Boussanelle, *Réflexions militaires* (Paris: Duchêne et Durand, 1764), p.2.
18 Boussanelle, *Réflexions militaires*, p.5.

on a forehead too large, he floats, he does the saw.'[19] The shock does not crush, it scatters. The cavalry, explains the Comte de Guibert, 'wins rather by frightening, by dispersing what opposes it than by shedding blood.'[20] The Marquis de Castries says it another way when he mentions the charge of a line of several squadrons: 'the object of the charge in line is more to move the bodies which are opposed to us than to destroy the individuals.'[21]

If we leave the scheme envisaged by the authors of the nineteenth century, the collision between two squadrons is theoretically possible. Was it so common? Avoiding the shock of impact is surely a human reflex? Numerous testimonies attest that it could not take place, that one of the adversaries, or both, escaped the shock of impact and shirked away before contact. The understanding of this 'avoidance phenomenon' inevitably leads us to question the psychology of the soldier. This is complex but essential, if only because of the obvious consequences on the conduct of the charge.

Several observations suggest that in this field the gap between the theory and the realities of the battlefield were sensitive. In 1776 Mottin de la Balme, for example, a firm believer in the existence and effectiveness of shock tactics, remarked that:

> So far the cavalry did not make use of the shock. There is much talk of shock action in military conversations, war books, memoirs, and ordinances. But it is by the abuse of this word and the misconceptions that we attach to this expression. Not long ago, the charge consisted of shooting each other, and as by convention, shots of pistol or carbine 30 steps away.[22]

Such an assertion seems sufficiently absolute, a condemnation of the old ways. The archaic nature of past practices was exaggerated to emphasise the extent of progress made by the new generation. However, this observation can be cross-referenced with others, emanating from prestigious officers. Maréchal de Duras made it a point to explain to Louvois that 'all those who tell him that one enters a squadron never knew what it was to go to the charge.' He added that forbidding men to use their pistol would only aggravate this state of affairs because 'of a hundred squadrons that will go to the charge and which will be expected by the enemy there are not two that approach them.'[23] In 1701 the Marshal de Villars is even clearer when he asserts that in entire battles 'there will scarcely be two or three charges where the squadrons enter into a melee, since it happens almost always that one of the two yield from fifteen paces and often farther.'[24] At the end of the same century the Prince de Ligne made a similar statement, although a little more radical: 'I have

---

19 D'Authville, *Essai sur la cavalerie tant ancienne que moderne*, p.270.
20 Guibert, *Essai général de tactique*, p.112.
21 SHD/DAT, 1MR 1731, f°56. 'Instruction pour M. le chevalier d'Abense, maître de camp commandant le régiment du Maître de camp général de la cavalerie', par M. le Marquis de Castries, 1770.
22 Augustin Mottin de la Balme, *Eléments de tactique pour la cavalerie* (Paris: Jombert, 1776), p.72.
23 Letter from Duras to Louvois, reproduced by Yves Durand, *La Maison de Durfort à l'époque moderne*, p.89.
24 SHD/DAT, 1MR 1725, f°1, 'Mémoire du maréchal de Villars sur la cavalerie', 1701.

not seen cavalry combat against cavalry in good faith; because apparently nobody wanted it.'[25]

These reflections lowering the frequency of cavalry combat are as recurrent as those which underline its importance. This is undoubtedly a considerable phenomenon that needs to be further questioned.

What these authors emphasise, beyond the somewhat rapid formulation of Mottin de la Balme, is less the impossibility of the shock than the fact that it occurred only rarely. They also found themselves considering the cause of this situation and describe what could be said to be an 'avoidance phenomenon'. One of the two adversaries, says Villars, yields before contact, avoiding the enemy. In the same way, Grandmaison, in an observation as brief as it is significant, remarks 'that ordinarily one of the two troops do not wait for the blow of chest and yields to the ardour of the other.'[26] This avoidance can even be simultaneous, by both sides, as if the fruit of consent, or of an implicit convention. 'I have seen troops stop as if it was an exercise, which may very well come from the habit, then run along each other parallel for a minute or two, and then leave for good', testifies the Prince de Ligne.[27]

The reason for this surprising behaviour is probably to be found in the psychology of the soldier. The officers or theoreticians of the sixteenth and eighteenth centuries rarely pushed the analysis so far, so it is towards the authors of the nineteenth century we must turn to consider these actions. Burnez states that 'the party that will have any inferiority – inferiority well felt by men – will turn around sooner or later but will turn around' and cites as an example an anecdote of the Habsburgs that perfectly illustrates the words of the Prince de Ligne. The scene takes place at Waren in 1806. The Prussians were roughly pursued by the French, so they detached 12 squadrons to give themselves some space. Opposing them are as many French squadrons. 'These two troops, although having put the sabre in their hand, did not approach and turned around after exchanging a few shots, which shows the short distance that separated them.'[28] The key to this phenomenon is, according to him, in the hearts or morale of men:

> Or seek elsewhere than in the human heart the cause that, when two lines of cavalry charge each other, one of the two almost always turned around 50 or 60 steps from the other and fled? Would it be disputed that many leaders, losing their cool and calm, shout instead of commanding, and thereby not only cause great confusion within their troops, but always end up losing their heads themselves?[29]

But the first to approach this subject in a systematic way is without a doubt Ardant du Picq. This is because he agrees to formulate basic remarks that most military dare only mention reluctantly. The first is the fundamental

---

25 Ligne, *Préjugés militaires*, p.15.
26 Thomas-Auguste Le roy de Grandmaison, *La petite guerre ou Traité du service des troupes légères en campagne* (n.p.: 1756), p.161.
27 Ligne, *Préjugés militaires*, p.15
28 Burnez, *Notes pour le cours de tactique*, p.380.
29 Burnez, *Notes pour le cours de tactique*, p.385.

recognition that must be given to fear. Fear, 'under penalty of misfortune, must enter as an essential element in every organization, discipline, plan.' Because 'the man does not go to fight for the fight, but for the victory, he does everything that depends on him to suppress the first and ensure the second.'[30] Moreover, Du Picq establishes the existence of a relative threshold beyond which the fear of struggle, and therefore of death, is stronger than the desire for victory. Thus, the combatant 'is capable of a given quantity of terror; beyond which he escapes combat.'[31]

But the charge of cavalry put a severe test on the courage of the soldiers. Unlike infantry combat, which allows the maintenance of a certain distance thanks to firearms, the charge implies that the soldier is almost obliged to go into contact. This is not in the nature of man, whose instinct seems, on the contrary, to try to avoid melee.[32] The man, analyses Alain Joxe, 'avoids face-to-face confrontation, two by two, as do the wild beasts of substantially equal strength. He hides or runs away as soon as the mechanism learned from the group's cohesion gives way to a panic assessment of the danger.'[33]

The shock, because it rests on the hypothesis of the direct struggle, is not therefore 'natural', and it is necessary to constrain the men. Much of the tactical thinking in the early modern period was therefore centred on this objective: to bring the rider as closely as possible to the enemy, until contact if necessary. This involves raising the threshold of fear, the 'amount of terror' bearable. Or to mask their fear, as did Charles XII and Frederick II, whose use of the gallop was partly based on this principle.

If contact between cavalry was infrequent, it is not because it was impossible, but it is precisely the idea of its possibility which frightened the riders and made them turn back before it took place. The soldier saw the enemy getting closer. Even if the pace remained moderate compared to a man of the nineteenth century, it nonetheless accelerates as they approach, and the distance reduces faster and faster. The terrible prospect of melee is emerging then, and fear increases even more.

What then makes the amount of terror bearable? There are several subjective elements, but also some points that objectively contribute towards shaking the soldiers. Let us consider for example the saturation of the senses in the midst of battle, the hearing, the smell, the sight: the sight of mangled corpses, or of a comrade hit by a cannonball or musket shot. The sensitivity of the soldiers obviously varies according to his experience or his state of fatigue, perhaps because of the many marches that often preceded a battle. We can still include among the elements that destabilise the rider the manifestations of fear among others, visible within the squadron itself: gaps that open between the files, the second rank that let itself fall behind, the feeling of collective nervousness. Finally, the external signs of confidence and moral force, or at least interpreted as such in the approaching enemy.

---

30 Ardant du Picq, *Études*, p.39.
31 Du Picq, *Études*, p.94.
32 Du Picq, *Études*, p.94.
33 Joxe, *Voyage*, p.289.

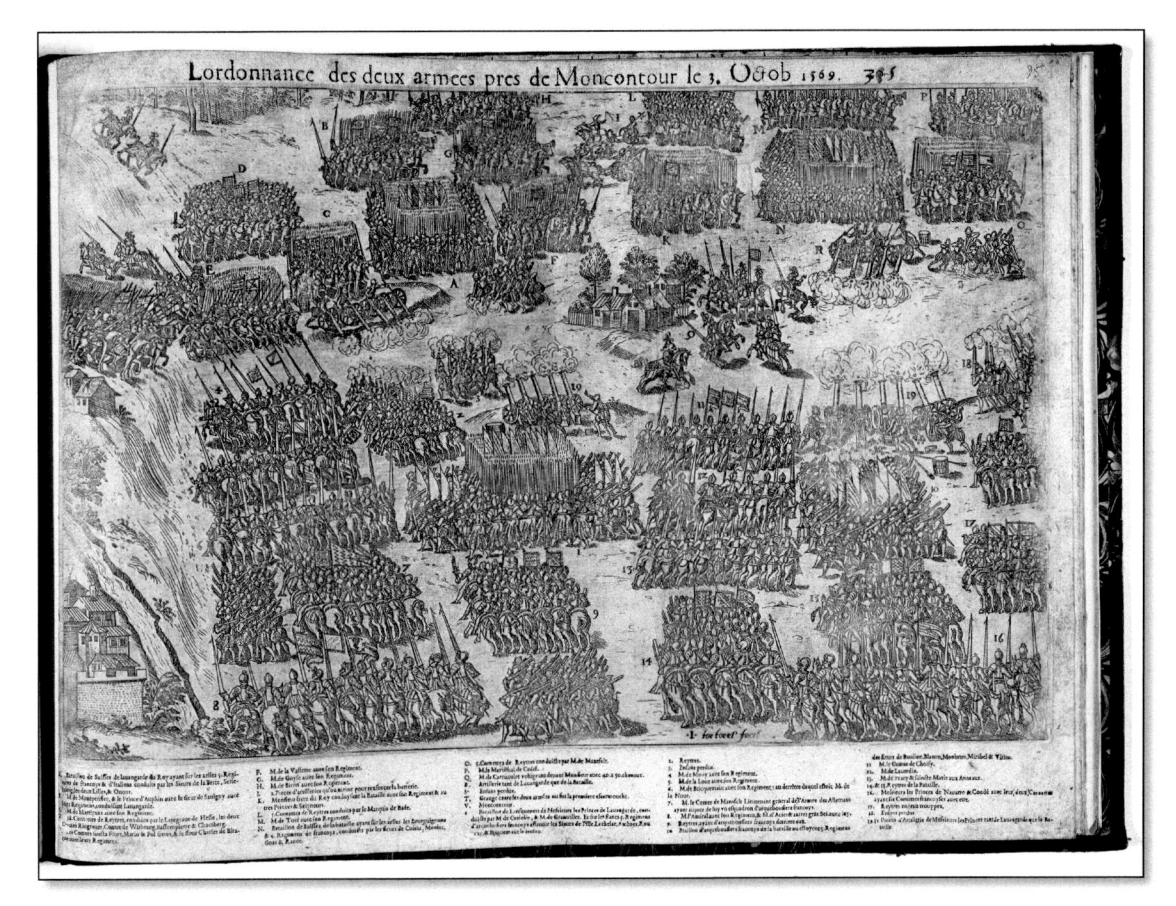

Battle of Moncontour in 1569. Jacques Tortorel, 1569–1570. (Rijksmuseum)

Then, a few metres from the enemy, fear and panic become stronger than discipline or the will to win. Some men hold their horses back, often those of the flanks who are the most exposed, and those who have the space available to turn around.[34] Then it is the whole squadron that disintegrates and turns back if there is still time. There will be no impact. The strength of cavalry is not in the impact, 'but in the terror of impact.'[35] It is also the meaning of the expression used by Guibert when he explains that cavalry wins 'by frightening' the enemy.

These considerations about fear and avoidance may lead us further, to one of the essential principles of the cavalry charge: in many cases, the success of a charge is decided before contact. 'The moral impulse of one of the adversaries almost always overthrows the other in advance, a little further or a little nearer; even nose to the nose, before the first sabre blow, one of the two troops is already beaten and is tangled for the flight.'[36] If one of the two squadrons flee before impact it is because the winner has been able to control their fear longer, because their moral strength is greater and that consciously or unconsciously, the loser has accepted this state of affairs and decided their fate. Men 'understand that before them they have a moral impulse greater

---

34   Following the pattern of the 'geometry of fear' developed by Joxe, *Voyage*, p.290.
35   Du Picq, *Études*, p.154.
36   Du Picq, *Études*, p.152.

than their own, and they are troubled and hesitant; hands instinctively pull horses aside. There is no more frankness in the attack … three quarters have already tried to avoid the shock.'[37] This point of view expressed in this way may appear to be caricatured, yet a few rare accounts of charge support this view. So, this cavalry fight in the First World War, albeit so far from our period, and yet so close:

> The two platoons are facing each other. The horses get upset; the nerves are tense to break. Now we distinguish the adversary with sharpness … But also, the trained eye of our dragoons realise, the almost imperceptible signs, that there is a slight fluctuation in their ranks; we see daylight between the ranks and files; one guesses that instinctively each one of them feels attracted to the left, towards the fields which separate them from the road to Liege.[38]

These are 'signs' that do not deceive. The French dragoons began their charge and, even before they reached the enemy, he had already fled.

Without theorising as far as Ardant du Picq does, some authors of the early modern period have understood this basic fact. Jean de Tavannes thus gives a reflection that testifies to his experience of combat: 'the gaps seen in the squadrons, a part of the horses turning to the flank, then the head here and there, and advancing unequally … all this testifies horror and irresolution. On the other hand, firmness, unity, speech, silence, equal movement, like large machines driven by a single spring with little noise, denotes resolution and conduct.'[39] At Moncontour (1569) a glance is enough for his father, Gaspard de Saulx, to measure the degree of trust of the Huguenots. He judges them 'in fear because no squadrons were walking by bulk and these squadrons leaved gaps in their midst'. 'They are yours!' he exclaimed to the Duc d'Anjou.[40] Louis XIV himself recognised the importance of this fact. 'Good order gives us confidence', he explains to the Dauphin, 'and that seems to be enough to sound brave, because most of the time our enemy does not wait until we are close enough to him so that we have to show him that we are indeed.'[41] He was thus convinced that 'many battles were won more by the good order of the march and the good countenance than by the sword and the musketry.'[42]

In the middle of the following century d'Authville still very clearly formulates this principle:

> The experts in cavalry judge, seeing two squadrons march against each other, which of the two will be beaten, in spite of the equality that may exist between them for their numbers and the quality, here is what they are based on and it is an almost infallible rule: the impetuosity of the shock of one breaks the other which

---

37 Du Picq, *Études*, p.151.
38 Marcel Dupont, *Cavaliers d'épopée* (Paris: Lavauzelle, 1985), p.15.
39 Tavannes, *Mémoires*, p.342.
40 Tavannes, *Mémoires*, p.338.
41 Louis XIV, *Mémoires*, vol. II, pp.112–113.
42 Louis XIV, *Mémoires*, vol. II, pp.112–113.

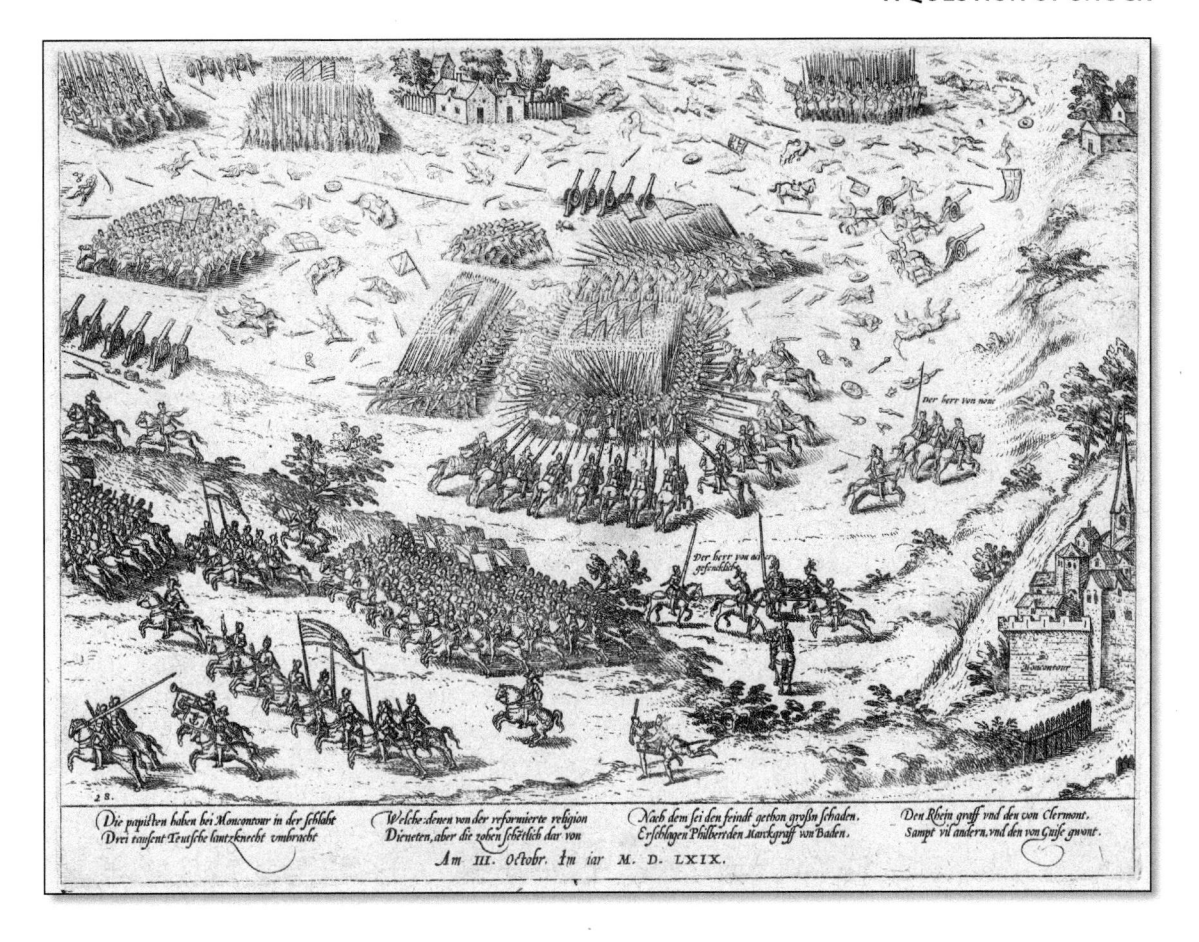

Battle of Moncontour in 1569. Workshop of Frans Hogenberg, 1570-1573. (Rijksmuseum)

has less strength, and this because it walks softly, it is open, disunited, or else because, being on an over-extended front, he falters and pulls back.[43]

On the contrary, where the advance of the opposing squadron was safe and confident, 'it often imposes so much that his enemy prevents his charge by fleeing before him.'[44] A reflection soberly summarised by Mottin de la Balme in 1776: 'All things equal, it is in the more or less advantageous way to present oneself to the enemy that the victory is decided.'[45]

The stage immediately following the impact of two units is so closely linked that it risks presenting an incomplete analysis if it is considered only briefly. This phase is often characterised by the term 'melee'. The term melee evokes the idea of a confused fight, an uncertain set of disordered man-on-man combats. All this is obviously not untrue. Whether a quick passing clash of swords or a more prolonged combat, or somewhere between the two, it is important to understand these differences.

We can firstly consider a case, probably quite common, in which one of the opposing squadrons would have put itself in a position to be defeated

---

43 D'Authville, *Essai*, pp.269–270.
44 D'Authville, *Essai*, p.270.
45 La Balme, *Eléments de tactique*, p.194.

even before impact. Unnerved by the proud bearing of their opponent, this squadron had slowed its pace considerably. The wavering feeling that has invaded its ranks became more intense and controlling, and more and more gaps opened between the files. As the moment of impact approached the riders who could, those on the wings and the rear, tried to avoid contact. When the two units met there was no proper melee. Only a few men tried to fight, the others sought their salvation in flight. This situation looked more like a pursuit than a melee. Even if we consider a more positive hypothesis, of the officers managing to prevent most of the soldiers from turning around at the last moment, the melee would still not be very long. The apprehension of the imminent impact would almost inevitably create gaps which, added to the superior speed of the enemy, would cause the unit to break by a body more disciplined, compact, and faster. From that point the men think only of their salvation and any actual hand-to-hand combat would be rare.

It could of course be that both sides had the same will to close and fight, thinking for example of the sixteenth century and the charges of the gendarmes, who would not turn in the face of the enemy without fear of losing their honour. If one of the two formations disintegrated under the impact, losing its order and cohesion, it was forced to break rather quickly, no organised resistance being possible. Otherwise, the impact could be followed by a melee in the traditional sense of the word.

D'Aubigné does not hesitate to expand on some of this, citing the great battles won by Henri IV during the Wars of Religion. At Coutras (1587), while the charge of Joyeuse was broken by the gendarmes of the King, judiciously supported by the salvos of their musketeers, the melee that followed the impact was fierce. D'Aubigné, overthrown from his horse by a Catholic, saved himself by stabbing his sword into the visor of his enemy.[46] The King was not the last to put himself in danger at the heart of the fight. The Royalist pamphleteers knew how to take advantage of these feats of arms to forge the image of a warrior king. The *Discours*, recounting the Battle of Ivry (1590), thus describes him remaining 'a great quarter of an hour among them [the enemies] always fighting.'[47]

True melees, contested battles, are still encountered beyond the sixteenth century when the opponents are of equal strength and determination. This is the case, for example, at Marston Moor (1644). The left wing of Parliament's army, led by Cromwell, was opposed to the formidable horsemen of Prince Rupert. A Parliamentary officer described the fight: 'Cromwell's own division had a hard pull of it: for they were charged by Rupert's bravest men, both in front and flanks: they stood at the sword point a pretty while, hacking at one another; but at last (it so pleased God) he [Cromwell] brake through them, scattering them before him like a little dust.'[48]

This testimony should remind us that melees rarely degenerated into general chaos in which each rider, isolated from his comrades, had to fight individually. In such a context the squadron no longer existed as a tactical

---

46 D'Aubigné, *Histoire Universelle*, p.138.
47 Anon., *Discours véritable*, p.23.
48 Tincey, *Marston Moor*, p.64.

The Battle of Ivry in 1590. Workshop of Frans Hogenberg, 1590–1592. (Rijksmuseum)

unit and the officers were unable to control it. On the contrary, the victory was won for the side who knew how to keep the best order for as long as possible. It is likely that only a small proportion of the riders fought, the first or the first two ranks. The others remained in support to protect the flanks, plug gaps, or replace a fallen comrade. This is suggested for example by the Chevalier D'Hilaire. The firing, he says, 'should occupy only second rank riders who, lying on the neck of their horses, can fire the pistol against those enemies who fight their comrades in the first rank.'[49]

The melee therefore lasted until one of the two opponents was no longer able to preserve its cohesion sufficiently. This happened because the other side, who had kept more order at the moment of impact, gradually took the advantage, increased its pressure and infiltrated between the files of his opponent. It may also have been the result of outside intervention, such as a troop coming to take one of the squadrons in its flank or rear and thus causing of flight and panic on the part of the riders who saw themselves flanked.

But it could also happen that the shock of impact and the subsequent melee ended in a kind of 'draw'. This was the case when neither side managed to break the order of their opponent. The situation then seems strange, as

---

49 SHD/DAT, 1MR 1732, f°63, 'Mémoire contenant des réflexions sur quelques articles militaires, par M. le chevalier D'Hilaire, capitaine de cavalerie, 1771'. A similar observation is made at the beginning of the seventeenth century by Louis de Montgommery, *La milice Françoise*, p.138.

it appears rather unlikely that the two units could, as if by some mutual agreement, stop the fight, turn their backs, and then return to their starting positions. We cannot really think of it in that way. There was only one real possibility in this case, that being not to turn back, but rather to continue to move straight ahead. This is the phenomenon that Brent Nosworthy refers to as 'threading'.[50] The two units did not come to a halt to begin hacking at each other, they were not completely mixed up one unit inside the another, but passed through each other's ranks and emerged at the rear.[51]

This situation was entirely possible under two conditions. First, that both of the two squadrons managed to keep enough cohesion and order not to be disrupted by the enemy and then were able to reassemble without much difficulty. Second, somewhat paradoxically, they must also not be too closely ordered or their formations too compact. There must be enough space between the files of each to allow the opposing riders to make their way through. We can find examples of this phenomena in the sixteenth century. Tavannes stated to Moncontour (1569) that the French and Italian squadrons 'passing among each other'.[52] His son also mentioned riders who 'pass and pass again through the squadrons without knocking'.[53] However, this phenomenon must have been more frequent after the middle of the seventeenth century, when the squadrons became sufficiently loose ordered for their 'crossing' to be facilitated. One of the most explicit evocations of this 'threading' is in the work of La Colonie. He describes at Schmidmittel (1703) the clash of cavalry between the Bavarians and the Imperialists:

> The determination that was in these troops on both sides caused the shock to be extremely violent, we remained mingled for some time, but the cavalry having pierced each before it in the time that the infantry was still struggling, the two parties rallied on both sides, and came to the charge a second time. However, despite this obstinacy and after a long struggle, both having found themselves separated a second time, each retreated on his side after losing many people without knowing who was victorious.[54]

Guibert also gives an insight into this phenomenon: 'when the two squadrons are composed only of seasoned men and horses, here is how their charge goes: the ranks are mutually interlocking, the horses seek themselves intervals; the riders join in hand-to-hand combat, everything gets mixed up to the point where the squadrons pass behind each other.'[55]

According to Nosworthy, the frequency of 'threading' decreased during the eighteenth century. Advances in training made it easier to conduct 'knee-

---

50 Nosworthy, The *Anatomy of Victory*, pp.125–126.
51 We observe a similar phenomenon, although in a different context, in the writings of Xenophon when he evokes the *anthippasie*, a manoeuvre performed in the context of equestrian games. *Le commandant de la cavalerie* (Paris: Les Belles lettres), 1973, p.43.
52 Tavannes, *Mémoires*, p.338.
53 Tavannes, *Mémoires*, p.297.
54 La Colonie, *Mémoires*, p.212.
55 Guibert, *Essai*, p.385.

to-knee' charges.[56] The progress of which he speaks, however, was probably not in effect before the middle of the century and concerned mainly the Prussian cavalry.

One could think that the riders' swordsmanship played a crucial role and made the difference in melee. This is probably true, but it was not always the case. For Pierre Cantal, the use of weapons in the melee is almost illusory, the vast majority of soldiers were too excited to think of using their swords: 'On a hundred riders, said an officer of the first empire, two or three think only of to give a thrust; it is they who do all the useful work; Five or six block the blows that are stroke at them, and sometimes extend a thrust when they see the possibility, without running any risk. The rest is delivered to the enemy.'[57]

Without referring to the 'emotion' of the riders, the observations of Jean de Tavannes also refer to a reality quite similar to that put forward by Pierre Cantal. He denounces those who 'go through the squadrons without hitting, come out with their pistols still loaded and white swords, for lack to be admonished before the charges, at least to show that they struck a blow.'[58]

German standard bearer in full armour, 1577. Abraham de Bruyn. (Rijksmuseum)

It is true, on the other hand, that the actual combat phase was sometimes too short for them to engage in combat. From the second third of the seventeenth century, it was mainly expected that the riders would make their way through the enemy squadron. Most of them had to be preoccupied with getting through the enemy formation as soon as possible to get out and find themselves safe on the other side. It is very likely that few of them wanted to engage in real duels on horseback in the manner of knights. Given the difficulty of the exercise (it was necessary for the rider to control his horse while he was fighting) this possibility was in any case beyond the ability of inexperienced troops.

For this reason, many riders preferred to be content with a cut, even though the officers of the eighteenth century explicitly favoured the thrust. The argument for the latter is mainly based on the low lethality of the cut. D'Authville reminds us that it is not easy to give a sharp blow that is particularly dangerous. In order to be really effective, the cut must be applied carefully, because 'in the event that the wrist bends right or left the sword no longer opposes the cutting edge to the air column that it wants to split, this air column then finds a greater surface area and becomes more resistant, it brings the sword back on its flat.' On the other hand, 'defensive weapons often guarantee from it, or if they do not, the bones prevent it from penetrating,

---

56 Nosworthy, *The Anatomy of Victory*, p.126.
57 Pierre Cantal, *Études sur la cavalerie* (Paris: Lavauzelle, 1905), p.40.
58 Tavannes, *Mémoires*, p.192.

rather than the point penetrating only two fingers deep makes a mortal wound or one very difficult to heal.'[59] Recent studies on Swedish soldiers found on the battlefield of Poltava (1709) seem to go in this direction: the sharp blows, although powerful and often delivered to the head, do not seem to have been sufficient to lead directly to death.[60]

Although more deadly, thrusting involved a fencer's control, and self-control which was beyond the skills learned from the poor instruction given to most soldiers. They were therefore probably much more in agreement with the words of Jeney, one of the few authors of the eighteenth century to defend the use of cutting. He does not deny that the thrusts are more deadly but points out that this is not the main objective during a cavalry fight. The rider who thrusts at his opponent is forced to stop to pull his blade out, but during this time another will have sabred and wounded three of his enemies, 'if not mortally at least they will be hors de combat: that is what must seek in battle, both for the interest and the glory of the sovereign.'[61] This state of mind is undoubtedly the one that dominates the simple riders. They do not seek at all costs the death of their enemy; it is enough for them to be hors de combat.

To define the shock or impact factor it is first necessary to forget the image created in the nineteenth and twentieth centuries of two masses of cavalry launched at full gallop and hitting each other at full speed. Except for the chivalrous charge, which disappeared at the beginning of the sixteenth century, the shock during our period was more of a free-for-all, the violence of the contact being less important and more diffuse. The two squadrons were not brick walls. They were groups consisting of ranks and files that were extremely difficult to keep solid because of the movement inherent in the squadron's march; as well as the poor instruction of most riders. Thus, gaps were created, 'daylight' appeared within the formations. This explains why, when two squadrons managed to come together, one of them could be broken, or they passed through each other in a kind of 'threading'. Admittedly, not all charges ended in impact, far from it, but that does not diminish the fundamental importance of it. Indeed, is precisely the fear of the shock of impact which made a squadron falter. Its effect acted both physically and morally, which explains why success was sometimes decided even before contact.

---

59   D'Authville, *Essai*, p.257.
60   Englund, *Poltava*, pp.208–209.
61   Louis Michel de Jeney, *Le partisan ou l'art de faire la petite guerre avec succès selon le génie de nosjours* (La Haye: Constapel, 1759), chapter 3; edition consulted online in 2005 on <stratisc.org>.

Part III

An Essential Place on the Battlefield

8

The French Wars of Religion

The specifications of the cavalry charge underwent a radical transformation in the second half of the sixteenth century, but did they upset the main principles of tactics and organisation? During the first half of the century the armies were usually divided into three corps, within which the cavalry and infantry units operated without supporting each other or coordinating their actions. Is it possible that the emergence of reiters and their pistols led commanders to adapt? More than general tactics, it is how cavalry were employed which should be questioned. The tactical developments referred to above did not take place over night, and the lancers' charge in line did not suddenly disappear from the middle of the century. The different categories of heavy cavalry, to which are often added the mounted arquebusiers, had to work together on the battlefield. The tactical doctrines became more complex since it was necessary to reconcile radically different modes of operating: the men-at-arms and the chevau-légers charged in line with the lance and at the gallop while the reiters attacked with the pistol and at the trot. These different tactics may have complemented each other, but this was often difficult exploit.

The question of the place of heavy cavalry on the battlefield is also particularly acute. The move towards the preference for fire tactics did appear to signal its decline. It is therefore necessary to consider how this new role for cavalry would be integrated into the tactical doctrines of the Wars of Religion. So apart from the knights and men-at-arms, did this affect the ability of heavy cavalry to take its place on the battlefield?

A study of two famous battles, Dreux (1562) and Ivry (1590), taking place at opposite ends of the Wars of Religion, presents us with a broad view of the period. It allows us to measure the changes that occurred in these turbulent decades, and to fully consider the true metamorphosis of heavy cavalry. The art of war in this period is perhaps worth a little more than the quick glance that one might otherwise give it.

The Battle of Dreux (1562) was the first great confrontation of the Wars of Religion. It is a significant example in several ways. First, the armies were commanded by the greatest captains of the time: Guise and Montmorency for the Royal and Catholic Army, Coligny and Condé for the Huguenots. The battle also allows us to observe how the generals used heavy cavalry at

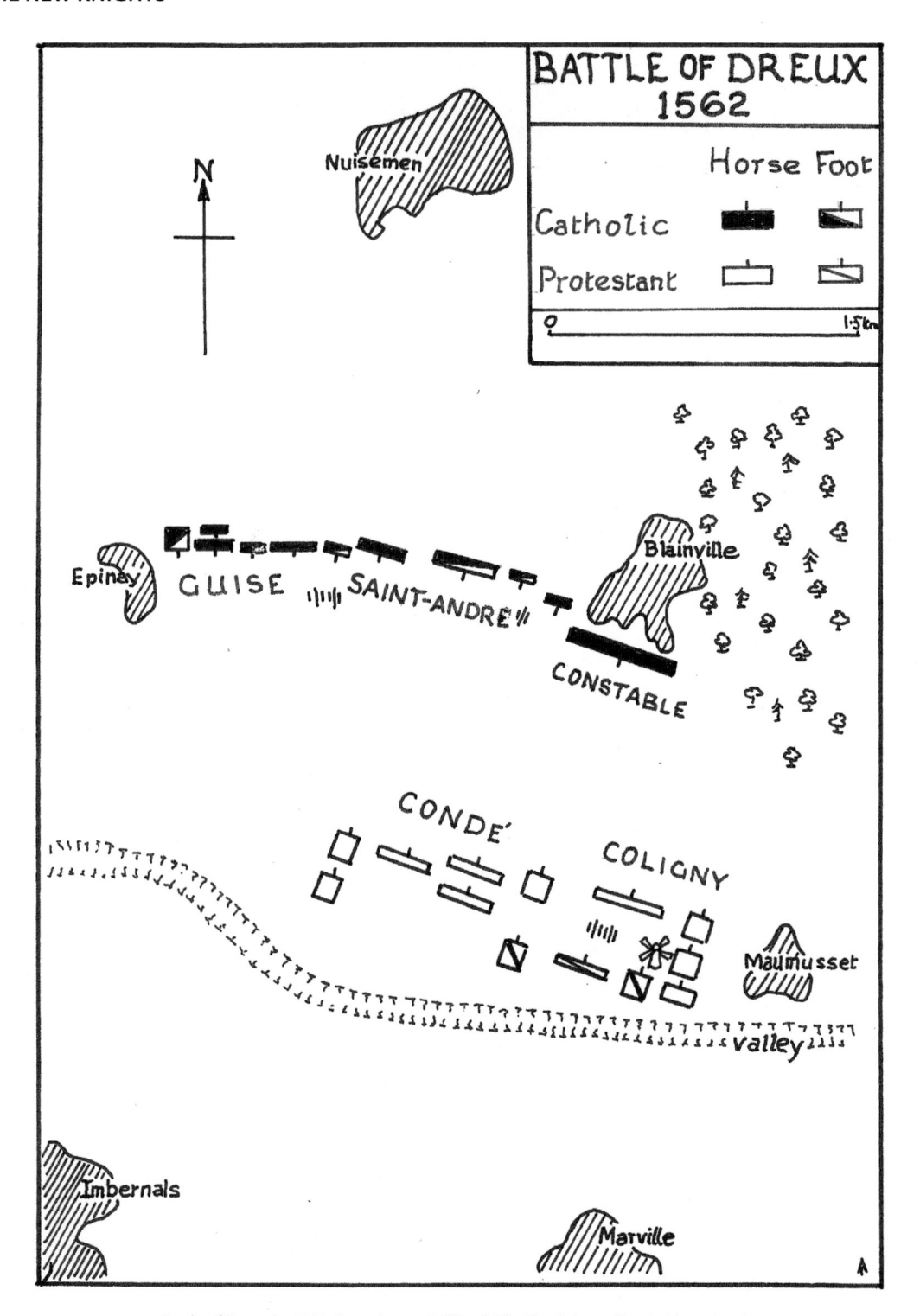

Battle of Dreux in 1562. From James B. Wood, *The King's Army* (Cambridge, 2002).

the beginning of the conflict. We see at work all the categories of mounted troops ordinarily to be found in armies of the period: men-at-arms and chevau-légers armed with lances, reiters, and mounted arquebusiers.

One of the main difficulties lay in the coordination of these different categories of riders. Army leaders ought to be able to take advantage of the unique characteristics of each type without hindering or creating disorder among the troops. Beyond the question of the combination of different cavalry types and the possible superiority of one or the other, the Battle of Dreux also lets us consider their tactics against enemy infantry. The Catholics had in their service 5,000 to 6,000 Swiss, formed in a massive square of pikes. Their clash with the Protestant cavalry was one of the key moments of this day.

The first year of the war was spent in indecisive operations marked by the capture of Rouen and Bourges from the Protestants. After campaigning around Paris during November, the Protestants decided to withdraw to Normandy to receive reinforcements from England. The Constable de Montmorency marched to block their way. On 19 December 1562 the Protestant army found the road to Normandy cut by the Royal Army, at Blainville, near Dreux.[1]

Unarmoured cavalry colonel, 1577. Abraham de Bruyn. (Rijksmuseum)

The Catholic army, about 22,000 strong (including more than 2,000 horsemen), was deployed in two corps. The vanguard under Guise occupied the right flank. On the far right, resting on the Épinay Wood, was the Spanish infantry. To his left were the gendarmes of Guise, then the old French 'bandes' (infantry), more gendarmes under Saint-André, the Landsknechts and gendarmes commanded by d'Aumale and Damville. To their left, almost on the same front, was the main body, commanded by the Constable. However, because of the narrow confines of the terrain, the Constable's troops were slightly ahead of those of Guise. Therefore, from left to right, we have the Swiss, the Constable's gendarmes, Picard and Breton infantry and finally the chevau-légers commanded by Sansac to the front of Blainville. The lance-armed gendarmes and chevau-légers were deployed in line.

This battle plan is characteristic of the Wars of Religion and differs from that of the previous era by the disappearance of a third body of troops, the reargard. It seems that in most battles, armies had become accustomed to dividing into only two corps: the vanguard and the main body. This arrangement represents a step backwards rather than progress. It was not adopted as a means of addressing changing circumstances but was almost

---

1 Jean-Paul Le Flem, article 'Dreux', in Jacques Garnier (ed.), *Dictionnaire des guerres*.

THE NEW KNIGHTS

Battle of Dreux in 1562.
Jean Perrissin, 1570.
(Rijksmuseum)

a systematic change, found for example in the order of march of the 38,000 strong army of the Duke d'Anjou in December 1567.[2]

Many of the orders of battle for the first half of the century are preserved. They mainly show the armies deployed in a single line (with rare exceptions as we will see with the Protestants). There was no question of deepening the deployment in order to allow retreating troops to reform. The two main battle corps, vanguard and main body, are deployed side by side, sometimes on the same line, sometimes echeloned; they fought separately. Another point of interest that can be seen is the intermingling of cavalry and infantry units. The cavalry was usually placed on both sides of the large infantry battalions. Alternating infantry and cavalry units became the norm in most of the battles of the Wars of Religion.

The Protestant army adopted a very different formation, probably resulting from the circumstances and characteristics of the army. It suffered from a significant numerical inferiority (about 12,000) but was superior in cavalry (about 4,500). Thus, if the army was divided into two corps, under Coligny and Condé, almost all the cavalry was in the front line: on the left Condé, on the right Coligny, each with gendarmes, chevau-légers and reiters, in the centre the gendarmes of Mouy and Avaret, preceded by *argoulets*

---

2   Wood, *The King's Army*, p.79.

THE FRENCH WARS OF RELIGION

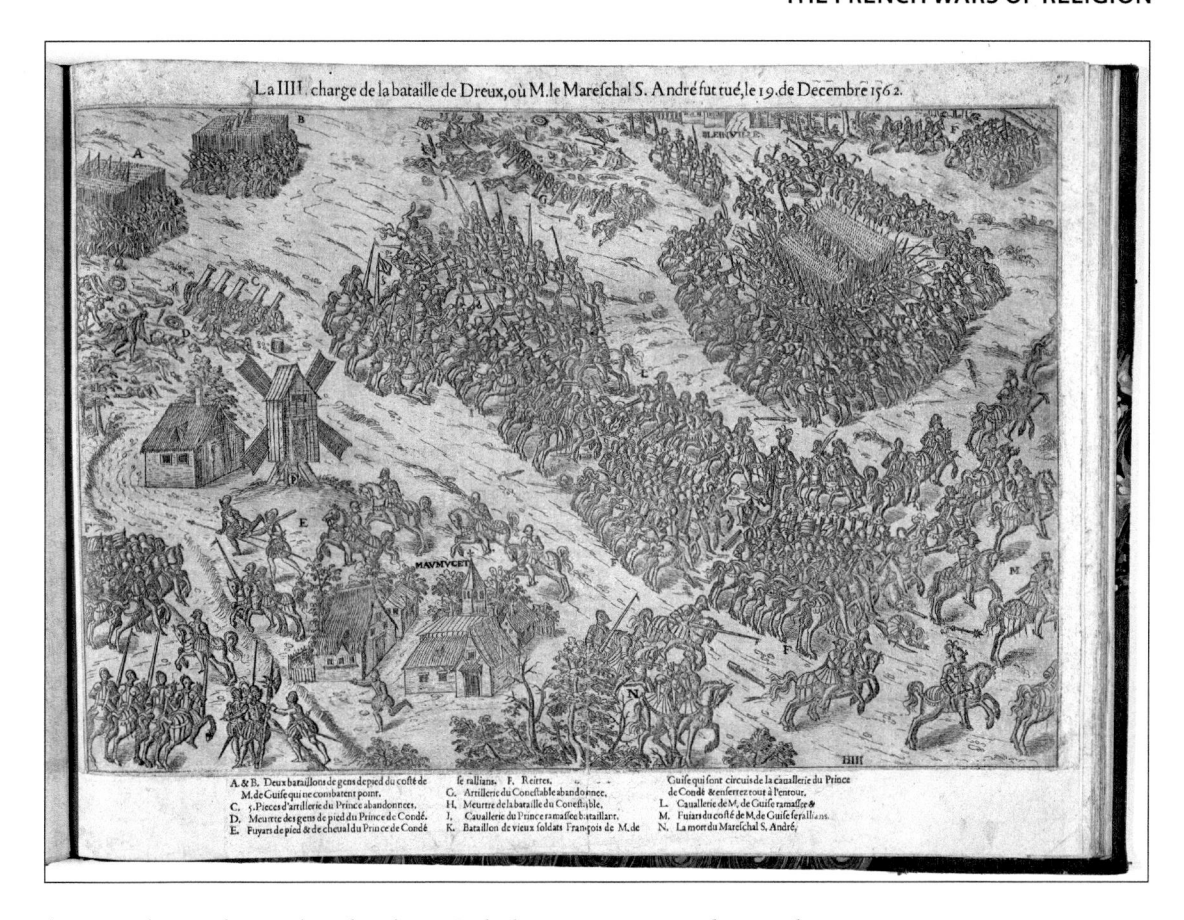

Battle of Dreux in 1562. Jean Perrissin, 1570. (Rijksmuseum)

(mounted arquebusiers). Like their Catholic counterparts, the gendarmes and chevau-légers of the Protestants were deployed in line and armed with lances. Reiters were organised as was usual in deep squadrons. Behind this cavalry was a thin second line composed of French and German infantry as well as a reserve of reiters. Dreux appears to be an exception, the Huguenots generally adopting later battle orders like those of the Catholics: the units split in a vanguard and a main body, placed in a single line with the cavalry and infantry intermingled.

The rather unorthodox deployment of Protestants did not mean that they intended to be outmanoeuvred by their opponents. They were under some pressure from Constable de Montmorency, who advanced his cannons to compel the Huguenots to advance into contact.[3] Montmorency was to be paid back in full. Towards one o'clock in the afternoon, while the preliminaries of the battle had begun nearly two hours earlier, the Prince of Condé gave the signal to attack. Immediately, all the Protestant cavalry ignored the Catholic vanguard of the Duke de Guise, and advanced towards the body of men commanded by the Constable.

The troops under command of Condé battle attacked the Swiss. Military captains and writers now know that infantry is not an adversary that

---

3 Duc de Guise, quoted by Périni, *Batailles françaises*, volume II, p.18.

THE NEW KNIGHTS

Battle of Dreux, 1562. To the right of the picture, the Protestant reiters put to flight the men-at-arms of the Constable of Montmorency. Jean Perrissin, 1570. (Rijksmuseum)

should be ignored, and military thinking gave it a little more space than in previous decades. La Noue recognised that the association of pikemen and arquebusiers was challenging for cavalry. Tavannes remarked that the latter generally avoided charging a battalion frontally and preferred to attack the flanks: 'The cavalry gladly attacks the corners of the battalions because it does not dare to sink in the middle.'[4] The tactical situation seemed more favourable at Dreux, since the Swiss did not have the support of arquebusiers.

Experienced captains knew that other elements came into play other than the weapons and armour alone. The horse was one of the main vulnerabilities of cavalry. Horses are sensitive, subject to fear, and 'few things hold it back'.[5] As part of a charge against infantry the horses' senses are particularly heightened. The sight of the pikes, the sound of firearms, the smell of powder, are all likely to upset and frighten a young or poorly prepared mount. The morale of the combatants themselves is also very important. La Noue suggested that part of the success of the charge is played out in the hearts of men. When infantrymen 'have the courage and confidence to stand firm', they can resist cavalry.[6] And indeed, it takes a lot of courage and assurance not to panic when the steel-clad men-at-arms start their charge at a gallop, or when the reiters trot towards them to discharge their pistol at point blank

---

4   Tavannes, *Mémoires*, p.84.
5   Tavannes, *Mémoires*, p.371.
6   La Noue, *Discours*, p.370.

range. It is obviously easier for the cavalry to charge inexperienced infantry, composed of newly raised soldiers.

But the battalion standing before the Protestant horsemen was of a different mettle altogether. Although their domination of the battlefield was no longer exclusive, the Swiss remained some of the best infantry in Europe. Their courage and their tactical doctrines were still their main assets. These qualities were about to be subjected to a severe test, and this right from the beginning of the combat. The Prince de Condé led more than 400 lances, nearly 1,500 reiters and the argoulets of La Curée. Each troop attacked according to its own tactics. Reiters and argoulets used their firepower to shoot at the Swiss at close range. The Swiss were not supported by any arquebusiers, so the riders could aim almost at leisure. Yet as deadly as their fire may have been, it was not enough to carry the combat in their favour. The objective of the charge against the infantry was not so much to kill the infantrymen as to destroy the battalion as a unit, and to hasten its disintegration. Once it was divided up and broken, it became completely vulnerable and would no longer able to put up any meaningful resistance. However, faced with infantry as experienced as the Swiss, it is highly unlikely that fire from the cavalry, even where well aimed and without any pressure from enemy shot, was enough to break the ranks of the Swiss pikemen.

It was then necessary to intervene with an attack by determined shock cavalry. This was the role of the Huguenot men-at-arms. Taking advantage of the confusion sown by the salvos of the reiters and argoulets, they attacked the Swiss. The gendarmes of Muy and Avaret charged ahead, supported by the Prince de Condé. They attacked 'with such fury that they strongly cut into the battalion', penetrating to the banners.[7] Seeing this, the gendarmes of d'Aumale and the chevau-légers of Damville left the vanguard of Guise and moved to support the Swiss, but they were repulsed by the reiters. The Swiss were in bad position, without any hope of immediate support.

Other infantry would have probably already broken. However, the Swiss did not give in to panic, and they rallied 'with great courage, without sparing blows of pikes to their enemies.'[8] Despite the harshness of this attack, the Swiss managed to prevent the disintegration of their formation. The enemy gave them a moment of respite. Noting the collapse of the rest of the Catholic formations, the Protestant horsemen abandoned their attack on the Swiss and turned towards easier prey.

While Condé was attacking the Swiss, the cavalry under Coligny were putting pressure on the other troops of the Constable de Montmorency. The latter advanced to meet the enemy at the head of his cavalry, 'with great boldness and assurance'. The combat is this time between two bodies of cavalry, with gendarmes and chevau-légers. But the Huguenots also counted reiters among their number. Their massive squadrons proved their superiority over the fragile lines of the men-at-arms. The caracole was a risky

---

7   Michel de Castelnau, *Mémoires de messire Michel de Castelnau*, in *Collection complète des mémoires relatifs à l'histoire de France, par M. Petitot*, Tome XXXIII (Paris: Foucault, 1823), p.244; Périni, *Batailles françaises*, vol. II, p.18.
8   Castelnau, *Mémoires*, p.244.

undertaking in this situation, so the reiters were content to move forward at a slow pace to not disrupt their formation. Having moved to within close range of the Catholic gendarmes, they halted, and the first two or three ranks delivered a devastating salvo.

Those who had not been injured or whose horses had not been killed saw the reiters advanced towards them into contact and hand-to-hand combat. The lances of the gendarmes were no longer of any use to them and instead had to rely on their swords. But here again, they found themselves under pressure, as La Noue points out: 'Reiters are never so dangerous as when we are mixed up with them because it is all fire.'[9] They had several guns already loaded that they used in the melee, and their defensive armament also allowed them to stand up to the gendarmes. Disorganised, lost in the smoke of the salvos, the survivors had to suffer the incessant fire of the reiters without being able to break their dense formation. They could only break off the fight and retreat.

Such combats, however, take a different turn depending on the units involved. If the chevau-légers of Sansac fled at the first impact, the Constable and his men-at-arms offered greater resistance. They also succumbed, however: 'The charge was so great and furious, so many horses were passing and passing again, so many shots of pistols, blows of lances and swords in his troops, that the Constable, notwithstanding the great duty as captain and valiant warrior he was, had his horse killed under him, and himself, wounded on the chin with a bullet which had pierced his armet, was finally taken.'[10] The Picard and Breton infantrymen had already taken to their heels, without waiting for the victors to charge them. The Protestants had more important things on their minds: they were either pursuing a personal enemy or engaged in looting.

Only the much-weakened Swiss were still in a position to fight. However, the Swiss infantrymen had hardly finished reforming their battalion when they had to suffer a new assault, by a squadron of reiters returning from plundering the Catholic camp. 'The brave mountaineers were again largely thrown on the ground and their ranks traversed, although it was difficult to penetrate into such hedgehogs; but the least wounded rallied in small troops and forced the Protestant horsemen to turn their backs to reload their pistols.'[11] It was then that Coligny launched his Landsknechts towards them. 'Seeing this, the Swiss, instead of being astonished, walked straight on them and put them to flight.'[12] But the enemy did not give them time to pursue their rivals. Reiters and Huguenot gendarmes, having rallied, again charged the Swiss. This last assault finally managed to break the square. The Swiss, broken into several small groups, but still fighting, then tried to retreat to the Catholic vanguard under the Duke of Guise.[13]

---

9   La Noue, *Discours*, p.361.
10 *Mémoires de Vieilleville*, quoted by Périni, *Batailles françaises*, vol. II, p.19.
11 Hardy de Périni, *Batailles françaises*, vol. II, p.20.
12 Castelnau, *Mémoires*, p.245.
13 Wood, *The King's Army*, p.193.

Imperial lancers fighting Turks during the relief of Vienna in 1529. Dirck Volckertszoon Coornhert, after Maarten van Heemskerck. (Rijksmuseum)

The battle had been going on for two hours, and the situation was very difficult for the Royal army. The main body was dispersed, its leader taken, and the Swiss had withdrawn. However, we should not forget that the vanguard was still intact. The Duc de Guise did not move, but the horsemen of d'Aumale and Damville tried, in vain to help the Swiss. Guise, 'in no way moved, he had overcome the impetuosity of his men, who wanted to force him to advance, telling everyone that it was not yet time, as so many attacks could not be made without the victor becoming as disordered as they were.'[14] Coligny moreover was not going to continue the attack, and to those who shouted victory to him he showed 'the big cloud' of the Catholic vanguard, motionless and worrying.[15]

Noting the retreat of the Swiss and the disorder of the Protestant cavalry, the Duke now judged the moment right to intervene. At the head of the troops of the vanguard, he advanced against the enemy infantry, which had not yet been engaged, they [Guise and Saint-André] made the attack with the gendarmes only, without encountering much resistance.'[16] According to Castelnau, the gendarmes of Guise were nonetheless accompanied by arquebusiers, who supported the charge of the men-at-arms with their fire.

Even alone, however, Catholic gendarmes would have likely overcome unreliable and weakly-armed infantry. The Huguenot infantry was rapidly dispersed, the Landsknechts meanwhile remained deaf to the exhortations of Andelot and fall back toward Blainville. Thus, ironically notes Castelnau, the Landsknechts 'used that day more their feet and legs than their pikes

---

14 Tavannes, *Mémoires*, p.266.
15 La Noue, *Mémoires*, Tome XLVII, p.150.
16 Guise, quoted by Périni, *Batailles françaises*, vol. II, p.21.

Imperial lancers fighting Turks during the relief of Vienna in 1529. Dirck Volckertszoon Coornhert after Maarten van Heemskerck. (Rijksmuseum)

and corselets.'[17] They are nevertheless caught by the French and Spanish infantrymen of the Duc de Guise, who make them 'big murder and butchery'.

This attack marked the turning point of the day. The Protestant infantry was swept away, the horsemen, 'separated and disbanded', were unable to react. Some of these, including reiters, even ran away in rout. Protestant leaders very quickly realised the seriousness of the situation: it was almost impossible for them to counter-attack. Condé could not bring himself to leave the battlefield and was forced to surrender his sword to one of Damville's men to have his life saved. Despite the dramatic turn that the battle then took, Coligny tried one last effort. He was helped in this by the Duc de Guise who 'thinks he has completely conquered everything' and pursued the Huguenots half-heartedly.[18] Taking advantage of this respite, Admiral Coligny assembled what he could of his cavalry (300 or 400 French and a little more than 1,000 reiters) in the shelter of a wood in the East of Blainville. After organising his squadron, he hurled himself on Guise's troops. The Catholic cavalry, numerically inferior, was quickly dispersed. But Coligny was stopped by the resistance of the veteran battalion under Martigues, which had not yet been engaged. The Huguenot gendarmes had used their lances and failed to break into the battalion, which was effectively supported by arquebusiers.[19]

As night fell, Coligny ordered a retreat. The Duke of Guise remained master of the battlefield. However, he did not undertake any pursuit and the retreat occurred in good order. The Protestants were not swept away. Moreover, the losses of the Royal army were at least as high as those of the Huguenots, about 5,000 (killed, wounded, prisoners), for the former against

---

17 Castelnau, *Mémoires*, p.246.
18 Tavannes, *Mémoires*, p.266.
19 Wood, *The King's Army*, p.197.

THE FRENCH WARS OF RELIGION

4,500 for the latter. The cavalry paid a heavy price. James B. Wood estimates Royal cavalry losses at about 1,000 killed, wounded and prisoners, or nearly 45 percent of the total.[20]

Some writers held the opinion that this battle did not have a real winner. This was not the opinion of La Noue, who believed that 'he who wins the battlefield, takes the artillery and the infantry signs has enough marks of victory.'[21] As incomplete as it may be, this victory of the Duc de Guise appeared rich in lessons learnt.

The first remark concerns the somewhat paradoxical situation of the men-at-arms. Their traditional mode of charge, in line with the lance, was visibly obsolete vis-à-vis the new tactics of the reiters. Whenever gendarmes or even chevau-légers had to face them, they were forced to give up the ground. These repeated failures illustrate in a severe but illuminating way the superiority of the charge of a squadron armed with the pistol in the fights between opposing cavalry. However, it would be inaccurate to say that the decline of the men-at-arms is absolute from this time. It is seen in the context of charges against the infantry. The lance, the weapon par excellence of the knights of the Middle Ages, was still an effective tool.[22] It showed its value by allowing the Huguenot men-at-arms to penetrate and pass through the massive 'hedgehog' of Swiss pike. On the other hand, after all their lances had been broken or lost, the same Huguenots were then unable to defeat the regiment of Martigues and were forced to withdraw.

The second point highlights precisely the balance of power between the infantry and the cavalry. The decline, again, is not obvious. Of course, the Swiss made an admirable defence, and it took at least three attacks to break their formation. However, it is also clear that these same Swiss were seriously abused by the cavalry. Mounted troops now using the arquebus as well as the pistol or lance, and able to combine these different weapons, meant the battalions of pikemen alone were unable to resist. Heavy cavalry appears neither helpless nor outmoded by the changes in tactics and troop types. On the contrary, combining the shock power of the men-at-arms with the firepower of the reiters, this evolving weapon retained its place on the battlefield. 'The main casualty of the new gun technology was not the cavalry, but the phalanx of the Swiss pikemen, whose ranks were mowed down by the salvos of pistols from the deep formations of the Germanic reiters.'[23]

Finally, the Battle of Dreux allows to return on the doctrine of the employment of cavalry, that is, the principles that governed its engagement on the battlefield. From this point of view, the judgments of contemporaries are generally harsh on Condé. His decision to attack the Swiss early in the battle earned him the criticism of Castelnau and Tavannes. 'If the Prince de Condé had used the charges made to the Swiss (uselessly) against the cavalry of M. de Guise, he had better advantage; he must have considered

---

20   Wood, *The King's Army*, pp.200–201.
21   La Noue, *Mémoires*, p.154.
22   Wood, *The King's Army*, p.204.
23   Wood, *The King's Army*.

that the cavalry being defeated, the infantry is very ill placed.'[24] This brief explanation from Tavannes shows that even if one does not attribute a particular place to the cavalry in the order of battle, there is a dominant tactical pattern: the cavalry must first confront the cavalry of the enemy and this is their main task, and only then should they turn against the infantry. Deprived of support, the infantry could not hope for any more than a retirement in good order, and it was therefore generally pointless to exhaust oneself in vain charges against the infantry from the very beginning of the combat. This is not a unique occurrence. At Ravenna (1512) the gendarmes and chevau-légers of Gaston de Foix defeated first the Italian and Spanish horsemen before charging the enemy infantry. This was also seen at the Battle of Ceresole (1544). Condé is criticised for having ignored this essential principle. In launching his cavalry against the Swiss, he left intact the horsemen of Guise, who were his real adversary, and who were then able to take advantage of the disorder which had overtaken the victorious Protestant troops.

And here we come to a second important point concerning the use of cavalry, and the occasion of another sharp criticism of the Prince: the exploitation of success. 'He [Condé] was so intoxicated with this cry of victory over the defence of the Swiss that he forgot all the rules and commands that must be observed by a commander of the army … mainly that he had not put on the road from Dreux to Orleans enough maréchaux de camp and sergeants to prevent the soldiers of his army from withdrawing with prisoners and booty.'[25] Condé did not know how to keep his cavalry in hand after the defeat of the Catholics, and his riders dispersed to pursue and loot. Some, as Vieilleville points out, even withdrew from the battlefield to take advantage of their good fortune. It is essential to exploit the success of the initial charges, and that the general limits the disorder that never failed to appear in the ranks of the victors, thus exposing them to the danger of being swept away by a possible counter-attack. Bayard's wise counsel in Ravenna testifies that experienced captains were well aware of the importance of this phase of the battle.[26]

In practice however cavalry leaders faced considerable obstacles. The failure of the Protestant cavalry can be explained by the conjunction of several issues. First, the lack of planning, which would enable a leader to give orders to reform and set rallying points. For if Coligny remained suspicious, apprehending the moment when the 'great cloud' of the Catholic vanguard would pour down onto the Protestants, Condé was carried away by the excitement of victory. Last but not least, we must not lose sight of the fact

---

24 Tavannes, *Mémoires*, p.267.
25 François de Scépeaux de Vieilleville, *Mémoires de la vie du maréchal de Vieilleville*, livre huitième, in *Collection complète des mémoires relatifs à l'histoire de France, par M. Petitot* (Paris: Foucault, 1832), Tome XXVIII, p.64.
26 Counsels given to Gaston de Foix: 'You won the battle, but do not push further and gather your gendarmerie in this place. One doesn't begin to pillage because it is not time.' 'le Loyal Serviteur '[Jacques de Mailles], *La très joyeuse, plaisante et récréative histoire du bon chevalier sans peur et sans reproche, le gentil seigneur de Bayart, composé par le Loyal Serviteur* (Paris: Garnier Frères, 1882), p.341.

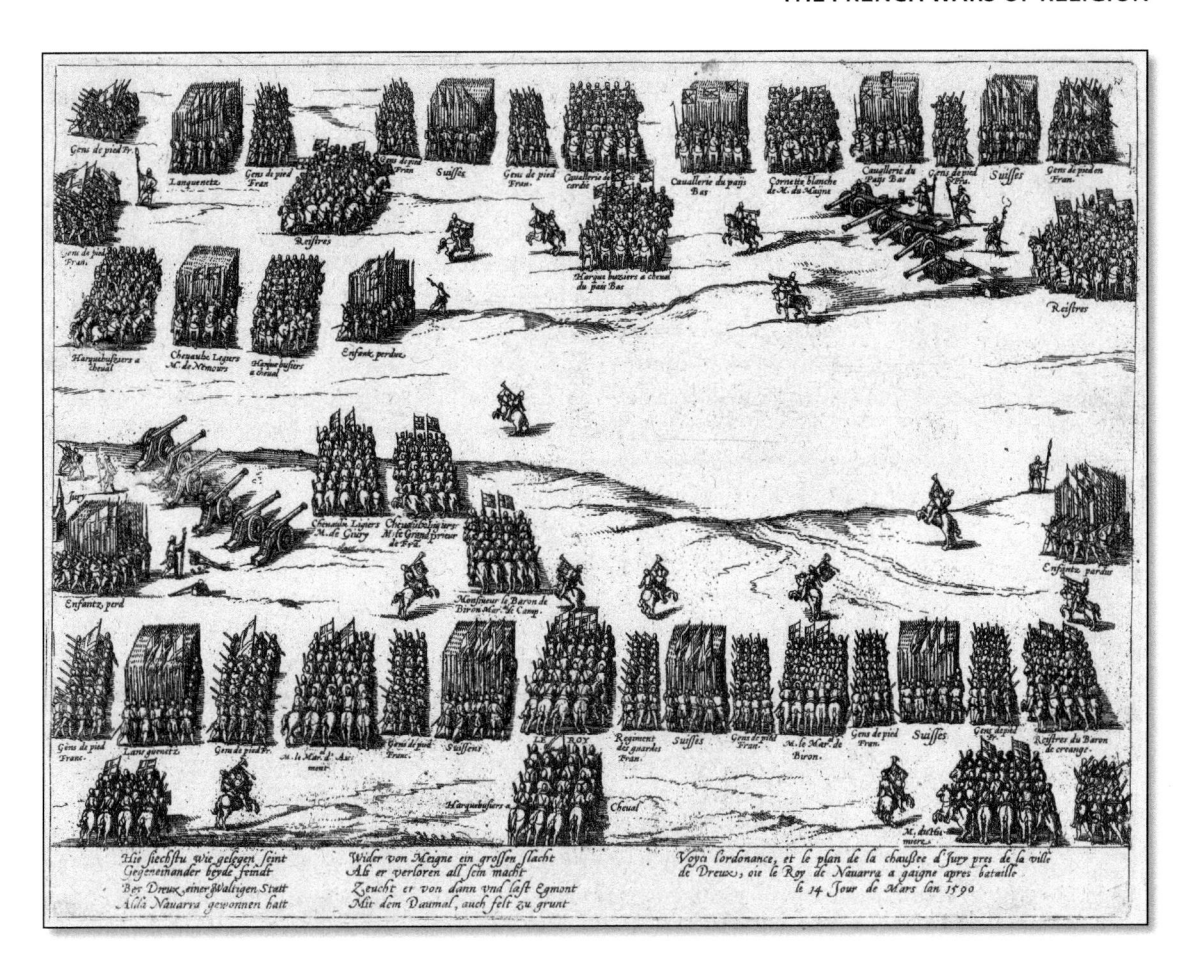

THE FRENCH WARS OF RELIGION

The Battle of Ivry in 1570. Workshop of Frans Hogenberg, 1590–1592. (Rijksmuseum)

that it is actually extremely difficult for a leader to keep control of his troops once the charge is launched. The rallying of cavalry, for example, is a very difficult thing to do in the heat of battle. Thus, when Condé realised the seriousness of the situation, immediately tried to rally his cavalry to carry out another charge. But his chevau-légers were scattered and did not hear the trumpet call to reform. As for the reiters, those who were not looting did not, or chose not, to understand the orders given in French.[27]

In general, the cavalry seemed to really dominate the battlefield. Its mobility, its power of shock and fire gave it an undeniable advantage.[28] From this point of view, the association of the reiters and gendarmes was a very important asset for the Huguenots. This element, added to the numerical superiority of the Protestant horsemen, could have allowed them victory. However, Condé's initial error and the limitations peculiar to the employment of cavalry prevented this.

In 1590, the war saw at Ivry the troops of Henry IV facing those of the Duc de Mayenne, leader of the Catholic League. The study of this battle is

---

27 Périni, *Batailles françaises*, vol. II, p.22.
28 Wood, *The King's Army*, p.204.

of obvious interest. It is a question, 28 years after Dreux, of measuring the changes that had taken place both from the point of view of the doctrine of employment and the weight of the cavalry on the battlefield.

The example of Dreux reminded us that the heavy cavalry with the lance still occupied an important place at the beginning of the Wars of Religion. However, the years between the two battles have seen the charge evolve significantly, especially among the Protestants. We know for example that the latter, both 'by default' and because they 'experienced the little usefulness of it', had gradually abandoned the lance. We can see, in the battles of Henry IV, that most men-at-arms fought with the pistol and the sword. Can we think that this considerable evolution diminished the strength of the Protestant heavy cavalry? Did it reduce, in general terms, the hitherto important role cavalry played on the battlefield?

Ivry also gives the opportunity to revisit some recurring questions. Firstly, it's known that Catholics now employ as many reiters as their foe. However, as the Catholic gentlemen were very reluctant to give up their lances, the captains were still faced with the delicate task of coordinating the actions of troops with very different tactics. Secondly, because of the tactical skill of Henri IV, the battle allowed him to approach the problem of rallying and the exploitation of victorious charges from a different perspective.

Before discussing the battle, it should be remembered that Henry IV's cavalry, which was distinctly different from that of his enemies, had already had the opportunity to prove its worth.

Henry was undoubtedly a great horseman. He was a pragmatic tactician who knew how to take advantage of his talent and experience to face the circumstances facing him and offset the weaknesses of his army. Thus, the heavy cavalry of the Catholics sometimes had a clear numerical superiority, and its men-at-arms were undeniably better equipped. The testimony of the Sieur de Saint-Auban supports this point of view. He reminds us in his memoirs that, if Henry's cavalry was well mounted, it was at a disadvantage from the point of view of armour, 'having only a simple cuirass … without armet or arm pieces.'[29] Nevertheless, Henry IV transforms the way his cavalry was employed to overcome these shortcomings, standardised through the transformations already underway.

The Battle of Coutras (1587), which we have already mentioned, is a very significant example. As La Noue advises, Henry had already organised his gendarmes and chevau-légers in squadrons, and no longer in thin lines. Each squadron was also accompanied by a group of arquebusiers 'of the stirrup', a tactic that Coligny had already proved the efficacy of. After the initial success of the Catholic cavalry of the left wing, which passed through the Protestant lines without exploiting its success, the decisive fight was played out in the centre. The formidable men-at-arms of Joyeuse, 1,200 men in a line, launched a furious charge against Henry's three squadrons.[30] Almost all without lances, the Huguenot gendarmes had orders to wait for the impact.

---

29   Jacques Pape, Seigneur de Saint-Auban, *Mémoires*, quoted by Love, 'All the King's Horsemen', p.513.
30   D'Aubigné, *Histoire Universelle*, Tome 7 (livres XI et XII), p.137.

THE FRENCH WARS OF RELIGION

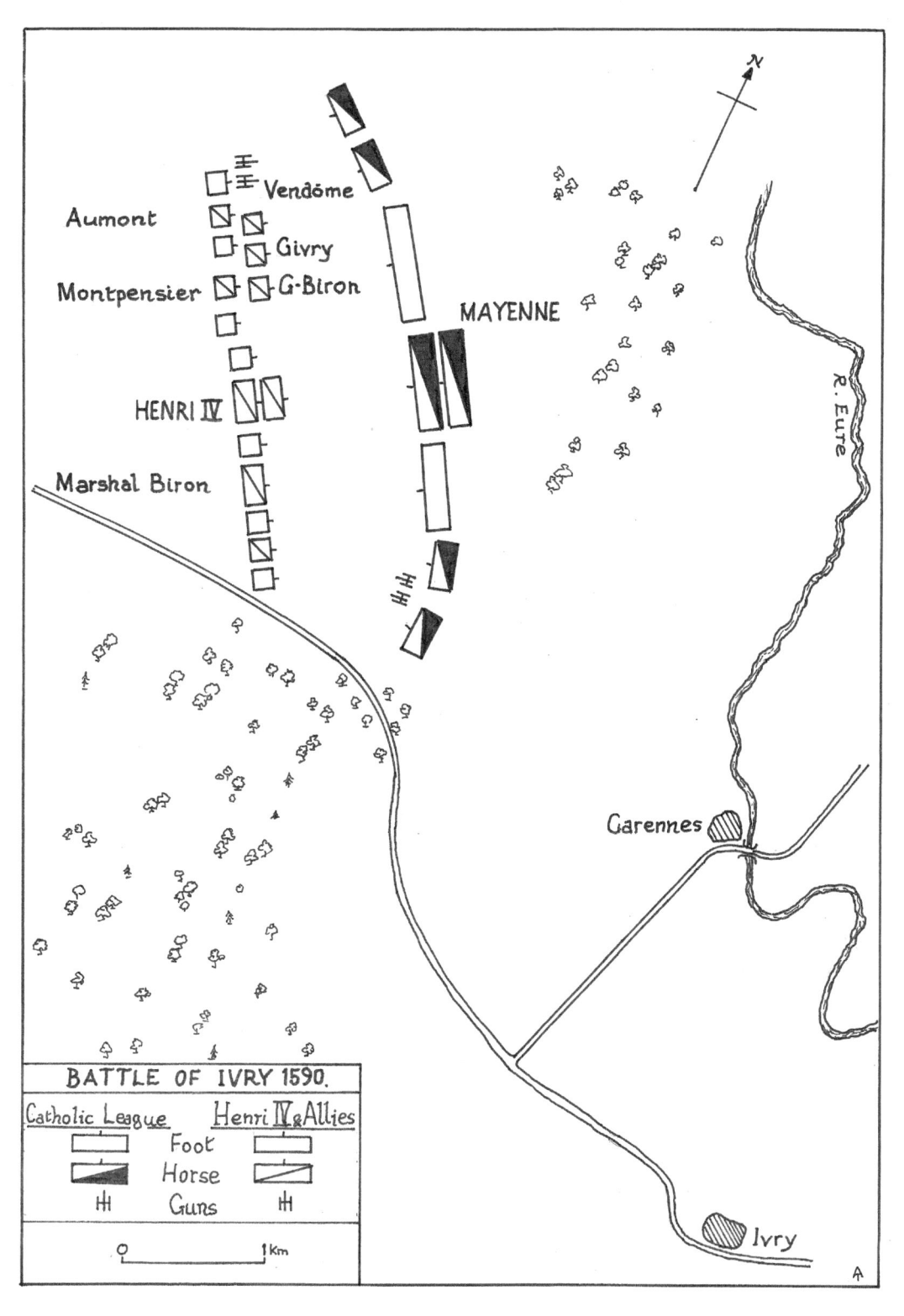

The Battle of Ivry in 1590. (Helion & Company)

Starting from too far away, with their breathless mounts and their disordered line, the Catholics suffered the salvo of the arquebusiers from a range of 10 feet. No sooner had they received the discharge than the Protestant horsemen opened fire as well and, trotting then galloping, hit the surviving enemy, who had not yet fallen 'nose on the mane'.[31]

In the ensuing melee, the Huguenots, fighting with the pistol and the sword, had an advantage over the Catholic gendarmes, some of whom, for lack of space, could not even lower their lances.[32] The fight finally turned to the advantage of the Protestants, and the Catholics fled, leaving 400 of them on the ground; the Duc de Joyeuse himself was killed during the pursuit. Seeing the success of their cavalry, the Huguenot infantry took to the offensive in their turn and threw themselves on the already shaken Catholic regiments. Only the return of Henry put a halt to the carnage.

But the resounding victory of Coutras did not put an end to the war. At the beginning of 1590, after another victory at Arques the previous year, Henri IV progressed towards the capital and laid siege to Dreux. The Duc de Mayenne could not let him take the city and he intervened to raise the siege. Afraid of finding himself in an unfavourable position, Henri retired to Nonancourt. Mayenne then followed in his wake along the valley of the Eure, persuaded to have a go at an army he thought was on the run. But the Royal army was prepared for battle and waited resolutely for their enemy in front of Ivry.

As at Coutras or Arques, the numbers of men in the two armies are not very important, with a considerable superiority of the Leaguers. Accounts differ as the actual troop numbers, but the Royal army fielded 2,500 horsemen and 6,000–7,000 foot soldiers, compared with 5,000 horsemen and 8,000–10,000 infantrymen under Mayenne. However, we see the return of an army organised in three bodies, vanguard, main battle, and rearguard, which had all but disappeared by the beginning of the Wars of Religion.[33] The Royal army was deployed in almost a straight line, backs to the sun and the wind. The rearguard occupied the right wing. It was composed of 300 reiters, a battalion of Swiss, the squadron of 250 gendarmes under Biron and another Swiss battalion, flanked by a regiment of infantry. The main battle had a little more depth. In the centre there was a large squadron of 600 gendarmes, flanked by the French Guard and a battalion of Swiss and Grisons. The line is supported by two companies of mounted arquebusiers and a squadron of 200 cuirassiers. Finally, the vanguard includes a squadron of 200 gendarmes and as many Norman gentlemen, a battalion of German pikemen and two regiments of French infantry. In front of the line, on the left, are two squadrons of chevau-légers (Givry and Auvergne) protecting the artillery. The order of Mayenne is quite like that of the King. He too has divided his army into three corps. However, his line is more of a semi-circle because he has a larger number of soldiers. In this case, as Aubigné remarked,

---

31 D'Aubigné, *Histoire Universelle*, Tome 7 (livres XI et XII), pp.137–138. See also Duplessis-Mornay quoted by Love, 'All the King's Horsemen', p.518.
32 D'Aubigné, *Histoire Universelle*, p.138.
33 Jean-Paul Le Flem, 'Ivry', in Garnier (ed.), *Dictionnaire des guerres*.

in order to keep an equal frontage a curved line is more suitable than a straight one.[34] Its main unit of gendarmes, although armed with lances, was arranged in squadrons, no doubt more to adapt to the circumstances than by true tactical choice.

The reappearance of the three corps of an army is not an illusion. Admittedly, this is an evolution from earlier years, when the armies were divided into two large corps (vanguard and main battle) generally distinguished on the battlefield and often fighting separately. However, this return to the practices of the first half of the century does not imply any real progress from the point of view of tactics. This division into three is largely formal, something especially true at Ivry, where the three corps were not autonomous divisions capable of fighting and manoeuvring separately. In fact, the different troops were formed only in one line.

Beyond this, there is much in common with the tactical organisation at the beginning of the Wars of Religion. First of all, there is still no second line, and the battle order usually has no depth. In addition, the cavalry does not yet have a fixed place in the deployment of the army, and the battle plan of Ivry shows the classic alternation of infantry and cavalry units. It was almost systematic in Henry's army, where each squadron is flanked by one or two formations of infantrymen. Again, the infantry and cavalry mix is not really intended to prepare for combined attacks. The idea is rather that both arms would support each other when needed. In practice, however, they usually fought on their own.

The use of cavalry and infantry units offers little in the way of any novelty. The same goes for the rules of engagement of the cavalry, as the beginning of the battle shows particularly.

It began, as was so often the case, for control of the artillery. The Duc de Nemours, who commanded the right flank of the Catholic League forces, was inconvenienced by the Protestant cannons placed to his front. He sent six cornets of reiters to silence them. The chevau-légers of d'Auvergne and Givry broke away from the Protestant line and made them turn back. This retirement was not carried without difficulty. The reiters wanted to slip between the squares of infantrymen to take shelter. However, the spaces left between the battalions of infantry are not sufficiently wide, and the reiters threw themselves against the Swiss and the Landsknechts, who were forced to lower their pikes against them. This placed the right wing of Mayenne's army in great disorder.[35]

This first failure did not dampen Nemours' fighting spirit, who decided to send his chevau-légers to take over from the reiters. The 200 cuirassiers of Biron and 200 gendarmes of d'Aumont left the line to flank them. After having pushed them to the edge of a wood, d'Aumont stopped his troops 'which had not changed order, neither for the melee of the charge nor for a grand fusillade on one side of the lansquenets' and returned to take his place beside the King's squadron.[36] In view of these successive failures,

---

34 D'Aubigné, *Histoire Universelle*, Tome 8 (livres XII et XIII), p.166.
35 Périni, *Batailles françaises*, vol. II, p.147.
36 D'Aubigné, *Histoire*, Tome 8 (livres XII et XIII), p.169.

the Catholic League launched another attack, this time by the formidable Walloon gendarmes. These manage to put d'Auvergne and Givry's troops to flight, and they seized the artillery. The King could not leave this advantage to the enemy. He committed his own squadron, placed in the centre of the line, to take back the cannons. The melee was confused. At the end of a quarter of an hour the Walloons had obtained an advantage and put the left of the Royal squadron in some difficulty.[37]

This, however, is not enough to shake the Huguenots, and the white cornet still floats above the right of the King's squadron. This was the moment chosen by the commander of the League army to intervene in person. 'The Duc de Mayenne having seen that it was time, marched towards the King with his main squadron of gendarmes. He is preceded by a troop of 400 *carabins* (light cavalry composed of mounted arquebusiers), who perform a discharge on the Protestant horsemen. This did not discourage the King's squadron, 'who, having swallowed this dragee, gives in a forest of lances.'[38] According to the *Discours véritable*, the King himself was seen 'to start twice the length of his horse in front of all the others, and to mingle ... furiously among the enemies.'[39] The melee was indeed very fierce, and Aubigné took the opportunity to emphasise the valour of the royal troops, such as the gendarme on whom 'three lances broke', or Fonslebon, who with a blow of his gun smashed the brain of the Comte d'Aiguemont.[40]

The outcome of the fight is uncertain, but a charge by Biron (at the head of his rallied troops) onto the flanks of the League cavalry certainly won a decisive advantage. As at Coutras, the numerical superiority of Catholics was not very useful to them. 'The first ranks of the Leagues,' says d'Aubigné, 'were badly damaged, but the rear feeling no harm, prevented the first to leave the game and disengage as soon as they wanted.'[41] 'This large body [the body of the Catholic gendarmes], which had been weakened, began to falter, and we saw the backs of those who had just so furiously presented their faces, and their heads and arms still all armed, borrowed help and assistance from their heels, which were not.'[42]

Once the swarm of Catholic gendarmes had scattered, three Walloon cornets reappear. But the Huguenots rallied and charged them energetically, and the sight of their comrades soon convinced them to turn back. The League infantry then remained alone on the battlefield. It was the cavalry who decided the day, and the battle was settled by a succession of confused and improvised charges and counter-charges. Henry's infantry hardly needed to intervene. But they are then facing the Catholic's intact infantry. Battalions of pikemen kept the place they occupied at the beginning of the battle, arquebusiers by their side. Henry would like to continue the fight, but Biron dissuaded him. He directed the artillery at the Swiss and thus obtained their

---

[37] Sully quoted by Périni, *Batailles françaises*, vol. II, p.147.
[38] D'Aubigné, *Histoire Universelle*, Tome 8 (livres XII et XIII), p.170.
[39] Anon., *Discours véritable*, p.23.
[40] D'Aubigné, *Histoire Universelle*, Tome 8 (livres XII et XIII), p.170.
[41] D'Aubigné, *Histoire Universelle*, Tome 8 (livres XII et XIII), p.171.
[42] Anon., *Discours véritable*, p.23.

surrender, as well as that of the French regiments. As for the Landsknechts, they were delivered to the King's Swiss and slaughtered without mercy in memory of the Battle of Arques.[43]

After Dreux, Ivry allows us to underline the correctness of the remark from Jean de Tavannes, who observed that 'it was very foolish to use the vigour of the cavalry to make charges against the Swiss or enemy footmen in the campaigns of France, especially since it is easy to judge that the cavalry being defeated, the infantry must be lost.'[44] During the Wars of Religion, as well as during the first half of the century, victory was generally obtained by breaking the enemy's cavalry. This had to be the first and main objective of any cavalry, and Condé made a serious error in disregarding this rule at Dreux.

Like many captains of his time, Henri IV was quite aware of this fact. Thus, to a reiter who pointed out to him before the battle the importance of the enemy's strength, he responded with knightly bravado: 'Good, more people, more glory. Besides, once the cavalry are defeated, it will be all very well for us to beat the footmen.'[45] This is just as revealing of the chivalrous spirit of the King as of the way in which the action and the role of the cavalry were considered. It's first objective had to be to beat the enemy cavalry, thus assuring the army an advantage against the opposing infantry. That is exactly how events had unfolded.

It was the actions of the cavalry that allowed the Royal army to obtain a decisive advantage. However, the rules of engagement were still rather rudimentary. Squadrons were often only engaged individually, or in small groups of two or three units, depending on the circumstances. A spectator would have the impression of a chess game in which the two opponents advance their pieces in turn, without any overall view of the bigger picture. This way of employing the cavalry, partially and somewhat improvised as it was, may appear inefficient, but it also had certain advantages. Indeed, the deployment for battle of this time are characterised by forming up in a single line. If all the units of the line charged together, the riders would know that they had no possible support behind them. By engaging them successively allowed at least the option to support any squadrons in difficulty. Thus, at Moncontour (1569), the Duc d'Anjou sent a squadron of reiters and the gendarmes of d'Aumale to support another formation of reiters being hard pressed by the Coligny's cavalry. This also allowed a command without a reserve to deal with any unexpected opportunities or to support comrades in difficulty.

Ivry also provides a fairly significant example of attempts to combine the charges of the different types of cavalry, highlighting some of the difficulties and limitations this entailed. These combinations were often rudimentary, since, for example, the gendarmes of the Duc de Mayenne were preceded by *carabins* which were supposed, by their fire, to throw the enemy into disorder and thus facilitate the task of the gendarmes at the moment of contact. The effectiveness of this tactic is far from obvious since the salvo of the *carabins*

---

43 Périni, *Batailles françaises*, vol. II, pp.149–150.
44 Tavannes, *Mémoires*, p.115.
45 Périni, *Batailles françaises*, vol. II, p.146.

did not succeed in disordering the squadron of King's cavalry, which made a determined counter-charge and broke through Mayenne's gendarmes.

Cooperation between different categories of mounted troops were sometimes risky, and this could particularly be the case with the reiters. Usually, after completing their caracole, they would wheel around to the left to reload. This manoeuvre could be hazardous for friendly cavalry units coming from behind. Mayenne later attributed his defeat largely to this. There was no doubt an attempt by the vanquished general to blame others for the shame of his failure. Nevertheless, this explanation is perhaps not without some truth. After having executed their caracole, his reiters collided with part of the long line of gendarmes who had just begun their charge. This mistake reduced the gendarme's momentum and rendered their lances useless, just as the enemy was engaging with his own squadrons.[46] It may be for this reason that Henry ordered the 250 reiters accompanying him not to perform their traditional caracole and to charge with the rest of his cavalry.[47]

Finally, the Battle of Ivry is an opportunity to return to an aspect of which we have already stressed the importance: exploiting a local success on the battlefield. At squadron level a charge is only really successful if their captain is able to rally the majority of his men. He must be able keep his men in hand to face a possible counter-attack or to gain a decisive advantage. But this task was not easy. As Tavannes remarks, 'every charging squadron, though victorious, breaks by charging.'[48] The disorder is rallied, facilitated by the impression that the hard work is done, and that the danger is past. It was even more difficult, of course, when the charge involved several squadrons or troops. The leader, himself caught in the midst of the action, has great difficulty in holding his men together. Riders scattered, too confident and attracted by the possibility of loot. This is what happened to the Protestants at Dreux; the Catholics at Coutras suffered a similar misadventure.

We can see that rallying riders after a charge is one of Henry's main concerns. At Ivry, before the beginning of the fight, he showed his officers three pear trees forming a distinct mass behind the right wing of the enemy: 'That is where we will have to meet, my companions, I will be there, and if you lose your cornets, rally to my white panache.'[49] The famous anecdote of the white panache takes on great importance. It had a political dimension first, emphasised by Hervé Drévillon. They managed to make the white banner, previously a rallying sign of the Huguenots, the symbol of rallying to the monarchy and the colour of France.[50] But beyond the political and symbolic stakes, we must also consider a more prosaic tactical dimension. The anecdote testifies to the King's willingness to do everything possible to

---

46 Love, 'All the King's Horsemen', p.519.
47 Love, 'All the King's Horsemen', p.519.
48 Tavannes, *Mémoires*, p.123.
49 Périni, *Batailles françaises*, vol. II, p.146.
50 Drévillon, *Batailles*, pp.103–104. War is not limited to the battlefield; the political field is also invested. Henry must gather and convince allies just as much as conquer.

keep control of his squadrons in the middle of the battle. The ability to rally as many riders as possible is one of the essential elements of victory. The King's precautions were not unnecessary. After having defeated the gendarmes under Mayenne, he stopped under the three pear trees and waited for his men to join him there, as per their orders. He is soon able to deal with the three intact Walloon cornets who attacked him.[51]

This ability to retain and rally his troops is one of the hallmarks of the King's superiority, and very few generals could demonstrate such skill. But Ivry gives the example of another fact quite rare for the time: the exploitation of the victory on the battlefield, the pursuit. Coutras gave rise only to a limited pursuit. The three princes of Bourbon, tells d'Aubigné, advanced only a quarter of a league (about 1 km) then returned to the battlefield.[52] On the contrary, at Ivry, Henry led an active pursuit. No sooner had he obtained the surrender of the enemy infantry than he organised his army to pursue their fleeing cavalry, and he was able to take many prisoners.[53] The cavalry was called upon to play an important role in the pursuit, even if the gendarmes were less useful in this respect than the chevau-légers. The King's great interest in the latter also gave him a definite advantage in the pursuit of the vanquished enemy.[54]

It must be noted that the conditions of engagement of cavalry during the Wars of Religion were little different from those seen in the first half of the century. Cavalry units were still most often intermixed with the infantry battalions, although the grouping together in the first line at Dreux is a special case. Charges were rarely triggered simultaneously, were instead engaged successively, individually or in small groups. They did not generally follow an overall plan but respond to the circumstances and initiatives of the enemy. There were no large tactical movements aimed, for example, at outflanking the enemy line of battle.

The combination of the different categories of cavalry were actually quite limited. Most often it was a question of preceding the charge of the heavy cavalry by *carabins* or *argoulets*, or to attach reiters to chevau-légers or gendarmes, with the inherent risks associated with the method of fighting of the former. In fact, if the combination of reiters and gendarmes proved fruitful against the Swiss at Dreux, it greatly inconvenienced Mayenne and his gendarmes at Ivry. Finally, the cavalry was still faced with the problem of rallying riders and of the proper exploitation of successful charges. These are quite important points that constitute real limits to the use of this arm in battle, and it took all the skill of Henry to avoid the mistakes of Dreux or Coutras at Ivry.

However, it is interesting to observe that the increase of firepower did not lead to the decline of heavy cavalry on the battlefield. There was certainly no question of denying that the infantry now played a considerable role, that it had increased its firepower and that the most experienced infantrymen were

---

51 Périni, *Batailles françaises*, vol. II, p.149.
52 D'Aubigné, *Histoire Universelle*, Tome 7 (livres XI et XII), p.141.
53 Périni, *Batailles françaises*, vol. II, pp.150–151.
54 Love, 'All the King's Horsemen', p.520.

quite capable of holding cavalry charges in check. However, it was rarely the infantry which was key to victory. According to a recurring pattern in the sixteenth century, the key element of victory lay in the confrontation between the opposing cavalry. During the Wars of Religion, the infantrymen sometimes even appeared as mere spectators. The infantry of the League was utterly powerless at Ivry, and the Protestant battalions hardly had any impact at Dreux.

But we must now go beyond the simple case of France and its civil wars and observe heavy cavalry in action in the context of a major Europe-wide conflict. The Thirty Years' War, the major conflict of the first half of the seventeenth century, is particularly suited to such an analysis.

9

The Thirty Years' War and New Ideas

The sixteenth century showed us that some military theoreticians needed to seriously redefine their views. The French Wars of Religion clearly put paid to the idea of a 'relative and absolute decline' of cavalry, as Geoffrey Parker believes. It is true that their employment was still limited and informal, but this was set to change in the next century. Indeed, the first half of the seventeenth century, especially during the Thirty Years' War, saw major changes in the art of war, both in the field of elementary tactics and in the arrangement of the units on the battlefield, that is the establishment of shallower formations and of the 'wings battle' (*la bataille d'ailes*). For Michael Roberts this is the major benefit of the 'military revolution'.

Although initially thought to be more focussed on the infantry, these evolving tactical doctrines cannot exclude the employment of cavalry. Combined with changes in the structure of the cavalry charge discussed in Chapter 5, the role of cavalry can be reaffirmed. The years from 1618 to 1648 are fundamental to this point of view. Around such figures of Gustavus Adolphus and other great commanders, cavalry reacquired its essential place on the battlefield.

To better understand the importance of this period, we first need to review the place of cavalry at the beginning of the conflict. We can then consider the conditions that led from Gustavus Adolphus' input to the establishment of the idea of the 'wings battle'. Finally, we will see the extension of these ideas into the various theatres of war in the decades that followed.

The Battle of White Mountain (1620) is an illustration of the rather erratic employment of cavalry. At the turn of the sixteenth century, Maurice of Nassau (1567–1625) strove to introduce tactical flexibility and increase the role of firepower. He deployed his battalions in shallower formations and extended this to the entire order of battle. This gave the army more depth, deployed in two or three lines, and allowed for the majority of cavalry to be deployed on the wings. This was above all to give the infantry the opportunity to make the most of its manoeuvrability and firepower. Cavalry was not seen as a priority in the Dutch model, and this could have had the consequence of reducing its role.

THE NEW KNIGHTS

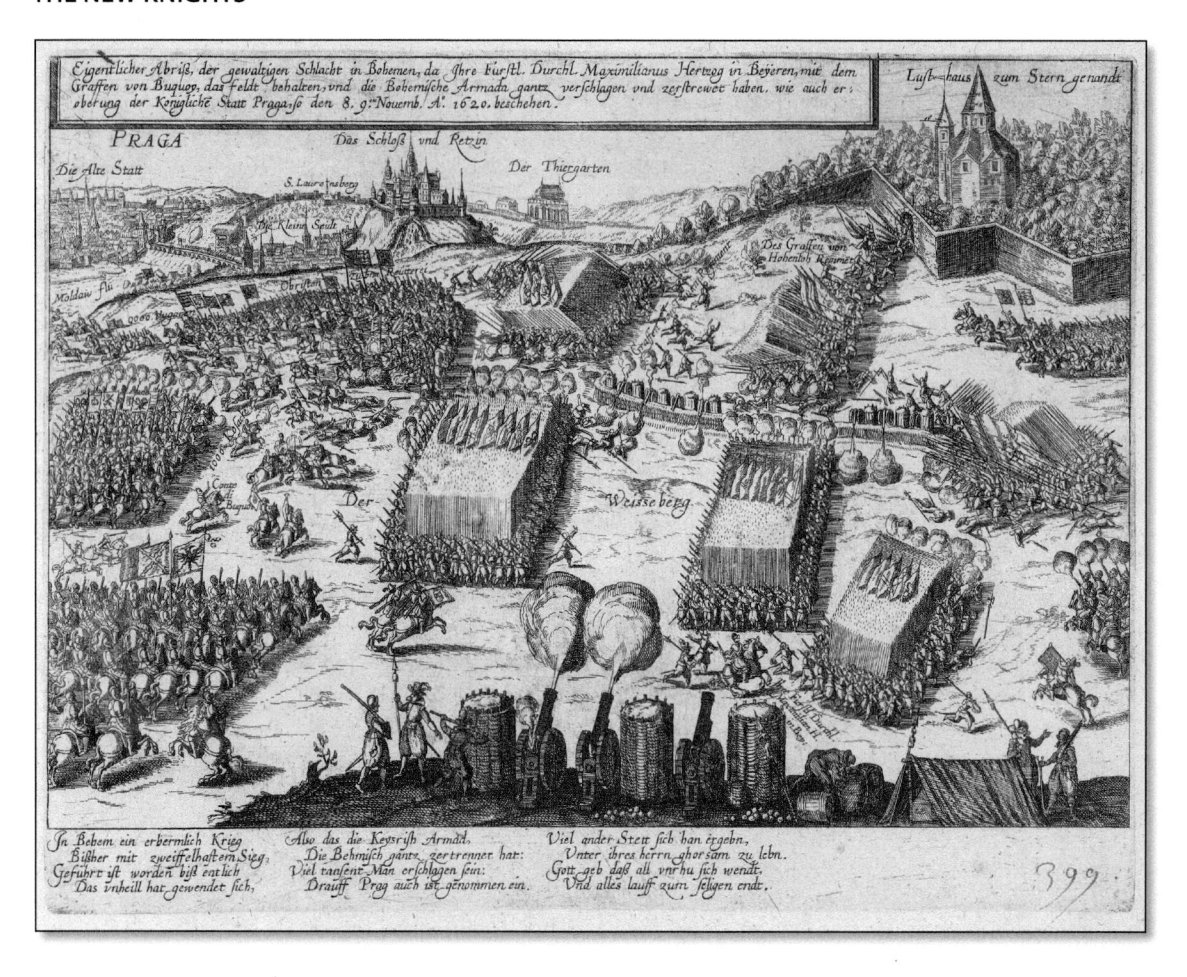

The Battle of White Mountain in 1620. Workshop of Frans Hogenberg, 1620–1622. (Rijksmuseum)

However, the most elaborate of tactical schemes are not necessarily, or usually, the easiest to implement in the field. Faced with the circumstances which led to the encounter, and the quality of the troops available, the generals took a pragmatic view. If Maurice's new doctrine was only introduced slowly, it suggests that the cavalry was never really relegated to a secondary role. We will therefore quickly consider the place of cavalry in military thinking at the beginning of the century before giving, with the example of the Battle of White Mountain (1620), a glimpse of his new doctrine.

When conflict begins it is influenced by different tactical models. The armies of Europe followed either the Spanish model or its competitor, the Dutch one, itself influenced by the French in their Wars of Religion. These different schools are relatively indifferent to the employment of cavalry. David Parrott emphasises for example that cavalry occupied a rather limited place in the tactical thinking of the Princes of Orange.[1] This principle is found elsewhere in the writings of authors inspired by the Dutch model.[2] It is the infantry that is at the heart of military thinking of the time, reflected

---

1   Parrott, *Richelieu's Army*, p.22.
2   Parrott, *Richelieu's Army*, p.34.

by its tactical organisation, the ratio of pikes to muskets and their handling. For Montgommery there was even too much cavalry in the French army, and the large numbers involved had several significant disadvantages. The difficulties of sourcing sufficient fodder compelled the squadrons to disperse themselves in camps distant from each other, which exposed them among other things to surprise attacks.[3]

There was also some reluctance to engage in battle. Strategic thinking was still in its infancy, but the preference of many authors was towards a war of attrition. 'The general,' says Billon, 'must conquer by length rather than by the chance of a battle, which is a perilous act to which one must come only by force and after the soldiers are prepared for perils and fights, because it's a place where novices are very surprised.'[4] This concept of war can only be to the detriment of the heavy cavalry, as a pitched battle was its principal reason for existing. And when authors ventured to consider the role of cavalry in battle, a clear hierarchy appears which favours the infantry. It is necessary, insists Praissac, 'that the cavalry is always arranged so that it always assists the infantry.'[5]

This preponderance of infantry should be considered carefully. First, because the theoretical innovations developed by the Princes of Orange, even supposing that they were truly revolutionary, were far from being applied in the field in their entirety. The tactical formations were not reduced in depth and lengthened as fast as the introduction of the Dutch model might suggest. Although they were less massive than in the previous century, battalions were still large. But above all, even in the Dutch army, it appears that the role of the cavalry in battle was far from a secondary one.

For Kees Schulten, Maurice of Nassau's victory at Nieuwpoort (1600) did not rely on his tactical and organic reforms.[6] It was the Spaniards, despite their giant *tercios* of pike and shot that were more massive than the Dutch infantry regiments, who adopted the most offensive tactics. Most of the fighting took place between the infantry of both sides, which were 'two hours continually in the hands, pikes with pikes', but it was the *tercios* which finally gained the upper hand and repelled Maurice's battalions.[7] Salvation came in the form of Maurice's cavalry. With great difficulty, he rallied a few squadrons and began a desperate charge that drove the Spaniards back and caused panic to break out among them.[8] It was therefore the cavalry that were decisive and which unlike that of the Spaniards, had abandoned the lance and relied instead on firepower associated with a relatively slower charge.

Maurice of Nassau was one of the first to deploy shallower units in a more elongated and deeper battle order, usually in three lines. This model may have been built with the infantry in mind, but it had obvious implications

---

3   Montgommery, *La milice françoise*, p.146.
4   Billon, *Les principes de l'art militaire*, p.155.
5   Du Praissac, *Les discours militaires*, p.20.
6   Kees Schulten, 'La bataille de Nieuport, 1600', *Revue Internationale d'Histoire Militaire* (n°78, 2000), pp.41–50.
7   G. Groen van Prinsterer, quoted by Schulten, 'La bataille de Nieuport, 1600', pp.46–47.
8   G. Groen van Prinsterer, quoted by Schulten, 'La bataille de Nieuport, 1600', p.47.

THE NEW KNIGHTS

Prince Maurice de Nassau at Battle of Nieuwpoort in 1600. Paulus van Hillegaert. (Rijksmuseum)

for the tactical use of cavalry, the most important of which being to group most of the available squadrons split between each wing. Their deployment on the wings allowed, at least in theory, a significant modification in the employment of the cavalry. Squadrons could then charge in line without the infantry getting in the way. They could also combine their attacks, support each other more easily or even conduct wide enveloping movements.

It is not certain that Maurice of Nassau really sought to fully exploit the new possibilities offered by the deploying squadrons to each wing, and that were smaller than the accepted deeper formations adopted by Reiters. The type of warfare waged in the Netherlands did not lend itself to the tactics practiced by the Dutch. Maurice's cavalry had abandoned the lance like the French, and relied mainly on fire tactics, and their cuirassiers advanced at a trot. Their use of the cavalry was a largely defensive one.[9]

One can question the influence that the Dutch model has had on the writings of the principal authors of the beginning of the century. Religion may undeniably have played a role in the case for French military writers. Montgommery, a Huguenot, was with Maurice of Nassau in 1600.[10] However, the lessons learned from the 'Holland militia' were mainly about the infantry. His observations on the use of cavalry were more marked by the French tradition. The association of arquebusiers or *carabins* with gendarmes or chevau-légers, advocated by Montgommery, was a frequent tactic during the Wars of Religion. Tavannes believed there were some similarities with Nassau's plans, notably in the grouping of squadrons placed as if on a chessboard in two lines. The Dutch influence is however not proven. Religion was not the issue here as Tavannes was Catholic. Furthermore, the writing of his memoirs was carried out over a long period of time, so it is difficult to

---

9   Roberts, *Cromwell's War Machine*, p.149.
10 Parrott, *Richelieu's Army*, p.28.

THE THIRTY YEARS' WAR AND NEW IDEAS

Squadrons of Dutch cavalry at Turnhout in 1597. Wenceslaus Hollar. (Wenceslaus Hollar Digital Collection, University of Toronto)

know when this passage was written. This observation may be more simply the result of his actual battlefield experience and/or his readings.

These two authors were not very thorough in their research. The details about how to lead a squadron in a charge are frequent, but little is said in the way in which one must dispose and employ all the cavalry of the army. This issue can be also observed in the two other major authors of the period leading up to the Thirty Years' War: Billon and Praissac.[11] These two writers are, perhaps even more than Montgommery, influenced by the Dutch school. Both advocated placing the greater part of the cavalry on the wings. Du Praissac, for example, who was well versed in the tactics of Maurice de Nassau, distributed 10 squadrons as follows: four are mixed with the infantry in the centre, the six others were divided between the two wings, each arranged in chevron and in two lines. However, these works do not take the analysis further than the previous ones. They suffer from the limitations of the Dutch model, where tactical thinking about cavalry was poorly developed. It may be added that Du Praissac did not seem to have any personal experience or familiarity with this arm, unlike Tavannes or Montgommery, and to a lesser extent Billon.

To a certain extent these works had the same theories and conclusions of two further authors who advanced ideas in the use of cavalry in combat at that time: Basta and Wallhausen. It is in Wallhausen's work that the general organisation of cavalry units appears to be the most advanced. This is shown, for example, by the two-line arrangement in chessboard formation, with reserve of a third line. Perhaps the Dutch influence played a role here. Wallhausen was the director of Siegen's school, created by Jean of Nassau, one of Maurice's cousins. Such influence would not be experienced by Basta, who was one of the leading generals of the Holy Roman Emperor. Wallhausen, however, does not

---
11   Billon, *Les principes de l'art militaire*; Du Praissac, *Les discours militaires*.

Spanish cavalry, Battle of Mariakerke (Leffingedijk) in 1600. Floris Balthasarsz. van Berckenrode, 1600. (Rijksmuseum)

fully espouse the model since the lancers he refers to were no longer used by this time by the cavalry of the United Provinces. Just as with the rather archaic reference to lancers, how to use them is also problematic. Wallhausen's work is too speculative. The 'fights' are carried out under the conditions desired by the author, and the enemy reacts according to his wishes. He did not take account the complex realities experience in battle.

If reflections on the organisation and use of cavalry has undeniably progressed by the beginning of the seventeenth century, there are still some important gaps. However, they were still incomplete and far too theoretical. Finally, it appears from the analysis of these different authors that there was a real difficulty in theorising about cavalry combat. This would include experienced men like Tavannes and Basta. This limit of theoretical thinking found its downfall on the battlefield, where it was difficult to rationalise how best to use cavalry.

The Thirty Years' War was born out of the revolt of the (Protestant) Czechs against the (Catholic) House of Habsburg. In 1618 they offered Frederick V, Protestant Elector of the Palatinate, the crown of Bohemia. The Battle of White Mountain ended the first phase (the so-called 'Palatine' phase) of the conflict.[12] This first great battle of the Thirty Years' War offered the opportunity for some useful practical experience to be gained. Facing each other were three very different armies. The army of the Bohemian State first, commissioned by the Prince of Anhalt on behalf of Frederick V, new King of Bohemia. Facing them were the combined armies of the Catholic League (an alliance of German Catholic States) and of the Emperor Ferdinand II.

This battle enable us to measure how far the Dutch model had been adopted and how it was applied in battle. The three armies adopted substantially different methods of deployment. The army of the Bohemia, about 21,700 strong, was arranged on two long lines, composed of small tactical units. This deployment may have been inspired by the desire to take advantage of the reforms of Maurice of Nassau, but other elements were also important,

---

12   Chaline, *La bataille de la Montagne Blanche*.

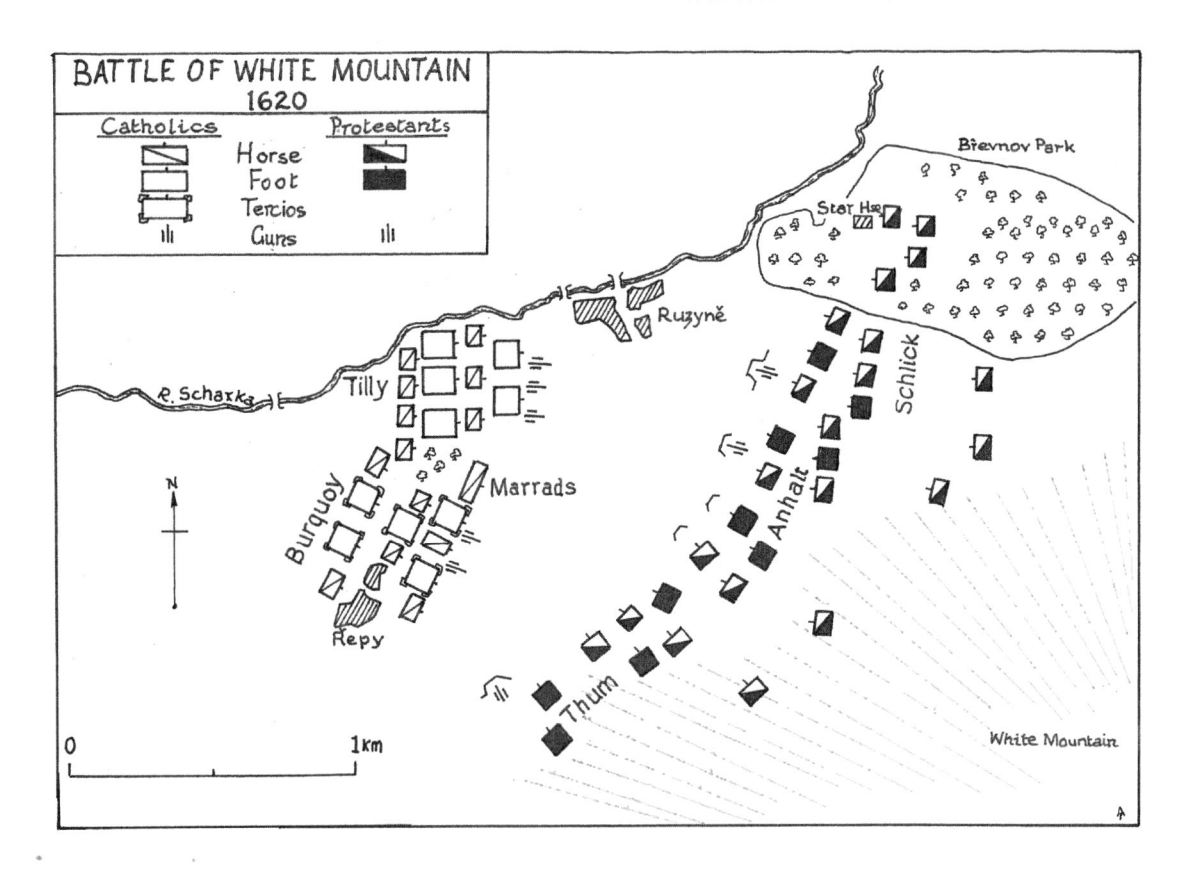

Battle of White Mountain in 1620. (Helion & Company)

such as the nature of the terrain and the numerical superiority of the enemy, which undoubtedly played a significant role.[13] Moreover, we notice that the Prince of Anhalt did not follow Maurice's doctrine as to the disposition of the cavalry. Maurice would not hesitate to deploy a few squadrons of horse within the infantry lines, but most of the mounted troops would be grouped on the wings. But at White Mountain, cavalry units alternated with infantry battalions. Did the commander of the army choose to disregard the new doctrine for using cavalry as developed by the Dutch, or did this deployment result from other external constraints?

In fact, it is difficult to determine precisely what led to this deployment. It is known, for example, that the troops arrived on the battlefield in a disorderly manner, which would not have facilitated the grouping of the cavalry on the wings. On the other hand, Anhalt was absolutely convinced of the unreliability of its units. It may therefore have been tempting to alternate between trusted companies and those over which there were doubts.[14] Finally these dispositions did not allow for any real reserve, and the 5,000 Hungarians placed behind the second line cannot be classed as such. As a result, the Bohemian army did not follow the Dutch 'model' very closely.

---

13   Chaline, *La bataille de la Montagne Blanche*, p.114.
14   Chaline, *La bataille de la Montagne Blanche*, p.115.

THE NEW KNIGHTS

Rather extreme cases of cavalry hand-to-hand combat, from J.J. Wallhausen's *Ritterkunst*. (Michał Paradowski's archive)

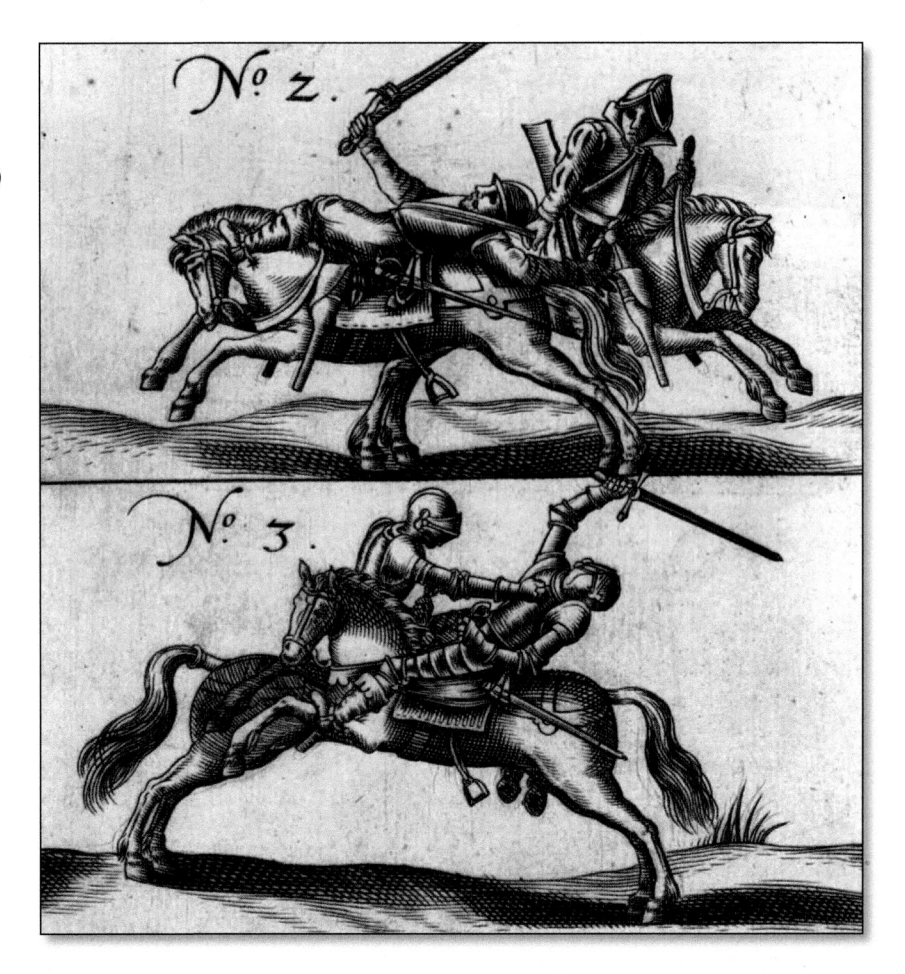

The deployment of the Catholic armies did not obey any simple principles either. It was divided into two large corps, corresponding to the Imperial troops and their League allies. Bucquoy,[15] who commanded the former, chose to deploy in a manner very close to the traditional Spanish model. At the heart were five massive squares, each from 1,300 to 2,800 men. These big units were arranged in chessboard formation to support each other. The cavalry was placed between these blocks and on the wings. This tactical pattern, says Olivier Chaline, was already considered somewhat dated at the time.[16] Bucquoy also defended himself after the battle, arguing that the errors of Tilly[17] (who commanded the army of the League) had forced him to adopt this formation. The army of the League, to the left of the Imperialists, was composed of units a little less massive but still larger than those of the Bohemians. The deployment was compact, and deep, with a first line of two

---

15 Charles-Bonaventure de Longueval, Comte de Bucquoy (1571–1621). Born in the Spanish Netherlands, he served first Spain then the empire. In 1618, Ferdinand II gave him the supreme command of his troops.
16 Chaline, *La bataille de la Montagne Blanche*, p.131.
17 Jean Tserclaes, Comte de Tilly (1559–1632), born in Wallonia, was one of the principal generals of the Catholic League and the Emperor.

infantry battalions, the second of only cavalry, the third of three infantry battalions and the last again with cavalry. Such an arrangement made mutual support between the squadrons difficult and suggests a predominantly defensive use of the cavalry. There is a distinct difference with the Imperialists' deployment. The positioning of most squadrons on the flanks of the *tercios* gave the Imperial cavalry greater mobility than that of the League. They could charge without having to weave their way around the infantry battalions and had the opportunity to support each other.

The Bohemians, the Catholic League and the Imperialists had cuirassiers and mounted arquebusiers. Neither side genuinely grouped their flanking squadrons, even if the deployment of the Imperialists allowed it, more so than that of the Bohemians and the League, to enable coordinated offensive action by the cavalry. However, despite these unfavourable conditions and a doctrine of attacking favouring the use of firepower and a slower charge, the squadrons did more than just stand fast. This was primarily due to the poor mobility of the infantry. The *tercios* were no longer like those of the first half of the sixteenth century, but they still contained substantial numbers of men. Added to this the nature of the terrain (the slope was unfavourable to the Imperialists), it is evident that the Bohemian cavalry, including the heavy cuirassiers, had a certain advantage.

It was these men who engaged first. To the right of the Catholic army, the squadrons (cuirassiers and arquebusiers) of the first Imperial line overtook the slow-moving *tercios* and advanced alone, in two groups, towards the Bohemians. The squadrons of the first line on the left of the Bohemian army broke away from their formation to meet the advancing Imperialist horsemen. They succeeded in defeating the first of these two groups, composed of arquebusiers and cuirassiers. The two squadrons of arquebusiers of the Imperialist second line then intervened and pushed the victors back in disorder. The second group, comprised of cuirassiers (under Marradas), were more successful and forced their opponents to retreat. Thus, the combat of the cavalry of the first line, supported effectively by that of the second, allowed Tieffenbach's Imperialists to open the way towards the heart of the Bohemian army. By contrast, the Bohemian second line cavalry did nothing to support their comrades or to address these setbacks. Faced with the danger represented by the advance of the Imperialists, the Prince of Anhalt planned to engage all of his left and centre. However, the success of the Imperial cavalry and the slow but imperturbable advance of the *tercios* had a considerable negative effect on the morale of his troops. So, when the Prince decided to order the counter-attack, many units fled, leaving the attack to falter.[18]

It is at this terrible moment that the charge of young Anhalt took place. Realising the danger of the situation, he put himself at the head of his regiment of mounted arquebusiers and led them in an impressive counter-attack. Located to the right of the Bohemian first line, he rushed at a gallop and crossed the battlefield to intervene on the left where his men were routing.

---

18 Chaline, *La bataille de la Montagne Blanche*, p.170.

THE NEW KNIGHTS

Imperial cavalry at the Battle of White Mountain in 1620. Workshop of Frans Hogenberg, 1620–1622. (Rijksmuseum)

This initiative was successful at first. He charged and defeated the cuirassiers of Marradas, then overthrew the other cavalry units of the Imperialists' first and second lines. He then turned against the German *tercio* to the left of the enemy first line. His riders seized an enemy battery and pointed it towards the enemy infantry. Then, supported by a regiment of Bohemian foot, they attacked the *tercio*. It suffered very heavy losses and was partly swept away. Fortune seemed to change sides and favour the Bohemians.

Thanks to its mobility, this cavalry was able to intervene quickly at any point of the line of battle and was thus capable of reacting quickly and decisively. It was a precious tool in the hands of a bold and determined leader. However, Anhalt's counter-attack failed. His regiment was not joined or supported by any other squadrons. The Imperial units could therefore reform and, reinforced by some of the League cavalry, repelled the arquebusiers who were now clearly outnumbered. Thus, the breaking of the German *tercio* did not bring about the defeat of the rest of the army and the Catholics were soon able to counter-attack in their turn. Here again the cavalry is in the first rank. The League horsemen sent to the rescue the situation did their job and the Imperialist rallied. Finally, the charge of the Catholic reserve, the Tuscan cuirassiers and the Polish 'Cossacks', completed the transformation of the Bohemian army into a crowd of panicked fugitives.[19]

---

19 Chaline, *La bataille de la Montagne Blanche*, p.170, pp.194–195.

The Imperial deployment, mixing infantry and cavalry, did not prevent any effective action by the cavalry. The squadrons did not fight directly alongside infantry but left their positions to fight separately. The fact that they were deployed in several lines, in a relatively loose order, allowed the units of the second line to come to support those of the first when they were in difficulty. They restored the situation and gave the opportunity to the defeated Imperialists to charge again.

The units at the disposal of the Prince of Anhalt were not of the same class as the Imperial cavalry. However, it also appears that the Bohemian cavalry was not used as efficiently as that of their opponents. Although the army was deployed thinly in two lines, with the cavalry, interspersed with the infantry, it seemed to act as it would have done in the previous century. In addition, support for units committed to the battle was not assured. This battle also reminds us of the paramount importance of the quality and experience of combatants. For David Parrott this factor may even have counted more than the tactics adopted.[20] His opinion is not shared by all, but it was nonetheless true that the Catholic army, with a somewhat denser and old-school order of battle was composed of determined veterans whose high morale had undoubtedly made the difference.

Finally, we saw that the arquebusiers fought in line alongside the cuirassiers. The example of young Anhalt shows that, although this was not common, these two troop types could sometimes face each other directly. The way charges had evolved encouraged this phenomenon. Firepower and trotting were favoured, as were tactics based on the caracole and its derivatives, which made it possible to avoid or mitigate the shock of frontal impact. This confirms the remark made by Wallhausen a few years earlier. 'No one keeps his rank or place [in the fighting], but everything goes backwards: the arquebusier serves as corasse, the corasse as musketeer, without any consideration of quality or quantity.'[21]

The Battle of White Mountain shows that there were different ways to deploy cavalry at the beginning of the Thirty Years' War. The Dutch model was far from dominant and in reality, the principle was often at odds with tactical doctrines. The persistence of traditional ideas did not prevent the cavalry from playing an important role on the battlefield, but it was nonetheless obvious that its actions were limited. The evolution of cavalry combat was also a factor. Heavy cavalrymen advanced at an often slow and very controlled pace. They avoided direct contact with the enemy, preferring to rely almost entirely on firepower. Perhaps the old processionary caracole was no longer in very common use, but its variants still constituted the main tactics of a charge at the beginning of the war.

---

20 'As a last resort, the Spanish, Imperialist and Swedish armies won battles, not so much because of their innovations and tactical practices, as because they saw themselves as elite forces, carrying a military national reputation for which they were prepared to go much further, in individual commitment and in sacrifice, than their opponents.' David Parrott, 'Strategy and tactics in the Thirty Years' War', in Rogers, *The Military Revolution Debate*, p.234.

21 Wallhausen, *Art militaire*, p.83.

THE NEW KNIGHTS

BATTLE OF BREITENFELD 1631.

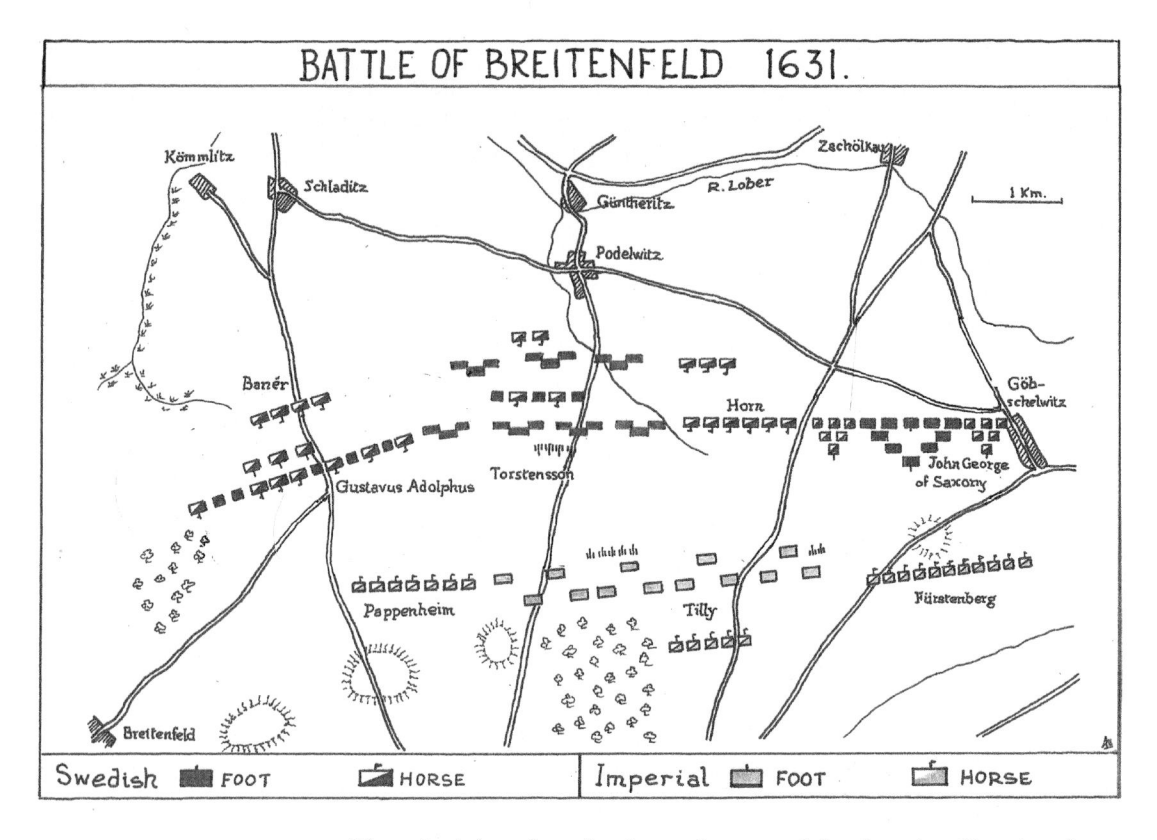

The Battle of Breitenfeld in 1631.

The principles of conducting a charge and the doctrine dictating the use of cavalry probably evolved in the following years, but the changes were marginal, and we must wait for the 1630s to observe a real turning point.

At Breitenfeld (1631) we see a new doctrine emerge. After the innovations of the Dutch, the next step in the progress of deploying and organising armies was taken by Gustavus Adolphus. With the Swedes, the thin and linear organisation was becoming more and more the reality of military practice. From the point of view of the cavalry, it is important to see how the improvements made by Gustavus in tactical organisation would modify the employment of cavalry on the battlefield. We have seen that the disposition of squadrons in lines grouped on the wings of the army was far from being general practice at the beginning of the Thirty Years' War. Yet this principle had become one of the foundations of European tactics by the end of the conflict. Could the 1630s be a turning point? To what extent would it have been encouraged by Gustavus's innovations?

The King personally only engaged in two major battles during the Thirty Years' War, but both have left a singular mark in the history of warfare. Breitenfeld, his greatest victory, will allow us to assess the originality of his deployment and of his doctrine in the use of cavalry. We may then consider more precisely the role played by Gustavus in the emergence of new tactical ideas: the battle of the cavalry wings and the charge in line.

THE THIRTY YEARS' WAR AND NEW IDEAS

Gustavus officially intervened in the conflict in 1630, standing as the defender of Protestant German freedom against the Emperor.[22] In July, he landed in Pomerania, then marched south, reaching Frankfurt on the Oder in April 1631. He then tried to prevent the capture of Magdeburg by Tilly. Unable to prevent it, he then confronted him at Breitenfeld.

The numerical advantage was with the Swedes. To their own troops (14,800 infantry and 8,000 cavalry) was added a corps of Saxon allies, 17,300 men in all, making a total for the combined army of a little more than 40,000 soldiers. Against them the army of Tilly gathered troops under the Duke of Bavaria and the Catholic League, numbering 31,400 men (21,400 infantry and 10,000 horse). It should be noted that most of the Saxon units were newly raised and/or poorly trained soldiers, far below the quality of the Swedes who were among the most formidable combatants of the time.[23] The high proportion of cavalry in the armies of the time was characteristic of the Thirty Years' War in this theatre of operation and is probably the first indication of the future role to be played by cavalry.

Medal celebrating Swedish victory at Breitenfeld. Sebastian Dadler, 1631. (Rijksmuseum)

There were some peculiarities in the Swedish deployment. First, the army was arranged in two main lines. The first had four infantry brigades and nine cavalry regiments, the second three infantry brigades and six cavalry regiments. Then there was a reserve deployed behind the centre of each line. The first line had a considerable reserve of two brigades and two cavalry regiments. The second was supported by two cavalry regiments. Finally, the bulk of the cavalry was grouped on the wings. The idea that the two arms could be mutually supportive was fully understood by Gustavus and he did not hesitate to place a few squadrons in reserve behind the infantry lines and to interpose platoons of 'commanded shot', musket-armed infantrymen, between his squadrons. Cavalry regiments and infantry brigades usually acted separately, and this was one of the basic tenets of Swedish tactics. This separation of roles, already advocated by Maurice of Nassau, was entirely in agreement with Gustavus's ideas. But the King went beyond Dutch doctrines. His army had a much larger proportion of horsemen, and he developed above all a far more offensive vision of the role of the cavalry.

The organisation and deployment of the Saxon army remained much closer to the Dutch model. The two wings were, as with the Swedes, composed of cavalry, and the centre composed of infantry, but the units of each of these three bodies were arranged in a chevron.

The deployment adopted by Gustavus's opponents is also illuminating. Tilly deployed his army in such a way as to reflect the old and the new of

---

22 Geoffrey Parker, *La guerre de Trente Ans* (Paris: Aubier, 1987), p. 197.
23 Barker, *The Military Intellectual and Battle*, pp.174–175.

THE NEW KNIGHTS

Swedish cavalry in 1631. From *Theatrum Europaeum*. (Michał Paradowski's archive)

the Spanish model. Notably, compared to the Battle of White Mountain for example, was the grouping of his cavalry on the wings, a significant indicator of the active role that he wanted to give to the cavalry, led here by the bold and enterprising Pappenheim. But the main body of the army, composed of infantry, suggests that Tilly was still hanging on the old principles of Spanish tactics. His infantry were grouped into seventeen large squares each of 1,500 to 2,000 men. These massive squares were arranged in groups of three in a single line, without a reserve.[24]

Some historians do not agree on the disposition of the cavalry. According to J.F.C. Fuller, Tilly ordered his squadrons to form up in two lines, like Gustavus. Thomas M. Barker, relying on the writing of Montecuccoli, instead said that the cavalry, like the rest of the army, was deployed in a single line. This is also the opinion of General de Grimoard, who wrote at the end of the eighteenth century.[25] The second hypothesis of a single line throughout, appears to carry more weight and it is on it that which we use to support our analysis.

If the principle of the distribution of the cavalry on the wings seems almost adopted by the early 1630s, the disposition of individual squadrons within each wing does not seem yet fixed: The Swedes arranged their squadrons in two lines, in a chessboard formation, the Saxons were in chevron and the Imperialists in a single line. The strength of the squadrons also varies from one army to another. The Swedes fielded units a little weaker (250 men on average) than those of their opponents and arranged them in three or

---

[24] J.F.C. Fuller, *Les batailles décisives du monde occidental* (Paris: Berger-Levrault, 1980, French edition), pp.90, 93. Several cavalry regiments were, however, placed behind the centre according to Barker, *The Military Intellectual and Battle*, p.179.

[25] Philippe Henri, Chevalier de Grimoard, *Essai théorique et pratique sur les batailles* (Paris: Desaint, 1775), p.123; Barker, *The Military Intellectual and Battle*, p.178.

four ranks, against six to eight ranks for the larger (between 300 to 400 men) German cuirassier squadrons. In doing so they benefited from lighter, faster and more manoeuvrable squadrons.

These differences should not make us forget the consequences of concentrating the cavalry on the wings. This positioning implies a doctrine for the use of cavalry very different from that which prevailed at the beginning of the war. It is no longer a question of successively engaging the squadrons (individually or in groups) by detaching them from the line of battle where they were intermixed with the infantry. These are larger masses of cavalry that will now be used en masse. More importantly, because of their placement on the wings, the squadrons are no longer bothered by their infantry getting in the way. They had a large space to manoeuvre. From then on, flank attacks and enveloping movements become possible, even decisive, as was shown at Breitenfeld.

The battle began in the morning mist with the first cavalry skirmishes, while Gustavus crossed the Lober, a small stream that separated him from Tilly's army. The latter did not take advantage of this favourable moment, choosing instead to wait until the enemy was within range of his cannon. This choice quickly proved to be an unfortunate one. Indeed, after a cannonade of two and a half hours the superiority of the Swedish artillery was proven. It was then, according to J.F.C. Fuller, that Pappenheim (who commanded Tilly's left wing) exasperated by the fire of Swedish cannons, took the decision to go it alone and attack.[26] So as not to be left behind Fürstenberg on the right wing also ordered his squadrons forward. In fact, it seems quite difficult to determine with certainty the way the assault started. Did the initiative really come from Pappenheim or did Tilly implement a preconceived plan?[27]

The fact remains that both wings attacked simultaneously. Pappenheim led all his squadrons to charge Banner, in command of the Swedish right wing. This movement alone illustrates the significant evolution in cavalry tactics since the beginning of the seventeenth century. The squadrons are no longer engaged in small groups, and the attacks now involve very large numbers. Here Pappenheim could count on nearly 5,000 horsemen. What we know of these men, as well as the tactics of their Swedish adversaries, allows us to reconstruct the combat between the two bodies of cavalry. We will content ourselves with 'following' a squadron from each side and observing how their confrontation unfolds. The size of the squadron is most relevant to understand the originality and effectiveness of the reforms operated by Gustavus.

Gottfried Heinrich von Pappenheim (1594–1632). Pieter de Jode (II). (Rijksmuseum)

---

26 Fuller, *Les batailles décisives*, p.92.
27 Nor is it impossible that the forward movement of the Swedish right to escape the wind and dust that came into their eyes led Tilly to engage.

Our Swedish squadron is deployed in three or four ranks, a platoon of musketeers standing at its side. They first advance towards the enemy at walking pace. The Imperial riders are getting closer. They are cuirassiers, formed in a massive squadron of six or eight ranks, advancing at no more than a trot. Highly protected, although not all necessarily had a complete set of equipment, they are undoubtedly quite impressive. Conversely, the Swedes do not seem especially imposing. Their armament classifies them among the mounted arquebusiers. Like their leader, Tilly, the cuirassiers have probably never taken seriously the use of such mounted troops in the face of heavy cavalry.[28] They expect these light cavalrymen to fire a salvo, perhaps two, and then break off from the fight. The Swedish front rank have unholstered their pistols, but is not shooting yet, not before the enemy. Finally, the cuirassiers arrive within range of the supporting musketeers and the platoon fires its salvo. This is unexpected, and even if it is not necessarily murderous, surprises the cuirassiers. Disconcerted, some hold their horses back, while others continue to advance. The disorder begins to spread in the Imperial ranks, and their cohesion is undermined.

Part of the Imperial squadron responds in a disorderly manner to the fire of the musketeers, but their shots are not very effective. In any case, they are not enough to damage the Swedes. The Swedish first rank then fire their pistols. Then, immediately, in accordance with Gustavus' orders and without waiting to see the result of their shooting, they discard their pistols and the whole squadron quickly falls on the enemy with the sword in hand. It is too much for the cuirassiers of the rear ranks. They have seen how their comrades were greeted by the musketeers' discharge. The salvo from the Swedish cavalry and the brutal attack which follows it is enough to convince them. They have in front of them an opponent resolved to close to hand-to-hand combat, not content to simply fire some salvos but intending to take the advantage by hand-to-hand combat. The morale effect produced by this vigorous action is doubtless added to by the enveloping moves undertaken by other Swedish squadrons. These are indeed on average smaller than their opponents, but their deployment in three or four ranks allows them to benefit from a more extended frontage. Attacking quickly, they try to outflank the Imperialists. Discouraged, the cuirassiers at the rear turnabout and flee. Those in front, mainly in the centre, do not have this opportunity. While they are trying to turn back the Swedes are already upon them.

The combat itself is then quite short. Gustavus's men reach the now disintegrating Imperialist squadron. The Swedes benefit from greater cohesion, and they complete the destruction of the enemy squadron. The speed gained during the final acceleration of the charge allows them to knock over the Imperialists who try to oppose them. The Swedes are much less protected than their opponents, so this superior shock is therefore a significant asset in the hand-to-hand combat. The heavy cuirassiers are less favoured in such a situation. The weight and bulk of their armour, and their limited field of vision, are disadvantages that should not be underestimated. With their

---

28 Roberts, *Cromwell's War Machine*, p.150.

sword, the Swedes can thrust into the weak points of the cuirassiers' armour: the visor, armpit, and lower abdomen (at the junction of the breastplate and tassets). The horse is obviously a prime target, and the Swedish swords are thrust deeply, turning the blade to widen and tear the wound.[29] Once dismounted, the cuirassiers, hampered by their armour, are particularly vulnerable. Guns are also used, fired at point-blank range which increases their effectiveness. The fight does not drag on, and the Imperialists flee and leave the field. If the enemy was strong and the conditions of a pursuit are not good, the Swedish squadron would not chase the fleeing cuirassiers. The Swedish riders regroup and return to take up position alongside the musketeers again. The latter have taken advantage of the charge to complete the slow process of reloading their weapons, and they are ready to deliver a second salvo if the enemy attacks again.

According to J.F.C. Fuller, the squadrons of Pappenheim still made six charges, all unsuccessful. At the last attempt, Gustavus decided to engage his second line, probably by a making a turning movement on the left flank of the enemy and managed to push them back.[30] The account of Grimoard differs somewhat as to how the Swedes finally won on the right wing. According to him, after his first failure against the Swedish squadrons and their platoons of musketeers, Pappenheim ordered the two squadrons placed at the left end of his line to outflank the Swedes. With squadrons now deployed in line, this type of manoeuvring becomes critically important. If the movement succeeded, the Swedish squadrons on the right would be charged both front and flank, and they would be unable to resist. Once these were put to flight, Pappenheim's men would have been able to 'roll up' the Swedish line. The flexibility of Gustavus Adolphus' tactical scheme, however, allowed him to thwart this attack. He deployed his second line on the flank of his first, and slightly behind, so as to block any attempt by the Imperialists to turn this flank.[31]

Another more limited manoeuvre of his squadrons then allowed him to take a decisive advantage. The Imperialists' failed enveloping attempt created a gap between the two manoeuvring units and the rest of the Pappenheim's line. Banner threw two squadrons into the gap to outflank these two isolated units. Already attacked to the front by the second Swedish line, they were now almost completely enveloped and had to fall back in disorder. Their escape

Spanish officer, siege of Breda 1624–1625. Jacques Callot, 1628. (Rijksmuseum)

---

29 Instructions given by Gustavus Adolphus himself on the eve of Breitenfeld. Brzezinski, *The Army of Gustavus Adolphus*, p.33.
30 Fuller, *Les batailles décisives*, p.92.
31 Grimoard, *Essai théorique*, p.123; Barker, *The Military Intellectual and Battle*, p.178.

THE NEW KNIGHTS

Swedish cavalry in 1631. From *Theatrum Europaeum*. (Rijksmuseum)

left the rest of Tilly's left wing uncovered and weakened. It was now the turn of the Imperialists to be exposed to an enveloping manoeuvre. This new blow, added to the fatigue and effects of the leather cannon[32] that accompanied the Swedish squadrons, completed the destruction of Pappenheim's men, and they withdrew from the battlefield, abandoning the ground to the Swedes.

While there may be differences about the course of the fighting, there is no doubt that the manoeuvring superiority of the Swedes was the decisive factor in their victory on the right wing. Their squadrons were a little smaller and less heavy than those of their opponents. They contain well trained and more lightly armed riders than the Imperial cuirassiers. Finally, only the squadrons of the first line were accompanied by platoons of musketeers and light cannon, and the others were free to their move more quickly. More mobile squadrons and less heavy riders gave Gustavus's men the opportunity to manoeuvre faster than their opponent. They were able to counter the enveloping attempt before carrying out a similar manoeuvre of their own. The fact that Tilly did not allow for a second line in his deployment is of course an aggravating factor. He did not have the necessary forces to repair the damage done by the first setbacks nor to protect his flanks.

Thus, a principle already well-known at the squadron level is confirmed on a higher tactical scale in the essential role of flanking attacks. Tavannes advocated very clearly at the beginning of the century their importance. A squadron that manages to attack their opponent in this way is assured

---

32 Developed by the Swedes, these small guns (three- or four-pounders) were made of a copper bore hooped with iron and covered with leather. They were easily transportable and had an impressive rate of fire for the time.

of victory. This truth retains all its strength if we now consider a group of squadrons. He who can outflank his opponent or take him in the flank gets a certain advantage. Pappenheim knew this very well, but the deployment and organisation of his squadrons and their slowness and their excessive depth, did not allow him to succeed in his manoeuvre. By comparison Gustavus adopted a tactic more adapted to the new doctrine used by his cavalry. Faced with opponents he knows are formidable, he combined defensive and offensive tactics. The former, based first on the co-ordination of squadrons of cavalry and attached musketeers and on the actions of his second line, allowed him to break the frontal charges of Pappenheim and defeat his outflanking attempt. The latter permitted him to take the initiative to attack the flanks and the rear of the enemy.

On the other wing, however, where the Saxons were deployed, the situation quickly turned to disaster. The cavalry of Fürstenberg repelled the squadrons of Elector John-George without much effort, leaving the Saxon battalions unsupported. Tilly understood the benefit he could gain from this situation. He removed some of his battalions from the centre and sent them to the right wing to cement the advantage won by his cavalry.

The Saxon infantry, mostly inexperienced, panicked and fled, abandoning their cannons to their adversaries. The Swedish army was in great danger. The rout of the Saxon corps exposed their left flank and rear. Victory would therefore belong to the one who could manoeuvre the fastest. From this point of view, the flexibility of the Swedish system again proves decisive. Horn, who commanded the Swedish left wing, first tried to gain time by launching an immediate counter-attack. Meanwhile, troops removed from the second line and from the reserve were moved to the left and are placed in a 'T' shape, forming a 90° angle with the Swedish first line. These measures allowed the Swedes to block the attempted encirclement initiated by Tilly. The fighting was fierce, but the Imperialists could not get through.

The recovery from the situation on the left gave Gustavus the opportunity to exploit his success on the right. The use of the cavalry by the King was a model of its kind. While some squadrons pursued Pappenheim's fugitives, the rest of the cavalry on the right wing began a rapid enveloping movement. First, they reached the heights that dominated Tilly's rear and seized his artillery, which was immediately turned against his former owners. At the same time, other squadrons from the second line wheeled and attacked the flanks and the rear of the Imperial infantry.[33]

The Imperial battalions were already in a certain level of confusion. Attacked now on all sides, they saw their salvation only in flight. The defeat of the Imperialists was completed without the intervention of the main corps of the Swedish infantry. Only nightfall saved the vanquished Imperial army from complete massacre. Gustavus instructed detachments of cavalry to lead the pursuit, and the harassed survivors of Tilly's army as they fell back in disorder to Leipzig.[34]

---

33 Grimoard, *Essai théorique*, pp.124–125.
34 Barker, *The Military Intellectual and Battle*, p.180.

Imperial officers and cavalry, siege of Magdeburg in 1631. Pieter Meulener, 1650. (Nationalmuseum, Stockholm)

The outcome of the battle allows us to draw some conclusions. One can of course, as David Parrott does, insist on the important question of tactical reserves. According to him, the Breitenfeld disaster is explained largely by the absence of an Imperial reserve, fresh troops that might have allowed Tilly, who was too sure of himself, to resist the Swedish offensive.[35] On the contrary, Gustavus Adolphus made very skilful use of his own reserves. The systematic use of reserves is one of the characteristics of seventeenth century battles. We are in a pivotal period. Furthermore, the example set by Tilly shows that the advantages of deploying in a single line, in terms of concentration of shock power, do not compensate for the disadvantages of such an arrangement.[36]

But above all, one can see the emergence at Breitenfeld of a new doctrine for the use of cavalry. The Swedish squadrons, shallower and more mobile, were now deployed predominantly on the wings, in chessboard formation and in two lines, with a reserve if the numbers allowed. It would be wrong to say that Gustavus was the creator of this model, but he structured a scheme that had probably been simply sketched out by Maurice of Nassau. The Swedish squadrons were arranged in line, and it was in line that they charged and manoeuvred. The ability to envelop the opponent, and to outflank his line, became essential. Finally, we see that it was on the wings that the battle was won. If each of the two armies won on one of the wings, then victory was assured by the one that was able to take advantage of their victory and exploit it. From this point of view, failure was obvious for the Imperialists. Tilly was unable to take advantage of the flight of the Saxon army to force the decision on the right. Thomas M. Barker sees it mainly as new proof of the tactical superiority of the Swedes, who know how to manoeuvre quickly to mitigate

---

35 Parrott, 'Strategy and tactics', p.232.
36 Parrott, 'Strategy and tactics', p.232. A principle reaffirmed by the Duc de Rohan, *Le parfait capitaine* (Paris: Houze, 1636), p.257.

THE THIRTY YEARS' WAR AND NEW IDEAS

the flight of the Saxons. Grimoard believes it was instead the competence of the general-in-chief that was in question, his indecision giving time to the Swedish left to be reinforced.[37] These two viewpoints are not mutually exclusive. Still, it is the superiority of the Swedish cavalry (to which the platoons of musketeers contributed) and the insight of Gustavus in its use which ensured victory on the day.

The tactical framework of the early 1630s is therefore marked by the adoption of a linear order, characterised by the arrangement of units in two or three more and more elongated lines, with most of the squadrons being grouped on the wings. Maurice of Nassau had initiated this pattern at the turn of the century, but White Mountain shows that it was far from being broadly adopted at the beginning of the Thirty Years' War. In 1631 thing have changed significantly. At Breitenfeld, although the Imperialists formed up in only one line, Gustavus and Tilly both placed their cavalry on the wings. The conditions were right for the model to appear, a model quickly adopted by most Western European armies, giving battles a very stereotypical character that great generals learned to use to the best. A model, finally, which gave the cavalry a considerable role in the outcome.

Swedish cavalry in 1631. From *Theatrum Europaeum*. (Rijksmuseum)

The expression (in the singular 'wing battle'), was used by Hans Delbrück to describe tactic whereby a general choose to attack on a wing using his best troops while he refused, in one way or another, his centre and the other wing.[38] It seems reasonable to reuse the term here since we have one of the essential principles, that is the battle is decided on the wings. However, it is necessary to modify the term slightly and to widen the scope. Indeed, unlike the concept put forward by Delbrück, there was an unwillingness to refuse a part of the army. The plural ('the battle of the wings') is the idea that both wings would attack at the same time, even where the success of just one of them would be enough to ensure victory.

The stripped-down theory is that from the 1630s battles were often won on the wings, and that victory rested largely on the performance of the cavalry. This phenomenon was, according to David Parrott, dictated by the changes seen in the use and effectiveness of the infantry. The development of firearms, their coordination with the pikemen and the use of field entrenchments could make the centre of the army virtually invulnerable to

---

37 Grimoard, *Essai théorique*, p.127.
38 Delbrück, *History of the art of war*, vol. IV, pp.274–275. This is the idea, summed up by Delbrück, that 'one seeks the decision in the battle not by a direct frontal attack but by an attack on a wing or a flank'.

a frontal attack.[39] The defensive power of the infantry forced the generals to seek a solution on the wings, where squadrons would have every opportunity, after defeating the opposing cavalry of course, to exploit their mobility and manoeuvrability.[40]

This pattern appears quite clearly from Breitenfeld onwards. At Lützen the following year, if the battle was tactically indecisive, it can be seen that Gustavus initially intended to carry the battle by a broad enveloping movement of his right wing. In addition, on the opposite wing, Bernard of Saxe-Weimar's cavalry twice threatened to outflank Wallenstein's right.

This evolution of tactics in play did not go unnoticed. At the end of the decade, Montecuccoli drew lessons from the battles he witnessed. He insisted on the importance of the army's wings, which became the key to victory, 'since if the enemy's wing is broken, he is vulnerable on his flanks and his rear, and it is impossible for him to resist.'[41] Battalions of infantry were more easily defeated without the protection of the cavalry supporting them on the flanks. Success on one of the wings, however, was not enough to guarantee victory, 'because an army is often victorious at one wing and defeated at the other.'[42] In this case, success would more surely go to the commander who was able to keep control of his troops and keep them in good order. Thus, at Breitenfeld, 'because the Imperialists, having dispersed the Saxons, went into disorder, and because the Swedes, having defeated the Imperial left wing, stood together, they won the battle and the Imperialists lost it.'[43]

The deployment of cavalry on the wings was, as we have seen at Breitenfeld, organised into two lines of squadron in chequerboard formation, and the squadrons of each line would normally attack at the same time. Gustavus's pattern of deployment became widespread in European armies. Military theoreticians, however, took a long time to take account of this evolution. Even in Lostelnau, which explicitly evokes Swedish tactical models, it remains difficult to identify clear principles on the organisation and action of the cavalry.[44] Only La Vallière offers a vision a little closer to the new tactical organisation of the cavalry. He specifies that 'one puts the infantry in the middle and the cavalry on the wings'. The squadrons of the second line are placed 'opposite the intervals' of the squadrons of the first line, in order 'that the troops of the vanguard [first line] being broken, they can pass between the intervals between the squadrons from the first line without overthrowing them'. He reports that, 'this interval is the width of the front of the squadron

---

39　Parrott, 'Strategy and tactics', pp.234–235.
40　This idea was already exposed by General Colin, *Les Transformations de la guerre* (Paris: Economica, 1989; 1st ed. 1911), pp. 91–92.
41　Thomas M. Barker, *The Military Intellectual and Battle*, p.84.
42　Thomas M. Barker, *The Military Intellectual and Battle*, p.153.
43　Thomas M. Barker, *The Military Intellectual and Battle*, p.120.
44　Colbert de Lostelneau, *Le maréschal de bataille, contenant le maniement des armes, les évolutions, plusieurs bataillons, tant contre l'infanterie que contre la cavalerie, divers ordres de batailles* (Paris: Mignon, 1648).

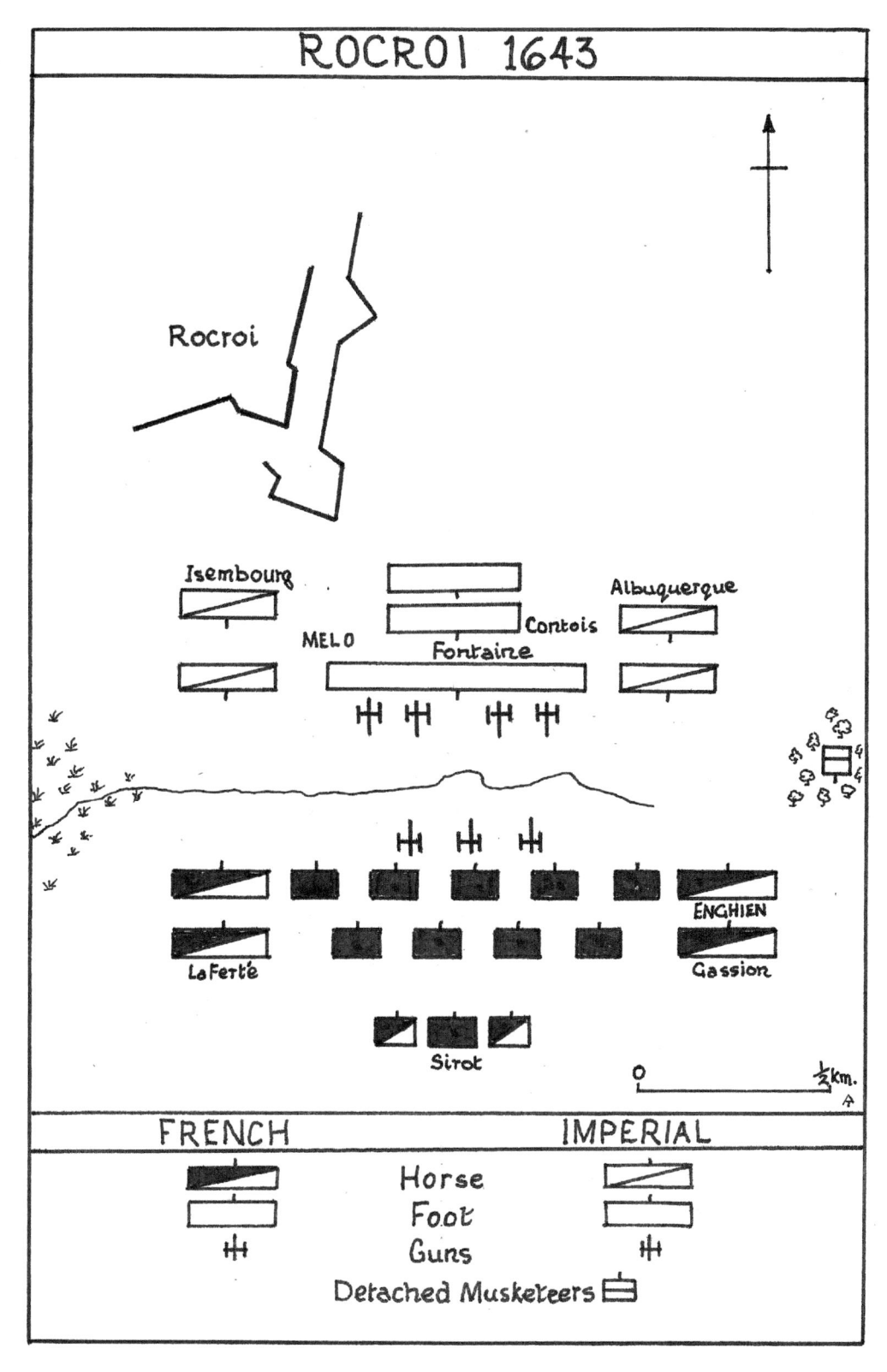

The Battle of Rocroi in 1643. (Helion & Company)

plus eight or 10 paces on each side.'[45] But his work was not published for the first time until 1652, some years after his death in Lérida in 1647.

However, in the field, the generals took note of these evolutions in the doctrines dictating the use the cavalry. The last decade of the war saw armies confronting each other who had all adopted the same organisation. Rocroi (1643) constitutes an example of this point of view.

Generals adopted this tactical scheme rather quickly, and the battle of the wings became the dominant model on the battlefields of the Thirty Years' War. One of the most famous is of course the Battle of Rocroi (1643), which could be considered as an archetypal example of the battle of the wings.

The circumstances of this battle, in the last years of the Thirty Years' War, are well known. Abandoning the traditional routes for invading France, the Spanish commander Francisco de Melo chose to enter France along the axis of Marienbourg–Rethel–Reims, a road barred only by the fortress town of Rocroi, which was protected by unexceptional defences. On 13 May he laid siege to the city. After a lively debate between the principal French leaders, it was decided, in accordance with the opinion of the Duc d'Enghien, that the Spanish army should be confronted and brought to battle. On the morning of 18 May the French army arrived on the Rocroi plateau where the Spanish was waiting, already deployed for battle.

The two armies were of roughly equal strength: 23,000 for the French and 25,000 for the Spaniards (who were only a minority in this motley army). The Spanish were also awaiting the arrival of reinforcements under Beck. The deployment of the two armies presents obvious similarities, proof of the convergent evolution of tactical doctrines in Europe. On both sides the infantry was in the centre of the battle line, with the cavalry grouped on the wings. The French and Spanish were also arranged in several lines plus a reserve, although views differ on the number of lines of troops in the Spanish centre.[46] The main difference was in the way the infantry units were deployed. The French battle array is more open and more flexible than the Spanish, whose five massive *tercios viejos*, had few intervals between them, forming almost a single mass.[47] This positioning had consequences on the frontage of both armies. Although less numerous, the French were deployed on a front of 2,500 metres, as opposed to 2,000 metres for the Spaniards.[48]

The cavalry was deployed similarly on both sides, in chequerboard formation in two lines. The French left had eight squadrons in the first line and five in the second. On the right, d'Enghien led 10 squadrons in first line and five in second. Opposite them, the Spanish had 14 squadrons on the

---

45 François de la Baume Le Blanc, Chevalier de La Vallière, *Pratique et Maximes de la guerre* (Paris: Loyson, 1652), pp.35, 37. It is in fact Jean de Laon, Sieur d'Aigremont, who published the manuscript by attributing to himself ownership of the work. The first edition on behalf of La Vallière dates to 1661.
46 Jean-Paul Le Flem considers only two lines, without reserve ('Rocroi', in Garnier, *Dictionnaire des guerres*). The Duc d'Aumale describes a deployement on three lines (*Histoire des princes*, vol. IV, pp.85–86). Finally, Périni thinks that the infantry was in two lines with a reserve of cavalry (Périni, *Batailles françaises*, Tome IV, p.23).
47 Laurent Henninger, *Rocroi, 1643* (Paris: Socomer, 1993), p.41.
48 Laurent Henninger, *Rocroi, 1643*, p.23.

The Battle of Rocroi in 1643. Solmon Savery. (Rijksmuseum)

right wing (two lines of seven each) and 15 on the left wing (eight in the front line and seven in the second).[49] The first lines were stronger than the second, because the latter had to be able to provide sufficiently wide intervals for the squadrons of the first line to retreat if necessary. The author Tjere was also of the view that because it was considered that the success of the first line could be the decisive factor in winning a battle, and therefore it was important to make it the stronger of the two.

The two armies faced each other, but despite the untimely movement of La Ferté Senneterre on the left, Melo refused to be drawn into the fight, preferring to wait until the arrival of Beck's 6,000 men. The battle only started the next day. Having learned from a deserter during the night of the imminent arrival of Beck, the Duc d'Enghien decided to engage without delay. At four o'clock in the morning, the squadrons on the right, led by the Duke himself, began to move. Taking advantage of the great flexibility allowed by their deployment in line, Enghien made changes to his deployment in order that the right wing could attack quickly and to the greatest advantage. He began by doubling his front, advancing with his 15 squadrons on one single line. At the agreed distance, the line then split in two. D'Enghien charged the Spanish front with eight squadrons. With the remaining seven, Gassion

---

49   D'Aumale, *Histoire des princes*, Tome IV, pp.85–86.

made a turning movement to take them in the flank. It was, however, the latter move which the Duke d'Albuquerque, in command of the Spanish left wing made up of Flemish horse, reacted to. Albuquerque began to turn his squadrons to face this attack on his left flank but was then caught by Enghien while manoeuvring, who charged his disorganised units in the flank. The first enemy line was bowled over.[50] D'Albuquerque, however, still had his second line, and he did not intend to give any ground. His squadrons rallied and a second fight began. The melee was tough, but charged from two directions by the French, the Flemish horsemen eventually gave up and fled. The Spanish left wing had been scattered in less than an hour.

However, as Montecuccoli very accurately observed, one can be victorious at one wing and defeated on the other, and that is exactly what happened to the French army. While the young general fought resolutely at the head of the squadrons of the right, those on the left under La Ferté, were swept away by the Alsatian veterans under the command of Isembourg. The latter immediately took advantage of his victory and turned against the French centre. The French cannons are taken, and several the infantry battalions were disordered in the confusion. The French army was now so compromised that La Vallière recommended retiring. Fortunately for the French, Sirot, who commanded the reserve, did not see it that way.

Raimondo von Montecuccoli (1609–1680). Christiaan Hagen. (Rijksmuseum)

The resistance offered by the French centre won d'Enghien precious time. He found himself atop a small mound and immediately seeing the seriousness of the situation, decided on what action to take. Rather than abandon the ground his men had won and turn back to rally his squadrons, he chose to exploit the situation and hit the enemy where they least expected it. Leaving Gassion with a few squadrons to prevent the return of the defeated Spanish cavalry, he ordered the remaining squadrons to almost about face and then charge onto the rear of the unsuspecting Spanish infantry.[51]

In a few minutes, the Walloon and German battalions were broken. Charging on, the French squadrons swung to the left and fell on the Italian battalions placed to the right of the *tercios viejos*. Engaged to their front by Sirot, who had seen the movements of his commander, and attacked in the rear by d'Enghien's cavalry, the Italian infantry fell back in disorder. The Alsatian cavalry tried to intervene, but they were too scattered to have any impact and were crushed between the victorious squadrons of d'Enghien

---

50 D'Aumale, *Histoire des princes*, Tome IV, p.101.
51 D'Aumale, *Histoire des princes*, Tome IV, p.106 f.

Imperial cuirassiers and Croats charging, Battle of Nördlingen 1634. Pieter Snayers. (Nationalmuseum, Stockholm)

and some of La Ferté's scattered squadrons that had rallied and returned to the fight.[52]

The last phase of the battle is famous, brilliantly portrayed by Bossuet. There was still 'this formidable infantry of Spain', which was of a different class than the Walloons, Germans, and Italians. The *tercios viejos*, the elite of the army, were arranged in massive squares, 'in big tight battalions, similar to so many towers'. They resisted the combined attacks of the French cavalry and infantry furiously. Finally, after three unsuccessful attacks, it was the devastating effect of the French artillery and their own dwindling supply of ammunition that overcame the Spaniards. The French cavalry alone would probably have been unable to do anything against these large squares of pikemen, flanked by musketeers and supported by cannons. Rocroi demonstrates however that in the hands of a skilled and inspiring leader cavalry could still be decisive, as their mobility and speed allowed d'Enghien to save the day, rescue the army from a very compromising situation and win the battle.

The main features of this style of battle are also found at the second Battle of Nördlingen on 3 August 1645. The ferocious infantry fighting that took place in the centre for control of the village of Allerheim did not impact on the final outcome. It was on the wings that the battle was won. The battle went the opposite way to Rocroi. On the right wing that the French were on the verge of disaster. The cavalry of Jean de Weert swept away the French squadrons. Fortunately for d'Enghien and Turenne, the victors did not exploit their success, and busied themselves in the pursuit of the fleeing enemy cavalry in search of ransoms and loot. On the left wing the French squadrons managed to put the Imperial cuirassiers to flight. They did not

---

52 D'Aumale, *Histoire des princes*, Tome IV, p.113.

lose themselves to the urge to pursue the enemy in seek of plunder, but attacked, supported by the captured Imperial cannon which were turned on the enemy infantry. When Jean de Weert and his cavalry wing returned to the battlefield as darkness was falling, it was too late for him to intervene and try to reverse the situation.[53]

The examples of Rocroi and Nördlingen, to which we can also add those of Marston Moor (1644), and Lens (1648) confirm the prominence of the use of the wings of the army, as put in place by Gustavus Adolphus at the beginning of the 1630s. Even if the idea of having the cavalry on the wings was not entirely his, he was the one who knew how to develop the practice and modify it to make the best use of it. His arrangement with the wings deployed in two lines was also effective enough to be quickly copied by most European armies. This gave a far greater importance to the cavalry in contributing to the desired victory. It allowed them to better utilise their natural advantages, speed and mobility. Although the exploitation of these assets was still limited by the frequent use of trotting and fire, the cavalry arm was now the decisive weapon on the battlefield. Deployed to the wings of the army and charging in line, the basis of the tactical doctrines adopted for the use of cavalry in later centuries can be seen to have their beginnings in the Thirty Years' War.

---

53 D'Aumale, *Histoire des princes*, Tome IV, p.440.

10

Cavalry During the Wars of Louis XIV

From the mid seventeenth century to the beginning of the eighteenth century, Europe experienced the many wars that marked the reign of Louis XIV. These conflicts were characterised by the importance accorded to siege warfare and by the considerable increase in the strength of armies in the field, but the nature of warfare did not experience any truly revolutionary upheavals. Of course, one could highlight the progressive replacement of the pike and the matchlock musket with the flintlock musket and the bayonet together with the reduction in the depth of infantry battalions, but the tactical framework remained one of a shallower deployment, as was first seen in the Thirty Years' War.

This relative stability is equally marked when considering the cavalry. The dominant tactical choice remained characterised by the placement of the bulk of the cavalry on the wings, with the squadrons arranged in two or three lines. Although it may be difficult to imagine that this organisation would be called into question in the second half of the century, it is not a waste of time to wonder to what extent it increased the manoeuvring capability. It is more in terms of permanence that questions relating to the weight of the cavalry in battle must be considered. The infantry, sometimes consecrated as the 'Queen of Battles' since the middle of the seventeenth century, did not seem able to play a decisive role on its own, especially as the pattern of the 'battle of the wings' continued. The relative weight of the cavalry tended to decrease by the end of the century. However, the stability of the tactical doctrines and of the role of cavalry in battle was at least valid until the War of the Spanish Succession. This conflict is often presented as an illustration of the limits of a shallow deployment and the 'wings battle', which could potentially have important consequences on the use and the role of cavalry.

Charging in line continued after the end of the Thirty Years' War, but there are still certain questions to be asked. The victories of Gustavus Adolphus, says Hervé de Weck, showed that the new way of employing cavalry gave it more mobility, and allowed it to manoeuvre more easily and more quickly.[1]

---

1 Hervé de Weck, *La cavalerie à travers les âges* (Lausanne: Edita S.A., 1980), p.95.

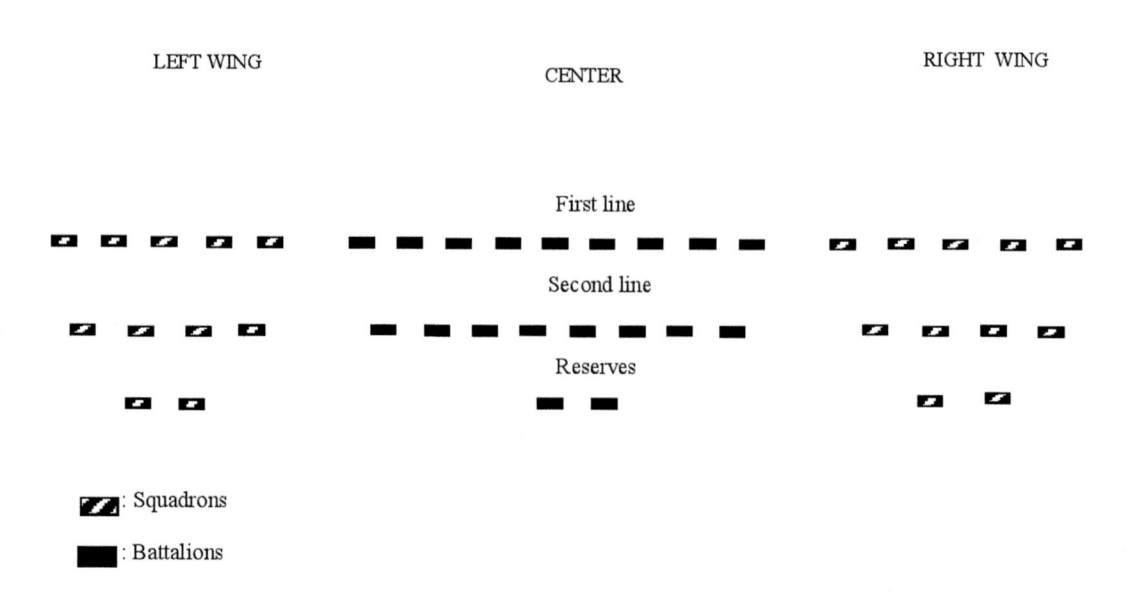

Army in battle according to the rules of "linear order", second half of the seventeenth- late eighteenth century.

LEFT WING   CENTER   RIGHT WING

First line

Second line

Reserves

: Squadrons

: Battalions

An army in battle according to the rules of 'linear order', second half of the seventeenth-late eighteenth century. (Author's diagram)

The tactical constraints and the limits of the cavalry of the time must not be neglected, even when under the leadership of prestigious leaders such as the Maréchal de Luxembourg. Consideration of these elements lead to the desire for a relatively simple doctrine, advocating more frontal attacks rather than manoeuvring.

The cavalry of Gustavus was clearly distinguished, at Breitenfeld perhaps even more than at Lützen, by its manoeuvring superiority. It must be said however that this superiority was much helped by the tactical choices of Gustavus's adversaries. Tilly still lined up big old-fashioned squadrons, heavier and less mobile than their Swedish counterparts; a disadvantage aggravated by the deployment of squadrons in a single line. The defensive deployment of Wallenstein's squadrons at Lützen also made things easier for the Swedes. In short, Gustavus faced enemies who had not yet adopted to the new mode of employing the cavalry. The shape of cavalry combat changed as soon as all the battle cavalry of the Western Europe's armies began to be deployed into two or three thin lines, consisting of small squadrons of about 150 men. It then became a little difficult to envisage large flanking movements as at Lützen or envelopment as at Breitenfeld. In both cases the presence of a second line made it possible to counter attempts such as these.

To this must be added the tactical constraints already mentioned in previous chapters. What all have in common is to considerably slow down manoeuvring. The slowness of deployment in line is the first issue. To surprise the enemy and try to outflank them, you must at least be able to deploy faster than him, and to charge before they have been able to organise their squadrons. But the armies of this era marched in columns, and the passage from column to line was done on the battlefield. Most important, in the second half of the seventeenth century and until the mid eighteenth, this passage from column to line was commonly carried out by a particularly slow processional movement.[2] To the slowness of the initial deployment was added that of the speed of the advancing troops and in the charge. The approach was a very delicate movement. The charge in line implies that the squadrons kept their alignment and kept their distance until the moment of contact. There had to be no wavering nor the appearance of gaps that the enemy could exploit to attack squadrons in the flank and break the whole line. This is why the advance was very slow, usually at no more than a walking pace.

This essential principle is barely mentioned in contemporary accounts. D'Aurignac is one of the most explicit on the subject: 'By marching towards the enemy, … every 50 paces, let us stop to give time to the squadrons and battalions to straighten up their lines as well as their ranks and their files.'[3] However Turenne is even clearer in his account of the Battle of the Dunes (1658): 'It was also clear that more diligence to walk would bring a great advantage, always taking a time away from the enemy to get himself in order: but an army corps which is walking in battle formation can only go a well ordered pace, and often it is necessary to wait a little for one and the others to be able to line up.'[4] These same reasons also dictated the pace of the charge. Given the quality of the recruits and the limited level of training they had received, the speed of the charge rarely exceeded a fast trot.

These constraints were accentuated by the considerable increase in the number of squadrons engaged in battles. While the Duc d'Enghien had barely 30 squadrons at Rocroi (1643), Turenne had 62 at Entzheim (1674), Luxembourg 80 at Fleurus (1690), and Marlborough and Eugene 250 at Malplaquet (1709). The battle lines lengthened in proportion; the first lines of the right wing and the left wing of Luxembourg at Fleurus contained 23 and 22 squadrons respectively, almost twice more than those of Turenne and Condé in Nördlingen. This lengthening of the lines not only increased the length of the overall deployment but also the difficulty in maintaining alignment.

Special conditions were needed for manoeuvres to be attempted and be successful. For example, d'Enghien created the conditions of surprise at Rocroi by launching his enveloping movement at four o'clock in the morning. But only commanders of high quality could order moves such as these and get away with them, and they needed experienced and well-trained riders to execute them. In Rethel (1650), Turenne, then in revolt against Cardinal Mazarin (first minister of the young Louis XIV), had a force of cavalry a little smaller than that of the royal army he faced. Interpreting the criss-crossing of some of the Royal infantry regiments as symptoms of confusion and

---

2   For a column that wants to deploy in line on its right, the first squadron makes a quarter-wheel to the right, advance to the location assigned to it and then goes in line by a quarter-wheel to the left. The squadrons who follow it then perform one by one the same manoeuvres and line up in succession on the left.
3   Azan, *Un tacticien du XVIIe siècle, d'Aurignac*, p.65.
4   Andrew-Michael Ramsay, *Histoire du vicomte de Turenne, Maréchal Général des Armées du roy* (Paris: Mazières et Garnier, 1735), Tome second, p.165.

serious disorder, Turenne decided to leave his position, however favourable, to exploit the situation he perceived.[5] His goal was to outflank the enemy right wing with the cavalry of his left wing. The balance of numbers was slightly unfavourable to him, since he could count on only 20 squadrons (twelve French squadrons in first line and eight Lorraine squadrons in second) against 23 of the enemy (fifteen in first line and eight in second).[6]

To compensate for this inferiority, he 'doubled' his first line by deploying six of the Lorraine squadrons from the second line to the left of the French. In a way, he is repeating d'Enghien and Gassion's manoeuvre at Rocroi.

The operation was accomplished quickly enough, and the enemy had no time to counter it.[7] The Lorraine squadrons constituted a solid and experienced body of cavalry, quite capable of this kind of movement. Turenne was thus left with a line of 18 squadrons facing the 15 royal squadrons. These were overwhelmed as each of the last three squadrons of the right of the line was facing two Lorraine squadrons. Turenne won this combat, but the right wing of the royal army did not collapse. Defeated squadrons from the first line retired to rally behind their infantry and return to action. Above all, Turenne had only two reserve squadrons in the second line, while the enemy had eight fresh ones. Exhausted and outnumbered, his squadrons ended up breaking off from the fight.[8]

The example of Rethel shows the limits of flanking manoeuvres. Although perfectly executed, it was not enough to ensure victory on the left wing. The enemy was too stubborn. Despite their defeat the first line rallied and returned to the fight, and the second line was not demoralised by the defeat of the first. There are, however, examples of successful manoeuvres. At Fleurus (1690), against Waldeck, Luxembourg undertook a much wider enveloping movement. The Marshal intended to take advantage of the ground, which concealed his movements from the enemy, to turn their left. At the head of his right wing, formed in column, he began a perilous march with only the cover of hedges and wheat fields, 'which were very high'.[9] Meanwhile, the left (commanded by Gournay) and the centre engaged to fix Waldeck's army, allowing Luxembourg to continue his turning movement. Having reached the desired position, beyond the enemy's left, he deployed his 37 squadrons in two lines (23 in the first, 14 in the second). Waldeck, seeing his army outflanked, ordered the second line of his left wing to counter the French squadrons. However, this cavalry was inferior in numbers and 'intimidated by its critical situation' and was easily broken.[10] Reinforcements from the second line of the right wing also failed to save Waldeck's left.

We can see that the effect of surprise, even if it was important, was not necessarily quite sufficient to guarantee the complete success of the operation, partly impeded as it was by the slow deployment of the cavalry columns, which

---

5 Périni, *Batailles françaises*, vol. IV, p.144.
6 Périni, *Batailles françaises*, vol. IV, p.144; Ramsay, *Histoire*, Tome second, p.68.
7 Ramsay, *Histoire*, Tome second, p.68.
8 Périni, *Batailles françaises*, vol. IV, pp.145–146.
9 Quincy, *L'histoire militaire*, Tome II, p.254.
10 Périni, *Batailles françaises*, vol. V, p.271.

gave Waldeck time to deploy his second line. Finally, despite Luxembourg's success, it appears that outflanking or enveloping manoeuvres remained tricky operations. They required daring commanders and experienced men. In addition, if they made it possible to gain the advantage initially, this was not always enough to obtain a decisive victory. Slow movement and the possible or more likely probable intervention of the second enemy line are the main factors that limited its effectiveness.

Even if they were sometimes used, flank movements and other enveloping manoeuvres were probably not the basis for the use of cavalry in the second half of the seventeenth century. For Brent Nosworthy, 'once the cavalry deployed with the enemy more or less in front of it, it finally engaged it directly. From this point of view, the action of two opposing regiments was reminiscent of medieval jousting, each unit representing a knight.'[11] The simplicity of shock, direct and brutal, is observed. At Montes Claros (1665), the right wing of the Franco-Portuguese was attacked by two lines of Imperial cuirassiers, supported by a third. These formidable riders literally rode through the enemy cavalry as if they were not there. They overthrew the first line and then put the second one to flight. Only the third offered any resistance, but it too ended up giving way.[12]

Brent Nosworthy's metaphor is interesting to a large extent, but it is not enough to accurately convey the proceedings of charges between opposing cavalry lines. The comparison that comes to mind rests in the field of dance. The fighting lines can be compared to a sort of warriors' ballet. Following the tactical norm of the time, the squadrons followed a sequence in which each cavalryman knew what he had to do and knew the movements that his opposite number would try to accomplish. The rules of this 'ballet' appear infrequently in writing, even if Vallière very quickly called to mind the principles.[13] These were based essentially on the successive engagement of lines. In a somewhat idealised manner, the 'ballet' could be described as follows: the cavalry, in two lines, advanced at the walk towards each other, when each of the first lines then charged at a trot. Before or after the impact, one of the two might yield, and the defeated squadrons would then run between the intervals of their second line in order to rally. This second support line advanced in its turn and charged the victors who, in disorder after the first combat, were also forced to move back behind their second line. This would then charge the advancing second enemy line to try to restore the situation.

This description is fine in theory, but the pattern laid out can be observed, at least partially, in a number of battles. At Entzheim (1674), according to Feuquières, the first line of cavalry on the left wing of Turenne's army was overthrown by that of the enemy's right. But the situation was re-established by the forward movement made by his second line, which contained the enemy and forced them to abandon the ground they had won, that initially had been occupied by the first French line, which then had time to rally.[14]

---

11 Nosworthy, *The Anatomy of Victory*, p.126.
12 Périni, *Batailles françaises*, vol. IV, pp.294–295.
13 La Vallière, *Pratiques et Maximes de la guerre*, p.39.
14 Feuquières, *Mémoires*, vol. III, p.244.

THE NEW KNIGHTS

Figure : charge in line by two cavalry wings : example of progress

Phase 1: The first line of the Gray is routed by the Whites.
Gray squadrons pass between the intervals of their second line to reform

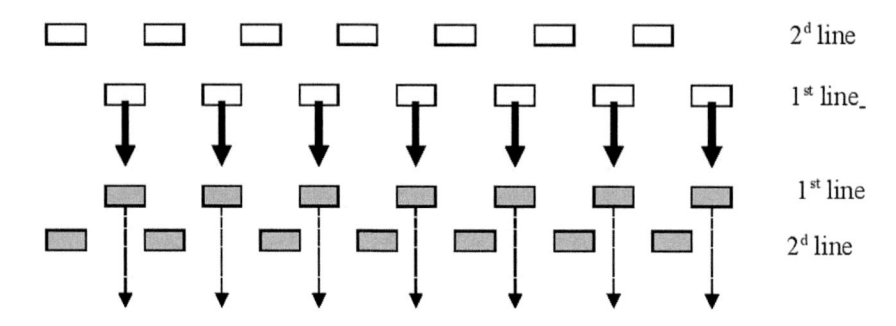

Phase 2: The second line of the Grays charges the victorious white line. This one, put in disorder by its success, beats a retreat and passes through its second line

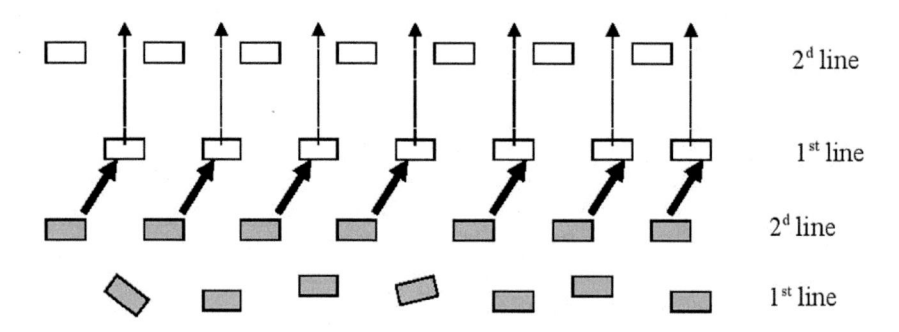

Phase 3: The second line of the Whites is shaken by the defeat of its first line, the officers can not retain the squadrons, the whole wing takes flight. The second gray line starts the chase.

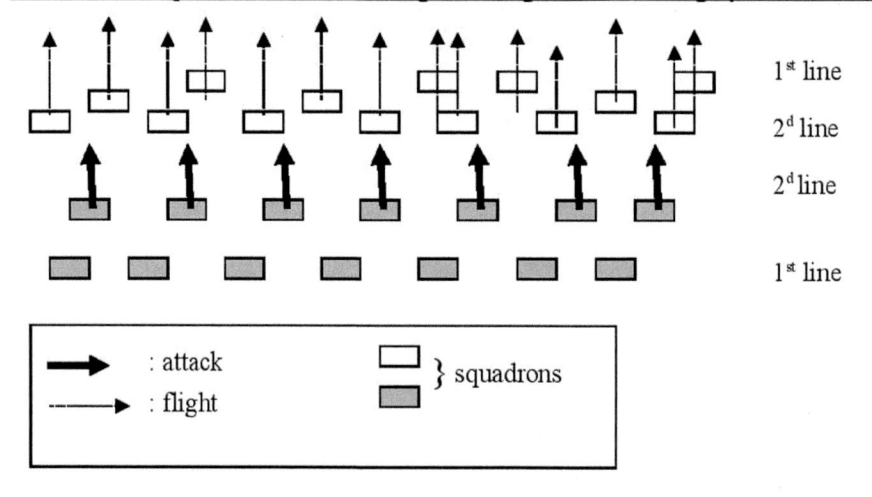

→ : attack
--→ : flight
▭ ▬ } squadrons

Charge in line by two cavalry wings: Example of progress. (Author's diagram)

At Staffarda (1690), the first line of Catinat's left, made up of squadrons of dragoons, were victorious when they charged the Savoyard squadrons. But they then had to face a solid second line of Imperial horsemen. The dragoons were pushed back and being unsupported (the second line was bogged down in the marshes), they had retreat far enough from the battle to reform safe from interference from the enemy. Once rallied they charged again and stopped the Imperialists. However, they would have needed the support of an infantry brigade to take a decisive advantage of the situation.[15]

In such a simple tactical scheme, it appears that victory is won most often by the side that has preserved its order the best. It was important to maintain good order and alignment before contact, so to approach the enemy with an advantage. But it was also necessary to reform quickly after the melee, whether the outcome was favourable or not. The winner must be prepared to face the second enemy line; the defeated to reform for a new attempt. In the case of opponents of equal quality and determination, the charges may come one after another until one of them could no longer reform properly or quickly enough due to the losses and disorder caused by the combat. This level of disorder would then be irreparable, and the unit was effectively out of the battle. So, rallying the squadrons after the charge became a crucial point.

Even when victorious, a line of cavalry remains fragile, exposed to a return of the enemy cavalry and from the fire of its infantry. It was therefore essential to have support from the second line. This is, in theory, the advantage of the tactical formations adopted from the mid seventeenth century. It was not uncommon, however, that the second line could not play its role. The squadrons that composed it, especially where they might consist of inexperienced troops, could be caught up in the panic of the first line, and ridden over and carried away with it in flight. Poor placement of the lines, without considering any constraints due to the ground, could also prove disastrous. It was for example a natural obstacle, the marshes, which at La Marsaglia (1693) prevented Quinçon's second line from coming to the assistance of the first.

The way the charges were conducted also sometimes deviated from the theory of the 'ballet' because the two 'partners' would shirk at the last moment. This is the case, for example, on the right wing of Turenne's army at Rethel, and on the left wing of Villars' forces at the first Battle of Höchstädt (1703). This phenomenon is raised in the context of the imminent impact between two squadrons, but it is also true for two lines of squadrons. At Rethel, the two lines turned back without approaching each other, and, according to Le Plessis, without even realising that their adversary had done likewise. It was ultimately the French Royal army who profited from this failure, their leaders managing somehow to rally their men and overcome the initial panic; on the contrary, the squadrons of the Comte de la Fauge fled without returning.[16]

---

15 Périni, *Batailles françaises*, vol. V, pp.287–288.
16 Périni, *Batailles françaises*, vol. IV, p.147.

David Parrott had observed that for the period covering the Thirty Years' War, the quality of the troops was often a major determining factor in the victory.[17] This remark remains valid for the years covered in this chapter. The experience of the riders and their self-confidence were essential to ensure the smooth process of the charge. Tactical strokes of genius are extremely rare, and generals were usually content to follow the principles of what was routine and what they had always done. In this context it is obvious that when two opposing squadrons faced each other, deployed in the same way and charging in the same way, it would the most experienced and the most determined who would be expected to prevail. The model of the charge in line is finally quite simple, adapted to the characteristics and limitations of the cavalry of time. It was based mainly on the 'ballet of the lines', and the enveloping and outflanking manoeuvres were little used.

The tactical doctrines changed very little, so it is not really necessary to discuss the evolution of the role of cavalry in the battles of the second half of the century. It would be more relevant to consider the question from the point of view of the balance between arms. The infantry, now an essential weapon, had seen continuous evolution of its armament and organisation. These transformations may have changed the balance of power within the cavalry, while helping to reinforce the pattern of the battle of the wings.

The evolution of infantry tactics during the seventeenth century is marked by two major phenomena, the reduction in the number of ranks and the very gradual disappearance of the pikes. At the beginning of the seventeenth century, the tactical formations of the infantry were marked by there being a relative diversity of ideas. If the shallow order took shape in the Dutch army, the Spanish school retained relatively massive and deep units (although the *tercios* are not now as imposing as their ancestors of the sixteenth century). The Thirty Years' War marks a first step towards the standard organisation of units. In the second half of the century, the coming together of the tactical arrangements for the infantry of the main European armies becomes more and more evident. At the end of the century, the battalions saw their manpower reduced to 715 men in France, 600 for the Swiss and Imperialists, formed up most of the time in five ranks.[18] In all armies, musketeers were now usually (but by no means always) placed on the flanks of pikemen. Throughout the century, the battalions were therefore affected by both a reduction strength and in the linear formation reducing the number of ranks, so extending the unit's frontage.

The evolution of the armament of the infantry is one of the keys factors allowing us to understand these changes. At the beginning of the seventeenth century, the pike remained an essential weapon. It was for many 'the queen of arms of the infantry', as Montecuccoli still said in the 1670s.[19] The pike however had to work with the musket, which replaced the arquebus. The limits of the musket are obvious. It was heavy, slow to reload, had a short

---

17 Parrott, 'Strategy and tactics', p.234.
18 Puységur, *L'Art de la guerre*, Livre I, p.57; Jean Nouzille, 'Les Impériaux aux XVIIe et XVIIIe siècle', in Bérenger (ed.), *La révolution militaire en Europe*, p.92.
19 Montecuccoli, *Mémoires*, p.17.

range and the firing mechanism were all weaknesses. These were only partially resolved with the growing adoption of the flintlock musket by the end of the century. However, even before these became the norm there was a gradual increase in the proportion of musketeers in battalions at the expense of pikemen. Maurice de Nassau was the first to establish a parity between the two arms within his units. Most European armies then followed his example. The decline in the proportion of pikemen accelerated sharply from the middle of the century, no doubt favoured by the introduction of the new model of musket. In the Austrian army for example, from the first years of the reign of Leopold I (1658–1705), there was only about one pikeman for every two musketeers. The decline of the pike is further increased with the introduction of the flintlock musket in 1684 and the socket bayonet in 1699 and pikemen disappeared from the Imperial infantry battalions by 1703.[20]

The logic behind this change is undoubtedly the same as that which led to the increase in the number of arquebusiers in the sixteenth century. Muskets could be produced in large numbers, they required only limited instruction and training, and they were ultimately easier to use than pikes. A State could easily equip large numbers of their men. The weapon was certainly not very accurate, but the quantity compensated for the quality. The tactical consequences were considerable and partly explain the changes observed previously. The generals quite logically wanted to make the most of their firepower, so they were tempted to thin and extend their formations, to enable as many musketeers to fire as possible at the same time. The decrease in the strength of battalions may also be a consequence of this phenomenon.[21] Before the adoption of the socket bayonet the protection offered by the pikes remained essential for the musketeers. It was necessary not to extend the ranks of musketeers so far as to be too far away from the decreasing number of pikemen, so smaller formations allowed them to better protect the musketeers.

Do these changes have any significant impact on the ability of infantry to effectively resist a cavalry charge? For Jean de Billon, whose writings reflect the art of warfare as it was practiced in the first decades of the century, there is no ambiguity. 'I blame all the soldiers who fear the cavalry for lack of judgment and to know the little harm it does,' he says without nuance.[22] The pikemen play a central role. Their defensive strength allowed the musketeers to fire while remaining under the protection of the pikes. It was even possible to integrate the pikes within the ranks and files of the muskets. However, these concepts were equally valid for the period when relatively large battalions were still in use and included an equal number of pikemen and musketeers.

Brent Nosworthy is of the view that the changes that took place in the second half of the century altered the situation dramatically. The drastic reduction of the proportion of the pikemen considerably weakened the

---

20 Montecuccoli, *Mémoires*, p.17; Nouzille, 'Les Impériaux', pp.92–93.
21 Other factors of course played a fundamental role: the manoeuvrability of the units or, more prosaically, the increasing difficulty for captains to recruit and maintain their manpower.
22 Billon, *Les principes de l'art militaire*, p.13.

infantry against the cavalry.[23] If we consider a French battalion of the end of the seventeenth century, with 650 men in five ranks, the pikemen (120) are in the centre in 24 files, the musketeers (530) are arranged in two wings of 52 files each (including grenadiers at each end). This formation makes the protection of the musketeers by pikemen much more difficult. When the cavalry charged, the musketeers sought shelter under the pikes, but with a ratio greater than one for four this operation appears to be rather complex. For the same reason, it was very risky to pass the files of musketeers between those of pikemen as such movements may have disordered the pikemen. This could also create dangerous gaps between their files, through which the enemy riders would seek to penetrate and break the battalion order.[24] The risk was even greater as the pikemen were no longer formed up then ranks deep. Their formation was much weaker and could be attacked more easily. The safety of the musketeers was not assured as the wings were vulnerable to cavalry charges, which would by extension weaken the entire battalion, as with the musketeers defeated or running away, the flanks of the pikemen would then be exposed.

Montecuccoli's observations in the early 1670s are not entirely consistent with this pessimistic view. According to him, the infantry retained a real capacity for resistance. 'A block of tight pikes is impenetrable to the cavalry, whose shock they themselves withstand at twenty-two feet of distance; and they push it even by the continual discharges of the musketry they cover.'[25] It is true that at the time Montecuccoli writes, the ratio between pikemen and musketeers was still about one to two, which perhaps allows a relatively acceptable level of protection. If we follow Montecuccoli's argument, do we think that the evolution suggested by Brent Nosworthy is not relevant?

At the end of the seventeenth century, the writings of Puységur leave little doubt as to the vulnerability of the infantry. A battalion equipped and deployed in this period would have little luck against cavalry. Although normally covered on its flanks by other battalions, to prevent or limit any possibility of envelopment, the outcome was often predictable. 'If the pikemen are firm, what is opposite [the riders who charge against the pikes] can stop when it is near, and the other squadrons go straight to the sleeves of the muskets, without the pikes to protect them; and if the sleeves are overturned, the pikemen then being turned, taken behind and in flank, can no longer defend themselves. In this formation the pikes were of no use against the cavalry.'[26] Maizeroy's judgment, in his *Théorie de la guerre*, also moves in this direction.[27] The rather unbalanced vision of the combat between cavalry and infantry that is described must be qualified. The human factor is most important, since we know that infantry made up of experienced soldiers would be much more difficult to shake or outmanoeuvre than panicked recruits. The terrain too

---

23 Nosworthy, *The Anatomy of Victory*, pp.29–30.
24 Nosworthy, *The Anatomy of Victory*, pp.30–31.
25 Montecuccoli, *Mémoires*, p.24.
26 Puységur, *L'Art de la guerre*, Livre I, p.69.
27 Paul-Gédéon Joly de Maizeroy, *Théorie de la guerre* (Lausanne: Aux dépens de la Société, 1777), p.lvii, lviii.

CAVALRY DURING THE WARS OF LOUIS XIV

Battle of Seneffe in 1674. Romeyn de Hooghe, 1674. (Rijksmuseum)

should be considered, where it is evident that infantrymen advantageously deployed or entrenched could offer considerable resistance to cavalry.

The last quarter of the century seems to coincide with a weakening of the infantry's ability to withstand cavalry. Mentioned by several military writers, this appears to be confirmed on the battlefield. The Battle of Seneffe (1674) repeatedly put the cavalry of the Prince de Condé in a position to confront the enemy infantry battalions. These events allow us to measure the relative superiority of the horsemen. In the second phase of the battle (between noon and two o'clock), the Dutch infantry established itself in the orchards and enclosures of the Saint Nicholas Priory. Condé ordered the Maison du Roi to drive it away. The Gardes du Corps, commanded by Fourilles, took the lead in the attack. Their losses were significant, the squadrons were forced to withdraw, but Fourilles managed to make a gap in the enemy line.[28] The Gendarmes and the Chevau-légers of the Guard, accompanied by the Cuirassiers du Roi, moved immediately to exploit the advantage won by the Gardes du Corps. The infantry was defeated, and the survivors fled in disorder to the village of Fay.[29]

Admittedly, this action involved the elite of the King's cavalry, and the Gardes du Corps bought their success dearly, but we remember the victory as one

---

28 D'Aumale, *Histoire des princes de Condé*, volume VII, p.510.
29 Périni, *Batailles françaises*, vol. V, p.97.

THE NEW KNIGHTS

The Battle of Fleurus in 1690. Jan Luyken, 1704. (Rijksmuseum)

of cavalry against an experienced and advantageously posted infantry.[30] Also of note, the attack was conducted in two stages in accordance with generally accepted principles. The squadrons were deployed in deep formations, the Gardes du Corps were at the front and charged first, while the other units held back, waiting to support them or take advantage of their breakthrough.

The last part of the battle, around the Fay (from two o'clock until nightfall), still saw horsemen and infantry fighting. On the French right, for example, the four squadrons of the Gardes are at the head of a turning movement. The three enemy battalions who oppose their attack, less favourably deployed this time, offered only very weak resistance.[31] The horsemen had been fighting since the beginning of the day, but they managed to push the infantry back quite easily.

Of course, cavalry did not always have it so easy. At Neerwinden (1693), the Anglo-Dutch troops of William of Orange were very strongly entrenched. After two failures by his infantry, Luxembourg, in command of the French army, sent his cavalry to assault these entrenchments 'that we could hardly

---

30 Fourilles himself had argued that the terrain was unfavourable for cavalry and to delay the charge. Scolded by Condé, he led the attack, where he was fatally wounded.
31 Le Pippre, *Abrégé chronologique*, Tome I, p.375.

climb on foot'.[32] Shot at from within pistol range, the cavalry was forced to retreat. Two other attempts had the same result. According to Saint-Simon, however, Luxembourg did not intend to order his cavalry to actually assault the entrenchments, 'but he hoped, by a general and audacious movement of this cavalry, to make the enemy abandon these entrenchments.'[33]

At the end of the Battle of Fleurus (1690), 14 elite Anglo-Dutch battalions, formed in a large square covered with *chevaux-de-frise*, managed to keep French infantry and cavalry in check. They escaped from the battlefield, leaving many dead on the ground.[34] This formation of a mobile square, the fire of experienced and determined soldiers, who did not panic despite their losses, were the main reasons for their successful escape. The Anglo-Dutch battalions were more manoeuvrable than the cumbersome *tercios* of Rocroi, immobilised on the battlefield. They also benefited from receiving the effective support of a few squadrons of rallied Allied horse. It is also probable that the French, seeing the battle won, and having already endured several hours of marching and fighting, did not display the same fury as the battalions of Enghien had, and who knew they had to win before the arrival of Spanish reinforcements under Beck. It is also noteworthy that the battalions of the reserve, sent by Waldeck at the beginning of the battle to contain the enveloping movement of Luxembourg, did not offer the same dogged resistance to the French squadrons.[35]

We can thus conclude that if the cavalry lost an important element of its shock power in the abandonment of the lance, this was compensated, in the last decades of the century at least, by a relative weakening of the infantry. The cavalry did without the lance and learnt to use their firearms and cold steel, as well as relying on their speed and manoeuvrability.

It is surprising that the authors of the second half of the seventeenth century give only a brief mention of the concept of the battle on the wings. In fact, very little is said at all. D'Aurignac for example, merely noted in 1693 that 'most battles have always been won when one was able to attack enemies by flanks.'[36]

Is this so surprising? All armies of the time now adopted the classic arrangement of units in two or three lines, with the infantry in the centre and the cavalry on the wings. Given the characteristics of these two arms, and the relative ineffectiveness of artillery, battles could hardly be conducted otherwise than by following the principles already discussed. Perhaps this was the reason authors did not consider it necessary to linger on this point? Montecuccoli also hints at the rather mechanical aspect of this tactical model: 'In modern ordinances, where all the infantry is usually put in the middle of the battle and the cavalry on the wings, that extend on several thousand paces,

---

32 Louis de Rouvroy, Duc de Saint-Simon, *Mémoires de Saint-Simon, nouvelle édition augmentée des additions de Saint-Simon au journal de Dangeau et de notes appendices par A. de Boislisle* (Paris: Hachette, 1879), Tome I, p.244.
33 Saint-Simon, *Mémoires*.
34 Périni, *Batailles françaises*, vol. V, pp.272–274.
35 Périni, *Batailles françaises*, p.271.
36 Azan, *Un tacticien du XVIIe siècle, d'Aurignac*, p.89.

it is clear that the wings being beaten, the infantry, who remains abandoned and have their flanks discovered cannot fail to be defeated.'[37]

The fact that the 'wings battle' model is not the subject of much thought or research does not prevent it from being a reality of warfare. There are further indications of the way generals thought and prepared for battle. This tactical doctrine serves as the basis for the organisation of manoeuvres and exercises. This is what occurred very clearly during the course of the great manoeuvres of Compiègne in 1698. The Chevalier de Quincy participated in the left wing of the 'army' which was expected to 'win':

> our two lines have charged with so much impetuosity those of our enemies that we routed them, and without losing for a moment a part of our cavalry folded away on our right to charge the enemy's infantry on its flank, while the other vigorously pursued their cavalry. The enemy infantry, finding themselves abandoned by their cavalry, was formed into a square battalion which we could never cut into, which obliged our generals to bring in cannon, which, by its continual and lively discharges, opened it so loudly that we entered with sword in hand.[38]

This story proves that practitioners incorporated in their exercises the tactical model of the wings battle as well as recognising the important role played by the cavalry. This role did not escape contemporary authors' eyes, since Mannesson-Mallet said in 1684 that 'it is from the cavalry that usually depends on the success of the battles and the most important undertakings of the war'.[39]

Many battles of the reign of Louis XIV prove that this scheme was also valid on the field of battle. At Cassel, in 1677, we see the battle unfolding in a very classical way. The two armies of the Duc d'Orleans and William of Orange, were deployed with their cavalry on the wings and the infantry in the centre. D'Orleans took the offensive, and the army was engaged along the whole line, after a premature move by Humières on the right wing.[40] The two French wings prevailed against their opponents, but the centre was in difficulty. Order was restored by the action of d'Orleans, who intervened with his second line. Meanwhile, the two victorious wings exploited their successes and turned against the enemy centre. Attacked in their front by the infantry, and on their flanks by the cavalry of d'Humières and Luxembourg, the Dutch battalions were forced to withdraw in disorder. At the Battle of Marsaglia (1693), it was also the success of the cavalry on the wings that allowed Marshal Catinat to emerge victorious.[41]

In most battles, however, the usage of cavalry remained very traditional. Few leaders could plan and execute manoeuvres of the scope of those carried out by Luxembourg at Fleurus. Noting the strength of Waldeck's position,

---

37 Montecuccoli, *Mémoires*, p.192.
38 Quincy, *Mémoires*, vol. 1, p.96.
39 Manesson-Mallet, *Les travaux de Mars*, vol. 3, p.87.
40 Périni, *Batailles françaises*, vol. V, p.194. Périni is inspired here by Feuquières (*Memoires*, vol. III).
41 Quincy, *Histoire militaire*, Tome II, pp.688–699; *Relation de la bataille par Catinat*, cited by Périni, *Batailles françaises*, vol. V, p.325.

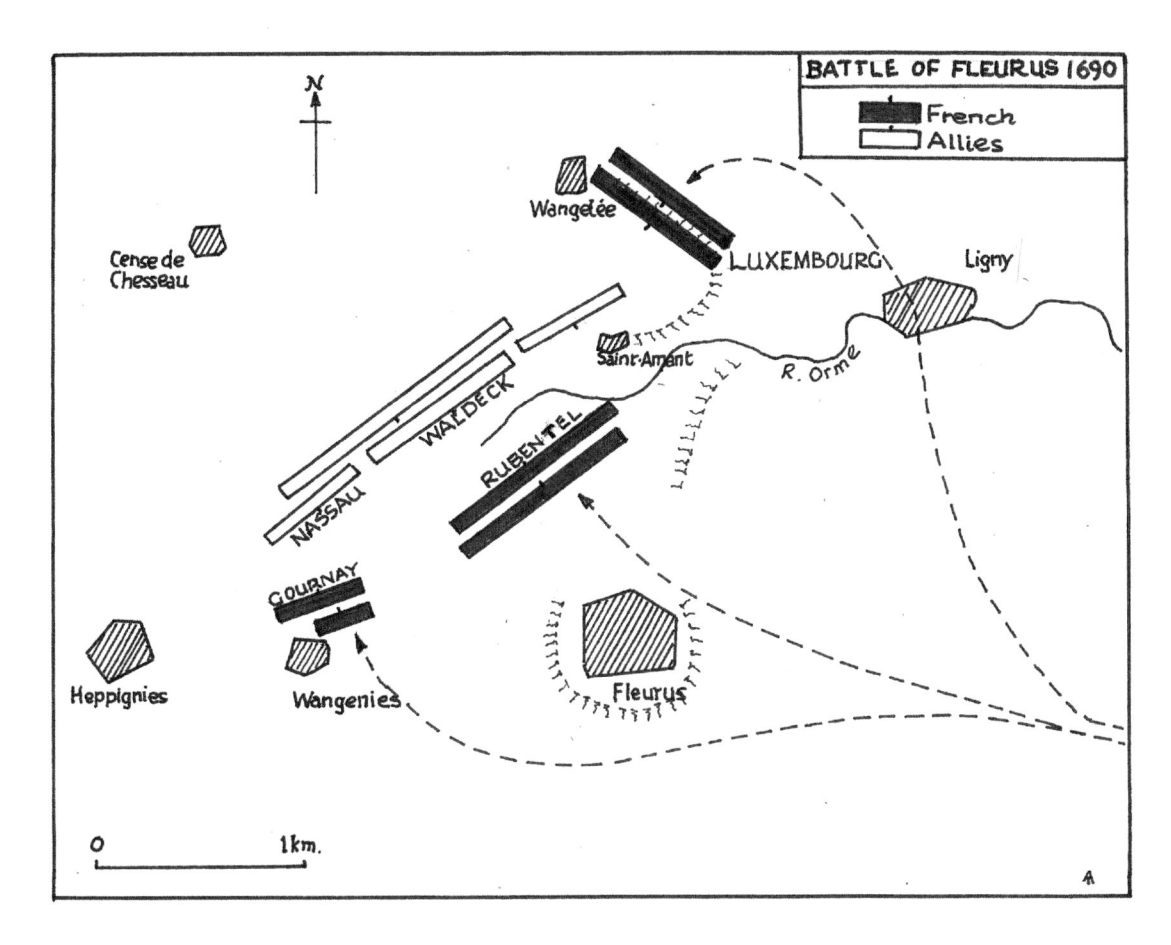

The Battle of Fleurus in 1690. (Helion & Company)

where 60 cannon supported the front line, which was also protected by two streams, Luxembourg decided to make a large turning movement that would outflank the enemy left wing.[42] The mission in the French centre and the left was to 'amuse' the enemy, to gain time to allow the cavalry column of the right to perform its movement. It was, according to Jean Perré, one of the first examples of the separation of divisions of an army.[43] The operation was not without risk since the French army was separated into two. Had he been aware of the situation, Waldeck could have exploited the gap between the two corps. But the fighting that took place along his front took his full attention, and he did not see Luxembourg's movement, masked as it was by the terrain. When he realised what was happening it was too late, and Luxembourg's men had extended around his flank and rear.

Waldeck was therefore in a very difficult position and was quickly defeated by the French cavalry. This manoeuvre was decisive in discovering the left of the enemy and preventing Waldeck from exploiting the partial successes won on his right against the French left. The latter then went on the

---

42 Périni, *Batailles françaises*, vol. V, p.267; Louis-François du Bouchet, Marquis de Sourches, *Mémoires du Marquis de Sourches sur le règne de Louis XIV* (Paris: Hachette, 1882–1893), Tome III, p.256.
43 Jean Perré, *La guerre et ses mutations, des origines à 1792* (Paris: Payot, 1910), p.288.

counter-attack, supported by the infantry of the centre which resumed the offensive. Attacked both from the front and on the flanks, the Allied army disintegrated. Soon there remained only the famous and aforementioned square of 14 battalions. They offered stubborn resistance but had no option other than to leave the battlefield. Luxembourg did not begin a vigorous pursuit on the evening of the battle, as the fatigue of his troops prevented it.

'This victory,' observes Jean Paul Le Flem, 'like so many others during the War of the League of Augsburg (Nine Years' War), was not exploited.'[44] Bertrand Fonck reminds us that the accepted practices of war and material issues multiplied the constraints on a victorious general. The army must be able to march, rally and regroup dispersed units, restore discipline and limit looting. There was also a real logistical log jam. For example, after Neerwinden supply problems prevented Luxembourg from pursuing the enemy. Finally, the strategic concepts held by Louis XIV and his entourage were sometimes another hurdle, as it was the King who imposed the delay on Luxembourg after Fleurus.[45]

The model of the wings battle favoured the actions of cavalry and allowed them to continue to play a considerable role on the battlefield. This was reinforced in the last quarter of the century by a relative weakening of the infantry. However, the place of the cavalry were closely linked to the tactical framework established from the end of the Thirty Years' War. But it was precisely this system, this tactical 'routine' that was challenged by the first great conflict of the eighteenth century.

The War of the Spanish Succession is often considered as the symbol of the ponderous nature of the art of war inherited from the seventeenth century. The shallow order is particularly questioned. Extending and thinning the armies in formations that were ever more extensive and difficult to move would have made battles as bloody as they were indecisive, as illustrated by Malplaquet (1709). It is important to understand to what extent the cavalry has been affected by these difficulties. Its doctrine of use is based on the charge in line of squadrons and on its placement on the wings within the framework of wings battles. However, it has often been considered that this tactical scheme, traditionally associated with the thin order, was neglected during the conflict, diminishing the role of the cavalry.

It must be said at once that the charge in line has remained an essential element in the use of cavalry on the battlefield. Neither the changes introduced in the morphology of the charge of the main European cavalries, nor the sprains made to the pattern of the wings-battle questioned this model, which remains valid throughout the war.

This tactical organisation, which constituted a line of squadrons in chessboard formation in two lines (possibly with a reserve) was still the most suitable for the cavalry mode of combat. It is not surprising then to find, as in the preceding conflicts, examples of these 'ballets' of the lines so characteristic of the cavalry clashes of this time. On the occasion of the

---

44 Jean-Paul Le Flem, 'Fleurus', in Garnier (ed.) *Dictionnaire des guerres*, p.321.
45 Bertrand Fonck, 'Les campagnes du maréchal de Luxembourg en Flandres, 1690–1694: bataille et stratégie', *RIHM*, n°76, 1997.

Battle of Blenheim (1704), Prince Eugene, who commanded the right wing of the allies, emphasised the succession of charges and their character little decisive:

> The cavalry of our right wing was repulsed by their second line, while their first line rallied, which we had defeated, our infantry was obliged to retreat too, it was brought back to the charge, and during that time our cavalry was repulsed a second time; but we rallied her immediately afterwards. The right wing then remained 60 paces away from the enemy for half an hour … We then charged them for the third time, and our cavalry was again repulsed.[46]

Another rather significant point of view is given to us by the Baron de Montigny-Languet, who took part in the same battle. Towards the beginning of the attack on the right, he rallied some squadrons of the gendarmerie who were fleeing and relaunched them in a charge against the English squadrons. 'Having defeated an English squadron, some gendarmes who accompanied me having been killed, I received two sabre blows on the head, a sword blow that pierced my arm and a bruise of a bullet in the leg, and my horse was injured.' He was then surrounded and, without hope of salvation, taken prisoner.

At the same time there was another charge of the gendarmerie, which was also repulsed.

> but some squadrons having made the English cavalry bend, those who took me were obliged to retreat at a gallop and to suffer all the musketry of M. de Tallard who was in the village, which broke them … The Englishman who had taken me in hand, having received a blow which made him fall from his horse and forced him to release the bridle of mine, I took it back as soon as possible to return to our people; but what sorrow for me when I saw that the English mounted grenadiers, who had already been repulsed, returned to the charge with the English cavalry, and once more overthrew all our gendarmerie and the cavalry which supported it.[47]

The testimony of this officer allows us to dive deep into the heart of 'ballet'. We observe the lively rhythm of the movements, the confusion that sometimes followed for the rider lost in the middle of charges and counter-charges. Confusion increased by the fact that, if a line could be completely pushed back, some squadrons could still rally and gain a local success.

There is therefore no significant change in charging in line. The need to maintain control of the squadrons during the advance of the line continues to preoccupy the generals. Even Marlborough, though an advocate of charging with cold steel refused to let his squadrons charge at a gallop. The fear of disordering the line of squadrons led him to permit only a quick trot.[48] Only

---

46 Letter from Prince Eugene, 25 August 1704, reproduced in *Mémoires relatifs à la succession d'Espagne sous Louis XIV, extraits de la correspondance de la cour et des généraux par le lieutenant général de Vault* (Paris, imprimerie royale, 1841), vol. IV, p.595.
47 De Vault, *Mémoires relatifs à la Succession d'Espagne*, pp.586–588.
48 Chandler, *The Art of War in the Age of Marlborough*, p.53.

Charles XII was sure enough of his men and their abilities to launch his lines at such a pace.

Innovations are ultimately marginal, although they could be very effective. Thus, Marlborough did not hesitate to gather large masses of squadrons, in order to have a clear numerical superiority to defeat the enemy cavalry at the desired moment.[49] At Blenheim, he employed no less than 80 squadrons in four lines, against 60 of Tallard's squadrons deployed in two lines.[50] As for his habit of inserting battalions between the cavalry lines, it reinforced the effect of the charge in line more than it modified the basic principle. Thus, at Blenheim again, entire battalions supported the cavalry attempting to cross the Nebel. However, care was taken to leave between them a space wide enough if it was necessary for the cavalry to reform under their protection.

The second half of the seventeenth century could not have been more conservative in the field of grand tactics. Generals were reluctant to innovate, and only the most brilliant attempted original tactics or bold initiatives. Thus, at the beginning of the eighteenth century, we arrived at the establishment of a fixed and reassuring tactical routine. Guillaume Le Blond exposed it in the *Encyclopédie* in 1751: seven maxims set the rules to form up an army in two lines, separated by 300 paces, with a reserve behind the second. The units of the second line were arranged opposite the intervals of the first, the infantry was in the centre and the cavalry on the wings.[51] This tactical scheme induced a model of battle with an often stereotypical outcome: the 'wings battle'. It was therefore in this order that the action of the cavalry on the battlefield was set. But this framework seemed to reach its limits during the War of the Spanish Succession.

The last conflict of the reign saw the progressive adoption of the flintlock musket and the bayonet. This modernisation increased the firepower of the infantry and increased resistance to cavalry attacks. We also saw a significant extension of the deployment area, due to the linear order and to the considerable increase in an army's strength.

The combination of these different elements led to a form of tactical stalemate. Quite paradoxically, the increase in firepower resulted in troops being almost tactically immobilised[52.] No doubt the stopping power of infantry and artillery made it possible to counter an assault by enemy cavalry, but the armies now no longer had any significant attacking capability.[53] The fighting took the form of murderous but not decisive frontal attacks.[54] Folar compared the battles of the War of the Spanish Succession with those of 'two naval fleets which flow reciprocally without ever coming alongside each other.'[55] The inability of the winner to pursue the vanquished and exploit his victory completed this impression of stalemate.

---

49 Chandler, *The Art of War in the Age of Marlborough*.
50 Grbasic and Vuksic, *L'âge d'or de la cavalerie*, p.53.
51 Guillaume Le Blond, 'Armée', Diderot and Le Rond d'Alembert, *Encyclopédie*, vol. I, p.89.
52 Bois, *Maurice de Saxe*, p.208.
53 Jean-Pierre Bois, *Les guerres en Europe 1494–1792* (Paris: Belin, 1993), p.249.
54 Perré, *La guerre et ses mutations*, p.302.
55 Quoted by Eric Muraise, *Introduction à l'histoire militaire* (Paris: Lavauzelle, 1964), p.161.

Battle of Malplaquet in 1709. Jan van Huchtenburg, 1727–1729. (Rijksmuseum)

The most commonly cited example to illustrate this phenomenon is the Battle of Malplaquet (1709). The numbers engaged are considerable: 65,000 French confront 90,000 allies (in comparison, at Fleurus there were 41,000 and 37,000 respectively), arranged on a front of more than three miles.[56] The lines were very long, but we see especially that neither side adhered to the 'classical' battle order. The French adopted a defensive position. Their left wing was covered by the Bois de Sart, their right rested on the Bois de Lainières, and the centre occupied the gap between the two. The troops in this gap were protected by entrenchments. It was therefore logic that the infantry that occupied the first lines, with the cavalry deployed in the second. The Allies did the same. The wings are the scene of long and bloody fighting. The Allies managed to drive the French out of the Bois de Sart, but they could not take any decisive advantage from this gain. The fate of the battle was to be in the centre, where the Allies took the entrenchments and cannon that occupied them. They were then able pass their cavalry across the entrenchments and exploit this success. The squadrons of the Maison du Roi executed several

---

56 Corvisier, *Histoire militaire de la France*, Tome I, p.540.

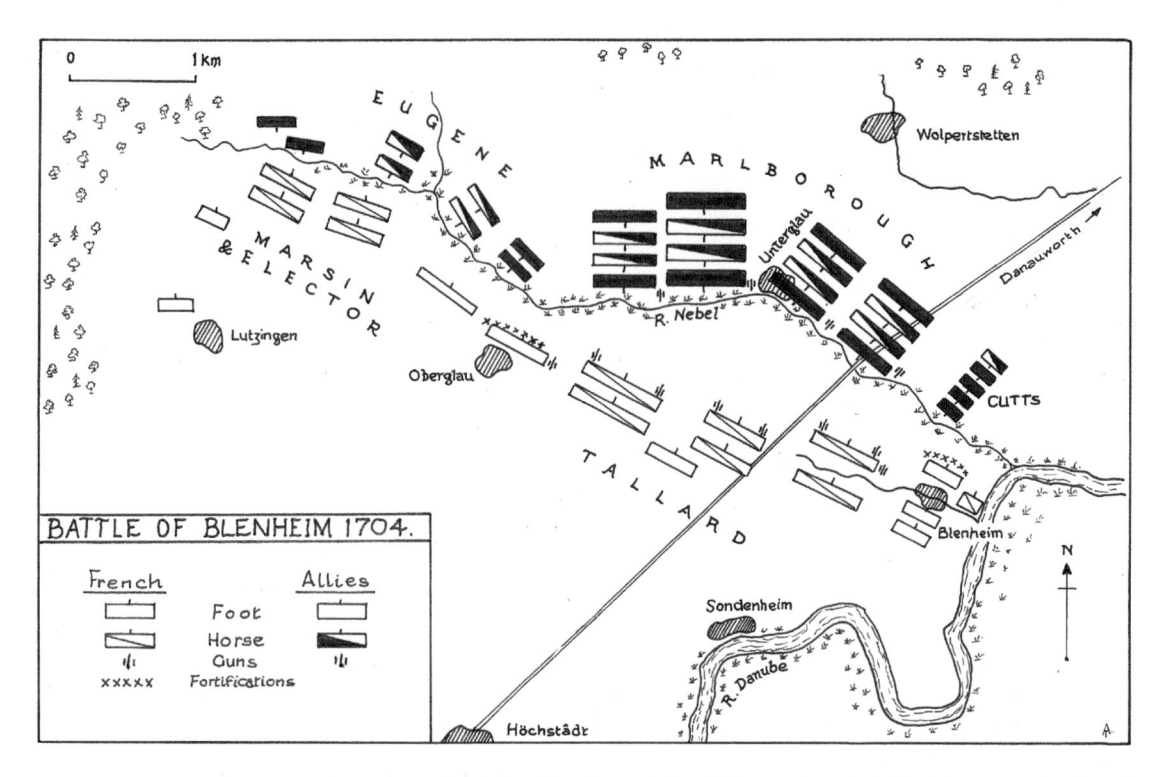

The Battle of Blenheim in 1704: same limited use of cavalry? (Helion & Company).

charges against the Dutch and English cavalry, but they are repulsed each time by the infantry now occupying the entrenchments. The French had no option other than to retreat.[57]

The tactic stalemate here is quite obvious. The cavalry had only a secondary role, manoeuvring was impossible, and the battle was decided by a deadly frontal attack with no decisive result (in the short term at least). However, the situation was perhaps more complex than it seemed, and it would be dangerous to make sweeping generalisations based on the sole example of Malplaquet. The model of the wings battle is found again and again in other battles. This is the case for example in Höchstädt (1703), Almanza (1707), and Villaviciosa (1710). But above all, to judge the reality of any tactical stalemate and a possible weakening of the cavalry, it is necessary to turn to the greatest battles of the war.

Höchstädt-Blenheim (1704), Ramillies (1706) and Oudenaarde (1708) have a number of similarities with Malplaquet. The strengths first,[58] the extent of the battlefield then (a little more than three and a half miles in the case of Blenheim and Ramillies), which complicated the task of effective command. Finally, the relative freedom taken with the tactical 'routine', mainly at Blenheim, should be highlighted. This phenomenon can be explained by the circumstances and the tactical choices made by the commanders. At Blenheim, each of the two armies were divided into two technically

---

57 Jean-paul Le Flem, 'Malplaquet', in Garnier, *Dictionnaire des guerres*, pp.525–527.
58 More than 100,000 men engaged in the first, 120,000 in the second, 160,000 in the last. Corvisier, *Histoire militaire*, p.540.

autonomous corps.[59] The infantry–cavalry mix also favoured Marlborough's tactical ideas, where, for example at Blenheim, entire battalions supported the cavalry attempting to cross the Nebel.[60]

Beyond these common points, are there signs of tactical indecision, and the same limited use of cavalry? Blenheim is perhaps the battle which at first glance is closest to Malplaquet. The principles of the accepted tactics of the time were followed a little at both. Moreover, the attacks of the two armies was also frontal, and there were no attempts at flanking manoeuvres. The difference is, however, in the outcomes: at Blenheim, Marlborough won an indisputable victory, out of all proportion to the costly and indecisive success of Malplaquet. In addition, the cavalry played a leading role in securing the victory. The initial attacks on Blenheim and Oberglau did not capture either, but they fixed a very large part of the enemy troops, which were sucked into the fighting, and diverted the attention of the French and Bavarian generals. Marlborough was free prepare the decisive attack, which focussed on the open space separating the two villages, at the centre of the French battle line.[61] In order to do this, he concentrated a considerable cavalry corps, 80 squadrons in four lines, which is opposed to 60 French squadrons.[62] The French cavalry were defeated, refusing to engage again and dispersed. The breakthrough was made. The French lost 38,000 men, killed, wounded and prisoners, against 12,000 casualties among the Allies' army.[63]

The impression of a tactical stalemate is therefore relative. These battles did not lead to an end of the war, but their consequences were no less significant. Blenheim delivered Bavaria to the allies, Ramillies won them the greater part of the Netherlands, whereas Villaviciosa definitively ensured the throne of Spain went to Philip V. From a strictly tactical point of view the model of the wings battle was a little out of fashion but it was not yet obsolete. In addition, the cavalry remained a fundamental player on the battlefield. Marlborough made particularly effective use of it, concentrating on one point of the enemy line with enough squadrons to obtain local numerical superiority and make a decisive impact on the battle.

Thus, the reign of Louis XIV was in many ways characterised by continuity. No clear break emerged from the hitherto accepted tactics. Charging in line, following the procedures of the 'ballet of lines', remained the preferred model of engagement for cavalry. These charges were most often frontal, it proved difficult to realise any enveloping manoeuvring. Despite the very relative tactical experiences of the War of the Spanish Succession, the cavalry retained an essential place on the battlefield, in whichever army it was serving. Even the adoption of the bayonet at the beginning of the eighteenth century still did not make an impression on its ability to be a commander's decisive tool.

Apart from or despite this, it is possible to highlight a peculiarity of this period, linked to the increase in the strength of the armies. This trend,

---

59 Nosworthy, *The Anatomy of Victory*, p.89.
60 Nosworthy, *The Anatomy of Victory*, p.90.
61 Nosworthy, *The Anatomy of Victory*, p.90. It seems that this attack was planned by Marlborough.
62 Grbrasic and Vukscic, *L'âge d'or*, p.53.
63 Corvisier, *Histoire militaire*, p.532.

observable in the armies of all belligerents, led to the deployment of more and more squadrons, the consequences of which must not be neglected. First, the lines lengthened considerably, increasing the difficulty of the manoeuvring such large bodies of men and horses all the more.[64] On the other hand, this evolution also pushed the generals to form groups of squadrons, in two, three or four lines, something hitherto unseen. Only the best of them, however, like Luxembourg or Marlborough, were able to make effective use of such large formations.

---

64 Tallard lined up 30 squadrons in a single line at Blenheim. At the rate of a theoretical frontage of about 49 yards per squadron, we have more than 1,400 yards for the whole line.

Conclusion

This investigation into the heart of the charge reminds us that the cavalry was far from the conservative and archaic weapon sometimes described. It evolved considerably over this period of just over 150 years. To confirm this, it is enough to compare the charge of the men-at-arms of the first half of the sixteenth century with that of the cavalrymen of the War of the Spanish Succession.

Of course, there are similarities between the two. The charge was of course the *raison d'être* of the heavy cavalry. There was the will, at least in theory, to charge into contact. But are they the same? Ignoring the differences in equipment, and the sources of recruitment for example, there was a significant difference. They were no longer aristocratic warriors who had learned to ride and fight, bringing individual courage to the forefront. They were men of the people, peasants, townspeople or bourgeois, who had to learn everything about cavalry combat. These men were no longer lined-up, side by side with their peers. They fought in squadrons and were only one element of a greater tactical organisation whose order and discipline had to be preserved at all costs in order to win a victory.

This simple reminder highlights the importance of the transformations made in heavy cavalry between the mid sixteenth and early eighteenth centuries. It is not in itself a novelty. The history of the cavalry shows that it has experienced since its creation many important changes. Without even referring to the knightly charge, one can recall many technical evolutions such as the adoption of the sarissa, the *contus* and the improvements in saddlery in ancient times, or the adoption of stirrups in the early Dark Ages. But the changes observed during our period are considerable. They mark a clear break with the charge such as heavy cavalry had practiced since the twelfth century. The origin of this was an attempt to adapt to an imbalance introduced by a number of factors, such as the great strides seen in technology and tactics, the wide adoption of firearms and the rise in power of the infantry. In addition, there was the dropping of many social barriers to serving in the cavalry and the massive increase in the numbers of men and horses. Denison thought this was more about adapting than amnesia, who would have thought the cavalry would have 'forgotten … that its main advantage lay in the impetuous charge and shock.'[1]

---

1 Denison, *A History of Cavalry*, p.191.

THE NEW KNIGHTS

Heavy cavalry of a new type took shape, armed with the pistol and formed into squadrons. Of course, the old knightly charge with the lance did not disappear immediately. For both socio-cultural and military reasons, the adoption of the charge with the pistol formed in squadrons did not take place overnight, and the two doctrines coexisted during all the French Wars of Religion. Evolution was no less inevitable, and the firearm took precedence over swords, the trot over the gallop, avoidance tactics over the brutal shock of direct contact. Then by the beginning of the seventeenth century the charge of the pistoleers, the cuirassiers or reiters, predominated.

The first decade of the Thirty Years' War saw no significant changes. Some generals were well aware of the limitations of this doctrine, but the changes, however moderate, concerned only the elite units. Ordinary riders were content to charge at a gentle trot, relying on their firepower to avoid or limit the shock of actual contact. Their lack of instruction did not really allow for more. On the other hand, since the enemy followed the same practice, there was no urgency to change this doctrine. It is this status quo that Gustavus Adolphus broke. He innovated, accelerated and standardised and proposed a new model. To counter him, his enemies had no choice but to adapt to these same new standards. His allies imitated them and spread them. At the end of the conflict the new doctrine had become widespread. Cavalry charged in shallower squadrons, the speed of the charge had increased slightly, and the fire of pistol and carbine only prepared the way for contact.

There is a new status quo, which will continue until the beginning of the next century. Once again, the limits of instruction for both men and horses, constituted a powerful obstacle to change. In France, only the Maison du Roi was able to charge at a gallop and with cold steel. All European cavalry were satisfied with this period of inertia, and none really took the initiative to introduce further change. Some modifications were emerging by the late seventeenth and early eighteenth centuries, but they were limited. The dazzling innovations of Charles XII were without immediate heir and the doctrine of the charge evolved only very slowly during the first half of the eighteenth century.

Our period is therefore the story of a long mutation, starting with the upheavals of the second half of the sixteenth century, continued with the search for a new level playing field achieved in the first decades of the eighteenth century. Clifford J. Rogers, writing about military evolution, suggested that these changes were 'a series of military revolutions, each trying to remedy an imbalance introduced by the previous one.'[2] This process would be marked by 'sudden and rapid changes, interrupted by long periods of stability.'[3]

If it seems out of place to assert that the wide adoption of the use of firepower in the sixteenth century was in itself a backward step, it is not untrue that cavalry experienced from this time a 'relative and absolute decline', or that heavy cavalry no longer carried as much weight when deciding the course of

---

2   Clifford J. Rogers, 'Military revolution of the Hundred Years War', in Rogers (ed.), *The Military Revolution Debate*, p.57
3   Clifford J. Rogers, 'Military revolution', p.77.

CONCLUSION

the battles. The increased role of the infantry and the artillery did not mean that the cavalry was relegated to a position of a spectator. Gendarmes and pistoleers played a considerable role in the battles of the Wars of Religion. Consider too that despite its progress and even if it had learned to stand up to the cavalrymen, the infantry remained relatively immobile and still had difficulty in combining the use pikes and firepower. If the heavy cavalry was only one of the tools available to the general, it remained capable of carrying the day. He who could defeat the enemy cavalry was certain, if not of total victory, then at least of not losing.

This was bound to strengthen with the evolution of the orders of battle operated during the Thirty Years' War. The use of the linear order, which placed the cavalry on the wings, allowing it to better exploit its mobility. While the defensive power of the infantry strengthened, the cavalry wings were able to make decisive moves on the flanks and rear of the enemy army. The squadrons that managed to put their opponents to flight found themselves able to manoeuvre freely and undisturbed. The enemy infantry, abandoned by its own cavalry, could rarely turn the situation around. The pattern of the wing-battles continued without modifications until the end of the century. Commanded by great horsemen like Turenne, Condé or Luxembourg, the French cavalry performed brilliantly in the main battles during the reign of Louis XIV.

The eighteenth century seems to begin under less favourable auspices. The infantry made a considerable technical advance by the adoption of the bayonet. Yet the cavalry still carried particular tactical weight at the beginning of the century. Although he sometimes thought 'out of the box', Marlborough knew how to use his cavalry as a battle winning weapon, repeatedly playing the role of a massive hammer to bludgeon its way through the enemy army, and we cannot forget the considerable contribution made by the cavalry of Charles XII to his victories.

Thus, the conduct of the charge and the tactical use of heavy cavalry stabilised at the beginning of the eighteenth century. The upheavals of the second half of the sixteenth century were integrated by the mounted troops, which gradually evolved to correct, in part at least, the limits of the new methods of carrying out a cavalry charge. A number of constraints still remained however, which prevented the cavalry from making the most of its hard-won advantages. It will be up to Frederick II of Prussia, by a new rupture in the equilibrium, to bring heavy battle cavalry to its highest level and to impose upon Europe yet another new model of the cavalry charge.

Bibliography

I. Handwritten sources: Service Historique de la Défense, Château de Vincennes

The archives of the Service Historique de la Défense are very useful for the beginning of the eighteenth century. The A1 series first, which brings together correspondence and battle narratives. The series 'Memoires et Reconnaissance' contain many memoirs of officers.

II. Published Sources

Alembert, Jean Le Rond d', et Diderot, Denis (ed.), *Encyclopédie ou dictionnaire raisonné des sciences, des arts et des métiers, par une société de gens de lettres, mis en ordre et publié par M. Diderot et d'Alembert* (Paris: Briasson, David, Le Breton, 1751–1765)

Amboise, Michel d', *Le guidon des gens de guerre* (Paris: Galliot du Pré, 1543)

Anon., *Discours véritable de la victoire obtenue par le roi, en la bataille donnée près le village d'Ivry, le quatorzième de mars, 1590* (Lyon: Ancelin, 1594)

Aubigné, Agrippa d', *Histoire Universelle* (Geneva: Droz, 1993)

Authville des Amourettes, Charles-Louis d', *Essai sur la cavalerie tant ancienne que moderne, Auquel on a joint les instructions & les ordonnances nouvelles qui y ont rapport, avec l'état actuel des troupes à cheval, leur paye, &c.* (Paris: Jombert, 1756)

Bardet de Villeneuve, P.P.A., *Cours de la science militaire, à l'usage de l'infanterie, de la cavalerie, du génie et de l'artillerie. Tome I. Les fonctions et les devoirs des officiers tant d'infanterie que de cavalerie* (La Haye: Van Duren, 1740)

Basta, Giorgio, *Le gouvernement de la cavalerie légère*, French translation by Théodor de Bry (*Il governo della cavalleria leggiera dal conte Giorgio Basta* (Venice: 1612)) (Rouen: J. Berthelin, 1627)

Berwick, Jacques Fitz-James, Maréchal Duc de, *Mémoires du Maréchal De Berwick* (Paris: Hachette, 1872)

Billon, Jean de, *Les principes de l'art militaire* (Rouen: Berthelin, 1641 [1st edition 1613])

Birac, Sieur de, *Les fonctions du capitaine de cavalerie, et les principales de ses officiers subalternes, avec un abrégé des ordonnances & reglemens du Roy, pour la cavalerie, depuis l'année en 1661 jusques en 1669. Et l'exercice de la cavalerie, par le sieur de B* (Paris: Quinet, 1669)

Birac, Sieur de, *Les fonctions du capitaine de cavalerie, et les principales de ses officiers subalternes, avec un abrégé des ordonnances et réglemens du roi et l'exercice de la cavalerie* (La Haye: van Bulderen, 1693)

Bohan, François-Philippe Loubat, Baron de, *Examen critique du militaire françois* (Geneva: 1781)

BIBLIOGRAPHY

Bohan, François-Philippe Loubat, Baron de, *Mémoires sur les haras, considérés comme une richesse pour la France, et sur les moyens qui peuvent augmenter les avantages de la cavalerie française*, édition posthume (Paris: 1804)

Bohan, François-Philippe Loubat, Baron de, *Principes pour monter et dresser les chevaux de guerre, formant le 3eme volume de l'ouvrage intitulé L'Examen critique du militaire françois (1781), suivis des extraits des tomes 1 et 2 qui ont paru les plus dignes d'être conservés* (Paris: Anselin et Pochard, 1821)

Boussanelle, Louis de, *Commentaires sur la cavalerie* (Paris: Guillyn, 1758)

Boussanelle, Louis de, *Réflexions militaires* (Paris: Duchêne et Durand, 1764)

Brézé, Gioacchino Bonaventura Argentero, Marquis de, *Observations historiques et critiques sur les commentaires de Folard et sur la cavalerie* (Turin: Les frères Reycends, 1772)

Brézé, Gioacchino Bonaventura Argentero, Marquis de, *Essai sur les haras, ou Examen méthodique des moyens propres pour établir, diriger & faire prospérer les haras* (Turin: Reycends, 1769)

Briquet, Pierre de, *Code militaire ou compilation des ordonnances des rois de France concernant les gens de guerre* (Paris: Prault père, 1761)

Bussy-Rabutin, Roger de, *Mémoires de messire Roger de Rabutin, comte de Bussy* (Paris: Anisson, 1696)

Castelnau, Michel de, *Mémoires de messire Michel de Castelnau 1559–1570*, in *Collection complète des mémoires relatifs à l'histoire de France, par M. Petitot*, Tome XXXIII (Paris: Foucault, 1823)

Chemnitz, Bogislav Philipp von, *Königlichen Schwedischen in Teutschland geführten Krieg*, vol. I (Stockholm: 1648)

Courtilz de Sandras, Gratien, *Les devoirs de l'homme de guerre* (La Haye: Van Bulderen, 1693)

Cruso, John, *Militarie Instructions for the Cavallrie* (Cambridge: printed by the printers of the University of Cambridge, 1632)

Daniel, Père G., *Histoire de la milice française et des changements qui s'y sont faits depuis l'établissement de la monarchie dans les Gaules jusqu'à la fin du règne de Louis le Grand* (Paris: Delespine et Coignard, 1721)

Des Cours, Nicolas Rémond, *Les véritables devoirs de l'homme d'épée. Particulièrement d'un gentilhomme qui veut réussir dans les Armées* (Amsterdam: Adrian Braakman, 1697)

Du Buisson, Nicolas (may be Courtilz de Sandras), *La Conduite de Mars nécessaire à tous ceux qui font profession des armes, avec des Mémoires contenant divers événements remarquables arrivés pendant la guerre d'Hollande* (La Haye: van Bulderen, 1693)

Du Praissac, *Les discours militaires du sieur du Praissac* (Paris: Guillemot et Thiboust, 1623)

Du Bellay, Martin, *Mémoires de messire Martin du Bellay*, in *Collection universelle des mémoires relatifs à l'histoire de France*, Tome 17 (London and Paris: privately published, 1786)

Drummond de Melfort, Louis (Comte), *Traité sur la cavalerie* (Desprez: Paris, 1776)

Feuquières, Antoine de Pas, Marquis de, *Mémoires du marquis de Feuquière, contenant ses maximes sur la guerre et l'application des exemples aux maximes* (Paris: Rollin, 1740)

Folard, Jean-Charles de, *Histoire de Polybe, nouvellement traduite du grec par Dom Vincent Thuillier, avec un commentaire ou un corps de science militaire enrichi de notes critiques et historiques, par M. de Folard* (Paris: P. Gandouin, 1727–1730)

Folard, Jean-Charles de, *Nouvelles découvertes sur la guerre dans une dissertation sur Polybe. Suivi du Traité de la colonne* (Paris: Josse et Labottière, 1724)

Fourquevaux, Raymond de Beccarie de Pavie, Seigneur de, *Instruction sur le fait de la guerre* (Paris: Galiot du Pré, 1548)

Gaya, Louis de, Sieur de Tréville, *L'Art de la guerre et la manière dont on la fait à présent* (Paris: Michallet, 1677)

Gaya, Louis de, Sieur de Tréville, *L'Art de la guerre et la manière dont on la fait aujourd'hui en France* (Paris: Michallet, 1689)

Giovio, Paolo, *Histoire de Paolo Govio sur les choses faites et advenues de son temps en toutes les parties du monde, traduite en français par Denis Sauvage, Historiographe du roi* (Paris: Olivier de Harsy, 1570)

Goulart, Simon, *Mémoires de la Ligue* (n.p.: 1602)

Grandmaison, Thomas-Auguste Le roy de, *La petite guerre ou Traité du service des troupes légères en campagne* (n.p.: 1756)

Grimoard, Philippe Henri, Chevalier de, *Recherche sur la force de l'armée française, les bases pour la fixer selon les circonstances* (Paris: Treuttel et Wurtz, 1805)

Grimoard, Philippe Henri, Chevalier de, *Essai théorique et pratique sur les batailles* (Paris: Desaint, 1775)

Guibert, Jacques-Antoine-Hippolyte, Comte de, *Essai général de Tactique* (Paris: Economica, 2004 [1st edition: 1772])

Guignard, M. de, *L'école de mars, ou mémoires instructifs sur toutes les parties qui composent le corps militaire en France* (Paris: Simart, 1725)

Guillet, Georges, *Les arts de l'homme d'épée, ou le dictionnaire du gentilhomme* (Paris: Gervais Clouzier, 1678)

Hay du Chastelet, Paul, *Politique militaire ou traité de la guerre, nouvelle édition revue, corrigée et augmentée de notes et de citations* (Paris: Jombert, 1757 [1st edition 1667])

Imbotti, Bernardin, *La milice moderne où sont comprises les évolutions tant de cavalerie que d'infanterie* (Paris: Camusat et Lepetit, 1646)

Instruction pour les Gardes du corps du roi, 1766 (Beauvais: Desjardins, 1767)

La Balme, Augustin Mottin de, *Eléments de tactique pour la cavalerie* (Paris: Jombert, 1776)

La Balme, Augustin Mottin de, *Essai sur l'équitation, ou principes raisonnés sur l'art de monter et de dresser les chevaux* (Amsterdam and Paris: Jombert et Ruault, 1773)

La Broue, Salomon de, *Le cavalerice françois* (Paris: Charles du Mesnil, 1646 [1st ed. 1593–1594])

La Colonie, Jean-François Martin de, *Mémoires de monsieur de La Colonie, maréchal de camp des armées de l'Electeur de Bavière [éd. Présentée et annotée par Anne-Marie Cocula]* (Paris: Mercure de France, 1992)

La Fontaine, Sieur de, *Les devoirs militaires des officiers de la cavalerie, contenant l'exercice des gens de guerre, par le sieur De La Fontaine, ingénieur ordinaire du roi* (Paris: Loyson, 1675)

La Guérinière, François Robichon de, *Ecole de cavalerie. Contenant la connaissance, l'instruction et la conservation du cheval* (Paris: Jacques Collombat, 1733)

La Guérinière, François Robichon de, *Elémens de cavalerie. Contenant la connoissance du cheval, l'embouchure, la ferrure, la selle, &c. avec un traité du haras* (Paris: Compagnie des libraires, 1754)

La Noue, François de, *Discours politiques et militaires*, ed. F.E. Sutcliffe (Geneva: Droz, 1967)

La Noue, François de, *Mémoires de La Noue*, in *Collection universelle des mémoires relatifs à l'histoire de France*. Tome 17 (London and Paris, privately published, 1788)

La Touche, Philibert de, *Les vrays principes de l'espée seule* (Paris: F. Muguet, 1670)

La Vallière, François de la Baume Le Blanc, Chevalier de, *Pratique et maximes de la guerre* (La Haye: Van Bulderen, 1693)

Langeais, Monsieur de, *Des fonctions et du principal devoir d'un officier de cavalerie, augmentées de réflexions sur l'Art militaire* (Paris: Ganeau, 1726)

Langeais, M. de, *Réflexions sur les tomes I et II des commentaires de Polibe faits par M. Follard et sur son livre de la nouvelle découverte. Avec des réflexions militaires et historiques* (Paris: chez Ganeau, 1728)

BIBLIOGRAPHY

Laon, Jean de, Sieur Daigremont, *Pratique et Maximes de la guerre, avec l'Exercice général et militaire de l'infanterie et un Traité des fortifications nouvelles* (Paris: Loyson, 1652)

Le Pippre de Noeufville, Simon Lamoral, *Abrégé chronologique et historique de l'origine, du progrès et de l'état actuel de la maison du roi et de toutes les troupes de France* (Liège: Kints, 1734)

Le Roy de Bosroger, *Principes de l'art de la guerre, développés d'après les meilleurs exemples et appliqués tant aux opérations d'un corps d'armée qu'à celle des détachemens particuliers* (Paris: Cellot et Jombert, 1779)

Le Roy de Bosroger, *Eléments de la guerre* (Paris: Costard 1773)

Lecoq-Madeleine, *Le service ordinaire et journalier de la cavalerie en abrégé* (Paris: Delatour et Simon, 1720)

Legrain, Baptiste, *Décade contenant la vie et gestes de Henri le Grand Roy de France et de Navarre IIIIe du nom* (Paris: 1614)

Ligne, Charles-Joseph, Prince de, *Les fantaisies militaires*, in *Œuvres du Prince de Ligne*, Tome II (Brussels: Van Meenen, 1860)

Ligne, Charles-Joseph, Prince de, *Préjugés militaires* (Paris: Champion, 1914)

Louis XIV, *Mémoires pour l'instruction du Dauphin, présentation par Pierre Goubert* (Paris: Imprimerie nationale, 1992)

Lostelneau, Sieur de, *Le maréchal de bataille, contenant le maniement des armes, les évolutions de plusieurs bataillons, tant contre l'infanterie que contre la cavalerie, divers ordres de batailles* (Paris: Mignon, 1648)

Mailles, Jacques de, *La très joyeuse, plaisante et récréative histoire du bon chevalier sans peur et sans reproche, le gentil seigneur de Bayart, composé par le Loyal Serviteur* (Paris: Garnier Frères, 1882)

Maizeroy, Paul-Gédéon Joly de, *Théorie de la guerre* (Lausanne: Aux dépens de la Société, 1777)

Machiavelli, Niccolò, *L'Art de la guerre*, in *Œuvres complètes* (Paris: Gallimard, coll. La Pléiade, 1954)

Manesson-Mallet, Alain, *Les travaux de Mars ou l'art de la guerre* (Amsterdam: Janson, 1684–1685 [1st edition 1671])

Melzo, Lodovico, *Les reigles militaires du chevalier frère Luis Melzo de l'Ordre de Malte pour le gouvernement et service particulier et propre de la cavallerie, traduictes d'Italien en françois par Paul Varroy* (Anvers: Verdussen, 1615)

Menou de Chernizay, René, Chevalier de, *La pratique du cavalier ou l'exercice de monter à cheval* (Paris: Loyson, 1656 [1st ed.1616])

Monluc, Blaise de, *Commentaires de Messire Blaise de Montluc, mareschal de France, Nouvelle collection des mémoires pour servir à l'histoire de France, Par Michaud et Poujalat*, Tome VII (Paris: chez l'éditeur du commentaire analytique du code civile, 1838)

Monro, Robert, *Monro, His Expedition with the Worthy Scots Regiment* (London: 1637)

Montbas, Jean-François Barton, Baron de, *Au service du roi, mémoires inédites d'un officier de Louis XIV, le baron de Montbas*, ed. Vicomte Henri de Montbas (Paris: Calmann-Levy, 1926)

Montecuccoli, Raimondo, *Mémoires de Montecuculi, généralissime des troupes de l'Empereur* (Amsterdam: Wetstein, 1752)

Montgommery, Louis de, Seigneur de Courbouson, *La milice françoise, contenant plusieurs belles et notables instructions sur ce qui doit être observé à bien ordonner des batailles, dresser des bataillons, situer places et forteresses, et le moyen de les attaquer et deffendre* (Paris: Corrozet, 1636)

Ordonnance du roi pour régler l'exercice de la cavalerie du 1er juin 1766 (Beauvais: Desjardins, 1767)

Pluvinel, Antoine de, *Le Maneige royal de M. de Pluvinel. Embelly de plusieurs excellentes figures gravées en taille-douce, par Crispin de Pas* (Paris: aux dépens de Crispin de Pas, 1623)

Pluvinel, Antoine de, *L'instruction du roy, en l'exercice de monter à cheval* (Amsterdam: Schipper, 1666 [1625])

Pontis, Louis de, *Mémoires du sieur de Pontis*, Tome II, in *Collection des mémoires relatifs à l'histoire de France, par M. Petitot* (Paris: Foucault, 1824)

Puerto, Alvaro Navia-Ossorio, Vicomte de (Marquis de Santa Cruz de Marcenado), *Reflexions militaires et politiques, traduites de l'espagnol de M. le marquis de Santa-Cruz de Marzenado (par M. de Vergy)* (Paris: J. Guérin, 1737–1738)

Puységur, Jacques-François de Chastenet, Marquis de, *L'Art de la guerre par principles et par règles, ouvrage de M. le maréchal de Puységur, mis au jour par M. le Mis de Puységur, son fils* (Paris: Jombert, 1748)

Quincy, Charles Sevin, Marquis de, *Histoire militaire de règne de Louis le Grand, enrichie des plans nécessaires. On y a joint un traité particulier de pratiques et de maximes de l'art militaire* (Paris: Coignard, 1726)

Quincy, Charles Sevin, Marquis de, *L'Art de la guerre ou maximes et instructions sur l'art militaire* (Paris: Coignard, 1740)

Quincy, Joseph Sévin, Comte de, *Mémoires du chevalier de Quincy* (Paris: éd. L. Lecestre, 1889–1901)

Ramsay, Andrew-Michael, *Histoire de Henri de la Tour d'Auvergne, vicomte de Turenne, Maréchal Général des Armées du roy* (Paris: Mazières et Garnier, 1735)

Richelieu, *Mémoires du maréchal de Richelieu, ouvrage composé dans la bibliothèque et dans les papiers du maréchal et sur ceux de plusieurs courtisans ces contemporains, chez Buisson* (Paris, 1793)

Rohan, Henri, Duc de, *Le parfait capitaine. Autrement, l'abrégé des guerres de Gaule des commentaires de Cesar, suivy d'un recueil de l'ordre de guerre des Anciens, ensemble d'un traité particulier de la guerre* (Paris: Houze, 1636)

Rohan, Henri, Duc de, *Mémoires du duc Henri de Rohan*, in *Collection des mémoires relatifs à l'Histoire de France, Par M. Petitot*, Tome XVII (Paris: Foucault, 1822)

Saint-Simon, Louis de Rouvroy, Duc de, *Mémoires de Saint-Simon, nouvelle édition augmentée des additions de Saint-Simon au journal de Dangeau et de notes appendices par A. de Boislisle* (Paris: Hachette, 1879–1831)

Saunier, Gaspard de, *L'art de la cavalerie* (Paris: Jombert, 1756)

Saxe, Maurice, Comte de, *Mes rêveries*, introduction de Jean-Pierre Bois (Paris: Economica, 2002 [édition de l'abbé Pérrau, 1757])

Sourches, Marquis de, *Mémoires du Marquis de Sourches sur le règne de Louis XIV* (Paris: Hachette, 1882–1893)

Tavannes, Gaspard de Saulx, Seigneur de, *Nouvelle collection des mémoires pour servir à l'histoire de France, par MM. Michaud et Poujoulat*, Tome VIII (Paris, 1838)

Turenne, Henri de la Tour d'Auvergne, Vicomte de, *Mémoires sur la guerre, tirés des originaux de M. de Turenne, par M**** (Paris: Rollin, 1738)

Turpin de Crissé, Lancelot, *Essai sur l'Art de la guerre* (Paris: Prault et Jombert, 1754)

Vault, François-Eugène de, *Mémoires militaires relatifs à la guerre de Succession d'Espagne sous Louis XIV, extraits de la correspondance de la cour et des généraux par le lieutenant général de Vault*, 11 vols (Paris: Imprimerie Royale, 1841)

Vernon, John, *The Young Horse-Man, or the Honest Plain-Dealing Cavalier* (London: printed by Andrew Coe, 1644)

Vieilleville, François de Scépeaux de, *Mémoires de la vie du maréchal de Vieilleville*, livre huitième, in *Collection complète des mémoires relatifs à l'histoire de France, par M. Petitot*, Tome XXVIII (Paris: Foucault, 1832)

Villars, Louis-Hector, duc de, *Mémoires du maréchal de Villars, Nouvelle collection des mémoires pour servir à l'histoire de France, par MM. Michaud et Poujalat* (Paris: chez l'éditeur du Commentaire analytique du Code civil, 1839)

Voltaire, *Précis du siècle de Louis XV*, in *Œuvres historiques, texte établi par R. Pomeau* (Paris: Gallimard, coll. La Pléiade, 1957)

Wallhausen, *Art de chevalerie, comprenant, après un advertissement nécessaire touchant l'estat douloureux de la chrestienté, l'instruction de touts avantages et dextérités nécessaire à chascun chevalier* (Frankfurt: Paul Jacques, 1616)

Wallhausen, Johan-Jacobi von, *Art militaire à cheval, instruction des principes et fondements de la cavalerie et des quatre espèces, ascavoir lances, corrasses, arquebus et drageons, avec tout ce qui est de leur charge et exercice ... par J.J. de Wallhausen, principal capitaine des gardes de la louable ville de Dantzig* (Francfort, imprimé par Paul Jacques aux frais de Théodor de Bry, 1616). Original edition: *Kriegskunst zu Pferd* (Frankfurt: privately published, 1616)

Wanery, Charles-Emmanuel de, *Remarques sur la cavalerie* (Paris: Anselin, 1828)

Xenophon, *Le commandant de la cavalerie* (Paris: Les Belles lettres, 1973)

III. Secondary Works

Ardant du Picq, Charles, *Études sur le combat* (Paris: Economica, 2004)

Ariès, Christian, *Armes blanches militaires françaises, 1er fascicule* (Paris: Librairie Petitot, 1968)

Arnold, Thomas F., *Les guerres de la Renaissance* (French translation: Paris: éditions Autrement, 2002)

Audouin-Rouzeau, Stéphane, 'Vers une anthropologie historique de la violence de combat au XIXe siècle: relire Ardant du Picq?', *Revue d'histoire du XIXe siècle,* n°30, 2005.

Audouin-Rouzeau, Stéphane, '"La mort de la bataille", La bataille d'hier à aujourd'hui', *Revue Internationale d'Histoire Militaire,* n°78, 2000.

Aumale, Henri d'Orléans, Duc d', *Histoire des princes de Condé pendant les XVIe et XVIIe siècles* (Paris: Calmann Lévy, 1886)

Ayton, Andrew, *Knights and Warhorses* (Woodbridge: Boydell, 1994)

Azan, Paul, *Un tacticien du XVIIe siècle, d'Aurignac* (Paris: Chapelot, 1904)

Barker, Thomas M., *The Military Intellectual and Battle. Raimondo Montecuccoli and the Thirty Years War* (Albany, New York: State University of New York Press, 1975)

Barrie-Curien, Viviane (ed.), *Guerre et pouvoir en Europe au XVIIe siècle* (Paris: Henri Veyrier, 1991)

Belhomme, Victor, *L'armée française en 1690* (Paris: librairie militaire L. Baudouin, 1895)

Bély, Lucien, *Les relations internationales en Europe XVIIe–XVIIIe siècles* (Paris: PUF, 2007)

Bély, Lucien (ed.), *Dictionnaire de l'Ancien Régime* (Paris: PUF, 1996)

Bérenger, Jean, 'L'influence des peuples de la steppe (Huns, Mongols, Tatares, Turcs) sur la conception européenne de la guerre de mouvement et l'emploi de la cavalerie', *Revue Internationale d'Histoire Militaire,* n° 49 (1980)

Bérenger, Jean, 'Les armées françaises et les guerres de Religion', *RIHM,* n°155 (1983)

Bérenger, Jean, *Turenne* (Paris: Fayard, 1987)

Bérenger, Jean, *Histoire de l'empire des Habsbourg* (Paris: Fayard, 1990)

Bérenger, Jean (ed.), *La révolution militaire en Europe* (Paris: Economica-ISC, 1998)

Black, Jeremy, *La guerre au XVIIIe siècle* (Paris: Editions Autrement, 2003 for the French edition)

Black, Jeremy, 'A Military Revolution? A 1660–1792 perspective', in Clifford J. Rogers (ed.), *The Military Revolution Debate. Readings on the Military Transformation of Early Modern Europe* (Boulder CO: Westview Press, 1995)

Blomac, Nicole de, 'Equitation de cour, équitation de guerre', in Daniel Roche (ed.) *Les écuries royales du XVIe au XVIIIe* (Paris: Association pour l'académie d'art équestre de Versailles, 1998)

Blomac, Nicole de, 'Le cheval de guerre entre le dire et le faire. Quelques variations sur le discours équestre adapté à la guerre', in Daniel Roche (ed.), *Le cheval et la guerre, du XVe au XXe* (Paris: Association pour l'Académie d'art équestre de Versailles, 2002)

Blomac, Nicole de, *Voyer d'Argenson et le cheval des Lumières* (Paris: Belin, 2004)

Bogros, Denis, *Les chevaux de la cavalerie française* (La Roche-Rigault: PSR éditions, 2001)

Bois, Jean-Pierre, *Les guerres en Europe 1494–1792* (Paris: Belin, 1993)

Bois, Jean-Pierre, 'Approche historiographique de la tactique à l'époque moderne', *Revue Historique des Armées*, n°2 (1997)

Bois, Jean-Pierre, 'L'homme dans la bataille à l'époque moderne', in *Cahiers du Centre d'études d'histoire de la défense*, n°9 (1999)

Bois, Jean-Pierre, 'Plaidoyer pour une histoire tactique de la guerre au XVIIIe siècle', in *L'armée au XVIIIe siècle, colloque d'Aix-en-Provence, 1996* (Aix-en-Provence: PUP, 1999)

Bois, Jean-Pierre, *Maurice de Saxe* (Paris, Fayard, 1992)

Bonin, Pierre, *Construire l'armée française. Textes fondateurs des institutions militaires*. Tome II: *Depuis le début du règne de Henri II jusqu'à la fin de l'Ancien Régime* (Turnhout: Brepols, 2006)

Bonnefoy, François, *Les armes de guerre portatives en France du début du règne de Louis XIV à la veille de la Révolution,* 2 vols (Paris: Librairie de l'Inde éditeur, 1991)

Brack, Fortuné de, *Avant poste de cavalerie légère* (Paris: Anselin, 1831)

Brioist Pascal, Hervé Drévillon, Pierre Serna, *Croiser le fer. Violence et culture de l'épée dans la France moderne (XVI–XVIIIe siècle)* (Paris: Champ Vallon, 2002)

Brzezinski, Richard, *The Army of Gustavus Adolphus, vol. 2: Cavalry* (Oxford: Osprey Publishing, 2003)

Brzezinski, Richard, *Lützen 1632, Climax of the Thirty Years' War* (Westport & London: Praeger, 2005)

Brzezinski, Richard, *Polish Winged Hussar, 1576–1775* (Oxford: Osprey Publishing, 2006)

Burnez, Pierre-Marie, *Notes pour le cours de tactique appliqué à la cavale*rie, monographie, 1888–89, bibliothèque de l'Ecole d'Application de l'Arme Blindée Cavalerie, Saumur

Cantal, Pierre, *Études sur la cavalerie* (Paris: Lavauzelle, 1905)

Cardini, Franco, *La culture de la guerre, Xe–XVIIIe siècle* (Paris: Gallimard, 1992)

Chagniot, Jean, 'La révolution militaire des temps modernes', *Revue Historique des Armées,* n°2 (1997)

Chagniot, Jean, 'Critique du concept de révolution militaire', Jean Bérenger (ed.), *La révolution militaire en Europe* (Paris: Economica-ISC, 1998)

Chagniot, Jean, *Guerre et société à l'époque moderne* (Paris: PUF, Nouvelle Clio, 2001)

Chaline, Olivier, *La bataille de la Montagne Blanche (8 novembre 1620). Un mystique chez les guerriers* (Paris: Noêsis, 1999)

Chandler, David, *The Art of Warfare in the Age of Marlborough* (Staplehurst and New York: Spellmount, Sarpedon, 1997)

Chauviré, Frédéric, 'La charge de cavalerie de Bayard à Seydlitz', *La nouvelle Histoire-Bataille 2, Cahiers du Centre d'Etudes Historiques sur la Défense*, n° 23 (2005)

Chauviré, Frédéric, 'La Maison du roi sous Louis XIV, une troupe d'élite, étude organique', *Revue Historique des Armées*, n°242 (2006)

Chauviré, Frédéric, 'A brides abattues, le problème de l'allure dans les charges de cavalerie du XVIe au XVIIIe siècle', *Revue Historique des Armées*, n°249, 2007

Chauviré, Frédéric, 'La Maison du roi sous Louis XIV, une troupe d'élite, étude tactique', *Revue Historique des Armées*, n°255 (2009)

BIBLIOGRAPHY

Chauviré, Frédéric, *Histoire de la cavalerie* (Paris: Perrin, 2013)

Chauviré, Frédéric and Bertrand Fonck (ed.), *L'âge d'or de la cavalerie* (Paris: Gallimard, 2015)

Childs, John, *La guerre au XVIIe siècle* (Paris: Editions Autrement, 2004 for the French edition)

Choppin, Henri, *Les origines de la cavalerie française* (Paris: Berger-Levrault, 1905)

Choppin, Henri, *La cavalerie française* (Paris: Garnier, 1893)

Colin, Jean, *Les transformations de la guerre* (Paris: Economica, 1989)

Contamine, Philippe, *La Guerre au Moyen Age* (Paris: PUF, Nouvelle Clio, 1999)

Contamine, Philippe (ed.), *Guerre et concurrences entre les Etats Européens du XIVe au XVIIIe siècle* (Paris: PUF, 1998)

Corvisier, André, *Louvois* (Paris: Fayard, 1983)

Corvisier, André (ed.), *Dictionnaire d'Art et d'Histoire Militaires* (Paris: PUF, 1988)

Corvisier, André, *Le soldat, la stratégie, la mort, Mélanges André Corvisier* (Paris, Economica, 1989)

Corvisier, André (ed.), *Histoire militaire de la France*; t. 1: *Des origines à 1715*; t. 2: *De 1715 à 1811* (Paris: PUF, 1992)

Corvisier, André, *La bataille de Malplaquet (1709), l'effondrement de la France évité* (Paris, Economica, 1997)

Coutau-Bégarie, Hervé, *Traité de stratégie* (Paris: Economica, 1999)

Croxton, Derek, 'La stratégie et la "révolution militaire" dans la guerre de Trente Ans: une révolution manquée?' in L. Henninger (ed.), *Nouveaux regards sur la guerre de Trente Ans, Actes du colloque international organisé par le CEHD à l'Ecole militaire le 6 avril 1998* (Paris: ADDIM, 1998)

Davis, R.H.C., *The Medieval Warhorse: Origin, Development and Redevelopment* (London: Thames & Hudson Ltd, 1989)

Desbrières Edouard and Maurice Sautai, *La cavalerie de 1740 à 1789* (Paris: Berger-Levrault, 1906)

Delbrück, Hans, *History of the Art of War*, 4 vols (Lincoln and London: University of Nebraska Press, 1990)

Denison, Georges T., *A History of Cavalry from the Earliest Time* (London: Macmillan, 1913)

Di Marco, Louis A., *War Horse: A History of the Military Horse and Rider* (Yardley, Pa: Westholme Publishing, 2008)

Drévillon, Hervé, 'L'héroïsme à l'épreuve de l'absolutisme, l'exemple du maréchal de Gassion (1609–1647)', *Cahiers du CEHD, Nouvelle Histoire Bataille (II)*, n°23 (2004)

Drévillon, Hervé, *L'impôt du sang, le métier des armes sous Louis XIV* (Paris, Taillandier: 2005)

Drévillon, Hervé, *Batailles. Scènes de guerre de la Table Ronde aux Tranchées* (Paris: Seuil, 2007)

Duby, Gorges, *Le dimanche de Bouvines* (Paris: Gallimard, 1985)

Dugué Mac Carthy, Marcel, *La cavalerie française et son harnachement* (Paris: Maloine, 1985)

Dugué Mac Carthy, Marcel, *La cavalerie au temps des chevaux* (Paris: EPA ed., 1989)

Dupont, Marcel, *Cavaliers d'épopée* (Paris: Lavauzelle, 1985)

Durand, Etienne de, 'De quelques difficultés de l'histoire militaire', *Cahiers du Centre d'études d'histoire de la défense*, n°9 (1999)

Durand, Yves, *La Maison de Durfort à l'époque moderne* (Fontenay-le-Comte: Lussaud, 1975)

Englund, Peter, *Poltava. Chronique d'un désastre,* translated from Swedish by Erik Harder (Paris: Esprit Ouvert, 1999)

Evans, John X. (ed.), *The works of Sir Roger William* (Oxford: Clarendon Press, 1972)

Fonck, Bertrand, 'Les campagnes du maréchal de Luxembourg en Flandres, 1690–1694: bataille et stratégie', *Revue Internationale d'Histoire Militaire*, n°76 (1997)

Franklin, Alfred, *Les grandes scènes du XVIe siècle, reproduction fac-similé du recueil de J. Tortorel et J. Perrissin, publié sous la direction de M. Alfred Franklin* (Paris: Fiscbacher, 1886)

Fratani Dominique, 'Les chevaux des Gonzague à la bataille de Fornoue', in Daniel Roche (ed.), *Le cheval et la guerre, du XVe au XXe siècle* (Paris: Association pour l'académie d'art équestre de Versailles, 2002)

Fuller, J.F.C., *Les batailles décisives du monde occidental* (Paris: Berger-Levrault, 1980, French edition)

Funcken, Liliane and Fred, *Le costume, l'armure et les armes au temps de la chevalerie* (Paris: Castermann, 1977)

Gaier, Claude, 'l'opinion des chefs de guerre français du XVIe sur le progrès de l'art militaire', *Revue internationale d'Histoire militaire*, n°29 (1970)

Gaier, Claude, 'La cavalerie lourde en Europe occidentale du XIIe au XVIe', *Revue Internationale d'Histoire Militaire*, n°31 (1971)

Gaier, Claude, *Armes et combats dans l'univers médiéval* (Brussels: De Boeck, 1985)

Garnier, Jacques (ed.), *Dictionnaire des guerres et des batailles de l'histoire de France* (Paris: Perrin, 2004)

Gladitz, Charles, *Horse Breeding in the Medieval World* (Dublin/Portland: Four Court Press, 1997)

Grbasic, Zvonimir and Velimir Vuksic, *L'âge d'or de la cavalerie* (Paris–Lausanne: La Bibliothèque des arts, 1989)

Gyllenstierna, Ebbe, 'Henri de Turenne et Charles-Gustave Wrangel. Stratégie et tactique pendant les dernières années de la guerre de Trente Ans', *Turenne et l'Art militaire*, Actes du colloque International sur Turenne et l'Art militaire, 1975 (Paris: Les Belles lettres, 1978)

Hale, J.R., *War and Society in Renaissance Europe 1450–1620* (Montreal and Kingston, London–Buffalo: McGill-Queen's University Press, 1998)

Hall, Bert S., *Weapons and Warfare in Renaissance Europe: Gunpowder, Technology and Tactics* (London: Johns Hopkins University Press, 1997)

Hardy de Périni, Edouard, *Batailles françaises*, 6 vols (Paris: Flammarion, 1894–1906)

Hatton, Ragnhild (ed.), *Captain Jefferye's letters from the Swedish army, 1707–1709* (Stockholm: P.A. Norstedt and Söner, 1954)

Henninger, Laurent, *Rocroi, 1643* (Paris: Socomer, 1993)

Henninger, Laurent, 'Une conséquence de la guerre de Trente Ans en Europe centrale et Balkanique: le renouveau de la cavalerie dans les armées occidentales', in L. Henninger (ed.), *Nouveaux regards sur la guerre de Trente Ans*, Actes du colloque international organisé par le CEHD à l'Ecole militaire le 6 avril 1998 (Paris: ADDIM, 1998)

Henninger, Laurent, 'Pour une nouvelle histoire bataille', *Cahiers du centre d'Etudes d'histoire de la défense*, n° 9 (1999)

Henriquet, M., and A Prévost, *L'équitation, un art, une passion* (Paris: Seuil, 1972)

Hoppe, Israël, *Geschichte des erstenschwediscen-polnischenkrieges in Preussen* (Leipzig: M. Toeppen, 1887)

Howard, Michael, *La guerre dans l'histoire de l'occident* (Paris: Fayard, 1988 for the French edition)

Humbert, E. *Cours d'art et d'histoire militaire appliqué à la cavalerie* (Saumur: Javaud, 1866)

Hyland, Ann, *The Warhorse, 1200–1600* (Stroud: Sutton, 1998)

Jeanjot-Emery, Pol, 'Les maladies, les accidents et les blessures du cheval de guerre', in Roche (ed.) *Le cheval et la guerre, du XVe au XXe siècle* (Paris: Association pour l'académie d'art équestre de Versailles, 2002)

Jeney, Louis Michel de, *Le partisan ou l'art de faire la petite guerre avec succès selon le génie de nosjours* (La Haye: Constapel, 1759)

Jouanna, Arlette, *Le devoir de révolte. La noblesse française et la gestation de l'Etat moderne, 1559–1661* (Paris: Fayard, 1989)

Joxe, Alain, *Voyage aux sources de la guerre* (Paris: PUF, 1991)

BIBLIOGRAPHY

Keegan, John, *The Face of Battle* (London: Jonathan Cape, 1976)

Keegan, John, *Histoire de la guerre, du néolithique à la guerre du Golfe* (Paris: éditions Dagorno, 1996, French edition)

Konstam, Angus, *Peter the Great's Army, 2: Cavalry* (Oxford: Osprey Publishing, 1993)

Kroener, Bernhard, *Les routes et les étapes, Die versorgung der französicher armeen in Nordostfrankreich, 1635-1661* (Münster: Aschendorff, 1980)

La Barre Duparq, Edouard de, *L'art militaire pendant les guerres de Religion* (Paris:Tanera, 1864)

Lacombe, Paul, *Les armes et les armures* (Paris, Hachette, 1886)

Léonard, Emile G., *L'armée et ses problémes au XVIIIe siècle* (Paris: Plon, 1958)

Love, Ronald, S., "All the King's Horsemen': the Equestrian Army of Henry IV 1588-1598", *The Sixteenth Century Journal*, 22, n°3-4 (1992)

Lynn, John, A.,'Tactical Evolution in the French Army, 1550-1660', *French Historical Studies*, XIV (1985)

Lynn, John, A., *Giant of the Grand Siècle, the French Army 1610-1715* (Cambridge: Cambridge University Press, 1998)

Lynn, John, A., *The Wars of Louis XIV, 1667-1714* (London: Longman, 1999)

Lynn, John, A., *Battle. A History of Combat and Culture* (Boulder CO: Westview Press, 2003)

Mc Neil, William, *La recherche de la puissance, technique, force armée et société depuis l'An Mil* (Paris: Economica, 1992, French edition)

Malfoy-Noël, Dorothée, *L'épreuve de la bataille 1700-1714* (Montpellier: Presse Universitaires de la Méditerranée, 2007)

Mantran, Robert (ed.), *Histoire de l'empire Ottoman* (Paris: Fayard, 1989)

Mulliez, Jacques, 'Le cheval d'arme en France au XVIIIe siècle: un fantôme?', in Daniel Roche (ed.), *Le cheval et la guerre, du XVe au XXe siècle* (Paris: Association pour l'académie d'art équestre de Versailles, 2002)

Mulliez, Jacques, *Les chevaux du royaume. Aux origines des haras nationaux* (Paris: Belin, 2004)

Muraise, Eric, *Introduction à l'histoire militaire* (Paris: Lavauzelle, 1964)

Nivet, Philippe (ed.), *La bataille en Picardie, combattre de l'antiquité au XXe siècle* (Amiens: Encrage, 2000)

Nosworthy, Brent, *The Anatomy of Victory, Battle Tactics 1689-1763* (New York: Hippocrène Books, 1990)

Nouzille, Jean, 'Les Impériaux aux XVIIe et XVIIIe siècle', in Jean Bérenger (ed.), *La révolution militaire en Europe* (Paris: Economica, 1998)

O'Connell, Robert, *Of Arms and Men: A History of War, Weapons, and Aggression* (Oxford: Oxford University Press, 1989)

Oury, Clément, *Les défaites françaises de la guerre de Succession d'Espagne, 1704-1708*, doctoral thesis directed by Olivier Chaline, manuscript, Université Paris IV-Sorbonne, 2011

Parker, Geoffrey, *La guerre de Trente Ans* (Paris: Aubier, 1987)

Parker, Geoffrey, *La révolution militaire; la guerre et l'essor de l'Occident, 1500-1800* (Paris: Gallimard, 1993, French edition)

Parker, Geoffrey, 'The Military revolution, a Myth?', in Rogers, C.-J. (ed.), *The Military Revolution debate: Readings on the Military Transformations of early Modern Europe* (Boulder CO: Westview Press, 1995)

Parrott, David, 'Strategy and Tactics in the Thirty Years' War', in Clifford J. Rogers (ed.), *The Military Revolution Debate. Readings on the Military Transformation of Early Modern Europe* (Boulder CO: Westview Press, 1995)

Parrott, David, *Richelieu's Army: War, Government and Society in France, 1624-1642* (Cambridge: Cambridge University Press, 2006)

Perré, Jean, *La guerre et ses mutations, des origines jusqu'à 1792* (Paris: Payot, 1910)

Phillips, Gervase, "of nimble service': Technology, Equestrianism and the Cavalry of Early Modern Western European Armies', *War and society*, XX, 2 (October 2002)

Pigailleim, Henri, *Blenheim 1704. Le prince Eugène et Marlborough contre la France* (Paris: Economica, 2004)

Roberts, Keith, *Cromwell's War Machine, the New Model Army, 1645-1660* (Barnsley: Pen & Sword, 2005)

Roberts, Michael, *Gustavus Adolphus* (London–New York: Longman, 1992)

Robinson, Gavin, 'Equine battering rams? A reassessment of cavalry charges in the English Civil War', *The Journal of Military History*, n°75 (2011)

Roche, Daniel (ed.), *Les écuries royales du XVIe au XVIIIe* (Paris: Association pour l'académie d'art équestre de Versailles, 1998)

Roche, Daniel (ed.), *Le cheval et la guerre, du XVe au XXe siècle* (Paris: Association pour l'académie d'art équestre de Versailles, 2002)

Roche, Daniel, *La gloire et la puissance. Histoire de la culture équestre, XVIe–XIXe siècle*, Tome 2ème (Paris: Fayard, 2011)

Roemer, Jean, *Cavalry: its history, management and uses* (New York: D. Van Nostrand, 1863)

Rogers, Clifford J. (ed.), *The Military Revolution Debate. Readings on the Military Transformation of Early Modern Europe* (Boulder CO: Westview Press, 1995)

Rogers, Clifford J., 'Military revolution of the Hundred Years War', in *The Military Revolution Debate. Readings on the Military Transformation of Early Modern Europe* (Boulder CO: Westview Press, 1995)

Rowlands, Guy, *The Dynastic State and the Army under Louis XIV. Royal Service and Private Interest, 1661-1701* (Cambridge: Cambridge University Press, 2002)

Schulten, Kees, 'Une nouvelle approche de Maurice de Nassau', in André Corvisier (ed.), *Mélanges André Corvisier. Le soldat, la stratégie, la mort* (Paris: Economica, 1989)

Schulten, Kees, 'La bataille de Nieuport, 1600', *Revue Internationale d'Histoire Militaire*, n°78 (2000)

Susane, Louis, *Histoire de la cavalerie française* (Paris: J. Hetzel et Cie, 1874)

Tincey, John, *Marston Moor 1644. The beginning of the end* (Oxford: Osprey Publishing, 2003)

Tincey, John, *Soldiers of the English Civil War, vol. 2: Cavalry* (Oxford: Osprey Publishing, 2004)

Tincey, John, *The British Army, 1660-1704* (Oxford: Osprey Publishing, 2005)

Tincey, John, *Ironsides: English Cavalry 1588-1688* (Oxford: Osprey Publishing, 2005)

Tuetey, Louis, *L'officier sous l'ancien régime, nobles et roturiers* (Paris: Plon, 1908)

Turenne et l'Art militaire, Actes du colloque International sur Turenne et l'Art militaire, 1975 (Paris: Les Belles lettres, 1978)

Venner, Dominique, *Les armes de combat individuelles* (Paris: Jacques Grancher, 1979)

Venner, Dominique, *Les armes blanches* (Paris: Jacques Grancher, 1986)

Weck, Hervé de, *La cavalerie à travers les âges* (Lausanne: Edita S.A., 1980)

Wood, James B., *The King's Army. Warfare, soldiers and society during the Wars of Religion in France 1562-1576* (Cambridge: Cambridge University Press, 2002)